International Law
National Tribunals
and the
Rights of Aliens

Volume 10, Procedural Aspects of International Law Series

The Procedural Aspects of International Law Series

RICHARD B. LILLICH, *editor*

International Law
National Tribunals
and the
Rights of Aliens

FRANK GRIFFITH DAWSON
and
IVAN L. HEAD

With the Collaboration of
PETER E. HERZOG

SYRACUSE UNIVERSITY PRESS

ISBN 0–8156–2152–3

Library of Congress Catalog Card: 76–155828

Copyright © 1971 by the Procedural Aspects of
International Law Institute, Inc.
New York, New York

FIRST EDITION 1971

Manufactured in the United States of America

To

HELENE AND BARBARA

And if a stranger sojourn with thee in your land, ye shall not vex him.

But the stranger that dwelleth with you shall be unto you as one born among you, and thou shalt love him as thyself; for ye were strangers in the land of Egypt: I am the LORD your God.

Leviticus 20:33,34

Editor's Foreword

This book, the tenth volume in the Procedural Aspects of International Law Series prepared by the Procedural Aspects of International Law Institute and published by Syracuse University Press, is the third of five studies which will be produced by the Institute's research project on "International Procedures to Protect Private Rights." This project, funded by a $160,000 grant from the Ford Foundation, has involved a four-year examination of a select number of procedural problems in three separate but interrelated areas: human rights; property rights; and, in a more limited sense, procedural rights (of aliens before national tribunals). The authors of the present study, Frank Griffith Dawson, formerly a practicing lawyer in New York and Caracas and now an investment banker in London, and Ivan L. Head, sometime Professor of Law at the University of Alberta, greatly assisted by Peter E. Herzog, Professor of Law at Syracuse University, have been responsible for producing this unique book on the rights of aliens before national tribunals. No published work to date has attempted to do what this volume sets out to accomplish.

To understand what makes this volume so unusual, some background information is needed, at least for the benefit of the general reader. When an individual's person or property is injured or taken by a foreign country, the old dogma that the individual is not a subject of international law still precludes him from immediate access to an international remedy. As the Supreme Court of the United States noted in the famous *Sabbatino Case,* "the usual method for an individual to seek relief is to exhaust local remedies and then repair to the executive authorities of his own state to persuade them to champion his claim in diplomacy or before an international tribunal." The main rationale of this Local Remedies Rule, as the authors relate, is "the premise that it is in the mutual interest of all nations, be they host States or potential protecting States, to promote the settlement of controversies at local court levels rather than allow them to grow into international disputes between sovereign States."

Unfortunately, the obvious inadequacy of local remedies in many countries today has contributed to the continued decline of the Rule's importance. Not only are remedies often lacking in many parts of the world, but even when they exist judicial and administrative bodies often fail to render impartial and unbiased decisions. In recent years, for instance, the intrusion of political considerations into the courtroom has been apparent not only in Communist nations but also in such countries as Cuba, Ghana, and South Africa. This situation, of course, is nothing new. Over a half-century ago Professor Borchard remarked upon the unwillingness of European countries to require their nationals to exhaust local remedies in "the more backward states in Latin America" adding that "this attitude of Europe is especially noticeable in cases where the Latin-American government is a party to the litigation." He expressed the hope that as those countries matured politically they would develop independent judiciaries, the existence of which would make foreign countries "submit the rights of their nationals and subjects to the decisions of the local courts, and to decline diplomatic interposition until local remedies have been exhausted."

This enlightened situation, unhappily, still has not arrived. Therefore, while agreeing with Borchard's hopes, one also must heed Professor Fisher's admonition that the discussion of procedural problems should proceed "realistically, with an eye to what is now possible, and not lose itself in reference to a distant goal." What has long been needed in this area of international law was not another volume discussing the many interesting theoretical problems raised by the local remedies requirement—there are an abundance of them already—but a practical, bread-and-butter comparative study of the various legal and nonlegal factors which actually preclude or limit the availability of effective remedies to injured aliens in foreign countries. This study ideally would be based upon firsthand familiarity with a wide sampling of countries and would include specific recommendations about how the availability and quality of local remedies might be improved. Only after a thorough examination of all aspects of the administration of justice as it effects aliens would the volume offer its views on the contemporary relevance of the Local Remedies Rule.

The authors of this study, in the opinion of the present writer, have produced such a book. Starting with an exhaustive examination of the written law of 25 leading countries representing the world's major legal systems, in many of which countries they have lived and worked, Dawson and Head, aided by Herzog, next visited all these countries to see how the law respecting remedies available to aliens actually works in practice. In 1967, for instance, Head visited the African countries of Ghana, Nigeria, Tanzania, and Kenya; Dawson visited the South American countries of Argentina, Brazil, Peru, and Surinam; and Herzog visited the European countries of Austria, France, and Germany. The following year Head visited the Asian countries of Pakistan, India, Ceylon, Malaysia, Singapore, and Australia, while Dawson subsequently visited Mexico, Venezuela, and the Central American countries of Guatemala, Honduras, and Costa Rica. In all the above countries, plus Canada, Great Britain, and the United States, they interviewed academic and practicing lawyers, trial and appellate judges and attorneys general, and other government officials charged with the administration of justice.

The result is a book of great assistance to individuals and corporations who venture abroad, plus the foreign offices of the countries from whence they come and to where they go. Corporate officials seeking a realistic evaluation of the judicial hurdles facing their operations in foreign countries, plus international lawyers representing individual and corporate clients, will find in it a handy and concise treatment of the major legal as well as nonlegal problems confronting the enforcement of rights by aliens in foreign countries. In the past, the Local Remedies Rule has been deemed not to apply when available remedies were inadequate, but no comparative data existed by which the adequacy of a given country's remedies could be judged. Now, some content for this aspect of the Rule exists in the form of this book, which for that reason alone should become the standard cited work in the area. Furthermore, if the recommendations contained in it are acted upon, over the next decade the world community will have gone a long way in restoring the Local Remedies Rule to its proper place in the international legal order.

RICHARD B. LILLICH

Charlottesville, Virginia
January, 1971

Preface

The purpose of this study is to provide laymen and lawyers alike with a guide to the procedural difficulties they can encounter when involved in litigation abroad. We hope that by pinpointing certain potentially troublesome areas of procedural law in various countries, scholars, bar associations, and legislators will be encouraged to seek practical reforms either by treaty or legislation before major international difficulties or conflicts develop. Finally, perhaps, this volume can serve as a reference book for lawyers with clients abroad, as well as for those government officials entrusted with protecting the rights of their citizens in foreign nations.

Since ancient times foreigners have been regarded with suspicion, if not fear, either due to their nonconforming religious and social customs, their assumed inferiority, or because they were considered potential spies and agents of other nations. Thus, the Romans refused aliens the benefits of the *jus civile,* thirteenth-century England limited their recourse to the ordinary courts of justice, and imperial Spain denied them trading rights in the New World. The impact of such restrictions until the last century was rather slight, since a relatively low number of persons, for one reason or another, chose to travel or live abroad.

Today, however, due to the twentieth-century revolution in transportation, communication, and international business, there are more individuals traveling and residing outside their own nations than ever before—be they ubiquitous German tourists on the beaches of the Mediterranean, Oklahoman drilling engineers living in the oil camps of Venezuela and Ecuador, or Italian businessmen conferring with potential customers in Prague. As a result, the alien has become a familiar figure in most parts of the world, and is no longer quite the object of distrust that he was in the past. Nevertheless, he is still, by virtue of his presence in the host country and his relationships with the people and institutions therein, subject to a wide variety of legal prescriptions of which he may be only vaguely aware, and which may have philosophical bases quite distinct from those of the legal system in his own nation.

In view of the increasing transnational movement of peoples, goods, and technology since World War II, we believe it timely to review the general background of the development of international law as it affects the procedural rights of aliens in foreign courts and tribunals (Chapters I–II), to describe the impact of extralegal forces upon the application of local law (Chapters III–IV), and then to explore on a comparative basis those aspects of selected legal systems which either could be applied adversely to an alien or which might not accord with the minimal requirements of procedural due process developed over the years through treaties, judicial decisions, and arbitral awards. (Chapters V–VIII.) Finally, in Chapter IX, specific recommendations are offered which might alleviate some of the procedural difficulties aliens could encounter in unfamiliar legal environments.

Fortunately, in none of the 25 countries in Europe, Africa, Asia, and the Americas studied herein does procedural legislation discriminate directly against foreigners purely on the basis of their alienage. All the nations examined provide open access to their courts and tribunals, except for occasional requirements that reciprocity of treatment exist in the alien's home State. Nevertheless, even if access is granted, the alien still could be disadvantaged or his rights under international law impaired either by the physical environment in which the legal process must function, or by strict application of local procedural rules incompatible with transnational litigation. Thus, political and economic turbulence may produce unjustified executive and legislative interference with an independent judiciary. Similarly, since in some nations constitutions are considered merely to reflect political aspirations, rather than to delimit governmental powers, constitutional guarantees of civil rights may be suspended during so-called "emergencies" without permitting adequate appeal or relief therefrom. Military regimes in Africa and Latin America provide recent examples. Therefore, while procedural safeguards may exist in theory they may not always be effective in practice. Moreover, even if the political and economic climate does not interfere with the judicial process, outdated codes of civil procedure may allow aliens located thousands of miles from where an action is brought only a few days in which to answer complaints, or they may require onerous security deposits from nonresident litigants. As a result, the availability of relief in local courts must be assessed anew in each particular situation, taking into consideration a multitude of factors, legal and extralegal, which may determine whether or not an alien will receive treatment consistent with international standards of due process.

Lack of space has forced us to be selective, both in the topics discussed and the countries examined. We have excluded problems of immigration, citizenship, and deportation. Criminal law and physical treatment while in custody are touched upon only marginally. Similarly, a limited number of countries were chosen for our survey, since international law as it relates to the treatment of aliens is historically associated with disputes involving the nations of Western Europe, the Americas, and their overseas possessions and spheres of influence. Therefore no attempt has been made to include Iron Curtain countries. Nevertheless, a comparative study of the rights of aliens in the Soviet Union and other similarly aligned nations is in itself a topic worthy of special, separate endeavor.

This study could not have been possible without the Ford Foundation's generous grant to the Procedural Aspects of International Law Institute, Inc., under the auspices of which our research was conducted. It would be impossible to thank in these few paragraphs all the practitioners, government officials, businessmen, and scholars who assisted us with our investigations in the countries visited. Special mention, however, should be made of the efforts of Professor Peter E. Herzog of the Syracuse University College of Law, who gave unstintingly of his time and is responsible for the basic research involving France, Germany, Austria, and Italy. We also wish to express our gratitude to Professor Henry de Vries of the Columbia University School of Law and to Frank Nahier of the New York Bar, both of whom made valuable suggestions concerning the structure of our project at its inception. In Latin America, a few of the attorneys who were especially helpful include Policarpo Yurrebaso Viale and Jorge Reinaldo Vanossi in Buenos Aires; Andrés A. Aramburu-Menchaca and Maximo Cisneros in Lima; Paul Griffith Garland and Nelson Pinto-Silva in São Paulo; Carlos Dunshee de Abranches in Rio de Janeiro; G. C. Van der Schroeff in Paramaribo, Surinam; Dr. Ramon Díaz in Caracas, Venezuela; Harry A. Zurcher in San José, Costa Rica; and Ruben Alvarez in Tegucigalpa, Honduras. In New York City, Luis Guillen of both the Salvadorean and New York Bars made available to us his comprehensive index to the Latin American official gazettes. In London we were greatly assisted by Professor J. N. D. Anderson and Mr. W. A. F. P. Steiner, Director and Secretary-Librarian, respectively, of the Institute of Advanced Legal Studies, who allowed us full use of the Institute's facilities. Finally, in the various Commonwealth countries visited we should like to record our thanks to the Canadian High Commissioners and their staffs, who were of such assistance in arranging our program, and the many judges and lawyers—too numerous to be mentioned by name—who contributed so generously of their experience and their time.

Above all, however, we are grateful to Professor Richard B. Lillich of the University of Virginia School of Law, who, assisted by his graduate students Stuart Macdonald and Bert B. Lockwood, Jr., edited in excellent fashion all the drafts which were prepared before going to press. His task was made especially arduous by the fact that the authors lived in four different countries during the preparation of the text, and consequently he had to cope with many communication problems. His discipline and sense of humor remained in perfect balance throughout a lengthy and trying project.

Finally, we should like to thank Mrs. Anne Taylor and Mrs. Iris Skrabec for typing various drafts of the manuscript, and the secretarial pool of the Publications Office of the University of Virginia School of Law for typing the final draft. We also appreciate the support and assistance of the entire staff of the Syracuse University Press, who shepherded the final manuscript through the last stages of editing and composition. Naturally, any errors of fact or law are attributable to the authors, rather than to the many kind people who helped them with this study.

FRANK GRIFFITH DAWSON
IVAN L. HEAD

London and Ottawa
January, 1971

Contents

International Law
National Tribunals
and the
Rights of Aliens

CHAPTER I

Diplomatic Protection and Procedural Due Process in Foreign Tribunals Prior to 1945

Traditionally, only nation-States have been considered subjects of international law with standing to present claims against other States. As a result, natural and corporate persons generally have been denied access to international tribunals to present claims against foreign States arising out of personal injuries or property damage, or out of failures to provide access to local courts or other remedial measures.[1]

In the early Middle Ages international commerce was so structured that few people lived abroad. Those persons that did had few real rights. In some places they could be treated as serfs and almost everywhere they could not pass property by inheritance. As trade and commerce expanded in the later Middle Ages, the position of foreigners improved, mostly due to increased protection given them by more powerful central governments against local feudal lords, and only quite incidentally to international agreement. Even the early colonial era did not lead to a great change, since most nations sought to limit trade with their newly acquired possessions to their own nationals.[2] In the New World, for instance, the Spanish sought

---

[1] Commentators have criticized this concept, which evolved from earlier theories that the primary function of international law was to restrain the absolute authority of princes and nation-States in their dealings with each other. In the nineteenth century this theory developed into a dualistic concept of international law entailing complete separation of two legal spheres: international law was to be applied in dealings between States; municipal law was to be applied within each State. Brownlie, *The Individual Before Tribunals Exercising International Jurisdiction,* 11 INT'L & COMP. L.Q. 701, 718–20 (1962); W. GORMLEY, THE PROCEDURAL STATUS OF THE INDIVIDUAL BEFORE INTERNATIONAL AND SUPRANATIONAL TRIBUNALS 23–35 (1966).

[2] P. ELLSWORTH, THE INTERNATIONAL ECONOMY ch. 2 (rev. ed. 1958). As to the development of the rights of aliens, see H. BATIFFOL, DROIT INTERNATIONAL PRIVÉ (4th ed. 1967).

to exclude English, Dutch and French merchants from their colonies by creating monopolies to handle trade.[3]

Notwithstanding these efforts, the successful colonization of the New World, then of Asia and to a lesser extent of Africa, and the development of regular trade with the Middle and Far East which began via the Cape of Good Hope in the sixteenth century, made international trade increasingly important to Western European economies. The mineral wealth of the New World was shipped to Spain, from whence much of it soon found its way to the Lowlands and other parts of Europe to finance both Hapsburg imperial ambitions and the manufactured products imported by Spain either for her own use or for her American colonies.[4] An international exchange economy, however primitive, was developing, and with it an increasing number of merchants were traveling to, and residing in, States not their own.

Not surprisingly, therefore, concern over the treatment accorded peaceful alien traders gradually became relevant to daily European life. In 1758, just as European economic theory began its transition from mercantilism to laissez faire, this concern was evidenced by the publication of Vattel's influential *The Law of Nations*. The author, who regarded the State as an organic unity composed of the sovereign and his subjects, advanced the thesis that a State has a duty to protect its subjects. Therefore a State that injured the person or property of the subject of another State committed an injury against that State for which it could be held responsible.[5] The techniques for protection, of course, varied from place to place and from century to century. In parts of Asia in the sixteenth, seven-

---

[3] J. PARRY, THE SPANISH SEABORNE EMPIRE 251–71, 292–306 (1966); H. HERRING, A HISTORY OF LATIN AMERICA 193–97 (1956).

[4] H. HEATON, ECONOMIC HISTORY OF EUROPE 247–50 (2d ed. 1948).

[5] "Whoever wrongs the State, violates its rights, disturbs its peace, or injures it in any manner whatever becomes its declared enemy and is in a position to be justly punished. Whoever ill-treats a citizen indirectly injures the State, which must protect that citizen. The sovereign of the injured citizen must avenge the deed and, if possible, force the aggressor to give full satisfaction or punish him, since otherwise the citizen will not obtain the chief end of civil society, which is protection." E. DE VATTEL, THE LAW OF NATIONS, Bk. II, ch. VI, at 136 (Classics of International Law ed., C. Fenwick transl. 1916). The context from which this famous quotation is abstracted, however, indicates that Vattel was discussing injuries to subjects by individuals rather than by States.

teenth and eighteenth centuries, for example, rather sophisticated agreements or *firmans* were executed by the great trading companies and local rulers. These agreements, also known as capitulations, often contained provisions for settling disputes between subjects or employees of the two parties.[6]

Vattel was writing for a more or less homogeneous, European, Christian society as yet untouched by the Industrial Revolution, a society composed of different States but nevertheless possessing a common civilization and a common moral code.[7] Hence, for Europe, Vattel's theories could provide a workable basis upon which theories of State responsibility for injuries to aliens could be built. Vattel's Europe, however, was not the whole world, as became clear in the nineteenth century. The acceleration of industrialization, the development of laissez-faire capitalism, the decline of State control over international commerce, the race for colonies, the stupendous increase in intra-European commerce and production, the emergence of new markets in the recently independent Latin American nations, the harnessing of novel sources of power and other far-reaching technical developments, plus increasingly rapid communications, new techniques in finance and corporate organization, and overseas investments in transportation, public utilities, mining and agricul-

---

[6] "The East India Companies and the local Rulers seem to have generally agreed on the formula 'actor sequitur forum rei'. Its adoption meant in practice that each contracting party would try its own nationals (subjects) for offences committed in the territory of the Ruler within which the Company had a settlement or other establishment. While this principle applied to a broad category of disputes (chiefly to criminal cases), it was not applicable in cases of breach of contract whenever local merchants and craftsmen were indebted to the Company or its merchants in connexion with the purchase or sale of goods. In this case the Company usually had the right of detention of the debtor up to the payment of debts or the delivery of goods. It must be presumed that the agency assuming jurisdiction normally applied its own law to its own nationals, but when it had to give a decision affecting the subjects of the other contracting party, the situation must have been much more complicated. There are provisions in several treaties (firmans) to the effect that the Company detaining a Ruler's subjects was under duty to consider the case of their liability according to local custom or usage. It has also been stated that the Companies assuming jurisdiction over their nationals extended it frequently to non-nationals in their service or to local converts under their protection." C. ALEXANDROWICZ, AN INTRODUCTION TO THE HISTORY OF THE LAW OF NATIONS IN THE EAST INDIES 112–13 (1967).

[7] F. DUNN, THE PROTECTION OF NATIONALS 49 (1932).

tural ventures to obtain raw material for the machines and man-power of Europe, all prompted as never before an increase in the numbers of Europeans traveling and living abroad, and thereby augmented the opportunities for controversy with the governments and nationals of foreign States.[8]

At the same time, international society broadened rapidly to em-brace foreign peoples whose experiences and cultures bore scant resemblance to those of the European soldiers, merchants and traders now swarming to their shores. Yet, while Grotius and other scholars had based their "law of nations" on the conviction that relations between nations were governed by certain immutable laws of nature, actual rules of conduct were in fact derived from Euro-pean experience. It soon became apparent, however, that the widely accepted presuppositions upon which the international economic order was posited within Europe and the United States—concepts of individual and economic liberty, freedom and sanctity of contract, and community respect for, and approval of, the acquisition of pri-vate economic wealth—were not necessarily shared to the same extent in the Middle East, Asia and Africa. Nevertheless, convinced of their natural superiority by Spencer and the other apostles of Social Darwinism, merchants and colonists of the wealthier, expand-ing Europe created by the Industrial Revolution always attempted to take with them their business customs and laws, and even their courts and governments as well.[9] "The European customs on which international law was based were to become, by force and fiat, the customs that others were to accept as law if they were to join this community as sovereign states."[10] Consequently, the Europeans established extraterritorial tribunals wherever possible and imported European procedural and commercial codes and concepts to prevent

---

[8] P. ELLSWORTH, *supra* note 2, at 49–57, 156–75; F. DUNN, *supra* note 7, at 53–54.

[9] The permeating influence of Social Darwinism upon the philosophy of the day is described succinctly in C. HAYES, A GENERATION OF MATERIALISM 9–13 (1941).

[10] M. KAPLAN & N. KATZENBACH, THE POLITICAL FOUNDATIONS OF INTERNA-TIONAL LAW 63 (1961). The impact of nineteenth-century nationalism and Hegelian philosophy upon the "Europeanization" of international law also was great. *Id.* at 64.

the impact of tribal and customary law upon themselves, at least in the commercial sphere.[11]

Colonial domination thus included the imposition by force of international commercial principles evolved in the crucible of laissez-faire European capitalism. "The ideas of justice and fair dealing incorporated in the accepted norms of conduct for European nations were carried over into the wide sphere of the international society of the nineteenth century," regardless of any incompatibility with the basic value structures of the subordinated societies involved.[12] It should not be surprising that, despite the intrinsic merit of many of the principles imposed, the manner in which they were transferred from Europe sowed a legacy of bitterness, a legacy from which the capital-exporting nations still reap an unpleasant harvest.

In contrast with other parts of the world, the legal heritage of the newly independent nations of Latin America approximated that of Western Europe; legislation and constitution reflected respect for private property, for the sanctity of contracts and for the protection of acquired rights, in addition to guaranteeing other basic political and economic freedoms. Moreover, these States reacted against the repressive Spanish colonial legislation which had prevented aliens from living or trading in the New World and which had prohibited "any type of contact with foreigners be it for purposes of trading or any other type of commerce on penalty of the loss of the life or property of whomever disobeys this Our Law."[13] Thus, Latin

---

[11] "The so-called extraterritorial rights, resting in their origin upon treaty, have in the course of time, particularly in Turkey, Morocco and other countries, gathered around themselves by custom an accretion of further encroachments upon the local jurisdiction, so as to constitute in some countries a veritable *imperium in imperio*." E. BORCHARD, THE DIPLOMATIC PROTECTION OF CITIZENS ABROAD 431 (1916).

[12] F. DUNN, *supra* note 7, at 54.

[13] Leyes de Indias, Titulo XXVII, Libro 9. This sixteenth-century legislation is quoted in L. BERTI, I COMPENDIO DE DERECHO MINERO VENEZOLANO 295–96 (2d ed. 1960). Other exclusionary legislation is quoted and commented upon in Runnebaum, *Condición Jurídica de los Extranjeros en Costa Rica*, 17 REVISTA DEL COLEGIO DE ABOGADOS 109, 120–25 (No. 2, 1961). Nevertheless, the exigencies of naval warfare in the late eighteenth century, and the consequent difficulty of supplying the colonies, led to a series of narrow exceptions by first permitting trade with foreign nations in slaves and then in other goods by means of neutral shipping. The colonists took full advantage of these limited legal excep-

Americans sought in their earliest post-independence legislation to attract foreign traders and immigrants, and to grant aliens equality before the law with nationals. "To govern is to populate," wrote Juan Bautista Alberdi, one of the draftsmen of the Argentine Constitution of 1853,[14] which guaranteed aliens the same individual freedoms as nationals and helped attract 4,900,000 immigrants to Argentina between 1857 and 1930.[15]

Similarly, the Constitution of the ill-fated Republic of Central America provided in 1824 that "the Republic is a sacred asylum for all aliens and the homeland of all who wish to live in its territory" and decreed the equality of aliens and nationals before the law.[16] Furthermore, the Costa Rican Constitution of 1859 expressly gave an alien equal access with nationals to the local legal process in order to redress injuries "to his person, property or honor."[17] In its 1847 and 1857 Constitutions, Mexico also granted (by implication) to aliens the same civil rights and guarantees as citizens.[18]

---

tions to create a brisk contraband trade to complement the legal traffic. This fact has led one commentator to observe that after 1778 "[t]he freedom of commerce urged by the Latin American governments after 1810 did no more than ratify the existing situation." Villalobos, *El Comercio Extranjero a Fines de la Denominación Española*, 4 JOURNAL OF INTER-AMERICAN STUDIES 517, 544 (1962).

[14] *Quoted in* T. MCGANN, ARGENTINA: THE DIVIDED LAND 29 (1966). Article 25 of the Argentine Constitution states: "The Federal Government shall encourage European immigration; and may not restrict, limit, or burden with any tax whatsoever, the entrance into Argentine territory of foreigners who arrive for the purposes of tilling the soil, improving industries, and introducing and teaching the arts and sciences." THE CONSTITUTION OF THE ARGENTINE REPUBLIC (Pan American Union ed. 1963).

[15] While approximately 800,000 immigrants were seasonal agricultural workers and eventually returned to Europe, the rest stayed. T. FILLOL, SOCIAL FACTORS IN ECONOMIC DEVELOPMENT: THE ARGENTINE CASE 26–27 (1961). The beneficial and adverse effects of this extraordinary tide of European immigration and European influence upon Argentine social and political patterns have been subjects of wide debate. *See* C. IBARGUREN, LA HISTORIA QUE HE VIVIDO 69 (1954); R. ROJAS, LA RESTAURACIÓN NACIONALISTA 53 (2d ed. 1922). *See also* T. DITELLA, ARGENTINA, SOCIEDAD DE MASAS 85–123 (1965). Manuel Galvez wrote: "In Buenos Aires there is a lack of an aesthetic sense, just as there is a lack of an ethical sense, because it is a city of immigrants. The immigrants came to the country with the single idea of wealth. They are hungry, demoralized people who worship money." EL DIARIO DE GABRIEL QUIROGA 185 (1910).

[16] Runnebaum, *supra* note 13, at 126.

[17] *Id.* at 129.

[18] Personal interviews in Mexico City in 1969. Also, these same constitutions

While aliens in Latin America generally were prohibited from participating in local political life and from holding public office, the formulation of this doctrine of equal treatment was nevertheless considered a great advance for the times, not only in limiting the territorial sovereignty of the State, but also in promoting human rights.[19]

Unfortunately, despite well-intentioned legislation, Latin American civil wars, political turbulence and general lawlessness in post-independence years often meant that the civil rights guaranteed by the constitutions could not be protected or enforced by the weak central governments, or by their court systems. While both nationals and aliens suffered, the latter, being strangers and supposedly wealthier, often were the special targets of marauding *bandoleros* and rebel armies. Again and again aliens suffered injuries to their persons and property which government officials were powerless to prevent, and for which judicial relief was not always available.[20] In Asia and Africa such events, or more often the fear of their occurrence, were invoked by protecting States to justify territorial acquisitions or the extortion of special trading and legal privileges.[21] However, the new Latin American States, while weak and anarchic, were nevertheless sovereign entities with legal and political systems

---

provided the basis for a writ of *amparo*, which in later years was developed to enable both nationals and aliens, through a device akin to habeas corpus, to protect basic civil rights from government usurpation, and even to challenge the constitutionality of legislation. *See generally* I. VALLARTA, EL JUICIO DE AMPARO Y EL WRIT OF HABEAS CORPUS (2d ed. 1896). The subject is discussed more fully at notes 52–102 of Chapter VII.

[19] "This equality has taken centuries to become a reality and today shines out as a great victory for modern civilization." Runnebaum, *supra* note 13, at 120.

[20] For an illuminating firsthand account of the confusion and anarchy permeating Central America in the early post-independence years, see generally J. STEPHENS, INCIDENTS OF TRAVEL IN CENTRAL AMERICA, CHIAPAS & YUCATAN (1841). *See also* T. KARNES, THE FAILURE OF UNION: CENTRAL AMERICA 1824–1960, at 12–95 (1961), and A. JAUREGUI, 3 LA AMERICA CENTRAL ANTE LA HISTORIA 137–58 (1949). For a description of Mexico see F. DUNN, DIPLOMATIC PROTECTION OF AMERICANS IN MEXICO 117–65 (1933).

[21] *See* page 3 *supra.* Some of these special conditions existed into the twentieth century. Turkey, in the Treaty of Lausanne in 1923, finally repudiated the capitulation system, but it remained in force in Siam, Persia, and Egypt until 1937. The special concessions which made possible foreign trading enclaves in China existed until 1943, when the concessionaire nations renounced their privileges. *See* Runnebaum, *supra* note 13, at 118.

too well established to be directly subdued or subverted. Moreover, the local governments, although disorganized, could command the loyalty of their unruly populaces against foreign invasion.[22] Meanwhile, both the Monroe Doctrine and the British Government's policy discouraged European territorial conquests, while preoccupation with the western frontier and with digesting the gains of the Mexican War somewhat blunted United States territorial appetites.[23] Nevertheless, because the non-Spanish aliens arriving from Europe and the United States came from nations much more powerful and stable than their host States, they often were able to circumvent the local laws to which they had submitted themselves, and to make demands for special treatment.

Since national tribunals were not always successful in assisting injured aliens to obtain relief, in the absence of international courts a new procedural device, diplomatic interposition, was perfected in the nineteenth century to bring a medium of order to what was no longer a relatively homogeneous, primarily European, international society. Using as a point of departure Vattel's thesis that an injury to a State's national vicariously injured his State, and that a sovereign which allows foreigners to enter his territory has an obligation to protect them, the European States found a convenient legal justification for intervention abroad to protect the lives and property of their citizens.[24] Pursuant to the legal thinking of the times, if a host State injured one of its own citizens, it incurred no international

---

[22] The expulsion in 1807 of invading English troops by the poorly armed populace of Buenos Aires, although it took place before independence, was a case in point. H. HERRING, *supra* note 3, at 270–71; J. PARRY, *supra* note 3, at 346–47.

[23] *See generally* D. PERKINS, A HISTORY OF THE MONROE DOCTRINE (1955). For similar reasons, the concept of extraterritorial jurisdiction was not utilized in Latin America as it was in Asia and Africa. *See* D. SHEA, THE CALVO CLAUSE 4–5 (1955).

[24] F. DUNN, *supra* note 7, at 51–52. Perhaps more meaning was ascribed to Vattel's words than their context would justify. Dunn has written: "He [Vattel] wrote of a world in which foreign property interests offered but few problems in national or international affairs. He viewed the state primarily in terms of personal sovereignty rather than of territorial jurisdiction. His personification of the state as an organic unity made up of the sovereign and his subjects (from which he derived his thesis that an injury to a citizen is an injury to the state) undoubtedly served a useful purpose in the juristic evolution of the modern state, but it is not easy to apply to the modern world of extensive international trade and intercourse, and easy and frequent changes of allegiance." *Id.* at 52.

responsibility. However, if the injury occurred to an alien or to his property, the alien's State could espouse his claim and demand compensation or other relief.[25] This theory has persisted. A former judge of the International Court of Justice concluded that

> [a]lthough international law does not at present recognize, apart from treaty, any fundamental rights of the individual protected by international society as against the State of which he is a national, it does acknowledge some of the principal fundamental rights of the individual in one particular sphere, namely, in respect of aliens. . . . The result, which is somewhat paradoxical, is that the individual in his capacity as an alien enjoys a larger measure of protection by international law than in his character as the citizen of his own State.[26]

At first, diplomatic requests for redress were presented on the basis of international comity. Gradually, however, with the evolution of a body of precedents, it became customary for protecting States to demand relief as a legal right, a practice encouraged by including in treaties provisions for the protection of the lives and property of the nationals of each contracting party in the territory of the other. In this regard, the early arrangements made by the European trading companies in South and South-East Asia supplied important precedents for subsequent practice. Alexandrowicz records that the "capitulation or pre-capitulation arrangements were the expression of international standards of equitable treatment of foreigners observed in the East Indies. Their conversion into irrevocable instruments derogatory to the sovereignty of the granting Ruler resulted in the deformation of an ancient custom which had been a constructive factor in the development of international trade in the East."[27] Thus by the middle of the nineteenth century govern-

---

[25] To a great degree this conception still prevails, although efforts are being made in multilateral agreements and conventions, such as the Universal Declaration of Human Rights and the European Convention for the Protection of Human Rights and Fundamental Freedoms, to set minimal standards of treatment to which States are obliged to adhere in dealing with their own citizens as well as with citizens of other States. Unfortunately, there still is a lack of adequate enforcement machinery. *See generally* J. CAREY, UN PROTECTION OF CIVIL AND POLITICAL RIGHTS (1970).

[26] H. LAUTERPACHT, INTERNATIONAL LAW AND HUMAN RIGHTS 121 (1950).

[27] C. ALEXANDROWICZ, *supra* note 6, at 230.

ments habitually treated problems of protection of nationals as legal questions and justified interposition by appeals to principles of international law and to the writings of publicists.

Diplomatic protection therefore became increasingly important in conducting international relations, and protecting States soon refined various means of assuring compliance with what came to be known as the "International Minimum Standard of Justice," that is, the standard of substantive and procedural treatment which aliens purportedly should receive in "civilized" States and which they thus should receive abroad under international law.[28] However, the standard of personal and property protection to which non-European States were expected to adhere was, as already indicated, European in origin, and local governments did not have the experience, courts, finances or internal control necessary to assure its implementation.

The procedures utilized to secure compliance with these standards in the absence of an international adjudicating and sanctioning authority reflected the inequalities in power between the European States and the States in which aliens were trading or investing. Basically, the system was one of self-help; that is, the protecting State itself would determine the gravity of the offense and the lengths to which it would go to protect its nationals' interests. The strategies at the disposal of a protecting State ranged from unofficial consular good offices in providing names of local attorneys and attempts to bring contending parties together for settlement, to diplomatic espousal involving formal protests, withdrawal of diplo-

---

[28] According to the "International Standard," the treatment accorded a State's own nationals is irrelevant so far as aliens are concerned, since aliens have a claim to a minimum standard of legal treatment that is not less than that promised by the "universal" standards of "civilized" States. The United States Secretary of State Elihu Root once defined the minimum standard as follows: "There is a standard of justice, very simple, very fundamental, and of such general acceptance by all civilized countries as to form a part of the international law of the world. The condition upon which any country is entitled to measure the justice due from it to an alien by the justice which it accords to its own citizens is that its system of law and administration shall conform to this general standard." Root, *The Basis of Protection to Citizens Residing Abroad*, 4 AM. J. INT'L L. 517, 521–22 (1910). This approach is quite simplistic and gives the "standard" no real content or substance. *See discussion in* F. DUNN, *supra* note 7, at 141–43, and Borchard, *The "Minimum Standard" of the Treatment of Aliens*, 38 MICH. L. REV. 445 (1940).

matic representation, blockades, threats of naval bombardment and, eventually, war.[29] Forcible self-help came to be considered, at least among the more powerful nations, as a legitimate, if ultimate, sanction to assure the protection of nationals and their property abroad.[30] This fact does not mean, however, that there was not "sharp disagreement between the larger and smaller powers as to the justifiable scope of the practice."[31] Examples abound of its abuse: in 1850 Palmerston supported the dubious claim of an English-born merchant in order to intimidate the Greek Government, and in 1898 Germany utilized the pretext of the violent deaths of several missionaries in China to seize Kiaochow.

Even in the nineteenth century, however, the right to protect one's nationals was not unlimited. Statesmen and foreign offices were unwilling to embroil themselves and their national prestige in ill-founded or inflated claims, and so exercised a restraining influence.[32] Notwithstanding its current image, for example, Great Britain actually exercised considerable restraint in pressing claims against foreign countries during the last century. According to Lillich, the

---

[29] E. BORCHARD, *supra* note 11, at 439–56.

[30] Lillich, *Forcible Self-Help by States to Protect Human Rights,* 53 IOWA L. REV. 325, 326–32 (1967).

[31] F. DUNN, *supra* note 7, at 55.

[32] Lillich, *supra* note 30, at 328 n.17.

"H.M.'s Govt. will support the just claims of British Subjects who have sustained losses or suffered oppression at the hands of those in authority in a foreign State, and they need only point to the measures which they have lately adopted towards Mexico as evidence of their determination to exact redress in all cases in which British Subjects may have suffered wrong.

"But while H.M.'s Govt. are firmly resolved to protect British Subjects in their lawful undertakings and to claim for them the rights secured to them by treaty stipulations with Foreign Nations, they will not think themselves called upon to interfere on behalf of those who may be proved to have mixed themselves up improperly in any of the political questions by which the peace of the Mexican Republic is disturbed; and in any case in which in the opinion of H.M.'s Govt. justice has been denied, H.M.'s Govt., while ready to claim such an amount of redress as, upon a consideration of the circumstances, may appear to them to be justly due, will be careful to exact no more: They would consider it degrading to this Country if her great power were to be employed in wantonly turning such assessments to the pecuniary benefit of complainants, who would thus find their advantage in undergoing an insult, and who would derive a positive pecuniary gain from having been robbed and plundered." Letter from Lord Malmesbury to Mr. Otway, April 16, 1859, in F.O. 97, vol. 276, at 148–50.

Foreign Office "repeatedly found it necessary to explain to indignant British subjects that it would not espouse doubtful or exaggerated claims."[33] Similarly, the United States Government consistently refused to espouse claims arising out of contractual disputes between its nationals and their host States on the theory that the Government should not be regarded by its citizens as an international debt collector, although unofficial good offices of consular and diplomatic representatives abroad always were available to promote amicable settlements.[34]

Furthermore, certain formal requirements evolved which were designed to weed out claims of lesser merit, such as requirements of a bond of nationality, of showing that espousal would not adversely affect national policy, and of evidence that claimants had sought in good faith to obtain relief in the courts of the offending States.[35] On the multinational level, the use of forcible self-help was limited somewhat when the Second Hague Conference in 1907 adopted and internationalized the thesis advanced five years earlier by the Argentine Minister of Foreign Affairs, Dr. Drago, that armed force could not be used to collect the contractual obligations of independent States.[36]

However, espousal of claims "never proved entirely satisfactory

[33] Lillich, *supra* note 30, at 328 n.17.

[34] E. BORCHARD, *supra* note 11, at 288–91. This policy is still the general rule observed by the Department of State. Bilder, *The Office of the Legal Adviser: The State Department Lawyer and Foreign Affairs*, 56 AM. J. INT'L L. 633, 662 (1962).

[35] *See* R. LILLICH, INTERNATIONAL CLAIMS: THEIR ADJUDICATION BY NATIONAL COMMISSIONS 76–101 (1962). *See also* R. LILLICH & G. CHRISTENSON, INTERNATIONAL CLAIMS: THEIR PREPARATION AND PRESENTATION 7–39 (1962).

[36] Convention For The Pacific Settlement of International Disputes, Oct. 18, 1907, 100 BRIT. & FOR. STATE PAPERS 298 (1906–07). In 1902 Drago submitted a well-reasoned note to the United States Department of State objecting to the joint intervention of Great Britain, Italy, and Germany against Venezuela upon the latter's default in the payment of government bonds in the hands of aliens. This protest led to a recommendation of a proposed policy, intended to become a corollary to the Monroe Doctrine, but which subsequently was given international validity at The Hague. E. BORCHARD, *supra* note 11, at 308–10. The Convention, however, in no way limited the right to use forcible self-help as a sanction in other situations. Waldock, *The Regulation of the Use of Force by Individual States in International Law*, 81 RECUEIL DES COURS (Hague Academy of International Law) 455, 467–68 (II-1952).

to either individual claimants or foreign offices,"[37] not only because the conditions precedent which a protecting State required to be observed prior to espousal—including the claimant's continued maintenance of his nationality and the exhaustion of local remedies—proved troublesome, but also because large groups of claims arising out of the same event often could be settled best if considered together. For this reason, commencing with the Jay Treaty of 1794 between Great Britain and the United States, nations began to allow claims to accumulate until they could be submitted, in bulk as it were, either to arbitration by mixed claims commissions or to adjudication by national claims commissions pursuant to lump sum settlements.[38] Out of the deliberations of these commissions has grown a large body of international judicial precedent relating not only to the substantive rights to be accorded aliens abroad, but also to the standards of procedural due process to be observed in local courts. By contrast, in some areas of the world disputes frequently were settled much more simply, albeit perhaps less impartially, by a combination of courts with extraterritorial jurisdiction and threats of harsh reprisal.

During these formative years in the evolution of the doctrine of diplomatic protection, there developed a counter-theory, more comprehensive than the Drago Doctrine, which came to be known as the doctrine of nonintervention.[39] The Latin Americans, if not the originators then certainly the most avid and articulate exponents of this counter-doctrine, gradually had become aware that diplomatic pro-

---

[37] R. LILLICH, *supra* note 35, at 5.

[38] Mixed claims commissions are composed of nationals of the protecting State, of the host State and of a third State. The mixed claims commission concept has not been an unqualified success, since deliberations have tended to be over-lengthy and the quality of decisions has "depended to a disproportionate degree upon the ability of . . . commissioners. Indeed, the very nature of the device was such as to produce commissioners of nonjudicious, adversary temperament." *Id.* at 7. National commissions, on the other hand, have tended to be more productive. They are composed of nationals of the protecting State whose function it is to distribute among claimants the lump sums paid by the offending State to the protecting State in full settlement of all claims. This device has been utilized by the United States since 1803, when the United States received a lump sum from France in settlement of various American claims. *Id.* at 7–10.

[39] Lillich, *supra* note 30, at 330.

tection often was abused and, if left unrestrained, might lead to the loss of territory either to a European power or to the colossus to the north. French expeditions to Mexico in 1838 and 1861, United States interventions in Central America and in the Caribbean after 1850, and the 1902–1903 German, British, and Italian threat to Venezuela seemed to confirm their worst fears.[40] Latin American jurists turned to Vattel, just as the European States had done, and seized upon yet another famous passage in his *Law of Nations* to justify their counterattack upon diplomatic intervention by stronger nations:

> [A]s the administration of justice necessarily requires that every sentence, pronounced in due form and by the court of last resort, be regarded as just and executed as such, when once a case in which foreigners are involved has been decided in due form, the sovereign of the litigants may not review the decision. To undertake to inquire into the justice of a definitive sentence is an attack upon the jurisdiction of the court which passed it. Hence a sovereign should not interfere in the suits of his subjects in foreign countries nor grant them his protection, except in cases where justice has been denied or the decision is clearly and palpably unjust, or the proper procedure has not been observed, or finally, in cases where his subjects, or foreigners in general, have been discriminated against. . . .[41]

Thus, the Latin Americans reasoned, local court decisions should be final and binding in all cases upon both aliens and nationals. Except where there might have been a "denial of justice," which they interpreted very narrowly, no foreign government should be allowed to review or protest the local decision.[42]

At the same time, the equal or national treatment doctrine, by which the Latin American nations initially had sought to encourage foreign immigration and investment by promising aliens equality of treatment with nationals, was revived to support the argument that foreigners were entitled to no better treatment than nationals.

---

[40] Dawson, *International Law, National Tribunals and the Rights of Aliens: The Latin American Experience*, 21 VAND. L. REV. 712, 720 (1968). "There seems little doubt that the great powers in their ready resort to ultimatums and threats of the use of force to exact the payment of pecuniary claims, particularly in Latin-America, have often abused their rights and have inflicted gross injustice upon weak States." E. BORCHARD, *supra* note 11, at 447.

[41] E. DE VATTEL, *supra* note 5, at Bk. II, ch. VII, at 139.

[42] F. DUNN, *supra* note 7, at 51.

Hence, what once had been exclusively a theory to encourage foreign investment and immigration became instead a protective device to shield weaker nations from the exactions of stronger States.[43]

The most articulate and famed proponent of the revised version of the doctrine of national treatment was Carlos Calvo, the erudite Argentine diplomat and legal scholar. Shortly before 1870 he began formulating a comprehensive theory to restrict diplomatic interposition, which he set forth in detail in a monumental, six-volume work published in 1896.[44] Briefly, the "Calvo Doctrine" is based upon two principles: (1) sovereign States, being free and independent, enjoy the right, on the basis of equality, to freedom from interference by other States, either through force or diplomacy; and (2) although aliens should be accorded equal treatment with nationals, they are not entitled to rights and privileges not accorded nationals and therefore must seek redress for grievances exclusively in local courts. These twin concepts of nonintervention and absolute denial of diplomatic protection are the core of the Calvo Doctrine which, as a corollary of the Doctrine of Equal Treatment, is accepted today as a principle of international law by most Latin American nations.[45]

Perhaps it was at this point, with the formulation of the Calvo Doctrine, that the Latin American nations began to assume a distinct, collective identity as a special legal system or suborder, with legal institutions within, yet in some aspects apart from, the Europeanized international law propounded by legal theorists in capital-exporting nations. Torn between allegiance to political, economic, and social ideals borrowed from Western Europe and the United States on the one hand, and submission to the harsh realities imposed by monocultural export economies and a stultifying heritage of unstable, authoritarian government on the other, the Latin American nations began to develop among themselves certain regional standards of international behavior. Many of these standards subsequently have been codified in bilateral and multilateral treaties covering diplomatic asylum, extradition, nonintervention, recognition of new governments and uniformity in the treatments of aliens. Latin American solidarity on these points, of course, has been greatly

---

[43] Dawson, *supra* note 40, at 718–21.

[44] LE DROIT INTERNATIONAL THÉORIQUE ET PRATIQUE (Paris ed. 1896).

[45] D. SHEA, *supra* note 23, at 19.

encouraged by geographical proximity, similar fears of alien economic domination, awareness of a shared intellectual heritage, and distrust of their large neighbor to the north. It is not surprising, therefore, that the Uruguayan essayist José Enrique Rodó could strike a deep responsive chord of sympathy throughout Latin America by contrasting unfavorably what he pictured as the materialistic, loutish Caliban, personified by the United States, with the idealism, refined taste and higher sensibilities of Latin America's Ariel.[46]

The coalescing Latin American opposition to diplomatic intervention coincided after 1870 with renewed foreign economic interest in Latin America. The development of strong industrial societies in the United States and Europe after 1870 brought increased demands for Latin America's traditional exports of sugar, coffee, and hides, as well as new products such as base metals, meat, wheat, and, eventually, gas and petroleum. However, large amounts of financing were required to assure an adequate supply of these materials and the construction of the necessary railway and harbor infrastructures. Since local capital and savings either were scarce or directed into socially prestigious investments such as land, foreign investors were invited to fill the economic vacuum. Many such investors responded because Latin America represented one of the few areas in the world still available to alien investors of varying nationalities. Investment elsewhere was largely restricted by this time to nationals of the colonizing States. The economic climate appeared attractive as well, since the strong governments of Porfirio Diaz in Mexico, Justo Rufino Barrios in Guatemala, Guzmán Blanco in Venezuela, and of the new oligarchy in Argentina brought a certain measure of political and economic stability.[47] As one they welcomed foreign investment with liberal economic concessions.[48] Nevertheless, many

---

[46] This essay, *Ariel,* was read widely throughout Latin America and may be considered the basic gospel of "Yankeephobia." It is the literary predecessor of THE SHARK AND THE SARDINES (1961), a vitriolic attack on the United States by Juan José Arevalo, former President of Guatemala.

[47] Vanger, *Politics and Class in Twentieth Century Latin America,* 49 HISPANIC AMERICAN HISTORICAL REV. 80 (1969).

[48] Porfirio Díaz, while he brought peace to Mexico, surrounded himself with financial advisers (known as the *científicos*) who were obsessed with material progress at the expense of all other goals. "Briefly, the intellectuals among the Díaz administrators were a product of their times; and their times were the

thoughtful Latin Americans began to look askance at the seemingly disproportionate amount of control which alien entrepreneurs were beginning to exercise over national economies. The theoretical, jurisprudential reaction by Calvo and his colleagues to these alien attempts to seek special advantages finally exploded on the political level with the Mexican Revolution of 1910. In the years to come, large amounts of foreign property were expropriated in Mexico, and the established legal order was challenged by assertions that deprived aliens were entitled to no greater consideration than were nationals in regard to the amount and timing of compensation.[49]

The nonintervention portion of the Calvo Doctrine was accepted in principle by the United States, at which it was aimed primarily, at the Seventh Pan American Conference in Montevideo in 1933.[50]

---

late 19th century when the rationalism of Spencer and Darwin had taken strong hold on the educated mind. In the Mexican setting of the time, Díaz' lieutenants sought to apply a series of unforgivable propositions. They took cognizance of the cultural inferiority of the Indian civilization and the productive inadequacy of the people it had nurtured; until development and growth lifted them out of the dust, according to the theory of the times, the Indians could not be expected to do much more than work as common labor in the fields and mines. Concurrently, the Díaz lieutenants accepted the proposition of the innate superiority of the European culture and the contribution which that culture could make to Mexico. To achieve development in the country, they gave the freest possible reign to the foreigner and pushed the Indian aside whenever he got in the way." Vernon, *An Interpretation of the Mexican View*, in How LATIN AMERICA VIEWS THE U.S. INVESTOR 95, 97 (R. Vernon ed. 1966). For example, a major part of railroad and telegraph construction in Guatemala after 1870 was accomplished by North American concessionaires. Rippy, *Relations of the United States and Guatemala During the Epoch of Justo Rufino Barrios*, 22 HISPANIC AMERICAN HISTORICAL REV. 597 (1942).

[49] The post-Revolution cult of *indigenismo*, of a conscious cultivation of national pride, of the exaltation of their pre-Columbian origins which so characterizes Mexican literature and art, is undoubtedly just as much a reaction to the Díaz era as was the nationalization of foreign oil companies and real estate. "La Revolución Mexicana is the all-embracing name for a vast social transformation, an attempt to give to the masses land, hygiene, education, to reshape the country completely, to create a true Mexican nation, to emancipate the Indian, who represents . . . more than 90 per cent of the population, and to liberate the peón through an economic and spiritual higher standard of living." Kunz, *The Mexican Expropriations*, 17 N.Y.U.L.Q. 327, 328 (1940). For a further discussion of the expropriations which followed in the aftermath of the Mexican Revolution, see Dawson & Weston, *"Prompt, Adequate and Effective"*: *A Universal Standard of Compensation?* 30 FORDHAM L. REV. 727, 740–41 (1962).

[50] H. HERRING, *supra* note 3, at 761–62.

However, the Latin American conception of nonintervention encompassed as well denial of diplomatic intervention on behalf of aliens. This broader definition is not acceptable to the United States or to most other nations which define intervention more restrictively, not considering themselves obliged to avoid such intervention on their citizens' behalf in circumstances where there has been discrimination or a "denial of justice."[51] The Latin American nations, nevertheless, persistently have sought to ensure acceptance of the second portion of the Calvo Doctrine through constitutional provisions, municipal legislation, and "Calvo clause" stipulations in contracts between aliens and Latin American States limiting recourse to diplomatic protection. Some of these attempts acknowledged the right to intervene in cases of denial of justice, while others did not.[52] However, even where Latin American commentators acknowledge a right of diplomatic intervention, it "should be expressed with the greatest prudence," states a Central American scholar, "taking into consideration that if this remedy becomes generalized it could place the foreigner in a privileged position with respect to nationals and would be a frequent cause of violations of the sovereignty of States."[53]

By contrast, the Calvo proposition that redress should be sought in local courts never has been considered objectionable in principle by protecting States. Before espousing a claim, they traditionally have demanded that their nationals first exhaust the remedies available in local courts. The origins of the Local Remedies Rule are somewhat obscure.[54] The principal motivation, however, would seem to be the reciprocal desire of States to avoid where possible situations which would justify interference by other States in their in-

---

[51] Arriving at an acceptable definition of intervention is no easy task. Lillich writes: "Thus, while all measures of forcible self-help may constitute intervention in the ordinary sense, when used as a word of art it denotes and condemns only those forceful coercive measures designed to maintain or alter the political situation in another state." Lillich, *supra* note 30, at 330. *See* 1 L. OPPENHEIM, INTERNATIONAL LAW § 134, at 305 (8th ed. H. Lauterpacht 1955).

[52] Dawson, *supra* note 40, at 721–22.

[53] Runnebaum, *Condición Jurídica de los Extranjeros en Costa Rica*, 17 REVISTA DEL COLEGIO DE ABOGADOS 35, 58 (No. 3, 1961).

[54] See T. HAESLER, THE EXHAUSTION OF LOCAL REMEDIES IN THE CASE LAW OF INTERNATIONAL COURTS AND TRIBUNALS 19–20 (1968).

ternal affairs, combined with the general proposition that aliens entering foreign countries may be presumed to have submitted themselves voluntarily to the jurisdiction of the local courts.[55] If procedural rights accorded aliens by international law could be vindicated in local courts, disputes would be terminated at that stage without need to invoke another State's protective apparatus.

As a result, nations generally have encouraged one another to open their courts to aliens and to establish effective municipal legal machinery which permits them to do justice to claimants before being called to account to the claimant's State on the international level.[56] As a procedural device for allocating jurisdiction between the national and international legal orders, proper application of the Local Remedies Rule resulted, in the nineteenth and during the first half of the twentieth century, in the disposal of the great majority of aliens' complaints at the local level where "justice, if available,

---

[55] Many policy justifications for the rule have been given by commentators. Borchard suggests five: "[F]irst, the citizen going abroad is presumed to take into account the means furnished by local law for the redress of wrongs; secondly, the right of sovereignty and independence warrants the local state in demanding for its courts freedom from interference, on the assumption that they are capable of doing justice; thirdly, the home government of the complaining citizen must give the offending government an opportunity of doing justice to the injured party in its own regular way, and thus avoid, if possible, all occasion for international discussion; fourthly, if the injury is committed by an individual or minor official, the exhaustion of local remedies is necessary to make certain that the wrongful act or denial of justice is the deliberate act of the state; and fifthly, if it is a deliberate act of the state, that the state is willing to leave the wrong unrighted." E. BORCHARD, supra note 11, at 817–18. Lillich states that "the main rationale behind the rule remains the same: the desire to settle disputes between aliens and states on the local level rather than make them matters of international concern." Lillich, *The Effectiveness of the Local Remedies Rule Today*, 58 AMERICAN SOC'Y INT'L L. PROCEEDINGS 101 (1964).

[56] "The purpose of the local remedies rule is exemplary. It is to permit a state to have full opportunity to do justice to a claimant before it is called upon internationally to answer to another state." Head, *A Fresh Look at the Local Remedies Rule*, 5 CANADIAN Y.B. INT'L L. 142, 151 (1967). As early as 1834, a Secretary of State of the United States wrote: "Although a government is bound to protect its citizens and see that their injuries are redressed, where justice is plainly refused them by a foreign nation, yet this obligation always presupposes a resort, in the first instance, to the ordinary means of defence, or reparation, which are afforded by the laws of the country in which their rights are infringed, to which laws they have voluntarily subjected themselves by entering within the sphere of their operation, and by which they must consent to abide." *Quoted in* E. BORCHARD, supra note 11, at 818.

is bound to be more swift and less costly" and "[i]ncidents of potential international irritation are contained within reasonable bounds."[57]

When injured aliens seeking substantive remedies were denied recourse to local tribunals, or when recourse would have been fruitless, non–Latin American commentators agreed that the rule need not be observed; instead they contended that a direct appeal to the diplomatic arena could be made. Diplomatic interposition also could be invoked even when local remedies had been "exhausted" if the procedures involved did not meet international standards of due process as established by treaties or by state practice, or did not supply the relief which the claimant, under international standards of substantive law, should have obtained.[58] Only at this stage, when an alien suffered a denial of justice due to the refusal, abuse or nonexistence of a local remedy, or when the remedy did not conform to international standards, would international responsibility attach, in this instance regardless of whether the host State or a private party was the initial wrongdoer.

The expression "denial of justice" is admittedly vague, although various attempts were made before World War II to give it meaningful content, mainly in the decisions of mixed and national claims commissions and in committees of the League of Nations, which sought to determine the circumstances under which States would become responsible for injuries suffered by aliens.[59] Unfortunately, attempts to codify the law of State responsibility foundered on disagreements between the exponents of a minimum international standard of justice and persons who, like the Latin Americans, argued that, except in certain narrowly interpreted circumstances, foreigners were entitled to no better treatment in local courts than

---

[57] Head, *supra* note 56, at 151.

[58] The American Law Institute's RESTATEMENT, FOREIGN RELATIONS LAW OF THE UNITED STATES (1965) in Section 208 excuses compliance with the Local Remedies Rule when available remedies "would not satisfy the requirements of procedural justice," when "exhaustion would be clearly ineffective in view of one or more prior determinations made, on substantially identical claims, by the highest agency of the state that has authority to grant relief," or when "the state of the alien's nationality, which has espoused his claim, is asserting in its own behalf a separate and preponderant claim for direct injury to it arising out of the same wrongful conduct." *See also* E. BORCHARD, *supra* note 11, at 821–25.

[59] Dawson, *supra* note 40, at 726–27.

nationals. Typically, a resolution concerning State responsibility adopted by the Latin American States at the Seventh Pan American Conference in Montevideo in 1933 declared that aliens must seek remedies in local courts and not request diplomatic protection except in "the cases of manifest denial or unmotivated delay of justice, *which should always be interpreted restrictively,* that is, in favor of the State where the dispute has arisen. If within a reasonable time it is not settled by diplomatic means, it will be submitted to arbitration."[60]

In order for a denial of justice to exist, a Costa Rican commentator has written, "it is necessary to exhaust legal remedies for revoking the act or repairing the omission which has caused the injury, because otherwise the injury would not be consummated, a necessary requirement so that the intervention of the claiming State will not violate the sovereignty and independence of the host State."[61] In 1928, the Columbian commentator Julian Restrepo recorded with somewhat greater precision the restrictive Latin American view as to when there would be a denial of procedural due process: "(1) the refusal of a judge to give judgment on the grounds that the law is silent, obscure or insufficient; (2) refusal, or negligence or delay in the administration of justice; (3) the failure to execute a final judgment; (4) denial of a remedy; (5) denial of evidence; (6) violation of the basic propositions of judicial procedures; (7) not applying the law or applying it in an irregular manner; (8) flagrant arbitrariness; (9) the injustice of a decision."[62] The Latin American preoccupation with equality between aliens and nationals, however, required the foregoing defects to be measured by local criteria, for violation of which nationals also would have some right to object, rather than against the criteria employed in the alien's nation or in light of some "international" standard.

To Latin American and other unstable nations most likely to be the objects of diplomatic intervention or self-help, a denial of procedural justice thus would arise only when a State denied an alien access to its remedial process, when local courts applied pro-

---

[60] *Quoted in* Runnebaum, *supra* note 53, at 56 (emphasis added).
[61] *Id.* at 57.
[62] J. RESTREPO, DERECHO INTERNACIONAL PRIVADO 106 (1928).

cedural rules in a discriminatory manner against alien litigants, or when there were basic defects in procedure. Equal treatment, in normal circumstances, would be all that an alien could expect. Great Britain and the United States, on the other hand, opposed such blanket commitments to standards of local justice and insisted upon an international minimum which might or might not be satisfied by equality of treatment with nationals. Professor Borchard, writing in 1915, noted that:

> The European countries and the United States invoking the right to protect their subjects abroad, upon which right the municipal law of Latin America, they assert, can place no limitation, pass upon each case as it arises and determine for themselves whether it appears probable that a resort to local courts will afford an adequate remedy. Their unwillingness to remit their citizens unreservedly to the local courts of the more backward states of Latin America seems to arise out of a lack of confidence in the impartiality of those courts and in their disposition to accord justice to the foreigner. This attitude . . . is especially noticeable in cases where the Latin-American government is a party to the litigation.[63]

The authors of the 1929 *Harvard Convention on Responsibility of States for Damages Done on their Territory to the Person or Property of Foreigners,* prepared in anticipation of the First Conference on the Codification of International Law held at The Hague in 1930, also sought in vain to phrase an acceptable definition of "denial of justice," stating in Article 9 that a "denial of justice exists when there is a denial, unwarranted delay or obstruction of access to courts, gross deficiency in the administration of judicial or remedial process, failure to provide those guaranties which are generally considered indispensable to the proper administration of justice, or a manifestly unjust judgment."[64] However, words such as "unwarranted," "gross," and "manifestly unjust" are equivocal and leave to whoever invokes the Article the task of referring to yet a third standard (perhaps to his own intuition, values, and prejudices) to determine when delay is "unwarranted," when a deficiency is "gross," and when a judgment is "manifestly unjust." The definition

---

[63] E. BORCHARD, *supra* note 11, at 821.
[64] 23 AM. J. INT'L L. SUPP. 133, 134 (1929).

proved unacceptable and the draft convention was stillborn into a hostile, nationalistic world.[65]

Happily, the decisions of mixed and national claims and arbitral commissions up to World War II provided some suggestion of what was and was not considered procedural due process in individual cases, including instances of denial of access to courts, physical mistreatment while awaiting trial, and refusals to pay judgments.[66] Such precedents were undoubtedly useful to foreign office legal advisers who, in the absence of an organized adjudicatory system with global competence to review the shortcomings of national law, were and still are called upon to advise whether another State has failed to provide aliens with adequate procedural remedies for the enforcement of substantive claims. In general, foreign offices assume a much more important role in the process of deciding international claims than either national or international tribunals.[67] Their legal advisers

[65] *See generally* Hackworth, *The Responsibility of States For Damages Caused In Their Territory To the Person or Property of Foreigners,* 24 AM. J. INT'L L. 500 (1930).

[66] See for example the cases collected in F. DUNN, *supra* note 20, and in J. MOORE, INTERNATIONAL ARBITRATIONS (1898) (6 vols.).

[67] One commentator, writing about the practice of the United States, has remarked: "It is not always appreciated . . . that the over-all influence of adjudicative agencies on international law is in general considerably less important than that exercised by foreign offices. The number of international law questions passed on by international or United States tribunals is probably no more than a fraction of the number of such questions passed on by the Office of the Legal Adviser in any equivalent period, and the types of such questions considered by courts are generally of comparatively minor significance in the broad context of international regulation." Bilder, *supra* note 34, at 668. More generally, a judge of the International Court of Justice has written: "[I]t is the advice tendered to governments by their legal advisers which, whether always acted upon or not, forms the main basis of state practice in the international field; and it is the practice of states which constitutes the immediate and proximate foundation of the customary rules of international law (even if the ultimate jurisprudential considerations which cause the validity of such rules to derive from state practice have necessarily to be sought for outside it)." Fitzmaurice, *Book Review,* 59 AM. J. INT'L L. 72 (1965). *See generally* LEGAL ADVISERS AND FOREIGN AFFAIRS (H. Merillat ed. 1964).

In the case of the United States, there seems to be a direct relation between the increase in the number of Departmnt of State personnel handling claims and the expansion of United States overseas investment. Secretaries of State Jefferson, Monroe, and Madison often personally handled the Department's legal work. The processing of claims, however, became so time-consuming that in 1848 Congress authorized the appointment of a special clerk to deal with these

exercise a dual function. Initially, they assume a quasi-judicial role in deciding whether or not local remedies have been exhausted and if, nevertheless, a claim exists under international law. In the latter event they then become advocates, urging the political department of their foreign office either to espouse the claim formally and to pursue it through traditional and diplomatic channels, including referral to a claims commission, or to set in motion the less formal procedures entailed in "good offices."[68] Despite their role as representatives of an exclusive national interest, legal advisers and foreign office officials, through traditional insistence upon the exhaustion of Local Remedies Rule, also represent the inclusive interests of all States in promoting settlements of disputes on local, rather than international levels.[69]

The power of foreign offices to make unilateral, nonreviewable decisions probably has been a factor in encouraging the formation of mixed claims tribunals and arbitration boards through which individual claimants have been able to obtain compensation for injuries or losses, and in stimulating diplomatic negotiations for lump sum settlements leading to the allocation of compensation by national commissions. There were, of course, other factors which encouraged settlement techniques of this nature, not the least of which was the apprehension in offending States that a protecting State might seek to enforce its unilateral determination that there had been a denial of procedural justice, for which reparation was due, by invoking one or more of the variety of available coercive strategies, including forcible self-help.

Thus, since a claimant was unable to bring suit in the Permanent

---

claims. The personnel involved expanded steadily until in 1866 a special official within the Department was appointed to supervise this activity with the title Examiner of Claims. Finally, a special Legal Adviser's Office was established for the Department in 1931, a great part of whose activity is devoted to international claims. Bilder, *supra* note 34, at 634–35.

[68] R. LILLICH & G. CHRISTENSON, *supra* note 35, at 91.

[69] Dawson, *International Law and the Procedural Rights of Aliens before National Tribunals*, 17 INT'L & COMP. L.Q. 404, 423 (1968): "Whether or not espousal is ultimately recommended where a denial of procedural justice is alleged depends upon the decision-maker's determination (a) of what local remedies exist; (b) if they exist, whether or not they are adequate as measured against an abstract standard which must be ascertained and identified; (c) if such remedies have been exhausted; and (d) in the event that a violation of procedural justice in light of the aforementioned standard is discovered, whether or not general policy reasons dictate espousal."

Court of International Justice because he was considered an "object" rather than a "subject" of international law,[70] or to sue his host State in the courts of his own nation because he was precluded by the doctrine of sovereign immunity, domestic courts of host States, foreign offices of protecting States, and occasionally ad hoc mixed and national claims commissions became the primary devices by which international concepts of due process were asserted and maintained. This legal order was horizontal rather than vertical.[71] That is, law-conforming behavior was promoted not so much by a vertical hierarchy of international tribunals modeled upon an internal municipal court system, as through the institutionalized interaction of foreign offices and domestic courts throughout the world. A stability of expectation of a minimum standard of procedural due process was assured claimants not through the sanctioning threat of an international writ of habeas corpus or a suit for damages in a international tribunal, but through promises of mutual restraint and threats of reciprocal retaliation within an established process of interaction, claim, and decision, constructed around the Exhaustion of Local Remedies Rule and sanctions ranging from diplomatic protest through self-help.

By the end of the first three decades of the twentieth century, however, the system by which procedural and substantive rights of aliens were assured respect abroad had come under severe strain. World War I and the Great Depression had destroyed the optimism and confidence which characterized social and business life in pre-1914 Europe and had shattered the existing political and economic system. The Peace of Versailles could do no more than paper over the fissures. Laissez faire and free trade were replaced by economic nationalism and restrictive trade practices, and the structure of the world's economy became irreparably undermined.[72] Concomitantly, as might have been expected, the international legal order, which had been posited upon Western European preferences, for the first time received a major challenge. With the Mexican Revolution, which gained momentum after the Constitutional Convention of

---

[70] *But see* W. GORMLEY, *supra* note 1, at 23–31.

[71] *See generally* R. FALK, THE ROLE OF DOMESTIC COURTS IN THE INTERNATIONAL LEGAL ORDER 21–52 (1964).

[72] P. ELLSWORTH, *supra* note 2, at 358–91; H. HALBORN, THE POLITICAL COLLAPSE OF EUROPE 111–32 (1955).

1917, and with the Bolshevik Revolution of the same year, a new pattern of State intervention and participation in national economies commenced, based on the principle that the economic necessity of the majority could take precedence over individual property rights. Wealth was alleged to have a new social connotation which seemed to render irrelevant existing legal concepts concerning the protection and acquisition of private property.[73]

Although the Mexican and Russian deprivation patterns were followed in "Succession States" of Eastern Europe, the challenge to traditional legal concepts nevertheless did not spread beyond control.[74] Despite these storm warnings, therefore, the international legal structure in 1939 remained much as it had been in 1914, with the same pretensions to universality and to European cultural and moral supremacy. It was only when Germany's panzer divisions smashed across the plains of Poland that the final process began which would collapse the already weakened political and economic structure and create a new reality of events and circumstances, a "new wisdom," to which traditional legal concepts and institutions have only recently begun to adjust. The Latin American States would be joined in the years following 1945 by a large number of newly independent nations in Asia and Africa, whose attitudes toward national treatment of aliens and of international responsibility would not be identical with the traditional concepts either of Western Europe or of North America.

---

[73] The exchange of notes between the Mexican and United States governments in the 1930s concerning the expropriation of agrarian and oil properties is illustrative of the impasse. Mexico pointed out the importance of the program of agrarian reform to the future of the Mexican people: "On the one hand, there are weighted the claims of justice and the improvement of a whole people, and on the other hand, the purely pecuniary interests of some individuals. . . . [T]he future of the nation . . . could not be halted by the impossibility of paying immediately the value of the properties belonging to a small number of foreigners who seek only a lucrative end." [1938] 5 FOREIGN REL. U.S. 680 (1956). The United States, however, took the position that "under every rule of law and equity, no government is entitled to expropriate private property, *for whatever purpose,* without provision for prompt, adequate, and effective payment therefor." 3 G. HACKWORTH, DIGEST OF INTERNATIONAL LAW 658–59 (1942) (emphasis added).

[74] Weston graphically describes the effects of World War I and the subsequent legal, economic, and political dislocation in *International Law and the Deprivation of Foreign Wealth: A Framework for Future Inquiry,* in 2 THE FUTURE OF THE INTERNATIONAL LEGAL ORDER 36, 49–51 (R. Falk & C. Black eds. 1970).

Chapter II

The Challenge of New Perspectives After 1945

The wave of political and ideological change precipitated by World War II and its immediate aftermath had little visible effect upon the exterior form in which disputes involving the procedural rights of aliens are either formulated or resolved. The legal position of the alien litigant remains largely as it has been for decades.

Although high expectations attended the creation of the United Nations in 1945, the individual's lack of capacity to bring suit in an international tribunal was not remedied by the Statute of the International Court of Justice. Despite pleas for reform by learned commentators, Article 34 of the Statute provides, as did the Statute of the Permanent Court of International Justice before it, that "only States may be parties in cases before the Court."[1] Plans to establish regional tribunals and to revive the defunct Central American Court

---

[1] I.C.J. STAT. art. 34. Rosenne, a leading authority on the International Court of Justice, has written: "It is possible that the direct representation of the individuals concerned in the proceedings before the [International] Court would have the effect, not only of stimulating public interest in the work of the court, but also, and this may be more important, of enhancing its prestige and public confidence in the reality of international justice." S. ROSENNE, THE INTERNATIONAL COURT OF JUSTICE 245 (1957). Today, persons as well as nations are participants in the international order, so that restrictive legal concepts which originated in another era are not necessarily appropriate for promoting and protecting legitimate human aspirations. As another commentator has written: "No longer limited to relations between governments, or even those between governments and foreign citizens, international law is coming to encompass also those private international activities of individuals and companies which are characteristically affected with a public international interest. These are activities which, individually or in their totality, have an impact on vital interests and policies of the foreign countries to which they extend and thus impinge upon relations between these countries and the home countries of the enterprises involved." Lachmann, *The Role of International Business in the Transfer of Technology to Developing Countries*, 60 AMERICAN SOC'Y INT'L L. PROCEEDINGS 31–32 (1966).

27

of Justice in which individuals could litigate against States have not yet been implemented.[2] Nor can private litigants denied access to international tribunals always be certain of relief in local courts. In some countries a plea of sovereign immunity, as before World War II, still may suffice to prevent litigants from suing governments or government agencies.[3]

There have been some limited breakthroughs. In 1952 the United States accepted the restrictive theory of sovereign immunity under which States may be sued for acts performed in a commercial or nonsovereign capacity.[4] Nevertheless, since State property normally is immune from execution, meaningful recovery may be unattainable even where suit is possible.[5] At the same time, the Act of State

---

[2] See generally Sohn, *Proposals for the Establishment of a System of International Tribunals*, in INTERNATIONAL TRADE ARBITRATION 63 (M. Domke ed. 1958). The Central American Court of Justice functioned between 1907 and 1917, "the first time in recent history that the individual was granted standing before an international tribunal." Parson, *The Individual Right of Petition: A Study of the Methods Used by International Organizations to Utilize the Individual as a Source of Information on the Violations of Human Rights*, 13 WAYNE L. REV. 678, 680 (1967). The court failed for political reasons rather than because it gave *locus standi* to individuals to sue sovereign States. See T. KARNES, THE FAILURE OF UNION: CENTRAL AMERICA, 1824–1960 (1961). See also Hudson, *The Central American Court of Justice*, 26 AM. J. INT'L L. 759 (1932).

[3] See generally R. LILLICH, THE PROTECTION OF FOREIGN INVESTMENT: SIX PROCEDURAL STUDIES 3–44 (1965).

[4] In the so-called "Tate Letter," the Department of State indicated its willingness "to follow the restrictive theory of sovereign immunity in the consideration of requests of foreign governments for a grant of sovereign immunity." 26 DEP'T STATE BULL. 984, 985 (1952). See Bishop, *New United States Policy Limiting Sovereign Immunity*, 47 AM. J. INT'L L. 93 (1953), and the cases collected in Comment, *International Law—Sovereign Immunity—The First Decade of the Tate Letter Policy*, 60 MICH. L. REV. 1142 (1962). See also *New Departures in the Law of Sovereign Immunity*, 63 AMERICAN SOC'Y INT'L L. PROCEEDINGS 182–203 (1969).

[5] The leading United States case which often is cited for this proposition is Dexter & Carpenter Inc. v. Kunglig Jarnvagsstyrelsen, 43 F.2d 705 (2d Cir. 1930). The rationale behind this apparent contradiction is that "[e]xecution against state property has been felt to be an offense against the dignity of the state to a far greater degree than submission to jurisdiction. There is more likely to be bad feeling and friction resulting from such seizures, which are likely to interfere with functions of the state. Therefore, the determination of legal rights and duties of the parties has been regarded as a good place to draw the line, so that execution against state property, as a general rule, be not per-

doctrine prevents both direct and indirect judicial challenges by private parties to the legislative, judicial, and executive actions of other nations on the theory that the courts of one country may not sit in judgment upon the acts of other sovereign States.[6] To be sure, these impediments are being slowly eroded, and not all nations are as reluctant as is the United States to permit satisfaction of a judgment by execution on State property,[7] or to refrain from passing upon the legality of the acts of foreign States.[8] Moreover, individuals are given restricted access to the Court of Justice of the European Communities by the Treaty of Rome and the Treaty of Paris, although judicial interpretation has narrowly circumscribed their scope.[9] The International Centre for the Settlement of Investment

---

mitted." Griffin, *Execution Against the Foreign Sovereign's Property: The Current Scene*, 55 AMERICAN SOC'Y INT'L L. PROCEEDINGS 105, 113 (1961). *See* Lowenfeld, *Claims Against Foreign States—A Proposal for Reform of United States Law*, 44 N.Y.U. L. REV. 901, 926–30 (1969).

[6] *See generally* R. LILLICH, *supra* note 3, at 45–113. In the United States, the so-called Sabbatino Amendment has lifted this bar in certain taking-of-property cases. *See* Banco Nacional de Cuba v. Farr, 383 F.2d 166 (2d Cir. 1967), *cert. denied*, 390 U.S. 956 (1968).

[7] Various European courts have permitted execution against State-owned property. *See, e.g.*, Société Commerciale de Belgique v. L'Etat hellénique (Tribunal Civil, 5e chambre, Bruxelles 1951), in 79 JOURNAL DU DROIT INTERNATIONAL 244 (1952); Decision No. 1690/1949 (Court of Appeal, Athens), in [1950] REVUE HELLÉNIQUE DE DROIT INTERNATIONAL 331; De Belgische Staat v. Société du Chemin de Fer International (District Court, Middelburg 1902), in Weekblad van het Recht No. 7812, at 1 (1902). *Cf.* Lalive, *L'Immunité de Juridiction des Etats et des Organisations Internationales*, 84 RECUEIL DES COURS (Hague Academy of International Law) 205, 272 (III–1953). "With the trend away from jurisdictional immunity, the execution question becomes of increased importance. To allow attachment but not execution is an irrational approach to the problem, for the sole purpose of the attachment is to have property from which a judgment can be satisfied." Note, *Collection of a Foreign Nation Debt by Attachment of an International Bank Loan*, 69 COLUM. L. REV. 897, 900 (1969). At least one lower court in the United States has allowed execution on sovereign property. United States v. Harris & Co. Advertising, Inc., 149 So. 2d 384 (Fla. Dist. Ct. App. 1963); Harris & Co. Advertising v. Republic of Cuba, 127 So. 2d 687 (Fla. Dist. Ct. App. 1961), 13 SYRACUSE L. REV. 169 (1961). *Cf.* Flota Maritima Browning de Cuba, S.A. v. Motor Vessel Ciudad de la Habana, 335 F.2d 619 (4th Cir. 1964).

[8] *See* Goldie, *The Sabbatino Case: International Law Versus The Act of State*, 12 U.C.L.A. L. REV. 107, 158–61 (1964).

[9] For an exposition of the case law in this area, see Angulo & Dawson, *Access by Natural and Legal Persons to the Court of Justice of the European Communi-*

Disputes, organized by the International Bank for Reconstruction and Development, also provides access to individuals engaged in controversies with sovereign States. However, the Centre is too recent a development to have borne fruit yet, and has not received universal support from capital-importing States.[10] The European Commission on Human Rights, while not a court in which an individual can sue his own State directly for violations of human rights, at least provides an indirect means whereby a private party's grievance can be brought to the attention of an international body.[11]

As a result of the impediments which so frequently prevent direct claims in national and international courts, injured aliens, in spite of the advances made, generally still must rely upon the espousal of their claims by their own foreign offices.[12] Accordingly, and also

---

ties, 36 U. CINN. L. REV. 583 (1967). *See also* Comment, *The Court of Justice of the European Communities: The Request for a Preliminary Ruling and the Protection of Individual Rights under Article 177 of the Treaty of Rome,* 18 SYRACUSE L. REV. 602 (1967).

[10] Latin American attorneys have indicated during the course of personal interviews that this lack of enthusiasm stems from the fact that contracting States are obliged to comply with awards in proceedings to which they have been parties and, it is feared, the particular arbitration panel involved may not be inclined toward the equal or national treatment theory and therefore will accord aliens more favorable treatment than nationals. However, in Broches, *The Convention on the Settlement of Investment Disputes: Some Observations on Jurisdiction,* 5 COLUM. J. OF TRANSNAT'L L. 263, 264 (1966), the General Counsel of the International Bank for Reconstruction and Development points out that "[t]he fact that a State has become a party to the Convention does not obligate that State or an investor who is a national of that State to make use of the facilities of the Centre [the International Centre for the Settlement of Investment Disputes established by the Convention]. No State and no investor can be brought before a conciliation commission or an arbitral tribunal without having consented thereto." Elsewhere, he seeks more specifically to allay Latin American fears that the Convention would violate "the constitutional principle of equality of citizens and aliens," or would introduce compulsory arbitration and thus infringe upon the sovereignty of the Latin American States, or would evidence "an unacceptable lack of confidence in the integrity and independence of the national courts." *The Convention on the Settlement of Investment Disputes,* 9 A.B.A. INT'L & COMP. L. SECTION BULL. No. 11, at 14–15 (1965).

[11] *See discussion in* W. GORMLEY, THE PROCEDURAL STATUS OF THE INDIVIDUAL BEFORE INTERNATIONAL AND SUPRANATIONAL TRIBUNALS 92–126 (1966).

[12] For example, the French Government espoused the compensation claim of the Compagnie Universelle du Canal Maritime de Suez against the United Arab Republic after the nationalization of the Suez Canal. Weston, *Postwar French Foreign Claims Practice: Adjudication by National Commissions—An Introductory Note,* 43 INDIANA L.J. 832, 836 (1968).

because the number of such claims is increasing, the practice of resolving groups of claims by lump sum agreements between the protecting and offending States has continued apace. Indeed, it has reached new heights of refinement with the establishment in the United States and in Great Britain of semi-permanent national commissions to adjudicate the claims of nationals against certain foreign States.[13] These international lump sum agreements occasionally have been supplemented by, or combined with, "value-tying" arrangements, including trading and barter agreements, to generate the funds from which compensation is to be paid.[14] Except in the area of lump sum agreements, however, deviations from past procedures to secure the protection of aliens' rights have been relatively small.

Despite this apparent lack of institutional development in the protection of individual rights, the context of conditions in which the pre–World War II procedures of interaction, claim and decision still are expected to operate has changed rapidly and radically. Consequently, even the most disinterested observer is left in grave doubt as to the present viability of traditional substantive and procedural legal norms.

The international legal order, which had developed in the late nineteenth century and had survived well into the twentieth century, was destroyed forever by the emergence after World War II of the two rival superpowers—the United States and the Soviet Union— and the simultaneous upsurge of anti-colonial sentiment in Africa and Asia. Stimulated by the East-West rift and encouraged by the

---

[13] Payments generally are made to nationals from the lump sums which the nationalizing State, by treaty, makes available to the protecting State. On the Foreign Claims Settlement Commission of the United States and the Foreign Compensation Commission of Great Britain, see R. LILLICH, INTERNATIONAL CLAIMS: POSTWAR BRITISH PRACTICE (1967); R. LILLICH, INTERNATIONAL CLAIMS: THEIR ADJUDICATION BY NATIONAL COMMISSIONS (1962); and Dawson & Weston, *"Prompt, Adequate and Effective": A Universal Standard of Compensation?* 30 FORDHAM L. REV. 727 (1962).

[14] The Procedural Aspects of International Law Institute, with the financial assistance of the Ford Foundation, has established a research project to study the lump sum settlement–national claims commission device. For a paper outlining the project and discussing the effect of such settlements on the compensation question, see Lillich, *International Claims: Their Settlement by Lump Sum Agreements, in* INTERNATIONAL ARBITRATION: LIBER AMICORUM FOR MARTIN DOMKE 143 (P. Sanders ed. 1967).

economic and political decline of the traditional colonial powers, a host of newly independent States of relative degrees of weakness appeared in the international arena, each demanding full participation in the community of nations. Although accorded equal status with older States in the United Nations, many of these new States eventually became, to greater or lesser degrees, economically and politically dependent upon one or another of the two superpowers. Meanwhile, the initial ideological rivalry between the United States and the Soviet Union assumed a more ominous image with the subordination of Eastern Europe to Soviet rule and the commencement of the Cold War, soon followed by a nuclear arms race of frightening proportions. This bipolarity of power has become somewhat decentralized in the past decade with the political and economic resurgence of Europe, with internal disagreements in the Sino-Soviet bloc, and with the weakening of the Western Alliance. Nevertheless, the basic reality today is one of political and ideological opposition which, despite efforts to close the breach, still divides the world community.

The new nations have increasingly come to challenge the validity of the expatriate legal systems that had been imposed on them. Many of these States have attacked, in addition, the substantive norms by which the legality of their behavior had previously been judged by the older States, as well as the international procedures traditionally utilized to secure law-conforming behavior from them. Indonesia offers one example. Prior to independence, the various population groups (Indonesians, Chinese, and Europeans) were subject to the same substantive criminal law but to two different criminal procedural codes—one for Europeans and the other for non-Europeans. Customary law was applied to Indonesians in civil matters, while Dutch civil and commercial law was applied to the Europeans. Chinese and non-native Moslems straddled the two systems, being subject with Indonesians to the same criminal code but assimilated to Europeans for commercial code purposes and, with family law exceptions, for civil code purposes as well.[15] The independence movement attacked this legal system as divisive and dis-

---

[15] Lev, *The Lady and the Banyan Tree: Civil-Law Change in Indonesia,* 14 AM. J. COMP. L. 282, 282–83 (1965).

criminatory, and the older legal divisions began to crumble as ideological emphasis was concentrated increasingly "on national self-identity, national unity, and the continuing revolution."[16] Finally, the remainder of the discriminatory civil code was annulled in 1963 and efforts were directed to the formulation of a unified legal system of equal application to all residents.[17] In the new African nations, too, post-independence structural problems often involve assuring the uniform application of the law to all citizens regardless of tribal affiliations. Other problems include making the procedural institutions imposed by colonial masters harmonize with the multiple, independent tribal court systems, and obtaining the unification and consolidation of customary law.[18]

The new, often uncritical, nationalism stimulated by rejection of the colonial past has combined with internal pressures for profound social and economic reform of archaic institutions and has motivated extensive expropriations and nationalizations of alien private property, accompanied to a varying degree by disregard for traditional compensatory principles. The nineteenth-century identification of the sanctity of private property with political liberalism, a link which had become an inseparable part of Western social mythology by 1945—especially in Great Britain and the United States—meant, however, that any threat to private ownership was tantamount to an assault upon the foundations of Western representative democracy. It followed that attempts to restructure colonial societies would encounter the enmity of influential sectors of Western public opinion.

---

[16] *Id.* at 289 .

[17] *Id.* at 293.

[18] It is extremely difficult to make new laws meaningful and relevant to the people living outside the capital cities of many African States. For instance, it is of little utility to pass a law declaring women to be of equal status with men if the administrative facilities for enforcing the new law outside the capital are minimal. One commentator, terming such laws "phantom legislation," eloquently describes the great diversity of legal systems prevailing in contemporary Africa. Allott, *The Unification of Laws in Africa*, 16 AM. J. COMP. L. 51, 52 (1968). *See also* L. GOWER, INDEPENDENT AFRICA: THE CHALLENGE TO THE LEGAL PROFESSION (1967); Milner, *The Development of African Law*, 1 INT'L LAWYER 192 (1967); Harvey, *The Judiciary in Ghana*, 21 THE RECORD 222 (1966); Merriam, *Traditional Cultures of Africa and Their Influence on Current Problems*, and Kamarck, *Economic Problems of the New States*, 55 AMERICAN SOC'Y INT'L L. PROCEEDINGS 146, 153 (1961), respectively.

Nevertheless, nationalization patterns inspired by the earlier Mexican and Soviet revolutions swept Eastern Europe after 1945 and erupted subsequently in Iran, Egypt, Indonesia, Cuba, and South America.[19] As a result, foreign wealth deprivations, once matters of only limited concern, are today subjects of national policy and a source of economic and political exacerbation between capital-importing and capital-exporting nations.

At the same time that they defy the compensation standards traditionally required by Western nations, many new States have asserted that the old practice of intervention in the otherwise domestic affairs of foreign States to protect nationals and their property is but the residue of nineteenth-century imperialism.[20] They contend that diplomatic protection and traditional compensatory norms are components of an international law in the formulation of which they were unable to participate, and which evolved and was imposed upon them solely to protect the economic interests of the great powers.[21]

---

[19] The more notable deprivations are listed in Weston, *International Law and The Deprivation of Foreign Wealth: A Framework for Future Inquiry*, in 2 THE FUTURE OF THE INTERNATIONAL LEGAL ORDER 36, 51 n.48 (R. Falk & C. Black eds. 1970). Even the Western European nations were not immune to the forces unleashed by ideology and economic necessity, as England, France, and Italy—albeit with higher standards of compensation than the Eastern European countries—nationalized basic industries. M. EINAUDI, NATIONALIZATION IN FRANCE AND ITALY (1955). Nevertheless, "there is no denying that socialist notions of economic rectitude have had a profound influence, particularly in the underdeveloped world where, rightly or wrongly—and to some extent borrowing from Lenin—capitalism has been equated with imperialism and colonialism. Planning, social welfare, collective controls, outright public ownership—each is testimony to the widespread conviction that government has a necessary role to play in the economic process. Whether we are talking about the foreign-wealth deprivations that have taken place in Great Britain or Ceylon, France or Algeria, this is a fact whose fundamental importance for policy determination needs neither sponsor nor justification." Weston, *supra*, at 64. *See also* Doman, *Postwar Nationalization of Foreign Property in Europe*, 48 COLUM. L. REV. 1125 (1948). A critique of the latest Peruvian and Bolivian nationalizations appears in Eder, *Expropriation: Hickenlooper and Hereafter*, 4 INT'L LAWYER 611, 619–25 (1970).

[20] *See* Falk, *Historical Tendencies, Modernizing and Revolutionary Nations, and the International Legal Order*, 8 How. L.J. 128, 133 (1962). *See generally* Guha Roy, *Is the Law of Responsibility of States for Injuries to Aliens a Part of Universal International Law?* 55 AM. J. INT'L L. 863 (1961).

[21] Thus, one non-Western commentator has written that "[t]he international community in its inception was confined to only some Christian states of

The new nations often find ready sympathizers among the older Latin American States. Fearful of alien economic domination, these nations have, since the time of Calvo, opposed unrestrained diplomatic intervention.[22] The purported universal applicability and relevance of Europeanized international law, therefore, has become less acceptable to a growing number of States, creating a further new source of disequilibrium in the international arena.

However, the tensions and preoccupations with which States now

---

Europe. It expanded within very narrow limits to embrace, first, the other Christian States of Europe and next their own offshoots in other continents. It thus retained until recently its racial exclusiveness in full and its geographical and other limitations in part. The international law which the world-wide community of States today inherits is the law which owes its genesis and growth, first, to the attempts of these States to regulate their mutual intercourse in their own interests and, secondly, to use made of it during the period of colonialism." Guha Roy, *supra* note 20, at 866. *Cf.* J. SYATAUW, SOME NEWLY ESTABLISHED ASIAN STATES AND THE DEVELOPMENT OF INTERNATIONAL LAW (1960). Dunn refuted the so-called "imperial hypothesis" nearly forty years ago when he noted that it "is frequently advanced as the basic driving force in the activities of strong nations in behalf of their nationals and property interests abroad." He concluded that it "has the signal advantage of great simplicity, both in the intellectual realm and in the realm of the emotions. Unfortunately, however, if one studies the situation carefully enough, one finds a great many phenomena that cannot be satisfactorily explained, either by this hypothesis or by its opposite. One is forced to conclude that this popular view is over-simplified, and rests upon some underlying assumptions of doubtful validity." F. DUNN, THE PROTECTION OF NATIONALS 22 (1932). More recently, Lillich has remarked that "[w]hile it is true that 'the ideas of justice and fair dealing incorporated in the accepted norms of conduct for European nations were carried over into the wider sphere of the international society of the nineteenth century,' there is no need to apologize for attempting to establish a universal consensus behind justice and fair dealing." *Forcible Self-Help by States to Protect Human Rights*, 53 IOWA L. REV. 325, 327–28 (1967).

[22] *See* text at notes 36–65 of Chapter I. Dunn, however, after pointing out that "[i]n other parts of the world, territorial conquest was then taking place on much slighter provocation than was being offered in some Latin American countries," concludes: "It seems quite probable that, had the practice of diplomatic protection not developed as a legal institution, some Latin-American countries would have had to pay much higher penalties than they did for the injuries and losses sustained by foreigners within their borders. While that institution did not always operate in the manner which Latin-American writers approved, it unquestionably served to delay or discourage the resort to forceful action by stronger states when their citizens sustained what was regarded as mistreatment in the territory of weaker states." F. DUNN, *supra* note 21, at 57–58.

must live cannot be attributed exclusively to the disruptive growing pains of the emerging nations or to the ideological gap between West and East. In some respects, the capitalistic world has created its own Frankenstein monster by astonishing technological achievements since World War II. Novel techniques of power-generation, of communications, and of transportation have exposed even the most remote and inhospitable parts of the globe to the blandishments and persuasions of the apostles and emissaries of an increasingly commercialized and materialistic Western society. The transistor radio urges the settlers of the upper Amazon to purchase detergents, while the jet airplane has made the salesman with his sample case a common figure in the new African republics. A recent fad in painting or dress spreads quickly from London to Bombay, from New York to Buenos Aires. The Asian and the African are now aware, thanks to television and motion pictures, of the products and luxuries of the "good life," and also of the apparent success of other nations in ousting unwanted foreign economic and political influence. They know that they need not be condemned forever to a life of unremunerative physical toil within a domestic political context in which they have no voice.[23] As a result of the creation of new desires and expectations, the peoples of the developing nations demand with increasing frequency and insistence greater enjoyment of all values: better education and nourishment, higher wages, more participation in government, access to more consumer goods. Traditional cultural, economic, and political structures are undergoing radical change, either in response to constant exposure to new ideologies, or to recently acquired needs for the comforts and products of modern technology.[24]

---

[23] Dawson, *International Law, National Tribunals and the Rights of Aliens: The Latin American Experience*, 21 VAND. L. REV. 712, 713–14 (1968).

[24] "The poor in Latin America are poorer today also because they want more than their forefathers did. Not only are there more of them, but they have learned to expect more of life. They want more of the gadgets we advertise. Most of them have seen our movies, heard the radio or seen pictures in newspapers and magazines (which they could not read). New roads, such as the very excellent ones in Peru, have opened the way to the great city, and large numbers of people have arrived in crowded buses or on foot. They have seen the wonders of the modern world and they want to participate in it." F. TANNENBAUM, TEN KEYS TO LATIN AMERICA 205–06 (1962).

The above developments have generated a movement to achieve, in the oft-publicized words of former Brazilian President Kubitschek, "fifty years' progress in five." Impatient demands have been inspired for industrialization and product diversification in order to limit dependence upon primary commodity exports as a source of foreign exchange. Local incentive legislation attracts foreign investment with promises of tax holidays, customs exemptions, and other privileges which may give new industry a competitive advantage.[25] In some areas, such as Venezuela, import replacement policies already have stimulated sufficient consumer-goods industries to warrant development of heavy industries, such as steel manufacturing, which often require even greater foreign assistance at inception. For their part, capital-exporting nations and international lending institutions, despite apprehensions concerning local monetary and political instability, actively seek investment opportunities for reasons of private gain and foreign policy.

Within the last 25 years, the consumer revolution has accelerated as never before the tempo and number of transactions involving the movement of wealth, people, and skills across international boundaries. This movement, in turn, has increased vastly the number and complexity of the legal interrelationships among aliens, foreign States, and foreign nationals, as well as the opportunities for disagreement and dispute. Despite insistence in States such as Mexico that foreign capital in some industrial areas form joint ventures with local capital, and despite limitations in certain countries concerning the number of aliens who can be employed on particular projects,

---

[25] For example, in Guatemala the *Ley de Fomento Industrial* accords new industries a ten-year exemption from customs duties on imports of necessary machinery, as well as a five-year exemption from any tax on profits. 78 RECOPILACIÓN DE LAS LEYES DE LA REPÚBLICA DE GUATEMALA 50, 51 (1959–60). Similar privileges are offered by Costa Rica's *Ley de Desarrollo y Protección Industrial*. See Ley No. 2426 (Sept. 3, 1959) and its implementing legislation. *See also* Nattier, *Latin American Incentives and Restraints, in* I DOING BUSINESS ABROAD 12–17 (New York P.L.I. ed. 1962). Sometimes, as in the 1950s in Latin America, foreign firms feel compelled to establish themselves in a market to which they formerly had been exporting in order to meet competition provided by newly established domestic industries. Wionczek, *A Latin American View, in* How LATIN AMERICA VIEWS THE U.S. INVESTOR 1, 24 (R. Vernon ed. 1966). Legislation similar to the laws discussed above also exists in African and Asian nations.

there are more aliens abroad today than ever before in history, engaged in a wide variety of activities either for their own private purposes, in connection with activities sponsored by their governments, or as employees of various international organizations. The legal systems within which these aliens live are as diverse as the projects on which they work. They include the sophisticated civil and common law systems of Western Europe, the newly independent African and Asian nations caught in the throes of harmonizing legal procedures of the colonial past with the modern requirements of independence, and the traditional Latin American legal environment currently beset by problems of streamlining procedural codes and relieving court congestion in order to provide the requisite machinery for accelerated international commerce.[26]

Since World War II a Third World has emerged, the exact contours of which are not yet clearly perceived. This new bloc is composed of economically retarded States whose new ideological orientations and economic aspirations render irrelevant both traditional national boundaries and the conventional dichotomy of collectivism versus individualism which once separated capitalist and socialist States.[27] However, despite massive transfusions of public and private capital and technical assistance by capital-exporting nations, the economic gap between have and have-not nations appears to be increasing. More heed obviously must be paid to such warnings as that of Professor Gardner that "[t]his wide and growing gap in living standards is a time-bomb which ticks ominously beneath the surface of contemporary affairs."[28] At the same time, the

---

[26] See Dawson, International Law and the Procedural Rights of Aliens Before National Tribunals, 17 INT'L & COMP. L.Q. 404, 411–15 (1968). See also Head, International Standards of Civil Procedure: The Alien in the Courts of Ghana, 12 ST. LOUIS L.J. 392 (1968).

[27] See Fatouros, International Law and the Third World, 50 VA. L. REV. 783 (1964). One scholar has called this area "the land of Bandungia"—Asia, Africa, and Latin America. V. DEAN, THE NATURE OF THE NON-WESTERN WORLD 13–16 (1957). "Plagued by poverty, antiquated institutions, political instability and a host of other grievances, the governments of Bandungia today strive not only to eradicate humiliating remnants of past political and economic subservience, but also to adjust to an age of mass consumption by overcoming complex frustrations generated by the disintegration of ancient ways." Id. at 67–68.

[28] International Measures for the Promotion and Protection of Foreign Investment, 53 AMERICAN SOC'Y INT'L L. PROCEEDINGS 255, 257 (1959).

cost of servicing even the low-cost loans which have been made available to those countries over the past 20 years absorbs an increasingly awesome percentage of the gross national products of the lesser-developed countries, making the cost of additional sorely needed economic assistance almost prohibitive. Many factors contribute to this development gap: excessive birth rates, improved health standards and consequent declining mortality rates, and the unprecedented economic boom in the industrialized world of the last decade.

Not surprisingly, the problems faced by the developing nations have given them a sense of identity and common purpose in international gatherings. At the two United Nations Conferences on Trade and Development, for example, these States sought Western (or, more accurately, Northern) concurrence to resolutions placing the more developed nations under an international obligation to grant increased aid and preferential treatment to imports from less-developed countries.[29] At the same time that they wish to stimulate and attract foreign investment, the underdeveloped nations also seek increasingly to control the nature and conditions of investment, to exclude aliens from certain industries, and to demand local capital participation in others.[30]

The identity of goals and interests of these nations, especially in Africa and Asia, leads them, through regional bodies such as the Organization of African Unity or the Asian-African Consultative Committee at the United Nations, to propose distinctive variations in the international legal order. These variations are rarely founded on Western European cultural or legal presuppositions and may not be "characterized by Christianity, a Greco-Roman past, and a respect for rationality expressed in political and legal ideas."[31]

---

[29] The specific measures proposed are discussed in Metzger, *Law and Policy Making for Trade Among "Have" and "Have-Not" Nations,* ELEVENTH HAMMARSKJOLD FORUM (J. Carey ed. 1968) and Kasdan, *Toward a Reorganization of International Trade—United Nations Conference on Trade and Development,* 19 THE RECORD 525 (1964).

[30] Thus, paradoxically, foreign investment in general may be openly encouraged by recipient States even while they are engaging, as in Peru, in campaigns against particular alien companies. *See Hearings on United States Relations with Peru Before the Subcomm. on Western Hemisphere Affairs of the Senate Comm. on Foreign Relations,* 91st Cong., 1st Sess. 89 (1969).

[31] Fatouros, *supra* note 27, at 787.

Meanwhile, the Latin American legal suborder which began to evolve in the late nineteenth century has been gaining both vitality and a new sense of purpose with the formation in 1960 of the Latin American Free Trade Association and the Central American Common Market.[32] Of great significance in this respect has been the creation of the Inter-American Juridical Committee and the Inter-American Council of Jurists which, as organs of the Organization of American States, promote the codification and evolution of a regional body of Latin American law on such matters as State responsibility, diplomatic asylum, the protection of human rights, arbitration, treaties, and the continental shelf.[33]

How the older nations adjust to the Third World, to its legal structures and to its political and economic demands, is one of the great issues of our times, transcending in importance and peril the sterile ideological rivalry between individualism and collectivism which prompts the expenditure of immense sums of money on

---

[32] The Latin American Free Trade Association (LAFTA) (Argentina, Chile, Brazil, Mexico, Peru, Colombia, Venezuela, Bolivia, Uruguay, and Paraguay) and the Central American Common Market (CACM) have been functioning since 1960 and their merger is now a distinct possibility. LATIN AMERICAN ECONOMIC INTEGRATION: EXPERIENCES AND PROSPECTS (M. Wionczek ed. 1966); LA INTEGRACIÓN ECONÓMICA LATINO AMERICANA (Banco Nacional de Comercio Exterior S.A. de Mexico ed. 1963). See also Hoagland, *The Latin American Free Trade Association,* and Nattier, *The Central American Program of Economic Integration,* in A LAWYER'S GUIDE TO INTERNATIONAL BUSINESS TRANSACTIONS 897, 923 (W. Surrey & C. Shaw eds. 1963), respectively. On the development and significance of legal suborders, see Fatouros, *supra* note 27, at 818–22. The shortcomings of the Latin American Free Trade Association have led to the formation of a five-nation subregional group, the Andean Common Market, composed of Colombia, Chile, Peru, Ecuador, and Bolivia. These nations are attempting to agree on a common policy, to be implemented by domestic legislation, toward foreign capital, technology, patents, and royalties. If measures on foreign investments scheduled to become effective June 30, 1971, are ratified by the five governments, foreign companies currently operating in Chile, Colombia, and Peru will have 15 years in which to become at least 51 percent locally owned, while foreign concerns operating in Bolivia and Ecuador will have 20 years to meet the same requirement. The measures also will put a 14 percent ceiling on remittances of profits abroad by foreign companies operating in the area. N.Y. Times, Dec. 25, 1970, at 47, cols. 3–4.

[33] *See generally* Freeman, *The Contribution of the Inter-American Juridical Committee and the Inter-American Council of Jurists to the Codification and Development of International Law,* 59 AMERICAN SOC'Y INT'L L. PROCEEDINGS 14 (1965).

defense and in so doing diverts precious wealth, energy and talent from the service of mankind. One commentator has written that "[t]he greatest challenge to contemporary mankind is presented by the realization that a minimum level of welfare and cooperation in the conservation of human resources is no less a matter of survival than the prevention of nuclear war, and that in both respects the organization of international society based upon the national sovereign state is disastrously inadequate."[34]

Fortunately, statesmen and lawyers have not been insensitive to the need to secure an equitable revision of legal norms and to accommodate them to new realities. However, while considerable success has been achieved, of benefit to all members of the international community, major emphasis has been on the substantive, as distinct from the procedural, side. Thus, post–World War II accomplishments in defining the substantive content of the law of State responsibility to aliens—which have included the impressive reports of the Special Rapporteur of the United Nations International Law Commission,[35] the draft convention prepared by the Harvard Law School,[36] the final version of the American Law Institute's *Restatement of the Foreign Relations Law of the United States*,[37] and the draft multinational convention of the Organization

---

[34] Friedmann, *Half a Century of International Law*, 50 VA. L. REV. 1333, 1354 (1964).

[35] *See, e.g.*, Garcia Amador, *(Sixth) Report on State Responsibility*, [1961] 2 Y.B. INT'L L. COMM'N 1, U.N. Doc. A/CN.4/134 and Add. 1 (1961). After 12 years of revising and resubmitting drafts, the United Nations' efforts have yet to win approval. Lillich, *Toward the Formulation of an Acceptable Body of Law Concerning State Responsibility*, 16 SYRACUSE L. REV. 721, 726–28 (1965).

[36] CONVENTION ON THE INTERNATIONAL RESPONSIBILITY OF STATES FOR INJURIES TO ALIENS (Draft No. 12 with Explanatory Notes, 1961). This convention was a revision, done at the request of the United Nations Secretariat, of the draft convention prepared by the Harvard Research in International Law in 1929. *See* 23 AM. J. INT'L L. SUPP. 133 (1929). Actually, what began as a revision became an entirely new convention. *See* Lillich, *supra* note 35, at 728–30. *See also* Sohn & Baxter, *Responsibility of States for Injuries to the Economic Interests of Aliens*, 55 AM. J. INT'L L. 545 (1961).

[37] RESTATEMENT, FOREIGN RELATIONS LAW OF THE UNITED STATES (1965). The Reporters who worked on the Restatement relied heavily upon the Harvard draft convention, note 36 *supra*. However, the Restatement, unlike either the Harvard or ILC drafts, did not seek to codify or to break new ground. Rather, stated Professor Covey Oliver, one of the Reporters, it was designed "to express what the law is, with a dash of what the law should be in certain situations."

for Economic Cooperation and Development[38]—"largely overlook or ignore the procedural problems of applying this body of law."[39] As one commentator has written in reference to the *Restatement*, "[t]his is unfortunate because a discussion of state responsibility would be incomplete without some analysis of international procedures. There is an intimate connection between substantive norms of international law and the institutional forms in which these norms can be applied."[40] Although the *Harvard Draft Convention* and the *Restatement* both seek to define "denial of procedural justice" and to enumerate standards of procedural due process of which aliens in foreign courts should be beneficiaries, the thrust of both studies is substantive: the machinery to enforce the standards is neglected.[41]

Agreement on substantive standards, while indeed vital, may be of limited utility if the means of application are lacking. At a time when opportunities for disputes between aliens, their host States

---

CORNELL LAW SCHOOL, PROCEEDINGS OF THE FIRST SUMMER CONFERENCE ON INTERNATIONAL LAW 152 (M. Cardozo ed. 1957).

[38] *See generally* A.B.A. COMMITTEE ON INTERNATIONAL TRADE AND INVESTMENT OF THE SECTION OF INTERNATIONAL AND COMPARATIVE LAW, THE PROTECTION OF PRIVATE PROPERTY INVESTED ABROAD 59–113 (1963). *See also* G. SCHWARZENBERGER, FOREIGN INVESTMENTS AND INTERNATIONAL LAW 153–69 (1969).

[39] *See* note 14 *supra.*

[40] Murphy, *State Responsibility for Injuries to Aliens*, 41 N.Y.U. L. REV. 125, 141–42 (1966).

[41] Article 7 of the Harvard Draft Convention and Section 181 of the American Law Institute's Restatement assert that to receive a fair trial an alien must: (a) have the benefit of an impartial tribunal or administrative authority; (b) receive specific information in advance of the charges against him; (c) have time to prepare his case; (d) have full opportunity to know the substance and source of any evidence against him and to contest its validity; (e) have the opportunity to obtain witnesses and evidence on his behalf; (f) have the opportunity to obtain and consult with legal counsel of his own choice, if necessary free of charge if this is provided to aliens; (g) have access to the services of an interpreter if needed; (h) be able to communicate with representatives of his own government and to have such a representative present at the proceedings; and (i) obtain disposition of his case with reasonable dispatch. The Draft Convention also would confer upon aliens "any other procedural right conferred by a treaty or recognized by the principal legal systems of the world." Other considerations might include denial of rights to appeal, executive interference in litigation or in the execution of judgment, unconscionably short limitations periods, stringent security deposits, or restrictions imposed by local codes upon admissibility of evidence.

and the nationals thereof are so great, and the possible consequences of dispute so drastic and perilous, it is unfortunate that the two traditional basic procedural strategies relating to the peaceful settlement of disputes—the doctrine of Diplomatic Protection and the Local Remedies Rule—have suffered severe erosion. The failure to devise an alternative to the first of these strategies and to strengthen the second should be of serious concern since, in the words of Friedmann, it is "utopian to assume that international law and affairs can ever dispense with conflict. Rather it is a question of (a) the level on which conflicts will occur and (b) the methods by which conflicts between nations will be settled."[42]

East-West rivalry has so stimulated the intensive development of weapons of mass destruction that a major war between the superpowers has become—absent miscalculation or madness—unthinkable. Each side is certain that the other, within minutes, could devastate it and a good portion of the rest of the globe as well. However, while the paramount nations now possess greater capacity for destruction than ever before, the consequences of the use of nuclear weapons dictate they be retained for deterrent, rather than offensive, purposes. The newer and weaker nations have profited to a great extent from this "nuclear neutralization" of the more economically and militarily powerful States. Some States have received military and economic assistance from one faction or the other as the price of loyalty. Other States, by aligning themselves ideologically from time to time with one of the superpowers, have been able to defy with relative impunity the policies and legal traditions of the rival power bloc, secure in the knowledge that fears of escalating a minor conflict into atomic confrontation will deter or limit retaliation.[43]

Thus, as the governments of Third World nations become more experienced and sophisticated, they desire and are able to effect increasing control over foreign investments made in an era of greater permissiveness and alien domination. Therefore, when England,

---

[42] Friedmann, *supra* note 34, at 1346.

[43] "This virtual neutralization of the big states gives effective reality to the sovereignty of the weaker states." R. FALK, THE ROLE OF DOMESTIC COURTS IN THE INTERNATIONAL LEGAL ORDER 18–19 (1964). *See also* Fatouros, *supra* note 27, at 790.

France, and Israel reacted with armed intervention to Egypt's nationalization of the Suez Canal in order to protect their "acquired rights," the international community, fearful of escalated conflict, immediately and successfully promoted a disengagement. Egypt, however, retained possession of the Canal. Anticipation of a similar outcome may have encouraged Castro to believe that as long as he attracted Moscow's ideological support he could safely expropriate the property of United States nationals in Cuba without regard to traditional international compensatory principles or fear of armed retaliation. Armed intervention still occurs, of course, especially in areas beneath strong great-power influence—witness Czechoslovakia and the Dominican Republic. Nevertheless, today "[p]owerful states are much less able to intervene in the affairs of weaker states to secure compliance with rules of international law, and especially with rules that are challenged by a consensus among weaker states."[44]

This new vitality given to the concept of sovereign equality by the nuclear stalemate has been assisted greatly by the postwar proliferation of international organizations which were formed, ironically, to overcome the weaknesses of the traditional State system as a peace-keeping device.[45] The members of the United Nations, by adherence to its Charter, have rejected "the threat or use of force against the territorial integrity or political independence of any state,"[46] and the Charter of the Organization of American States forbids inter-

----

[44] R. FALK, *supra* note 43, at 17. He points out, however, that "this general observation is inaccurate unless qualified." *Id.* at 17 n.5.

[45] Since the nations of the Third World are still individually weak, and any strength they may have will diminish if they cannot obtain support of one of the major powers, "it is to the interest of the third world states, as it has always been in the interest of the weaker, to strengthen the international legal order and promote the use of legal channels in interstate relations. This does not mean that the third world either desires or is prepared to strengthen the *status quo* in the present international society. On the contrary, its members want change, preferably peaceful and, if possible, legal—change of the factual situations through change of the legal rules concerning them. In achieving such change, however, it is clearly in their long-range interest to avoid weakening the international legal order." Fatouros, *supra* note 27, at 791.

[46] U.N. CHARTER art. 2, para. 4. In Article 2(7) intervention by the United Nations was forbidden in matters which are essentially within the domestic jurisdiction of any state, except for the application of enforcement measures under Chapter VII (action with respect to threats to the peace, breaches of the peace, and acts of aggression).

vention *"for any reason whatever,* in the internal or external affairs of any other State."[47] Membership enables even the weakest nations to challenge the assumptions of the stronger. For example, in 1959 the majority of the Inter-American Juridical Committee of the Organization of American States, interpreting the Charter, broadly defined intervention to include "acts by which it is attempted to impose or there is imposed upon a state the recognition of a privileged status for aliens beyond the rights, remedies, and guaranties granted to its nationals under local law."[48] The United States representative on the Committee vigorously dissented, stating that "normal diplomatic protection of the lives and property of citizens abroad under international law should not be included . . . under the guise of intervention. The use of the term intervention in this sense is a misnomer."[49] Unfortunately, the majority of the Committee did not agree.

Moreover, these supranational organizations provide their members, great and small, with powerful fora from which, with the aid of the new communications media, they can mobilize public support for their positions. The existence of these same media, assisted by newly developed private groups such as the International Commission of Jurists—which has publicized denials of fundamental human rights in Cuba, Spain, South Africa, and other nations—has fostered development of a global consciousness concerning the rule of law. A new urgency to considerations of public opinion now enters into the deliberations of world leaders who, limited in their ability to

---

[47] O.A.S. CHARTER art. 18 (emphasis added). The Charter, in Article 20, also provides that "the territory of a State is inviolable; it may not be the object, even temporarily, of military occupation or of other measures of force taken by another State, directly or indirectly, on any grounds whatever." These articles formerly were numbered 15 and 17, respectively.

[48] COMITÉ JURÍDICO INTERAMERICANO, VI RECOMENDACIONES E INFORMES 278 (1961).

[49] *Id.* at 283. A 1962 report of the Committee, again over the dissent of the United States representative, rejected the possibility of an international claim by an alien against a State once the alien is given access to any court. Professor Freeman has written that this interpretation "is not even good law in Latin America, for few qualified publicists there would agree with it, and not even Calvo if he were alive. Apparently, under that view a claim would not lie even where the decision of the court was flatly in violation of a treaty provision. No recorded case sustains such an outrageous result." Freeman, *supra* note 33, at 21.

employ naked force, increasingly must rely upon persuasion rather than coercion to attain their goals.[50]

Those exponents of nonintervention who in the pre–World War II years condemned diplomatic intervention and forcible self-help as infringements of sovereignty thus have been supported by the course of historical events. Deprived of its ultimate sanction as a result of the combination of nuclear stalemate and treaty limitation, the principle of diplomatic protection of nationals has been gravely weakened. Although, in fact, the use of forcible self-help to secure conforming behavior was the exception and not the rule, the possibility of its invocation in a variety of situations in earlier times must have been continuously present in the minds of decision-makers. Therefore its influence on the outcome of decision, while difficult to measure, would be impossible to deny. Today, however, even within a protecting State large segments of public opinion may oppose their government's employment of forcible self-help for a variety of reasons, ranging from apprehension over possible escalation of violence and distaste for violating treaty obligations to humanitarian feelings. The invasion of Egypt in 1956 and the landing of troops in the Dominican Republic in 1965 are recent examples. In short, the vast public support which in the past often encouraged forcible self-help may be difficult to muster today. Thus, while the use of force to secure conforming behavior cannot be eliminated entirely as a strategy in view of the present disorderly state of global affairs, its credibility as an ultimate sanction to which

---

[50] "All nations are interested in having a good public 'image'—to apply a Madison Avenue phrase to an international field. Undoubtedly, exposure to public attention at the United Nations, with the attendant press, radio and television coverage, has heightened the concern of nations for the good opinion of other peoples. Observance and respect for fundamental human rights and the essentials of due process under the rule of law furnish one of the bases for good public opinion. No nation wishes to be considered as oppressing its citizens or denying elementary justice to those within its borders." Debevoise, *Lessons from Organizations Like the International Commission of Jurists in Focusing Public Opinion,* 58 AMERICAN SOC'Y INT'L L. PROCEEDINGS 143, 144 (1964). While the importance of this rather amorphous concept can be exaggerated, and "no state is prepared to sacrifice its vital interests merely in order to obey an indefinite and partly artificial world public opinion, decisions on minor matters may be affected, and these often have a cumulative importance." Fatouros, *supra* note 27, at 797.

protecting States in practice may resort without question has been severely undercut in the postwar period.[51]

The necessity of relying upon persuasion rather than coercion has caused even the utilization of nonviolent strategies to become less acceptable. The broad definition of intervention implied in the Charter of the Organization of American States, for example, questions the utilization of strategies of economic or even ideological coercion. Thus Cuba in 1960 and Peru in 1968 protested that if the United States denied their sugar access to the profitable United States' market in retaliation for the expropriation of property of American nationals, it would be guilty of economic aggression in violation of the Charter.[52] As in the case of forcible self-help, employment of harsh economic strategies such as boycotts, embargoes, and suspensions of economic assistance with the aim of inducing conforming actions has received wide criticism within protecting States themselves.[53] Moreover, the bonds of ideological solidarity, which today need not depend upon geographical propinquity, and the precarious internal economic structure of various capital-exporting nations, may seriously impair the effectiveness of economic sanctions. The United States suspension of trade with Cuba, for example, has not produced the desired effect because of a massive compensatory Soviet aid program.[54] Threats to blacklist ships carrying cargoes to

---

[51] For a reasoned argument in favor of the legitimacy of a limited right of self-help by States to protect fundamental human rights, see Lillich, *supra* note 21, at 326–51. *See also* Lillich, *Intervention to Protect Human Rights*, 15 McGILL L.J. 205 (1969).

[52] *See* Dawson & Weston, *Banco Nacional de Cuba v. Sabbatino: New Wine in Old Bottles*, 31 U. CHI. L. REV. 63, 94 (1963). For background data on the Peruvian situation, see generally *Hearings*, note 30 *supra*.

[53] The wide range of available economic retaliatory strategies are discussed in Weston, *supra* note 19, at 145–48. For comments reflecting the growing skepticism of harsh economic and other reprisals, see J. DRIER, THE ORGANIZATION OF AMERICAN STATES AND THE HEMISPHERE CRISIS 32 (1962); M. KAPLAN & N. KATZENBACH, THE POLITICAL FOUNDATIONS OF INTERNATIONAL LAW ch. 8 (1961); Schachter, *The Enforcement of International Judicial and Arbitral Awards*, 54 AM. J. INT'L L. 1, 7 (1960).

[54] The sugar boycott was decreed in Proclamation No. 3355, 25 Fed. Reg. 6414 (1960), enacted pursuant to authority granted by Pub. L. No. 86–592, 74 Stat. 330 (1961). The trade embargo was decreed in Proclamation No. 3447, 27 Fed. Reg. 1085 (1962), enacted pursuant to authority granted by Pub. L. No. 87–195, 75 Stat. 444 (1961).

Cuban ports have had little deterrent effect even on the United States' ideological allies, some of which, such as Great Britain, have had severe balance-of-payments problems which can be redressed only by promoting increased exports, even at the expense of ruffled relations with Washington. Still other countries, such as Canada, refuse to regard trade in nonstrategic goods as other than a moderating influence in world politics.

The complexity and interrelationship of global politics and ideology, plus an increased concern about the national "image" both inside and outside a country, also have contributed to a certain reticence within foreign offices to support, either officially or informally, the claims of nationals. Even though the United States, as the world's principal supplier of foreign military and economic assistance, has at its disposal instruments of pressure which it could use on behalf of private investors abroad, it often possesses at the same time and in the same foreign country competing political interests which may take priority over private claims.[55] When the rules concerning diplomatic intervention, espousal, and the law of State responsibility first were developed it was not necessarily inaccurate to identify the values of private investors with the goals of their protecting nations, since the primary concern of both parties was the expansion of trade and the creation of world markets.[56] In the

---

[55] R. LILLICH & G. CHRISTENSON, INTERNATIONAL CLAIMS: THEIR PREPARATION AND PRESENTATION 90 (1962).

[56] "The practical conditions which first gave rise to the operative development of the Law of State Responsibility, on the other hand, largely describe the world arena from about 1850 to World War I. By and large, it was during this period that private foreign investment first assumed truly international proportions. With the acceleration of industrialization, improvements in agricultural technology, faster means of communication and increasing number and complexity of business and financial techniques, European people, capital and predispositions, to say nothing of goods, flowed as never before until the old mercantilist structure was finally dismantled. Inevitably, the appearance of the European trader and investor in sovereign foreign lands, notably in politically independent but unstable Latin America, produced the conflicts which helped generate the prescriptions today subsumed under the Law of State Responsibility.

"The prescriptions which evolved, however, although of purported impartiality, are demonstrably European in origin and bias. Principles of common justice and fair dealing which had been forged in the simpler pre-industrial era (e.g., notions of the sacredness of private property and of absolute freedom of contract) were transmuted into accepted patterns of expectation in the wider international community. Due in no small measure to the enormous expansion of British overseas

mid–twentieth century, however, this identification is much less realistic. Although the profit motive remains the predominant force generating private investment, the greatest problem now facing all nations is not the creation of wealth and markets, but the wider sharing and distribution of skills, goods, and services. By the year 2000 the already inadequate economic resources of the Third World, if present birth rates are maintained, will be forced to support some 80 percent of the then world population of 7.5 billion, a 100 percent increase over present population figures.[57] The rate of annual increase in the gross national product of the Third World, however, generally lags behind the growth rate of the capital-exporting nations.[58] Unless remedial action is taken at an early date to expand food and other resource production, the effect upon present world political structures could be disastrous. It therefore should not seem unnatural if a foreign office considered the over-all long-range goal of creating an environment of political and economic progress in a particular country as more important than the immediate pecuniary objectives of one or more private entrepreneurs.[59] Thus, we may be

investments backed by the largest empire and the most powerful fleet in the world, these principles tended to favor the capitalist economy of nineteenth century Europe. And as long as the international community was dominated by a European system of capitalistic individualism, this bias persisted. Beginning with the sweeping transformations of the Mexican and Russian revolutions, the twentieth century offered the initial and now constant challenge to these underlying values." Dawson & Weston, *supra* note 52, at 73–74.

[57] World Population, Report of a National Policy Panel of the United Nations Association of the United States of America 14 (New York, May 1969). The distinguished Argentine economist, Dr. Raul Prebisch, has prepared a study for the Inter-American Development Bank, in which he predicts that Latin America's present population of 280,000,000 will double by 1990. Three-fourths of these people will be concentrated in urban areas where, if present rates of industrial development persist, there will be great underemployment. International Herald-Tribune, March 28–29, 1970, at 9, col. 4.

[58] *See generally* the current economic developments part of the U.N.'s World Economic Survey for 1968, U.N. Doc. ST/ECA/119 (1970).

[59] Goodwin, formerly an adviser on Latin America to the late President Kennedy, when appearing before a Senate Subcommittee to testify on Peruvian–United States relations, stated with reference to the nationalization of the International Petroleum Company property: "It does not mean that those [IPC's] claims are not right, but, on the other hand, the interests of the oil company and the interests of the United States are not the same in many cases." *Hearings, supra* note 30, at 90. Lowenfeld, formerly Deputy Legal Adviser to the United States Department of State, has stated with reference to the termi-

witnessing the evolution of a new relationship between the private investor and his government from which the specter of Vattel has been exorcised by the complexities of modern developmental economics. This change may presage a new role for legal advisers in foreign offices as "problem solvers," assisting investors and their host nations to arrive at an equitable and mutually profitable modus vivendi, rather than as advocates and judges.[60]

The above trend does not mean that meritorious claims no longer will be espoused where local justice is denied, or that the good offices of the alien's consul in the host State will not be available. However, a congruency of interest between the protecting State and its national can no longer be presumed, and the alien may have a greater burden of proof to surmount in order to convince his foreign office of the merits of his claim and of its basic compatibility with national goals.[61]

Despite its affirmation as a "well-established rule of customary international law" by the International Court of Justice in the 1959 *Interhandel* case,[62] and its approval by the United States Supreme Court in the 1964 *Sabbatino* decision,[63] the Local Remedies Rule also is suffering an eclipse. Extensive transformations in global economic and political patterns have occurred since Borchard concluded 37 years ago that most international claims "generally have

---

nation of foreign aid under the Hickenlooper Amendment: "But the United States may have a whole series of other matters going either with country X directly or with a regional group of which X is a part. For an obvious example, it would be very difficult to establish and maintain an Alliance for Progress in Latin America if every investment dispute, large or small, threatened to terminate the aid program for an entire country." Lowenfeld, *Diplomatic Intervention in Investment Disputes*, 61 AMERICAN SOC'Y INT'L L. PROCEEDINGS 96, 98 (1967).

[60] *Id.* at 101–02.

[61] "Jurisprudential and political considerations aside, the personal adjustment of the alien to the local environment may also seriously affect the consideration which his claim receives from both national courts and from his own diplomatic representatives. Willingness to cooperate with municipal authorities, to observe the substantive laws of the host state even when nationals may not do so, and to abide by local court and administrative procedures and customs is not only the first line of defense before national tribunals, but also builds a record of good faith which the alien may eventually find indispensible in persuading his own state to espouse his claim." Dawson, *supra* note 23, at 741.

[62] Interhandel Case (Switzerland v. United States), [1959] I.C.J. 6, 27.

[63] Banco Nacional de Cuba v. Sabbatino, 376 U.S. 398, 422–23 (1964).

their origin in some isolated disturbance, event or incident compounded of disputed facts and law, which on that very account cannot normally give rise to an international claim until the local courts have had a chance to investigate the case and by denial of justice have laid the foundation for a formal claim."[64]

Governments today are directly involved at all levels of the national and international economic order, sometimes legislating vast nationalization programs in order to alter radically traditional patterns of wealth ownership. By so doing they have severely challenged the assumptions underlying the Local Remedies Rule. The majority of the post–World War II seizures have occurred in Communist or Socialist States and, since these programs were designed to restructure the entire national socioeconomic order, the implementing legislation usually did not permit deprived parties to contest the takings in local tribunals.[65] Even in Latin American States, where constitutional provisions provide for procedural due process, the efficacy or availability of local remedies on occasion has all but disappeared. The Guatemalan Agrarian Reform Law of 1952 did not provide meaningful review of expropriations, and judges who had agreed to hear an appeal against valuation procedures found themselves summarily dismissed.[66] More recently, members of the Havana Bar refused to defend expropriated United States firms in Cuba, citing the personal risks involved.[67] When the appellate review courts

---

[64] Borchard, *The Local Remedy Rule*, 28 AM. J. INT'L L. 729, 732 (1934).

[65] "The customary international rule regarding local remedies grew up in a day when countries had a common interest in respecting and preserving the integrity of every other country. In some respects changed political and economic conditions have modified the assumptions underlying the traditional view . . . . There is little reason to change the traditional rule requiring local remedies to be exhausted before espousal in relationship to Western-oriented countries. However, in relationship to communist or bloc countries, as it is generally futile to exhaust legal remedies in those countries, the increasing United States practice has been to negotiate *en bloc* settlements of claims of American nationals without mentioning local remedies. In relationship to underdeveloped or nonaligned countries, a United States practice has not evolved." Christenson, *International Claims Procedure Before the Department of State*, 13 SYRACUSE L. REV. 527, 538 (1962).

[66] Dawson, *Labor Legislation and Social Integration in Guatemala: 1871–1944*, 14 AM. J. COMP. L. 124, 140 n.76 (1965).

[67] UNITED STATES TRADE AND INVESTMENT IN LATIN AMERICA 43 (Columbia Society of International Law ed. 1963).

required by the Cuban Agrarian Reform Law were not established, the Department of State of the United States finally issued a memorandum indicating that if local remedies did not exist in Cuba no attempts at exhaustion need be made.[68] Such incidents have diminished steadily the stature of the Rule, with the result that since World War II deprived aliens more and more have appealed for relief directly to their own States, which in turn have attempted to secure compensation by negotiating lump sum settlement agreements with the depriving nations.[69]

The inapplicability of the Local Remedies Rule to extensive nationalizations has been rationalized as an exception to, rather than a denial of, the Rule, the theory being advanced that claimants never have been required to exhaust remedies which are nonexistent or insufficient. Other observers consider lump sum agreements to be implied "waivers" by the depriving State of the exhaustion requirement. This interpretation has been adopted by the Department of State and the Foreign Claims Settlement Commission in the United States, as well as by the Foreign Office and the Foreign Conpensation Commission in Great Britain.[70] Whatever the theory, current governmental practice in circumstances of large-scale nationalizations of alien property appears to have deprived the Rule of much practical relevance. The result of this and similar factors has been to place in doubt its continued vitality as a condition precedent for espousal, and as a desirable technique to prevent the escalation of essentially local, private issues into matters of international concern. This development is regrettable.

Claimants have not been unreservedly pleased with the results of lump sum agreements. Not only has the rate of compensation been low, but upon espousal claimants lose control over the conduct of

---

[68] *Reprinted in* Kerley, *Contemporary Practice of the United States Relating to International Law*, 56 AM. J. INT'L L. 165, 166–67 (1962). *See also* Lillich, *The Cuban Claims Act of 1964*, 51 A.B.A. J. 445, 447 n.26 (1965).

[69] *See* Lillich, *International Claims: A Comparative Study of American and British Postwar Practice*, 39 INDIANA L.J. 465 (1964). *See also* Lillich, *International Claims: A Comparative Study of United Kingdom and United States Practice*, in 17 CURRENT LEGAL PROBLEMS 157 (G. Keeton & G. Schwarzenberger eds. 1964).

[70] *See* Lillich, *The Effectiveness of the Local Remedies Rule Today*, 58 AMERICAN SOC'Y INT'L L. PROCEEDINGS 101, 102 (1964).

their case. Governments, which often have delayed negotiations with the offending State until a politically opportune moment, also have compromised claims for reasons of foreign policy of minimal relevance to the merits of the case. There is little a claimant can do in such an event since, in most countries, the government's compromise of a claim is not considered a deprivation of property without due process of law, and thus provides no basis for legal action by the claimant against his "protecting" government.[71] In addition, awards by national claims commissions entrusted with distributing the proceeds of lump sum settlements generally are not subject to judicial review.[72]

Since the relief obtainable by the executive branch was satisfactory to few persons in the United States with overseas investments, it was only natural that eventually they should seek assurances of protection from the legislative arm of government. In 1962, disappointed by the inadequate compensation obtained through lump sum compensation agreements, frustrated by the apparent inability or unwillingness of the executive branch to invoke traditional diplomatic strategies to prevent further assaults upon United States property abroad, and apprehensive over threats to private investments in Argentina, Brazil, and Ceylon, the United States Congress passed the so-called Hickenlooper Amendment to the Foreign Assistance Act.[73] This statute, as amended, requires the President to suspend foreign aid to any country taking the property of, or repudiating or nullifying existing contracts with, any United States corporation or citizen unless "appropriate steps" are taken by that country within six months to assure compensation "as required by international law." The legislation has been criticized severely since it links foreign assistance to the allegedly unrelated problem of wealth deprivation and, moreover, apparently has been but margin-

---

[71] See Aris Gloves, Inc. v. United States, 420 F.2d 1386 (Ct. Cl. 1970). See generally R. LILLICH, INTERNATIONAL CLAIMS: THEIR ADJUDICATION BY NATIONAL COMMISSIONS 23–40 (1962).

[72] See, e.g., 64 Stat. 16 (1950), 22 U.S.C. § 1623(h) (1964). See Lillich, Judicial Review and the FCSC, 15 AD. L. REV. 72 (1963). In Great Britain, limited judicial review now is permitted from the decisions of the Foreign Compensation Commission. Foreign Compensation Act 1969, c. 20, § 3.

[73] 76 Stat. 260 (1962), 22 U.S.C. § 2370(e)(1) (1964). The legislative history of the amendment is discussed at length in R. LILLICH, supra note 3, at 97–113.

ally effective either as a deterrent to wealth deprivations or as a threat to coerce the "prompt, adequate and effective" compensation traditionally demanded by the Department of State.[74] Most importantly, because the amendment does not specifically condition suspension upon the exhaustion of local remedies by deprived investors, it not only perpetuates the pattern established by lump sum settlement agreements, but immediately elevates an investment dispute to a matter of serious international concern regardless of the merits of the claim. In this respect it works in opposition to the laudable goals of the Local Remedies Rule.[75]

The Rule has been discredited still further by court decisions in the Soviet Union, Eastern Europe, Cuba, and South Africa which have reflected clearly the intrusion of political considerations into the judicial process, and by arbitrary executive action in Argentina, Brazil, and Ghana to remove judges considered unfavorable to the regime. Additionally, it must be recognized that while overtly discriminatory procedural legislation against aliens based upon ideological considerations is not now in vogue, it still exists in some forms even in developed nations. In the United States, rules in several states prevent legatees residing in Iron Curtain countries from obtaining the proceeds of property left them by United States decedents.[76] The decisions of some Canadian courts have led to the

---

[74] *Id.* at 134–46. *See also* Brown, *The Use of Foreign Aid as an Instrument to Secure Compliance With International Obligations,* 58 AMERICAN SOC'Y INT'L L. PROCEEDINGS 210, 212 (1964).

[75] The amendment, which makes no mention of the exhaustion-of-local-remedies requirement, contrasts sharply with the policy underlying the United States Investment Guaranty Program, which provides that in the event of expropriation the deprived investor must pursue local remedies in order to preserve his claim and to be assured of eventual payment in full by the United States. R. LILLICH, *supra* note 3, at 157–58. It also is interesting to compare the amendment with the Convention on the Settlement of Investment Disputes Between States and Nationals of Other States of the International Bank for Reconstruction and Development, Article 26 of which provides: "Consent of the parties to arbitration under this Convention shall, unless otherwise stated, be deemed consent to such arbitration to the exclusion of any other remedy. A Contracting State may require the exhaustion of local administrative or judicial remedies as a condition of its consent to arbitration under this Convention." The Convention is conveniently reprinted in 60 AM. J. INT'L L. 892, 899 (1966). The above article is discussed in Schwebel & Wetter, *Arbitration and the Exhaustion of Local Remedies, id.* at 484.

[76] For example, Section 2218 of the New York Surrogate's Court Procedure

same result.[77] Moreover, even absent formal discriminatory procedures, an alien whose government is not on friendly terms with
that of his host State may find his case unaccountably snarled
in red tape. Again, while many nations have adequate procedural
laws and codes, the day-to-day functioning of the frequently
underpaid staff upon which the judges must rely may leave a large
gulf between theory and practice. One result of these delinquencies
is that an increasing number of major firms involved in international
business activities now attempt to insert arbitration clauses into
contracts and agreements in order to avoid foreign litigation.

The present poor health of the Local Remedies Rule is not by any
means sufficient reason for its total abandonment. Indeed, the contrary is the case. The possible consequences of any drift towards
exclusive reliance upon the inadequate machinery of State intervention to vindicate the substantive and procedural rights of aliens
underlines the urgency not only of developing new settlement techniques but of improving local remedies as well. The same persuasive reasons which made the Local Remedies Rule so attractive a
century ago remain largely valid today. Additionally, the stimulant
effect of the Rule upon legal institutions in developing countries is
sufficient reason by itself to attract support for its retention from all
members of the international community.

Fortunately, the Rule is by no means defunct. For example, it is
preserved in the European Convention on Human Rights, Article 26
of which provides that an individual's petition is admissible before
the Commission only "after all domestic remedies have been exhausted according to the generally recognized rules of international

---

Act permits withholding funds from nonresident beneficiaries where it appears
that they will not have "the benefit or use or control of the money or other
property" they may have inherited. N.Y. Surr. Ct. Proc. Act § 2218(2) (Mc-
Kinney 1970). This and similar legislation in other states has been utilized to
prevent legacies from going to residents of Eastern Europe and the Soviet
Union. However, the Supreme Court of the United States recently declared a
similar Oregon statute unconstitutional as applied, and the future of such legislation is in doubt. Zschernig v. Miller, 389 U.S. 429 (1968). For recent
discussion of this point, see Note, *Alien Succession under State Law: The Jurisdictional Conflict,* 20 SYRACUSE L. REV. 661 (1969).

[77] *In re* Daniluk Estate, [1935] 1 W.W.R. 142, 143; *Re* Lukac, Hayzel v.
Public Trustee, [1963] 40 D.L.R.2d 120, 124.

law. . . ."[78] It is present as well in other international agreements, such as the United Nations Resolution on Permanent Sovereignty Over Natural Resources.[79] The Rule similarly is enshrined in a number of Latin American constitutions which permit recourse to diplomatic intervention only after local remedies have been exhausted,[80] a pattern endorsed by the 1948 Pact of Bogotá.[81]

While little can, or perhaps should, be done to restore the status quo ante as regards diplomatic protection, certainly the Local Remedies Rule can be revitalized as a means of settling both substantive and procedural disputes on the lowest possible levels of tension. This revitalization need not entail reiterating or reformulating abstract definitions of "procedural due process" or "denial of justice" or their component elements. Neither need it involve strident calls for immediate local legal reform. Rather, the objective, as in the following Chapters, should be to isolate those potential problem areas in domestic procedures where either discrimination against aliens does or could exist, or where reality does not coincide with theory, and, additionally, to suggest certain minimal strategies which could exert a realistic and persuasive influence upon the executive, legislative, and judicial decision-makers entrusted with the formulation and application of local law.

Before turning to an examination of specific procedural problem areas, however, it is important to remember the political and economic, as well as the institutional and legal, environments in which courts must function in the countries examined. Because a court may most easily, and at the same time least obviously, depart from normal standards by procedural rulings rather than by substantive denials, alien litigants and the international community itself should be aware of the extraneous, often extralegal, factors with which litigants occasionally have to contend, and of the potentially damaging influences they exert upon an otherwise impartial legal process.

---

[78] Nov. 4, 1950, art. 26, 213 U.N.T.S. 221. The Convention is conveniently reprinted in 45 AM. J. INT'L L. SUPP. 24, 31 (1951). See generally Waldock, The European Convention for the Protection of Human Rights and Fundamental Freedoms, 34 BRIT. Y.B. INT'L L. 556 (1958).

[79] G.A. Res. 1803, 17 U.N. GAOR Supp. 17, at 15, U.N. Doc. A/5217 (1962).

[80] See text at notes 18–40 of Chapter V.

[81] American Treaty on Pacific Settlement, April 30, 1948, art. VII, 24 Pan-Am. T.S. 15, 16.

CHAPTER III

Extralegal Problems Which May Intrude Upon the Judicial Process

The judicial process in the most sophisticated and cosmopolitan of societies never can be divorced entirely from the influence of extraneous pressures within the community which are irrelevant to the normal course of litigation. Since these influences may affect seriously an alien's ability to enforce his rights in municipal courts and tribunals, they should not be neglected in a study of this nature.

During periods of increased crime, any court may succumb to the clamor of the citizenry and pronounce criminal sentences of great severity, intended to be exemplary to the lawless elements. Alternatively, an attempt by a powerful corporate litigant to exact punitive damages from a relatively weak individual may fail, even though the legal claim is flawless, should the community rally behind the "small man" and create an atmosphere which a judge interprets as possibly destructive of the court's stature. Any number of other examples could be found.

It should not, therefore, be surprising that the injection of a foreign element into the judicial process, as by the presence of an alien litigant, under certain circumstances will produce results not entirely in harmony with previous jurisprudence. Because a court may most easily, and at the same time least obviously, depart from normal standards by procedural rulings rather than by substantive denial, an alien litigant and the community itself should be aware of the nature of the extraneous, often extralegal, factors with which litigants occasionally must contend, and of the potentially damaging influences they bring to bear upon otherwise impartial legal processes. The phenomenon is not new, but there is reason to suggest that the results have never been so potentially dangerous as at present, given the increased importance of local courts in maintaining international legal order.

Judicial and legislative discrimination against aliens is as old as society itself. Notwithstanding the biblical admonition that "ye shall have one ordinance, both for the stranger, and for him that was born in the land,"[1] foreigners have been feared and distrusted—and subjected to legal disabilities—in all lands, in every country. These disabilities and restrictions developed in both the civil and the common law. The origins of this differentiation are of interest today, because the recent emergence into the international community of a large number of newly independent States has recreated many of the conditions which influenced the development of European legal systems hundreds of years ago. Aliens were present in European feudal States either as invaders or merchants; today they appear in developing countries as technicians or businessmen. In both instances they stand out not so much because they are aliens, but because their actual or apparent advantageous positions in the community makes them the subject of envy. The experience of England in the Middle Ages facilitates our understanding of the modern phenomenon, for it provides an excellent example of similar circumstances in earlier times.[2]

England was settled by wave after wave of foreign invaders. As a result, English legal institutions faced a much more formidable task than did their Roman predecessors, which could in safety, being supreme, proclaim one law for the alien and another for the Roman citizen.[3] England, however, could not enjoy the relatively tranquil development of a body of law of its own making since it was a con-

---

[1] *Numbers* 9:14.

[2] The still earlier Roman example, by contrast, is not a good parallel. In the mid-twentieth century, no single State is supreme among its contemporaries, nor was England 800 years ago. The Romans, however, were. They were able to deny to foreigners the benefits of the *jus civile*. "Roman law, however backward, was good enough for Romans, and what was good enough for Romans was apparently too good for foreigners." C. KINNANE, ANGLO-AMERICAN LAW 191 (2d ed. 1952). A special body of law grew up for the foreigner, and a special office of magistrate for aliens—Praetor Peregrinus—was created in 242 B.C. This situation did not disappear for centuries. Rome, supreme in the world, could deal with aliens in a deliberate, obvious fashion.

[3] "Very ancient [English] law may regard every stranger as an enemy; but it will lay far more stress upon purity of blood than on place of birth; it will be tribal rather than territorial law." F. POLLOCK & F. MAITLAND, THE HISTORY OF ENGLISH LAW 460 (2d ed. 1898).

quered land, adjusting after the Norman Conquest of 1066 to the presence of a "foreign duke and his descendants [who] became kings of England and the ultimate lord of all the land in the country, without ceasing to be the duke of wide continental domains; and the leaders of the conquering army became the owners of much of the land of England, without ceasing to be lords of great estates on the continent."[4] Consequently, a purely English nationality was long impossible, and England, as would be the case with its colonies centuries later, could not evolve a logical and consistent body of laws respecting aliens.

As experienced in many countries in the nineteenth and twentieth centuries, English laws governing alien activity were prompted not by general distaste for all foreigners, but by dislike for the privileged alien occupant. In England this enmity first was directed toward Frenchmen. Once Normandy was severed from the king's realms, King John declared forfeit for treason the lands of those nobles who adhered to the French kings. However, non-French aliens were in large measure merchants and received better treatment. Far from being the objects of discrimination, they were protected by Magna Carta: "All merchants may enter or leave England unharmed and without fear, and may stay or travel within it, by land or by water, for purposes of trade, free from all illegal exactions, in accordance with ancient and lawful customs. This, however, does not apply in time of war to merchants from a country that is at war with us."[5] Magna Carta reflected the usefulness to the crown of these alien merchants; they lent money to the king and could pay for royal favors. Moreover, they were less dangerous than the French, who claimed title to English lands through their Norman forebears and therefore challenged the king's omnipotence.

Despite this protection the alien merchant nevertheless received discriminatory treatment as compared to his English competitor, the burgher. After all, the alien merchant's position was one of privilege granted by the sovereign, rather than right according to law. Additionally, Magna Carta apparently granted the same protection to the burgher as it did to the merchant.[6] Seeking to confine

---

[4] W. HOLDSWORTH, HISTORY OF ENGLISH LAW 73 (3d ed. 1926).

[5] MAGNA CARTA § 41 (G. Davis transl. 1963).

[6] *Id.* § 13.

the merchant's scope of activity, the burgher argued that the alien lived off usury—a mortal sin at that time.[7] The merchant attempted to ease the pressure upon himself by moving out of the city, but the dilemma which resulted is illustrated in the plight of a fifteenth-century printer: "The aliens affected the suburbs, where they were free from the exactions of the municipal officers, who with the connivance of the corporation employed malicious chicane of all sorts with the object of driving them out of the country. But in the suburbs they were liable to the unrestrained outbreaks of the mob. Such was the experience of Richard Pynson, himself a Norman, who petitioned the Star Chamber for redress against the violence of his neighbors of the parish of St. Clement Danes."[8] In 1464 a general petition was presented to Edward IV from the "handcrafty men and women" of London and "other good cities" seeking redress for these assaults. As the above shows, a position of privilege, real or imagined, still may result in discrimination against aliens whose nations are either wealthier or more politically powerful than the host States in which they live, work, or travel.

The Effect of Political Relations and Economic Disparity Between the Alien's Nation and the Host State

In many places today, as in England in the Middle Ages, extra-legal pressures may be brought to bear upon the alien and in some instances may affect his rights or his status as a litigant. These measures, as in the English-Norman dispute, may arise from the

---

[7] The status of the Jewish trader is distinct. As related by Bracton: "The Jew can have nothing that is his own, for whatever he acquires, he acquires, not for himself, but for the King. . . ." BRACTON, ON THE LAWS AND CUSTOMS OF ENGLAND folio 386b, *quoted in* F. POLLOCK & F. MAITLAND, *supra* note 3, at 468. The servility of the Jew extended only to the king, however, not to others. Certain dispensations were permitted him, chiefly the charging of interest on money lent (denied at that time to Christians). If the king's interests were not involved, the Jew's relationships with Gentiles were determined by law. The Jewish community was permitted to arrange its own affairs according to Hebrew law. *Id.* at 468–75. Thus, in a sense, a separate body of law existed for the Jew just as the Romans used a separate body of law for the foreigner.

[8] SELECT CASES IN THE STAR CHAMBER (Selden-Society, Vol. 16) I, cxxxviii. *See also* A. BEARDWOOD, ALIEN MERCHANTS IN ENGLAND, 1350 TO 1377, THEIR LEGAL AND ECONOMIC POSITION (1931).

relationship between the alien's nation and the host State. For example, there may be economic and political differences either in terms of their bilateral relations, or in terms of their ideological positions on more general global issues such as the Cold War, which are ultimately reflected in individual and governmental stances of direct impact on aliens. Or there may exist general and persistent characteristics of xenophobia, racism, or nationalism culminating in hostility to all aliens or to aliens of a particular nationality. In this context it may be relevant if the host nation is a former colonial possession of the alien's State or of any other State.

In these respects, the procedural position of alien litigants in various former Crown colonies offers some measure of an international standard of conduct or practice. The courts in these countries, as do courts elsewhere, reflect something not only of the political and economic climates in which they are placed but, in addition, a considerable echo of their colonial past. At the same time their role is not only one of interpreters of the values and the forces stirring in the breasts of newly independent, or relatively newly independent, countries, but also of guardians or interlocutors of the traditions and standards of the English juridical system. This secondary aspect, this role of courts *qua* Commonwealth, is as important to the maintenance of internationally acceptable standards of justice as it is peculiar to the individual countries involved.

There are at the moment 31 fully independent members of the Commonwealth of Nations, an immense expansion from the brave experiment launched by the Statute of Westminster in 1931.[9] These 31 countries remain, as were the original seven, "autonomous communities . . . equal in status, in no way subordinate one to another in any aspect of their domestic or external affairs, though united by a common allegiance to the Crown and freely associated as members of the British Commonwealth of Nations."[10] Contrasting with the situation of almost four decades ago, however, the strength of several individual links with the Crown has all but vanished.[11]

---

[9] 22 Geo. 5, c. 4.

[10] REPORT OF INTER-IMPERIAL RELATIONS COMMITTEE ch. II (Imperial Conference 1926) (commonly called the Balfour Report).

[11] Of the original seven members, only four remain. Newfoundland relinquished its autonomy and resumed colonial status in 1934, becoming a Canadian

Variations and changes in previous norms have removed elements once common to many Commonwealth countries until often they seem a heterogeneous collection of States.

India's acquisition of independence in 1947, for example, and that country's decision to adopt a republican form of government, while at the same time acquiring full Commonwealth membership, marked a singular departure from previous practice. For the first time Commonwealth membership extended to States whose connection with the Crown was measured not in terms of allegiance, but only by a cooperative relationship. In short order, India's dramatic move became precedent for other governmental variations. Pakistan opted for republicanism, as did several African States thereafter. Malaya (now Malaysia) chose to establish its own monarchy, and created in its constitution a unique technique for the election, by the Sultans, of a king. Other common features of Commonwealth States soon began to change. English, the *lingua franca* of the old Empire, came to share official status with other tongues. For example, Canada has recognized French as an official language for certain purposes since 1867. With varying degrees of acceptance and usefulness, official languages within one or more Commonwealth countries came to include Afrikaans, Hindi, Urdu, Bengali, Sinhalese, Malay, Swahili, Mandarin, and others.

Foreign policies of Commonwealth States differ widely, the most striking examples being, perhaps, not the periodic armed clashes between India and Pakistan, but the 1965 breach of diplomatic relations between Pakistan and Malaysia, and the 1967 recognition by Tanzania and Zambia of the independence of the breakaway Nigerian region of Biafra. While the practice continues of accrediting not ambassadors but High Commissioners from one country to another, several States have abandoned the term "external affairs" (understood, in Commonwealth practice, to embrace relations with both foreign and Commonwealth States) in favor of the less distinctive phrase "foreign affairs." Many other differences exist: there never had been a common religion, currency base, or manner of dress; the Judicial Committee of the Privy Council long ago ceased

---

Province in 1949, while Eire and South Africa withdrew in 1949 and 1961, respectively.

to be the final court of appeal for many Commonwealth members; no common element can be found in the several flags or coats of arms.

Despite their differences, the Commonwealth members possess in some considerable measure in their judicial processes similar attitudes toward aliens. They offer for that reason valuable examples when attempting to define any widely practiced and accepted norm or standard of conduct, especially since in many of them aliens reside in large numbers. Moreover, significantly, the great majority of these countries have underdeveloped economies, which rely excessively on one or two agricultural or mineral commodities for the bulk of their cash income, and which are woefully deficient in skilled or well-educated labor. Consequently, they depend upon massive injections of foreign capital and technical assistance in order to span in a single generation the several centuries which may separate them from Western society. The pride of independence, the spirit which attends upon *maîtres chez-eux,* and the memories of past abuses and indignities, however, occasionally combine to produce a climate ill-suited to attracting money and talent from abroad.

The former colonies of Europe today form part of the large number of economically underdeveloped but newly independent countries, the delegations of which throng the United Nations.[12] At the same time, a good number of the more developed United Nations members at one point or another in their history have occupied the role abroad of a colonial or quasi-colonial power in the eyes of the local inhabitants. This widespread web of colonial relationships means that most developing countries continue to engage in a broad spectrum of political and economic contacts and relations with countries which once played a dominating political or economic role either in their own pasts or in that of a neighboring country. While this continuity has beneficial aspects in terms of the exchange of goods and ideas, it also serves on occasion as an unpleasant reminder of times gone by, and affords opportunities to redress old grievances. Nevertheless, while discriminatory treatment of aliens and alien investment probably never can be eliminated entirely, its effect can be softened by providing adequate legal remedies to injured aliens.

---

[12] Thailand is a notable exception.

This facility exists in some measure in most Commonwealth countries.

The international fabric of relationships before World Wars I and II is rendered even more complex by those post-1945 ideological confrontations which affect so many countries without regard for age or economic maturity. The attitudes engendered by the Cold War are reminiscent of the much older attitudes toward usury. There is evidence in certain Western countries that aliens may be deprived of legal benefits because they are deemed guilty of what these countries regard as the contemporary sin of adherence to Communism. Consider the judgment of the Saskatchewan Court of King's Bench in a case denying a claim to an estate in that province by a Soviet citizen: "The little accurate information available to me would indicate that any right of succession and inheritance has been abolished in Russia, having had communism substituted therefor."[13] Or that of the Supreme Court of Alberta in an application under the Family Relief Act[14] made by an alien relative of a deceased, who was a resident of Czechoslovakia: "It is my view that a Judge should and would exercise his discretion against making any award where the dependant lives behind the Iron Curtain in a jurisdiction where the authenticity of information is doubtful and the disposition of funds more so."[15] Similar judgments have been rendered by courts in the United States pursuant to legislation designed to prevent beneficiaries in Iron Curtain countries from receiving the use of property left them by United States decedents.[16] One is compelled to observe that such decisions and legislation are not so much products of nonavailability or lack of authenticity of information about the foreign legal or economic systems in question as they are the result of prejudices against Communism. They are, in short, a reflection of the political relationship between the host State and the homeland of the alien litigant.

This ideological conflict which derives from the Cold War and affects legislation or court decisions also is present in Latin America, but to a somewhat lesser degree. To be sure, so-called "anti-Com-

---

[13] *In re* Daniluk Estate, [1935] 1 W.W.R. 142, 143 (1935).
[14] ALBERTA REV. STAT. c. 109 (1955).
[15] *Re* Lukac, Hayzel v. Public Trustee, [1963] 40 D.L.R.2d 120, 124 (1963).
[16] *Cf.* Petition of Mazurowski, 331 Mass. 33, 116 N.E.2d 854 (1954).

munist" legislation has been enacted, most notably in Argentina and
Brazil, pursuant to which alien or national "subversives" may be
deprived of basic procedural rights. However, these laws have been
primarily utilized to muzzle domestic political dissent, rather than
to defend the nation against foreign subversion. The Cold War,
in fact, merely provided an excuse for repressive legislation, a fact
obvious from its broad scope and from the proclivity of even mod-
erately conservative Latin American elements to brand as "Communist" anyone advocating alteration in the status quo. The 1967
Argentine Repression of Communism Act is illustrative.[17] It provides
imprisonment of one to eight years and, in the case of aliens or
naturalized citizens, expulsion from the country, for persons classified as "Communists,"[18] who are defined as "physical or legal persons who carry on activities proven to be of undoubtedly Communist
ideological motivation. Activities carried on prior to this law may
be taken into account."[19] While the preamble to the Act denies any
intent to penalize freedom of expression concerning "political and
social events," and states that it is only directed against Communist-

---

[17] Represión del Comunismo Ley No. 17,401, Boletín Oficial, Aug. 29, 1967.
See also the Brazilian Nova Lei de Segurança Nacional, Decreto Lei No. 314,
March 13, 1967.

[18] Ley No. 17,401, arts. 11, 14, & 15; Decreto 8329 of November 13, 1967,
establishes in greater detail the procedures to be followed in classification, 14
REVISTA DE LEGISLACIÓN ARGENTINA, JURISPRUDENCIA ARGENTINA 69 (Nov.,
1967).

[19] Ley No. 17,401, art. 1. An administrative agency first determines in secret
proceedings if persons are Communists, and then notifies the person involved of
its decision. The determination then may be appealed through administrative
channels to the executive power. (Arts. 3 & 4.) Once administrative remedies are
exhausted, an aggrieved party may appeal to a federal court, which will only
reverse the administrative decision if it indicates "manifest arbitrariness."
(Art. 4.) Natural persons classified as Communists may not, *inter alia*, become
citizens, hold public office, teach in public or private schools, receive state
scholarships, operate radio or television stations, acquire, direct or administer
publication activities, or hold offices in labor unions. (Art. 6.) Companies which
are being investigated under the Act may be "intervened" by the government
and their activities suspended. (Art. 9.) Aliens (except members of the diplomatic corps) "who, because of their backgrounds, are reputed to be Communists"
may be denied entry into the country. (Art. 7.) Persons classified as Communists
under the Act may, at the end of five years, petition for their "rehabilitation,"
offering evidence that during this period they have not engaged in subversive
activities. (Art. 10.)

inspired "activities disturbing to or subversive of the social order,"[20] the legislative standards seem unduly vague and susceptible to varying interpretations.

Hostility between the alien's State and the host State, of course, may spring from sources other than ideology. Ever since independence, Latin American nations have warred over disputed boundaries, since upon the break from Spain geographical barriers and technical incapacity prevented accurate demarcation of frontiers. Some disputes, as between Venezuela and Brazil, have been resolved peacefully. Often, however, conflicting claims have not been settled and are revived from time to time for political and other reasons, as is the case with Venezuela and Guyana, Surinam and Guyana, and Ecuador and Peru. An unsettled frontier was certainly one of the factors which precipitated the so-called "football war" between El Salvador and Honduras in the summer of 1969. As a result, nationals of one disputant may fear they will not be accorded completely fair treatment in the courts of the other.

Some incidents between an alien and his host State defy categorization. They flow neither from a colonial background nor a pattern of xenophobia. They admit some degree of description, however, in purely economic terms. Examples are the severe treatment of immigrant laborers in Malaysia, the withdrawal of work permits from noncitizens in Kenya, and the expulsion of immense numbers of persons from Ghana. These events all occurred in Commonwealth countries, which is perhaps a commentary of sorts on the limitations inherent in a parliamentary system with its strong doctrine of parliamentary superiority. The Ghanaian incident is particularly distressing in both social and legal terms. It is quite distinct from the Kenya situation, where most of those expelled were Asians. Ghana, once the very fount of the African unity movement—indeed, a country with a constitution which anticipates the creation of a single African State—expelled hundreds of thousands, perhaps millions, of Africans.

On November 18, 1969, the Ghanaian Government ordered all resident aliens to leave the country by December 2 unless by that

---

[20] BOLETÍN INFORMATIVO: ANALES DE LEGISLACIÓN ARGENTINA No. 26 at 7 (Sept. 11, 1967).

date they were in possession of residence and work permits. In order to obtain such permits, aliens were required to produce a passport or some other proof of nationality. The great majority had no such documents. They had come from other parts of West Africa decades ago and had considered Ghana their permanent home for many years. The embassies to whom passport applications were hurriedly made could not begin to cope with the flood in the time allowed. Ironically, the aliens at whom the ouster was purportedly aimed— Syrians, Lebanese, Indians, Chinese from Hong Kong—all were in possession of identification and the necessary residence and work documents and so none were affected. The heavy toll fell on persons from Upper Volta, Togo, Ivory Coast, Nigeria, Dahomey, Mali, Senegal, Sierra Leone, Niger, and Cameroon. Several hundred thousand came from Nigeria alone. In hours, these well-settled, employed aliens were turned into hapless refugees. Nor did their plight improve.

None of the expellees, who in total may account for one-quarter of the total population of Ghana, could leave the country without an exit visa, which was obtainable only on presentation of an income tax clearance, a health certificate, and a valid passport. The incredible hardship caused by this inhumane governmental activity and bureaucratic chaos is matched only by the loss suffered by the Ghanaian economy. Most of the African expellees were employed in occupations in which Ghanaians themselves refuse to engage, including cocoa-farm labor, mining, road construction, and garbage collection. Indeed, they had come to Ghana for this very reason.

The volume of persons affected in situations of this sort inevitably produces impotence in the courts. They are unable to protect the victims of the decree, or to secure compensation for deprivation of property. The incident exemplifies the severe limitations of judicial institutions in situations of massive social change.

Nationalism and Xenophobia in Developing Countries

Nationalism is by no means a twentieth-century product, but its incidence is unquestionably more widespread now than ever before in history. Independence has created for scores of newborn States a problem seldom encountered by more established governments: the task of creating a sense of common identity and purpose among diverse peoples and tribes who in the past often had nothing more in common than their arbitrary union for administrative purposes by the colonial powers. Once this imposed, external unifying force was withdrawn, a domestic substitute of voluntary quality was required, which has not always been easy to assure. Moreover, because common dislike for colonial administration was often the dominant adhesive among preindependent peoples, withdrawal of alien administration left in many places a legacy of centrifugal forces. In order to create an alternate sense of cohesion, the new governments have employed the traditional techniques of directing loyalties to recently created objects of pride—the national steel mill and the national airline; to newly established national institutions—the legislative assembly and the ports authority; to fresh initiatives and accomplishments in the world beyond—as hosts to international conferences and as sponsors of resolutions in the General Assembly.

This development may be called nationalism. It has proliferated in an era when in many respects it is out of date and woefully inappropriate for dealing with the problems of an interdependent world. Established nations—which themselves served as models for this phenomenon through past periodic appeals to patriotism and stimulation of emotional tributes to king and country—are ill-advised now, however, to warn recently independent States that nationalism is an evil influence and a historical anachronism. People whose societal concepts are tribal or village in structure require an immense adjustment simply to accept a relationship to any authority located more than a few miles distant. To expect the governments of these countries to provide the impetus for an even greater adjustment, for an acceptance of some vague form of internationalism, is as unrealistic as expecting these same young governments to forego voluntarily the trappings and privileges of sovereignty flaunted before them by decades of colonial administrators. This fact explains in part why the United Nations is far from a supranational institution. To the newly independent States the United Nations offers them their finest, and perhaps only, opportunity to compete equally with other States. Their airlines may consist only of a single airplane, their navies may be nonexistent, and their steel mills uneconomic, but in New York they command at a reasonable price all the panoply of a diplomatic unit. Here the vote of a small country in the General Assembly is equivalent to that of a superpower. Here such a State may register its views in committee as often and as forcefully as any country in the world. Here more than anywhere else the new nation is recognized as a State, as a full-fledged member of the world community. Thus, these countries view the United Nations not as a place to surrender a modicum of sovereignty to the commonweal, but instead as a stage where sovereignty can be demonstrated and possibly exploited.[21]

Nationalism, of course, may lead to discriminatory treatment against aliens, as has happened in some States. However, if the process of nationalism includes the creation or maintenance of national institutions patterned after similar institutions in developed countries, the courts and the judicial process need not be discriminatory. Indeed, it may be said with some degree of confidence that all Commonwealth countries have consciously pursued a policy of administration of justice almost identical to the system inherited from Britain. Nationalism in these respects has meant an attempt to create a new tradition in the image of the old.

This development should not be surprising. British justice and judicial fair play have long enjoyed enviable reputations. Even during the colonial era the wrath and the distrust of native peoples seeking independence throughout the empire were seldom directed at the courts, but rather at the executive, which also exercised legislative powers. If the laws interpreted in the courts were unpopular, the people correctly understood that the fault was not that

---

[21] Just how far this pure sovereignty leads to purity of voting practices, however, may be questioned. As the Deputy Assistant Secretary of State for International Organization Affairs has stated, "[a]nyone who believes that United States influence in the United Nations is measured by the fact that it has less than one-hundredth of the votes in the General Assembly fails completely to understand the realities of power as they are reflected in the world organization. These realities include the fact that the United States is the principal contributor to the U.N.'s regular budget, is by far the largest supporter of the U.N.'s peace-keeping and development programs, and is making by far the largest individual contribution to the defense and development of the non-communist world. On U.N. decisions of vital importance to the United States, the voting of other countries has been considerably influenced by U.S. views." Gardner, *United Nations Procedures and Power Realities: The International Apportionment Problem*, 52 DEP'T STATE BULL. 701, 703 (1965).

of the judiciary. For better or for worse, a parliamentary system in large measure makes the legislature supreme.

Following independence, the judicial structure remained remarkably unchanged in most Commonwealth countries. Appeals to the Judicial Committee of the Privy Council in London have been abandoned in many but not all instances.[22] Nor is there any discernible difference in this respect as between developed and developing States of the Commonwealth. Appeals do not lie from Canada, but do from Singapore; one can appeal in certain cases from Australia, but not from Kenya. In several countries, high judicial office is held by nonnationals because they are the most qualified persons available, and because there still remains such similarity in the laws of many Commonwealth countries that judges from one adjust easily to the laws of another. This interchangeability of the judiciary certainly is the case today in Tanzania, in Trinidad, and in Nigeria, and until recent years in other countries as well.

These common elements of law and procedure are not inconsistent with nationalism, but rather exert a moderating influence upon nationalistic extremes. The use of English as the *lingua franca* in the courts (and in the international marketplaces), and the employment of similar legal procedures, permit not only the exchange of judges but also reassure foreign businessmen who may be reluctant

---

[22] The Privy Council's role has not been applauded universally. One Canadian commentator has spoken of "the failure of the Privy Council frankly to acknowledge and admit, in its formal opinions accompanying its decisions, that it was engaging in constitutional elaborations that were neither expressly warranted by the text of the Constitution, nor supported by the original historical intentions of the Founding Fathers of the Constitution, in reaching the results that the Privy Council did, in the period from 1896 onwards, in relation to social and economic planning legislation and Dominion-Provincial relations generally. The judicial policy-maker surely has certain obligations of public candour, in order to expose the judicial policy choices to the democratic corrective of public discussion and criticism! The failure of the Privy Council, in relation to the Canadian Constitution, to be frank and explicit as to the policy bases of its opinions, meant that the reasons for the actual policy choices too often remained obscured and concealed, with the policy considerations necessarily operating as 'inarticulate major premises' to the final decision. . . . If we had judicial policy-making on the part of the Privy Council in relation to the Canadian Constitution, in the period from 1896 onwards, it was, necessarily, because of these very omissions, a species of policy-making in the dark—at best, impressionistic and rather hit-and-miss." E. McWHINNEY, JUDICIAL REVIEW IN THE ENGLISH-SPEAKING WORLD 232–33 (3d ed. 1965).

to invest abroad through concern about the quality of legal systems operative in certain countries. It is the rule rather than the exception that in most Commonwealth countries litigation is commenced, tried, and concluded by employing pleadings and following procedures which in most respects are almost identical to those used in the law courts in England. Even the names of the courts, the titles of the judges, and the dress of the barristers are patterned closely on the English model. Of course, English laws and techniques have not dispelled or replaced local laws. Instead, as with the medieval law merchant, the common law (English model) has flowed in to fill gaps, and now serves in a complementary fashion the needs of those countries.

The beneficial consequences should not be underrated. If the common law is firmly rooted, and if democratic legislative institutions perform their traditional roles, then the substantive laws of these former colonies may be expected to develop and to exhibit autonomous characteristics which will reflect the social requirements not of England, but the State in question. If Canada can be used as a model, the degree of departure from English substantive law will be in direct proportion to the period of independence. If the spirit of justice has been equally well-rooted as the law, however (and again using Canada as a model), then the procedures introduced into those countries in their colonial era should not be expected to be subject to the same pressures for major revision. They will continue to do the job required of them in their old form.[23]

Independence and a spirit of nationalism need not lead automatically to a rejection of laws and legal institutions inherited from colonial masters. Nor has the continued widespread use of laws of English origin in Commonwealth countries occurred unconsciously or by coincidence. While it is true that attainment of independence by Commonwealth members has the same legal effect as secession in

---

[23] It has been remarked, however, that "the dominant theme in North American philosophy of law today must be the concept of change or revolution in law. In Mr. Justice Oliver Wendell Holmes' own aphorism, it is revolting to have no better reason for a rule of law than that it was so laid down in the time of Henry IV. The prestige argument, from age alone, that because a claimed legal rule has lasted a certain length of time it must automatically be valid and binding at the present-day, regardless of changes in basic societal conditions and expectations, is no longer very persuasive." *Id.* at 229–30.

most instances, there is nevertheless an important distinction because in every instance independence has been granted by the mother country. No question of legality or illegality of independence exists, so that no stigma attaches to the adoption of English law and procedures.[24] Many statutes in these countries are almost identical in whole or in part to English legislation or, in East Africa, to both English and Indian legislation. In these instances, and where specific English statutes are incorporated into the local law, regard is paid to the way in which the original or "pattern" legislation has been interpreted in the country of origin. Yet another category of incorporation of external law is found in general reception statutes, which always cause some difficulty in interpretation. These statutes generally provide that the common law, doctrines of equity, and statutes of general application of England shall be in force in the country in question, so far as local circumstances permit, and subject to such qualifications as local circumstances may make necessary.[25]

In some instances, procedural law is incorporated as well; Ghana, for example, has done so. The Supreme Court (Civil Procedure) Rules[26] are almost identical to the English Rules of the Supreme

---

[24] This is not to say that some confusing situations do not exist. Singapore declared itself independent one day prior to its entry into the newly enlarged state of Malaysia in September 1963. Later, of course, it separated from Malaysia and is now an independent State. For a discussion of the legal issues raised by this particular event, see Green, *Malaya/Singapore/Malaysia: Comments on State Competence, Succession and Continuity,* 4 CANADIAN Y.B. INT'L L. 3 (1966).

[25] An example is the Federation of Malaya Civil Law Ordinance No. 5 of 1956. Section 3 reads: "(1) Save in so far as other provision has been made or may hereafter be made by any written law in force in the Federation or any part thereof, the Court shall apply the common law of England and the rules of equity as administered in England at the date of the coming into force of this Ordinance. Provided always that the said common law and rules of equity shall be applied so far only as the circumstances of the States comprised in the Federation and their respective inhabitants permit and subject to such qualifications as local circumstances render necessary." The importance of such a standardizing ordinance in Malaysia, where the remnants of no less than 43 different legal systems still form active parts of the country's jurisprudence, cannot be overestimated.

[26] Laws of the Gold Coast, 1954, Subsidiary Legislation, c. 4. The Chapter 4 referred to is "The Courts' Ordinance" of July 1, 1935, which was repealed and replaced by the Courts' Act, 1960, (C.A.9) which was in turn repealed and replaced by The Courts' Decree, 1966 (N.L.C.D.84). Throughout, however, the

Court as the latter stood prior to their revision in late 1954. Nevertheless, what has been borrowed may not provide for every contingency. The Ghanaian Rules state: "Where no provision is made by these Rules, the procedure, practice and forms in force for the time being in the High Court of Justice in England shall, so far as they can be conveniently applied, be in force in the Supreme Court of the Gold Coast."[27] Similarly, in Malaysia, the Rules of the Supreme Court provide: "All proceedings other than actions and all applications in the High Court or the Court of Appeal may, subject to these rules, be taken and made in the same manner as the like proceeding or application would be taken or made in the High Court of Justice or in the Court of Appeal in England, as the case may be."[28] On the west coast of Africa, in Ghana, Nigeria, the Gambia, and Sierra Leone, the English procedural practice came direct. Such was not the case in Tanzania in East Africa. Until October 1966, Tanzanian courts employed the Indian Code of Civil Procedure (1908), which itself is derived from turn-of-the-century English rules. The new Tanzanian code is a revised, refurbished version of English procedure received indirectly via India.[29]

This reliance by 31 countries—possessing among them 800 million people (almost one-fourth of the world's population)—upon a single source of substantive and procedural law is a remarkable phenomenon not often appreciated outside the Commonwealth. It does lead, however, to unexpected results, as indicated by Tanzanian civil procedure. Some of the English rules which formed the basis for the 1908 Indian Code have changed considerably in the past 60 years, and the Indian Code itself has been altered. Yet in Tanzania the clock in a sense stopped in 1908 and did not start again until 1966, when the old Indian Code was abandoned in favor of a Tanzanian code. Another example, this time in substantive law, is found in Canada, where until 1968 the divorce law[30] was based in large part

---

Supreme Court (Civil Procedure) Rules of 1954 have remained intact and have been subjected to amendment or modification on very few occasions, most of which have related to matters of form only. *See also* L. OKOGWU, THE LEGAL STATUS OF THE ALIENS IN NIGERIA (1969).

[27] Order 74.

[28] *Discussed in* Sundaram v. Chew Choo Khonn, (1968) 2 MALAYAN L.J. 40.

[29] TANZANIAN CIVIL PROCEDURE CODE, Act No. 49 (1966).

[30] Marriage and Divorce Act, CAN. REV. STAT. c. 176 (1952).

upon the English Matrimonial Causes Act of 1857,[31] a statute that had not been in effect in England for over a quarter of a century.

This continued adherence to English civil procedure in Commonwealth countries is of considerable significance, and not simply to the alien litigant. Rules of civil procedure are of wider consequence than the particular lawsuit which they may be governing. They promote respect for law and the orderly functioning of commercial intercourse and private contractual relationships throughout the community. The desire of society to dispose efficiently and quickly of litigation is reflected in the limitations statutes, attitudes toward res judicata and provisions for execution of judgments found in all the countries studied. There is a second, larger community which also benefits from orderly procedures in civil litigation. This community is the community of nations subscribing to the principles of international law and the exhaustion of local remedies requirement. The Local Remedies Rule, at its most basic or functional level, serves the world community by reconciling the conflicting interests of the respondent State and the plaintiff alien, permitting each to seek justice in the cheapest and most convenient fashion, so that incidents of potential international irritation are contained within reasonable bounds.

Nationalism is not synonomous with xenophobia, nor need it lead in that direction. Some evidence of selective xenophobia does from time to time appear, of course, but more often as a result of envy for a privileged position thought to be occupied by the alien. Extraterritorial courts were not common in the old British Empire. This fact meant, by and large, that a single judicial system—and in many instances a single body of law—applied to both alien and citizen. Nationalism, with or without a tinge of xenophobia, also is a potent force in the Western Hemisphere and may be assuming new dimensions as the Latin American nations seek a common front against what they consider to be the inequitable trade, investment, and foreign assistance policies of the United States. This attitude manifests itself in demands for joint foreign investor–local government

---

[31] The Divorce and Matrimonial Causes Act of 1857, 20 & 21 Vict., c. 85. By the English "short titles" statute passed in 1896, the name of this act was declared to be "The Matrimonial Causes Act." Short Titles Act of 1896, 59 & 60 Vict., c. 14.

ownership of basic income-producing activities (such as the copper mines in Chile), increased dissatisfaction over the treatment mineral and petroleum exports receive in United States markets, the actual or threatened expropriation of alien property (most recently in Bolivia and Peru), restriction on foreign banking activity as in Costa Rica, and demands (as in Ecuador, Peru, and Chile) that national sovereignty over maritime resources be recognized as extending well beyond traditional three-mile limits. Anti-Yanqui feeling is fanned by local news media, which could create an atmosphere prejudicial to the enforcement of legal rights by aliens in municipal courts, which in turn would only harm the long-run interests of the host State.

In some countries the effect of xenophobia upon the administration of justice is most visible in the concern expressed about participation of expatriates in the legal profession. Such concern, of course, is by no means peculiar to developing countries. Because lawyers have an influential position in a society, few nations permit noncitizens to practice law actively. Also, demands for restrictive bar regulations may be prompted not by reasons of security or apprehensions of foreign influence, but by pressure from the local bar which may fear loss of income to alien attorneys. Following its 1965 annual conference, the Nigeria Bar Association published a pamphlet which concluded:

> The Nigerian Bar Association is fighting:
> (a) for the survival of its members in their own country,
> (b) to end the last vestiges of colonialism in the legal profession,
> (c) to break the closed circle formed for foreign monopoly of our economy viz: Foreign Businessmen—using—Foreign Banks— using—Foreign Insurance Companies—using—Foreign Accountants—using Foreign Lawyers.

Nigeria is not alone in such sentiments. In continental Europe and in most of the states of the United States of America, only nationals can become members of the legal profession.[32] This situation perhaps is due more to the close relationship between attorneys and the courts, which are, after all, one of the instrumentalities

---

[32] In countries having a divided legal profession, nationality generally is a requirement for membership in all branches.

through which the State exercises its sovereign power, than to simple xenophobia.[33] However, a certain amount of xenophobia—or at least fear of excessive competition—even if unvoiced, usually exists as one of the motivating factors for such restrictions. It is particularly true where, as in France, naturalized citizens must wait five years before admission will be granted to one of the legal professions.[34] The importance of these rules, however, should not be overestimated. French courts, for instance, traditionally will permit a foreign attorney to appear before them *pro hac vice* if such appearance would be useful, if prior permission of the court is obtained, and if the foreign attorney is accompanied by a French lawyer. Furthermore, informal agreements between bar associations sometimes enable attorneys from one association to appear in courts within the territory of the other. Such an agreement exists between the Brussels and Paris bars.[35] In addition, the giving of legal advice traditionally has been unrestricted by governmental regulation in France and Italy.[36] As a result, a number of American law firms have been able to establish themselves in Paris and several other places on the continent. Finally, pursuant to Articles 52–58 on the right of establishment and Articles 59–66 on the free movement of services of

---

[33] It is interesting to note that the German statute regulating the legal profession, the *Bundesrechtsanwaltsordnung* (Law of Aug. 6, 1959, [1959] BGBl. 565), contains no express nationality rule, but incorporates such a rule by reference, since Section 4 of the statute requires the same qualifications for attorneys as for judges. Judges, however, must be German nationals pursuant to the Law of Sept. 8, 1961, [1961] BGBl. 1665, *as amended* by Law of Aug. 18, 1965, [1965] BGBl. 891, § 9.

[34] Ordonnance of Oct. 19, 1945, French Code of Nationality, [1945] J.O. 6700, [1946] D.L. 10, art. 81. Even the lapse of a five-year period after naturalization does not always guarantee admission to the bar. The bar associations which, subject to court review, control admission to the bar, sometimes check whether the candidate has a sufficient knowledge of the French language and is sufficiently integrated into French society. *See, e.g.*, X., Cass. req. June 2, 1937, [1937] D.H. Jur. 345. *See generally* 1 H. SOLUS & R. PERROT, DROIT JUDICIAIRE PRIVÉ 761–68 1961).

[35] *See generally* Hamelin, *Avocat*, 1 RÉPERTOIRE DALLOZ DE PROCÉDURE CIVILE ET COMMERCIALE at No. 303 (1955).

[36] Subject to a number of minor exceptions, nonprofessionals may not appear before a court. On law practice by nonprofessionals see P. HERZOG, CIVIL PROCEDURE IN FRANCE 66–67 (1967); M. CAPPELLETTI, J. MERRYMAN & J. PERILLO, THE ITALIAN LEGAL SYSTEM 92 n.28 (1967).

the Treaty Establishing a European Economic Community,[37] a draft directive is in preparation which, when finally enacted, will remove many of the existing restrictions preventing a Europe-wide practice of law.[38] Thus, aliens eventually may be able to be represented by a counsel of their own nationality if so desired.

Nevertheless, nationalism or the stimulation of pride in one's State and in its achievements and prospects is not necessarily destructive. There is an immense difference between the self-indulgent Nigerian proclamation referred to above and the dedication of purpose found in Tanzania's Arusha Declaration of February 1967, which resulted in the nationalization of several key industries. Tanzania's primary purpose was not to despoil foreigners, however, as evidenced by the eminently reasonable compensation provisions in the several nationalization statutes, but rather to promote the interests of the Tanzanian people. Enlightened self-interest should not be confused with xenophobia. The Declaration has been described as stressing that "the only people who were going to build Tanzania were the people themselves and it expressed a policy of self-reliance. . . ."[39] In the words of the declaration, "Tanzania . . . is involved in a war against poverty and oppression . . . , this struggle is aimed at moving the people of Tanzania and the people of Africa as a whole from a state of poverty to a state of prosperity." These words, presupposing sincerity, are not ones to which the international community should take exception.

In addition to the rather intangible, extralegal factors explored in this Chapter, and which may adversely affect an alien's successful participation in the local legal processes, there exist certain more tangible barriers of which aliens should be aware. The effective functioning of the judicial systems of all the nations studied are, to varying extents, susceptible to alterations in internal political and economic climates. Constitutional safeguards for basic human rights otherwise available both to aliens and nationals may on occasion be lacking. Moreover, unless the alien can rely upon an independent

---

[37] March 25, 1957, 298 U.N.T.S. 11.

[38] *See Attorneys to Argue in any Court in Community*, EUROPEAN COMMUNITY June 1969 at 21.

[39] TANZANIA TODAY 1 (1968).

judiciary, free of executive or legislative domination, he may find that even the most exemplary codes of civil or criminal procedure are of little avail. In such situations, denials of procedural due process may very likely result, providing legitimate bases for international claims.

CHAPTER IV

Political and Economic Instability
as They Affect Legal Institutions

Legal relations, whether between individuals or between individual and State, cannot function satisfactorily absent some degree of certainty. Without predictability of result, no individual can organize his business affairs wisely or plan his personal conduct satisfactorily. Laws or legal systems that fluctuate wildly lead to unjust results in their application. No one suffers so much in these circumstances as does the alien, for he is less able by virtue of his unfamiliarity with a foreign society either to anticipate changes or to accommodate to them. For these reasons, countries lacking basic constitutional guarantees and independent judiciaries are unattractive both to prospective investors and to immigrants.

Constitutional Safeguards of Fundamental Rights

Guarantees and safeguards relating to basic human freedoms entrenched in constitutions, in statutory law, or in judicial practices are especially valuable, since they can neither be suspended nor applied in a discriminatory fashion without attracting international attention and thereby offending foreign sensibilities. Suspension and discrimination thus become less likely. This is not to say that guarantees must be totally inflexible—that laws cannot provide temporary suspension in genuine national emergencies—but only that suspensions must be effected in a bona fide and evenhanded fashion. The Canadian Bill of Rights,[1] for example, which is a statutory as distinct from a constitutional instrument, provides that guarantees are all subject to the provisions of the War Measures Act,[2] that is, they may be suspended in certain circumstances. As recent events in

---

[1] Stat. Canada c. 44 (1960).
[2] Can. Rev. Stat. c. 288 (1952).

Canada have shown, such suspensions occur only upon genuine emergencies, determined by strict standards, and are not employed in a fashion discriminatory to alien friends.

The existence of suspensory provisions and the frequency of their invocation nevertheless must be weighed by persons considering investment or residence in foreign States. Such provisions, which are not difficult to find, affect nationals and aliens alike. The Peruvian Constitution declares that "when necessary for the security of the State" the executive branch may suspend totally or partially the provisions which guarantee the right of public assembly, the inviolability of home and correspondence from unauthorized search and seizure, as well as freedom from arrest without a warrant and from unauthorized detention.[3] In Argentina the same situation may result should Congress, or the President alone if Congress is not in session, declare a state of seige "in the event of internal disorder."[4] The President of Guatemala is empowered in the event of invasion, "serious disturbance of the peace, public disaster, or of activities against the security of the State," to suspend guarantees relating to activities normally protected against police interference.[5] Even wider power is contained in the Honduran Constitution, which permits suspension not only of guarantees but of remedies such as habeas corpus as well.[6] While similar suspensions are permitted by legislation elsewhere, the frequency of their occurrence in Latin America warrants close examination of the circumstances and conditions pursuant to which they may be decreed.

The procedures by which civil rights are curtailed pursuant to a *suspensión de garantías* or *estado de sitio* usually are established in the same constitution which guarantees enjoyment of the rights themselves, although, as in Honduras and Guatemala, the procedures may be supplemented by special legislation. In such situations, relief against abuses through writs of habeas corpus may be limited, either

---

[3] CONSTITUTION OF THE REPUBLIC OF PERU 1933, art. 70 (Pan American Union ed. 1967).

[4] CONSTITUTION OF THE REPUBLIC OF ARGENTINA 1853, arts. 67(26) & 86(19) (Pan American Union ed. 1963).

[5] CONSTITUTION OF THE REPUBLIC OF GUATEMALA 1965, art. 151 (Pan American Union ed. 1966).

[6] CONSTITUTION OF THE REPUBLIC OF HONDURAS 1965, art. 107 (Pan American Union ed. 1966).

because issuance of these protective writs has been forbidden, or because judicial deference to the excutive is taken for granted. The ample scope of Venezuelan provisions authorizing suspension of guarantees in "a commotion which could disturb the peace of the republic or in serious circumstances which could affect economic or social life," clearly extends to habeas corpus,[7] while the Mexican Constitution allows suspension of "the guarantees which may be impeding a rapid, easy solution to the situation" creating the emergency.[8] By contrast, habeas corpus may be suspended only in the event of civil war or invasion in the United States of America.[9] Costa Rica is even more liberal, entirely excluding habeas corpus from those guarantees which may be suspended.[10]

Primary constitutional authority to suspend guarantees rests with the executive branch in Brazil,[11] Guatemala,[12] Peru,[13] and Venezuela,[14] with congressional ratification required only subsequently. In Venezuela, however, Congress, in joint session, can declare that the circumstances which justified suspension no longer exist, thus restoring the guarantees suspended.[15] If Congress is not in session, declarations of a state of emergency usually require that the legislature be convened so that approval may be granted or withheld. In Argentina,[16] Costa Rica,[17] Honduras,[18] and Mexico,[19] the power to declare a state of emergency and suspend guarantees rests with the legislature according to the constitutions. The executive, how-

---

[7] CONSTITUCIÓN DE LA REPUBLICA DE VENEZUELA 1961, art. 241 (La Torre ed. 1969).

[8] CONSTITUCIÓN POLÍTICA DE LOS ESTADOS UNIDOS MEXICANOS 1917, art. 29, reprinted in CONSTITUCIÓN AMPARO Y ORGÁNICA JUDICIAL FEDERAL (Epoca S.A. ed. 1968).

[9] U.S. CONST. art. I, § 9. See also Ex Parte Milligan, 71 U.S. (4 Wall.) 2 (1866).

[10] CONSTITUTION OF THE REPUBLIC OF COSTA RICA 1949, art. 121(2) (Pan American Union ed. 1965).

[11] CONSTITUTION OF BRAZIL 1967, art. 152 (Pan American Union ed. 1967).

[12] Art. 151.

[13] Art. 70.

[14] Art. 241.

[15] Art. 242.

[16] Art. 67(26).

[17] Art. 121.

[18] Art. 164.

[19] Art. 29.

ever, may declare an emergency if the legislature is not in session. In Costa Rica such a Presidential declaration is equivalent to calling an emergency session of Congress, which according to the constitution must meet within 48 hours and approve the suspension by a two-thirds vote. Otherwise the guarantees are restored.[20] If no quorum exists, Congress may meet the following day and ratify the suspension by the vote of two-thirds of the members present. No other Latin American nation studied has delineated so carefully in its constitution the approval procedure to be followed, although Mexico's Article 29 requires that Congress meet "without delay" to ratify the executive action. Study of the legal environments in these nations suggests, however, that a legislature may be an ineffective supervisory control, especially when dominated by the executive. The impotence of the legislature is obvious, for example, in countries such as Argentina, where it is disbanded, or Malaysia, where at the date of writing it is suspended.

Restrictions on the scope of suspension sometimes may be found in constitutional provisions limiting the period of time for which suspensions may be decreed, as, for example, 30 days in Costa Rica[21] and Guatemala,[22] and 60 days in Brazil.[23] In Honduras suspension may last only 30 days if declared by the President when Congress is not in session, and 60 if declared by Congress.[24] Argentina[25] and Mexico[26] specify no precise restrictions, allowing suspensions for "a limited time." Of course, where the period can be extended for an additional 60 days, as in Brazil, these limitations are not effective.[27]

Not all guarantees may be suspended. For example, Venezuela's Constitution forbids suspension of guarantees against incommunicado detention, capital punishment, torture, or imprisonment exceeding 30 years.[28] The Constitution also permits taking limited emergency measures in situations which do not justify blanket

---

[20] Art. 140(4).
[21] Art. 121(7).
[22] Art. 152.
[23] Art. 153.
[24] Arts. 164 & 165.
[25] Art. 23.
[26] Art. 29.
[27] Art. 153.
[28] Art. 241.

restriction or suspension of guarantees.[29] In Argentina the Constitution provides that during suspension the President "shall not convict or apply punishment upon his own authority. His power shall be limited, in such a case, with respect to persons, to arresting them or transferring them from one point of the nation to another if they do not prefer to leave Argentine territory."[30] Costa Rica,[31] Peru,[32] and Brazil[33] list the guarantees that can be suspended, indicating by omission the ones that cannot. Of course, depending upon the gravity of the situation, some guarantees subject to suspension normally will be excepted from the decree proclaiming the state of emergency.[34]

The best protection for aliens and nationals alike against excesses committed in the name of national emergency is through the courts. This judicial review, in the opinion of Mexican commentator Hector Fix Zamudio, should not concern itself with the legitimacy of the political motivations behind the declaration of the state of emergency. Instead, it should ascertain whether the particular executive action is reasonably related to the elimination of the situation which created the emergency in the first place. The executive action should "not as, unfortunately, has happened frequently by using the pretext of an internal conflict, be disproportionate to the real danger and detrimental to human rights, thus denying the protection which the constitutional provisions afford to said rights."[35]

Judicial review, however, may not be obtainable if habeas corpus has been among the rights suspended. Of the Latin American nations studied, only Brazil,[36] Guatemala,[37] and Honduras[38] specifically

---

[29] Art. 244.

[30] Art. 23.

[31] Art. 121(7).

[32] Art. 70.

[33] Art. 152(1).

[34] In Guatemala, five different degrees of emergency situations are listed in Article 153 of the Constitution: State of Prevention, State of Alarm, State of Public Calamity, State of Siege, and State of War. The seriousness of the emergency determines the measures to be taken in accordance with the provisions of the Guatemalan *Ley de Orden Público*.

[35] Zamudio, *La Protección Procesal de las Garantias Individuales en America Latina*, 1967 REVISTA IBEROAMERICANA DE DERECHO PROCESAL 393, 456 (No. 3).

[36] Art. 156.

[37] Art. 154.

[38] Art. 172.

provide in their Constitutions for limited judicial relief against actions taken during an "emergency." In Brazil and Guatemala, for instance, judicial relief is only available after the state of emergency has ceased.[39] While Honduras allows suspension of habeas corpus, the Constitution specifically permits an action for relief if the executive detains persons for more than 10 days without arraignment, or decrees new crimes or penalties not in existence before the state of emergency was declared.[40] The Mexican Constitution does not provide for judicial review, but the Mexican Supreme Court, throughout the suspension of guarantees declared during World War II, heard relief petitions and declared unconstitutional certain governmental actions unrelated to national defense.[41] In contrast, Argentine courts, although the constitution is silent in this respect, generally hold that habeas corpus petitions must await conclusion of the state of emergency.[42]

It is remarkable that inhabitants of the Latin American States find nothing abnormal with decrees suspending constitutional guarantees, a phenomenon perhaps attributable to the frequency of occurrence. Indeed, from time to time in some nations, such as Guatemala in recent years, partial or total suspension constitutes normalcy, rather than the reverse. In such situations judicial relief may be limited, a situation which could justify an alien's immediate appeal to diplomatic protection absent effective local remedies.[43]

---

[39] Article 154 of the Guatemalan Constitution allows persons to appeal "unnecessary acts and measures not authorized by the Ley de Orden Público," and Article 156 of the Brazilian Constitution permits appeals if the correct procedures in declaring the suspension have not been followed, and a person has been deprived of rights other than one specifically classified in the Constitution as susceptible of suspension.

[40] Arts. 170 & 171.

[41] Personal interviews in Mexico City in 1969.

[42] Personal interviews in Buenos Aires in 1969. *See generally* Eder, *Habeas Corpus Disembodied: The Latin American Experience*, in XXTH CENTURY COMPARATIVE AND CONFLICTS LAW 463 (K. Nadelmann, A. Von Mehren & J. Hazard eds. 1961).

[43] The frequency with which guarantees are suspended, and the relative complacency with which the implementing decrees are accepted by a large segment of the community, perhaps can be explained best as products of two conflicting, yet coexisting, strains in Latin American culture, both of which are legacies of the authoritarian colonial past and of the turbulent, anarchical post-independence years. Adherence to abstract, purportedly universal, legal and social principles is

Suspensory provisions also are encountered in the constitutions of many newly independent States of the Commonwealth. While most of these countries protect fundamental rights and freedoms, many constitutions of States which achieved independence after 1960 contained comprehensive protective provisions. One exception was Tanganyika (now Tanzania), which contained a reference to fundamental rights in the preamble but not in the operative body of its constitution.[44] Another occurred upon the simultaneous independence of Singapore, North Borneo, and Sarawak as states of Malaysia.[45] In the latter instance, the somewhat limited guarantees already contained in the Constitution of the Federation of Malaya extended to the new components.[46] Prior to 1960, only the Indian Constitution included a bill of rights. The explanation is found in the fact that this constitution was enacted by a constituent assembly following independence. Other postwar constitutions contained only limited guarantees.[47]

The bill of rights included in constitutions subsequent to 1960

---

combined with an egocentric world vision in which each individual stands independent and at bay against the universe around him. This combination conflicts continuously with equally strong tendencies to ascribe, if not concede, to one powerful man or group the ability to recreate and maintain the relatively certain and stable political, economic, and social order once assured by the Spanish Crown and its emissaries in the New World. In some respects, the disorderly history of Latin America since independence is a constant, futile search for a symbol of legitimate authority to replace the Crown, interrupted by violent rejections of leaders and ideas found wanting. The difficulty, of course, is the impossibility of a consensus concerning the legitimacy of those persons who anoint the new leaders and select the new symbols of authority. At least in the monarchical period, the lines and rules of succession were rather clear. In few Latin American nations, most notably Mexico, Chile, and Uruguay, has the broadly based political party system functioned long and well enough to generate a widely acceptable mystique of nonviolent succession and peaceful transfer of power. Even so, the fabric is still fragile and may yet be rent again.

[44] The Tanganyika (Constitution) Order in Council, 1961, Preamble to the annexed Constitution (STAT. INSTR. No. 2274 of 1961).

[45] On August 31, 1963. Singapore subsequently withdrew from the Federation and declared itself independent on August 9, 1965.

[46] See note 47 infra.

[47] See, e.g., The Ceylon (Constitution) Order in Council, 1946, § 29(2) of the annexed Constitution; The Ghana (Constitution) Order in Council, 1957, §§ 31, 34 of the annexed Constitution (STAT. INSTR. No. 277 of 1957); The Federation of Malaya Independence Order in Council, 1957, §§ 5–13 and 149-151 of the annexed Constitution (STAT. INSTR. No. 1533 of 1957).

followed one of three basic models. The first, found in the Nigerian Constitution, is based upon the European Convention for the Protection of Human Rights and Fundamental Freedoms.[48] It was formulated by lawyers from common law jurisdictions. The second model is encountered in the Cyprus Constitution, drafted by lawyers from civil law jurisdictions.[49] The final model is the Trinidad and Tobago Constitution, which is based on the Canadian Act for the Recognition and Protection of Human Rights and Fundamental Freedoms.[50] Each model guarantees to the individual rights enforceable in the courts. The Cyprus model also includes protection for economic and social rights.[51]

Those constitutions patterned upon the Nigerian model permit suspensions of guarantees during periods of emergency. A declaration of emergency requires parliamentary approval, but there is considerable variation as to the size of the majority needed. Jamaica, for example, permits suspension during a "period of public emergency," which is defined as a time during which Jamaica is engaged in a war, when a state of emergency has been proclaimed by the Governor-General, and "there is in force a resolution of each House supported by the votes of a majority of all the members of that House declaring that democratic institutions in Jamaica are threatened by subversion."[52] Kenya, by comparison, requires that declarations of emergency be preceded by resolutions "of either House of the National Assembly supported by the votes of sixty-five per cent of all the members of that House, and every declaration of emergency shall lapse at the expiration of seven days, commencing with the day on which it was made, unless it has in the meantime been approved by a resolution of the other House supported by the votes of sixty-five per cent of all the members of that House."[53] The Swaziland Constitution provides that a declaration by the King of a

---

[48] The Nigeria (Constitution) Order in Council, 1960, §§ 17–32 of the annexed Constitution (STAT. INSTR. No. 1652 of 1960).

[49] The Cyprus Constitution, arts. 6–35, CMND. No. 1093 (1960).

[50] See note 1 *supra.*

[51] See note 49 *supra.*

[52] The Jamaica (Constitution) Order in Council, 1962, § 26(4) of the annexed Constitution (STAT. INSTR. 1550 of 1962).

[53] The Kenya Independence Order in Council, 1963, § 29(2) of the annexed Constitution (STAT. INSTR. No. 1968 of 1963).

state of emergency shall cease to have effect within seven days if Parliament is sitting, or 21 days if not, unless in the meantime "it is approved by a resolution passed at a joint sitting of the Senate and the House of Assembly."[54] Zambia requires only a bare majority vote in the National Assembly following the declaration.[55] A proclamation of emergency in Malaysia must be "approved by a resolution of each House of Parliament."[56] The Nigerian Constitution combines provisions found in the constitutions of Jamaica and Kenya requiring a pre-existing resolution "of each House of Parliament supported by the votes of not less than two-thirds of all the members of the House. . . ."[57]

The two most important constitutions of new, pre-1960 Commonwealth nations were the constitutions of India and Pakistan. The Indian Constitution, which contains an extensive article providing for the identification and protection of fundamental rights,[58] empowers the President to proclaim an emergency when he is satisfied that national security is threatened either by war, external aggression, or internal disturbance.[59] He then may order that "the right to move any court for the enforcement of such of the rights conferred . . . as may be mentioned in the order, and all proceedings pending in any court for the enforcement of the rights mentioned shall remain suspended."[60]

The Pakistan Constitution similarly declares fundamental rights,[61] and provides for proclamations of emergency by the President[62] and suspension of judicial remedies to enforce those rights during the time the proclamation is in force.[63] The Pakistan Constitution, how-

---

[54] The Swaziland Independence Order, 1968, § 18(2) of the annexed Constitution (STAT. INSTR. No. 1377 of 1968).

[55] The Zambia Independence Order, 1964, § 29(2) of the annexed Constitution (STAT. INSTR. No. 1652 of 1964).

[56] The Federation of Malaya Independence Order in Council, 1957, § 150(3) of the annexed Constitution (STAT. INSTR. No. 1533 of 1957).

[57] The Nigeria (Constitution) Order in Council, 1960, § 65(3) of the annexed Constitution (STAT. INSTR. No. 1652 of 1960).

[58] CONSTITUTION OF INDIA, part III, arts. 12–35.

[59] Art. 352.

[60] Art. 359.

[61] CONSTITUTION OF THE ISLAMIC REPUBLIC OF PAKISTAN, part II, art. 6.

[62] Id., part III, art. 30(1).

[63] Id. art. 30(10), as amended in 1966.

ever, does not include the limitation on the duration of an emergency proclamation found in the Indian Constitution. In the latter, such a proclamation "shall cease to operate at the expiration of two months unless before the expiration of that period it has been approved by resolutions of both Houses of Parliament."[64]

Several Commonwealth constitutions, such as that of Mauritius, specifically refer to discrimination.[65] In most instances no question of discrimination arises because provisions for suspension of rights in extraordinary circumstances apply equally to nationals and aliens. The interim Constitution of Tanzania, for example, refers to "the equality of all men,"[66] while the Constitutions of India and Pakistan distinguish between rights accorded citizens and rights enjoyed by "persons." Rights generally regarded as fundamental attach to individuals in the latter, broader category, which would include aliens as well as nationals.[67] This approach contrasts with Colombia, the Constitution of which explicitly permits a limited discrimination against aliens: "foreigners shall enjoy in Colombia the same civil rights that are accorded Colombians. But the law may, for reasons of public order, subject foreigners to special conditions or deny them the exercise of specific civil rights."[68] Such provisions are not uncommon in Latin America, but are generally directed either to limiting alien participation in the political process or to authorizing their summary expulsion in times of emergency, with little appellate recourse.

The Kenya Constitution declares that "every person in Kenya is entitled to the fundamental rights and freedoms of the individual, that is to say, the right, whatever his race, tribe, place of origin or residence or other local connection, political opinions, colour, creed

---

[64] Art. 352(2)(c).

[65] The Mauritius Independence Order, 1968, § 16 of the annexed Constitution.

[66] An Act to Declare the Interim Constitution of Tanzania, 1965, Tanzania, Act No. 43 of 1956, § 56.

[67] The Supreme Court of India found it necessary to examine the distinction between "persons" and "citizens" in an important constitutional case. It held that under the Constitution all citizens are persons, but all persons are not citizens. State Trading Corp. of India v. Commercial Tax Officer, Visakhapatnam, [1964] 4 India S. Ct. 99.

[68] CONSTITUTION OF THE REPUBLIC OF COLOMBIA 1886, art. 11 (Pan American Union ed. 1962).

or sex, but subject to respect for the rights and freedoms of others and for the public interest," then listing three categories which embrace the classical freedoms.[69] The section makes no reference to nationality, citizenship, or domicile, yet section 26 contains certain limitations which affect persons not citizens of Kenya. Non-Kenyans are protected, however, from "discriminatory" treatment, defined as "different treatment to different persons attributable wholly or mainly to their respective descriptions by race, tribe, place of origin or residence or other local connection, political opinions, colour or creed whereby persons of one such description are subjected to disabilities or restrictions to which persons of another such description are not made subject or are accorded privileges or advantages which are not accorded to persons of another such description."[70] Thus, a city council which rented market stalls on a priority basis to "Kenya citizens of African origin" was held to be acting in a discriminatory, and therefore unconstitutional, fashion because it had distinguished between citizens of different origins.[71] Similar judicial reasoning was employed when the Supreme Court of India considered a case involving alleged discriminatory treatment contrary to constitutional provisions. The court held that in order to establish denial of equal protection of the law under Article 14 of the Indian Constitution, a plea of differential treatment alone is insufficient. Rather, the complaint must show differential treatment from other persons similarly circumstanced, without the existence of any reasonable basis.[72]

It should be noted and emphasized that, unlike some Latin American nations, Commonwealth countries generally do not suspend access to judicial remedies during emergencies. Habeas corpus re-

[69] The Kenya Independence Order in Council, 1963, § 14 of the annexed Constitution (STAT. INSTR. No. 1968 of 1963).

[70] Id. § 26(3).

[71] Madhwa v. City Council of Nairobi, [1968] E. Afr. L.R. 406 (H. Crt. of Kenya).

[72] State of Madhya Pradesh v. Bhopal Sugar Industries Ltd., [1964] 6 India S. Ct. 846. See also East India Tobacco Co. v. State of Andhra Pradesh, [1963] 1 India S. Ct. 404; Ranjit Singh v. Commissioner of Income Tax, Uttar Pradesh, [1962] 1 India S. Ct. 966. For discussion of all aspects of constitutions of Commonwealth countries see S. DE SMITH, THE NEW COMMONWEALTH AND ITS CONSTITUTIONS ch. 5 (1964), and de Smith, Fundamental Rights in the New Commonwealth, 10 INT'L & COMP. L.Q. 83 & 215 (1961).

mains accessible to all persons regardless of citizenship and notwithstanding circumstances which have precipitated a declaration of a state of emergency or suspension of fundamental rights. One reason for this distinction is found in the common law heritage enjoyed by the overwhelming majority of the States of the Commonwealth. Another reason is that the United Kingdom Parliament is the source of the constitutions of the vast majority of the 31 countries. The combination of these two influences, plus the strong experience of an independent judiciary, has permitted in most places the retention of extraordinary judicial remedies despite the suspension of civil rights.

Habeas corpus, in legal systems derived from English common law, is one of the prerogative writs which accord courts a degree of effective control over executive acts.[73] Unless a constitution permits suspension, it may be assumed that in a Commonwealth country employing a presidential system of government guarantees remain in effect. Somewhat ironically, those Commonwealth States following a parliamentary system—in which the legislature is supreme—retain in parliament the right to suspend prerogative writs or otherwise diminish the jurisdiction of the courts by ordinary statute unless the constitution specifically provides the contrary. In Canada, for example, the executive cannot suspend access to the courts (by reason of the prerogative writ jurisdiction of the courts), but Parliament can achieve this result by passage of a simple statute.[74] In either system the courts are powerless to do more than review the constitutionality and application of the particular act challenged. They have no authority to restore fundamental rights which have been suspended by proper legal process. Nevertheless, the very existence of this independent and impartial assessment of the circumstances surrounding any particular administrative act assures citizen and alien alike that rights will not likely be taken from him illegally, capriciously, or in a discriminatory fashion.

Denial of individual freedoms through inappropriate means is not confined to newly independent States. Constitutions of older continental European States on occasion have been abused as well, espe-

---

[73] *See* text at note 114 of Chapter VII.

[74] *See, e.g.,* The War Measures Act, CAN. REV. STAT. c. 288 (1952).

cially in the period between the two world wars when emergency provisions sometimes were extended improperly. Consequently, suspensory provisions usually arouse mixed reactions in Europe, as witness the debate concerning the introduction of emergency legislation in Germany.[75] However, these provisions generally are felt to be necessary and are quite common. Perhaps because bills of rights in European constitutions are usually rather flexible, emergency provisions typically do not authorize the executive to suspend constitutional rights. Provisions enabling the executive to exercise legislative powers are more frequent.[76]

The most elaborate suspensory provisions are found in the French Constitution of 1958, which continues the long-standing power of the executive to declare a state of siege, permitting transfer of broad powers to military authorities. However, states of siege extending beyond 12 days require legislative ratification.[77] The rules relating to the state of siege have not been too important in the immediate past.[78] Article 16 of the present French Constitution is more important, and authorizes the President to take appropriate measures if the institutions of the Republic, the independence of the nation, the integrity of the territory, or the execution of French international obligations are in immediate jeopardy and the authorities instituted by the Constitution are prevented from functioning. In substance this authorization amounts to a grant of all governmental powers, legislative and executive, to the President. However, the President must consult the Prime Minister, the presiding officers of both houses of the legislature, and the President of the Constitutional Council concerning the emergency measures. There is no specific

---

[75] Emergency provisions of a very detailed nature were added to the Constitution of the Federal Republic of Germany by the 17th Law for The Amendment of the Constitution, May 30, 1968, [1968] BGBl. 709. For a detailed discussion of its provisions and the debate it provoked see Note, *Recent Emergency Legislation in West Germany*, 82 HARV. L. REV. 1704 (1969).

[76] Not infrequently, provisions in bills of rights are designed to protect only against arbitrary executive, but not against legislative, action.

[77] FRENCH CONSTITUTION OF 1958, art. 36. The rules concerning the state of siege are contained in the Law of Aug. 9, 1849, [1849] D.P. IV. 135, *as amended* by the Law of April 3, 1878, 16 Bulletin des Lois 338, No. 6827 (12th Series 1878), [1878] D.P. IV. 27.

[78] For a more detailed discussion in English see Kelly & Pelletier, *Theories of Emergency Government*, 11 SOUTH DAKOTA L. REV. 42 (1966).

authorization to suspend constitutional civil liberties. This lack would seem due to the peculiar nature of the French bill of rights and the Declaration of the Rights of Man and of the Citizen of 1789, which are considered statements of principles rather than legally binding instruments. Article 16 of the French Constitution was invoked during the 1961 rebellion against General De Gaulle,[79] when special courts were created to deal with political crimes, and increased rights of search and arrest were granted the police.[80]

A more cautious approach is assumed in the Italian Constitution, no doubt because memories of the Fascist era remain. Therefore the executive may not issue decrees having the force of law without legislative mandate,[81] and delegations of legislative power are restricted by requiring specific criteria to guide their exercise.[82] However, the Constitution assumes the existence of, rather than grants, emergency powers. It provides that temporary measures having the force of law adopted by the executive in cases of necessity and urgency must be submitted the same day for legislative approval. If the legislature is not sitting it must be convened.[83] No specific provision exists for suspension of constitutional civil liberties which in Italy, with some exceptions, are rights enforceable by law, rather than mere guiding principles of State policy.[84]

The Austrian Constitution follows a similar approach, though it is more specific in granting the executive the power to exercise legislative functions. Again, rapid legislative ratification is required. Some matters remain outside the scope of emergency decrees, such as the alteration of the Constitution itself, the alienation of public property, the imposition of financial burdens on the Republic or the provinces, and the protection of workers and tenants.[85] During the

---

[79] See Decree of April 23, 1961, [1961] J.O. 3874, [1961] D.L. 154.

[80] See generally Pickles, Special Powers in France—Art. 16 in Practice, [1963] PUBLIC LAW 23. Judicial review of measures taken pursuant to Article 16 of the French Constitution is quite limited. See Rubin de Servens, [1962] Rec. Cons. d'Et. 143, [1962] Sem. Jur. II 12613. But cf. Canal, [1962] Rec. Cons. d'Et. 552, [1963] Sem. Jur. II 13068.

[81] ITALIAN CONSTITUTION OF 1947, art. 77, para. 1.

[82] Art. 76.

[83] Art. 77(2), (3).

[84] See M. CAPPELLETTI, J. MERRYMAN & J. PERILLO, THE ITALIAN LEGAL SYSTEM 56–61 (1967).

[85] AUSTRALIAN CONSTITUTION OF 1929, art. 18(3)–(5).

inter-war period, these provisions did not prevent the abuse of emergency legislation, although no problems have arisen since 1945.

The Independence of a Well-Functioning Judiciary as a Safeguard of Fundamental Rights

Constitutional safeguards of fundamental freedoms or rights, while important in establishing the tone or the climate of the country, are of no lasting consequence without institutional means of enforcement. Courts of law provide this mechanism. The importance of properly functioning and independent courts is emphasized by the presence in many constitutions of provisions for suspension of specific fundamental rights in circumstances which only can be measured through judicial inquiry. Examples are found in the constitutions of Commonwealth countries which provide that suspensory features may be implemented only for specific purposes and only if justifiable in a democratic society. The Nigerian Constitution, for example, speaks of measures that are "reasonably justifiable for the purpose of dealing with the situation. . . ."[86] The Constitution of Jamaica employs a different test: that the law is "reasonably required" in the interests concerned.[87] The Constitution of Kenya combines the two concepts, providing that a law may be excepted from the requirements of the guarantee if it is "reasonably required" in the interests concerned, but only to the extent that it can be shown to be "reasonably justifiable in a democratic society."[88] The Constitution of Lesotho establishes a test of what is "necessary in a practical sense in a democratic society in the interests of any of the matters specified" in the exception.[89]

Because this close interrelationship of constitutional guarantees and judicial review exists, suspension or disappearance of safeguards

---

[86] *Supra* note 57, § 28(1).

[87] *Supra* note 52, § 22(2)(a).

[88] *Supra* note 53, § 20(2).

[89] The Lesotho Independence Order, 1966, § 15(3) of the annexed Constitution (Stat. Instr. No. 1172 of 1966). The Constitution of this tiny African State is of interest in still another respect. It includes rights which do not appear either in the Nigerian Constitution or in the European Convention upon which it is modeled. Equality before the law and equal protection of the law are both guaranteed in Section 18.

always involves a circumscription or reduction of the jurisdiction of the courts. It sometimes involves even more: a challenge to the independence of the judiciary, a much more serious event. Courts with limited functions and powers are nonetheless courts, but courts composed of judges subject to political influence and pressure are not courts at all. This principle is of the deepest significance to aliens, for any discussion of procedural safeguards for alien litigants must be premised upon the existence of a judiciary possessing both independence and integrity.[90] Most modern constitutions, fortunately, seek to protect the judiciary and to hold inviolate the holders of judicial office in the performance of their duties.[91] Nevertheless, a judiciary uncertain of its strength, in a State dominated by a political figure or group possessing almost absolute power, encourages unsatisfactory results. An illustration is found in an unhappy, but now concluded, period of Ghanaian history. Both as a model to be avoided and as a widely publicized incident, it bears examination in some detail.

The framers of the Ghanaian Constitution had sought to protect both the judiciary—which Ghana had inherited from Great Britain, complete with British traditions of impartiality and fair play—and the rule of law by placing restrictions on the office of the President. Article 12 required the President on assumption of office to swear that he "will preserve and defend the Constitution" and "do right to all manner of people according to law." Immediately after assuming office the President was required by Article 13 solemnly to declare his adherence to a number of "fundamental principles," which declared that freedom and justice be honored and maintained, that persons not suffer discrimination, that no person be deprived of freedom of religion or speech, the right to move and assemble, or the

---

[90] See Roberts-Wray, *The Independence of the Judiciary in Commonwealth Countries,* in CHANGING LAW IN DEVELOPING COUNTRIES 63 (J. Anderson ed. 1963); *African Conference on the Rule of Law,* 3 J. INT'L COMM. OF JURISTS 10 (1961).

[91] See, e.g., the Nigerian Constitution, *supra* note 57, § 106(2): "A person holding the office of Chief Justice of the Federation or a Federal Justice may be removed from office only for inability to discharge the functions of his office (whether arising from infirmity of body or mind or any other cause) or for misbehaviour, and shall not be so removed except in accordance with the provisions of this section."

right of access to courts of law, and that no person be deprived of his property except as provided by law.

These principles give the appearance of a bill of rights similar to ones found in other constitutions. It is not surprising, therefore, that several prisoners detained under the Preventive Detention Act[92] applied for habeas corpus on the ground that this Act was invalid as conflicting with Article 13. The courts refused the writ and dismissed the subsequent appeal. The Chief Justice of Ghana, Sir Arku Korsah, said the argument which likened the article to a bill of rights was misleading, that the provisions of the article were instead similar to the oath taken by the monarch of England during the coronation service.[93]

The court then held that the contention that Article 13 limited the legislative power of Parliament was in direct conflict with the express provisions of Article 20 of the Constitution, entitled "The Sovereign Parliament." Section 5 of that article reads "[n]o person or body other than Parliament shall have power to make provisions having the force of law except under authority conferred by Act of Parliament." Section 6 states that "[a]part from the limitations referred to in the preceding provisions of this article . . . the power of Parliament to make laws shall be under no limitation whatsoever." The court continued:

> In our view the declaration merely represents the goal to which every President must pledge himself to attempt to achieve. It does not represent a legal requirement which can be enforced by the courts.
>
> On examination of the said declarations with a view to finding out how any could be enforced we are satisfied that the provisions of Article 13(1) do not create legal obligations enforceable by a court of law. The declarations however impose on every President a moral obligation, and provide a political yardstick by which the conduct of the Head of State can be measured by the electorate. The people's

---

[92] Ghana, The Preventive Detention Act, 1958 (Act 17).

[93] "In one case the President is required to make a solemn declaration, in the other the Queen is required to take a solemn oath. Neither the oath nor the declaration can be said to have a statutory effect of an enactment of Parliament. The suggestion that the declarations made by the President on assumption of office constitute a 'Bill of Rights' in the sense in which the expression is understood under the Constitution of the United States of America is therefore untenable." *Re* Akoto, [1961] G.L.R. 523, 534.

remedy for any departure from the principles of the declaration, is through the use of the ballot box, and not through the courts.[94]

This approach reflects the doctrine of parliamentary supremacy, concisely and forcefully stated.[95] The underlying reasoning of the Chief Justice was that Ghana is patterned on the British model where Parliament is supreme, and the judiciary, though independent, is neither supreme nor in a position of shared supremacy with the legislature. This viewpoint is apparently supported in Article 41(2) of the Constitution, which states that the judicial power conferred on the courts is done so "subject to the provisions of the Constitution."[96]

For proper protection of the electorate, however, the theory of parliamentary supremacy requires the careful scrutiny of an opposition party. Without such opposition a strong leader may without publicity subvert even a carefully worded constitution and divest the judiciary of independence. Kwame Nkrumah, the first President of Ghana, proved strong enough for the task. Notwithstanding his disavowals of dictatorial conduct and his boast of establishing an independent judiciary,[97] Nkrumah quite effectively subordinated the

---

[94] *Id.* at 535.

[95] Rubin and Murray, in their treatise on the Constitution of Ghana, have taken issue with this judgment on the ground that the analogy to the coronation oath is false: "It is respectfully submitted that the Court erred in comparing the Presidential declaration under Article 13(1) with the Coronation Oath. It is surely the oath required by Article 12(1), the taking of which constitutes the assumption of office as President—not the declaration made *after office has been assumed*—which is analogous to the Coronation Oath." L. RUBIN & P. MURRAY, THE CONSTITUTION AND GOVERNMENT OF GHANA 227 n.65 (2d ed. 1964).

[96] These words have been interpreted by one scholar to mean that it is "within the competence of the legislature to annul a particular judicial decision or to divert some part of the judical power to bodies other than the courts, for example to administrative tribunals or even the National Assembly itself. These limiting words also embrace provisions in the Constitution expressly regulating the judicial power. . . ." F. BENNION, THE CONSTITUTIONAL LAW OF GHANA 169 (1962).

[97] *See* K. NKRUMAH, I SPEAK OF FREEDOM 44 (1961). T. ELIAS, GHANA AND SIERRA LEONE: THE DEVELOPMENT OF THEIR LAWS AND CONSTITUTIONS 137 (1962) quotes the Nkrumah Government as saying, on the occasion of the introduction of the concept of a Judicial Service Commission, that it desired to ensure constitutional security of tenure for judges and to remove "any occasion for questioning the independence of the judicature of the Gold Coast in the future."

judiciary to his will. Article 45(3) of the Constitution, guaranteeing security of tenure to judges, was amended in 1964 to permit the President "at any time, *for reasons which to him appear sufficient*," to remove from office a Judge of the Supreme Court or a Judge of the High Court.[98]

---

[98] The Constitution (Amendment) Act, 1964 (Act 224) § 6 (emphasis added). This amendment followed a direct confrontation between the President and the courts after the acquittal of persons charged with treason and conspiracy to commit treason. In 1961 Parliament had created a Special Criminal Division of the High Court to consist of a presiding judge and two others chosen by the Chief Justice at the request of the President, plus 12 jurors selected from a special list. The Criminal Procedure (Amendment) Act, 1961 (Act 91). The court's jurisdiction was defined as including those offenses against the safety of the State or against the peace proscribed by the Criminal Code plus any "offence specified by the President by legislative instrument." The procedure of the Division seemed designed to avoid, in the name of speed, the careful review provisions normally open to an accused. In the result, there were no preliminary hearings, juries and assessors were excluded; there were no appeals, or disclosure of any dissenting judgment. In addition, regulations permitted trying an accused in his absence but, unlike the 1960 Criminal Procedure Code, denied to courts power to set aside in absentia convictions.

The first trial under these procedures, held in March 1963, led to conviction of each accused. The second trial, held several months later, resulted in acquittals for three of the five accused, provoking a quick reaction from the government. Any remaining doubts about the official attitude toward an independent judiciary soon vanished. The Attorney General is reported to have labeled the judgment a "mockery of justice" and the Convention Peoples Party newspaper, the organ of the President's party which in 1964 was accorded primacy and protection by constitutional amendment, charged the sitting judges with "open subversion" and "treachery." It continued: "The courts, ideally an instrument of Socialist education and discipline, not of class insolence and subversion, ye have made a den of thieves, robbers, assassins and corruption. And the voices of the people say—Away with them! No more shall we entrust such vital machinery in the hands of the class enemy." [*sic*]. Accra Evening News, Dec. 12, 1963, at 1.

Two days after the decision, Nkrumah, specifically permitted by the Constitution, dismissed the Chief Justice, who had been a member of the offending Special Criminal Division. The deposed Chief Justice immediately resigned from the judicial service and in a few days another member of the same court did likewise. The President then dismissed from the judicial service the third member of the Special Criminal Division, two other judges of the Supreme Court, and a judge of the High Court. Steps were also taken to quash the acquittal. Legislation with retroactive effect was rushed through Parliament providing that "where it appears to the President that it is in the interest of the security of the State so to do, he may by an executive instrument declare the decision of the Court to be of no effect, and the instrument shall be deemed to be a nolle prosequi entered by the Attorney General before the decision in the

Following the February 1966 coup d'état, the new National Liberation Council suspended the now distorted Constitution and acted quickly to restore confidence in the judiciary as an independent arm of government, and in the law as an impartial instrument. A Legal Committee was established consisting of the Chief Justice of Ghana, the President of the Ghana Bar Association, a judge of the Court of Appeal, the Attorney General, the Solicitor General, the Dean of the Faculty of Law at the University of Ghana, and three others, who were charged with making suggestions respecting "any legal matters affecting the country, including matters preparatory to the setting up of a commission to consider a new constitution," examining the laws "with a view to determining which . . . are inimical to the well being of the people of Ghana," and suggesting such legislative and other measures as it might consider necessary for the reform of existing laws.[99] Most importantly, the Judicial Service Act was amended[100] to permit appointment of Judges by the National Liberation Council on the advice of the Judicial Service Commission,[101] and for removal the same way on the grounds of "stated misbehaviour or infirmity of body or mind."[102] Finally, and certainly worthy of mention, the Special Criminal Division was abolished, effective May 13, 1966.[103]

No evidence exists to suggest that since 1966 the superior courts of Ghana have been other than independent and impartial, composed

---

case was given. . . ." The Criminal Procedure (Amendment) Act, 1964 (Act 238). The President did so declare, and in a subsequent trial the accused were all convicted. For a more detailed discussion of the tensions which affected the Ghanaian judicial structure see W. HARVEY, LAW AND SOCIAL CHANGE IN GHANA ch. VII (1966).

[99] National Liberation Council (Legal Committee) (Appointment) Decree, 1966 (N.L.C.D. 38).

[100] The Judicial Service Act, 1960 (Amendment) Decree, 1966 (N.L.C.D. 39).

[101] Consisting (following an amendment found at N.L.C.D. 58) of the Chief Justice of Ghana, the most senior judge of the High Court, the Attorney General, two retired judges, and the Chairman of the Civil Service Commission.

[102] The amendment provided as well that judges' salaries are not to be diminished while in office, and that the retirement age of the Chief Justice was to be 65, and of all other judges 62.

[103] N.L.C.D. 43. For a more detailed description of the independence of the judiciary in newly independent States of the Commonwealth see Roberts-Wray, *supra* note 90; K. ROBERTS-WRAY, COMMONWEALTH AND COLONIAL LAW 496–505 (1966).

of well-qualified jurists confident in their security of tenure, dispensing justice in accord with the highest traditions of the law. The recent return of a civilian administration, and the inclusion of strong constitutional guarantees for the judiciary, supports this belief. Nevertheless, incidents such as the December 1969 expulsion of hundreds of thousands of aliens from Ghana emphasize the limited ability of courts anywhere to deal *practically* with complaints of aliens in immense volume.[104]

The pre-1966 Ghanaian experience is not unique, as was dramatically illustrated by the resignation and sudden departure from Zambia in 1969 of the Chief Justice after a decision of the court had been criticized as "political" by President Kaunda. The judiciary does not everywhere have assured tenure and independence, and so judges occasionally may be reluctant to admit complaints or appeals directed against governmental actions. For instance, in Argentina during the Peron era, judges who granted writs of habeas corpus were subject to reprisals. In Guatemala, members of the Supreme Court who had agreed to hear an appeal against the Agrarian Reform Law of 1952 were dismissed summarily.

As long as judges may be removed at executive or legislative whim, a truly independent judiciary will not exist, and a basic safeguard for a fair judicial process will be lacking. In Latin America, constitutional and legislative enactments establish procedures which seem on their face to inhibit arbitrary action against the judiciary, but which do not always function as intended. Life tenure, unlike in the United States of America, is a rarity. In Costa Rica, for example, where the judiciary in fact seems to enjoy great independence and respect, judges may be removed by a two-thirds vote of the legislature.[105] Despite this absence of life tenure, however, the essentially democratic and non-totalitarian Costa Rican tradition protects the judiciary from outside pressure. By contrast, the Guatemalan Constitution only permits removal for a felony, notorious bad conduct, or "manifest incapacity," pursuant to a decision of two-thirds of Congress after hearing the accused.[106] Nevertheless, a strong executive with a cooperative majority in Congress, a combination

---

[104] *See* text at pages 66–67 of Chapter III.
[105] *Supra* note 10, art. 165.
[106] *Supra* note 5, art. 242.

which has often occurred in Guatemalan history, may threaten judicial independence seriously.

The consensus in Costa Rica, Guatemala, and Honduras surprisingly seems to be that if judges were given life tenure they would become less, not more, responsible.[107] By contrast, the Brazilian Constitution guarantees judges life tenure, except where they are removed "in the public interest."[108] Removal is determined by a two-thirds vote of members of a court superior to that of which the accused judge is a member, meeting in closed session. Courts also may remove their own members in similar fashion, although in both cases the accused is assured a chance of interposing a defense. The "public interest" appears to be an extremely vague standard, susceptible of wide interpretation, so the fact that the removal procedure is conducted by the judiciary itself, rather than by the legislature, may provide scant consolation.

In Argentina, as in the United States of America, federal judges hold office "during their good behavior."[109] However, this provision did not prevent arbitrary dismissal of the entire Supreme Court when General Carlos Ongania seized power in 1966. In 1968 the rule of law was dealt another blow by the same administration when police denied permission to hold an anti-government demonstration in the city of Rosario. The organizers of the meeting then successfully alleged the unconstitutionality of the denial in the courts of the Province of Santa Fé. The court found that the police prohibition violated the right of assembly granted by the provincial constitution, since no state of seige or suspension of constitutional guarantees had been previously decreed. The decision was appealed by the Provincial authorities but confirmed on appeal.

Two judges subsequently proceeded to the meeting place on the date of the demonstration and ordered removal of the police cordon blocking entrance to the square. Alleging that they had received "superior orders," mounted officers charged into the crowd, making numerous arrests and injuring several persons, including one of the judges. The Supreme Court of the Province later issued a decision

---

[107] Personal interviews with practicing attorneys elsewhere in Latin America also suggest widespread support for this view.

[108] *Supra* note 11, art. 108(iii).

[109] *Supra* note 4, art. 96.

upholding the validity of the decree and condemning the police action. The Federal authorities then intervened in the province "to reorganize the judicial power," all pursuant to Article 6 of the Constitution which allows the Federal Government to intervene in the provinces "to guarantee the republican form of government." The following day the Provincial Supreme Court resigned en masse. To their great credit, the members of the Bar Association of Buenos Aires then published a statement declaring that Article 6 was inapplicable to this case and that the government had violated the pledge it had made when it assumed office "to restore the rule of true justice."[110]

As the Argentine illustration demonstrates, constitutional safeguards have not prevented harassment of judges by strong-willed executive branches, especially where, as has occurred from time to time in Latin America, legislatures cease to function or are subservient to executive pressure. Even where no overt intimidation exists, knowledge that executive displeasure has in the past and can in the future cause dismissal, imprisonment, or exile may greatly inhibit the judiciary and members of the bar in general.

The distinction between judicial independence in Africa or Latin America and Europe is found more in practice than in constitutional provisions.[111] In Western Europe, constitutions quite generally provide that the judiciary shall be independent and subject only to law.[112] While the judiciary in all West European countries is a career service, normal disciplinary procedures applicable to ordinary civil servants do not apply to judges. Instead, the French and Italian Constitutions provide that disciplinary powers over judges shall rest exclusively with a special body called the Conseil Supérieur de la Magistrature in France[113] and the Consiglio Superiore della

---

[110] *Argentina: Atropello al Poder judicial*, 35 BOLETÍN DE LA COMISIÓN INTERNACIONAL DE JURISTAS 15, 18 (Sept. 1968).

[111] "In England, judicial independence is maintained in spite of, rather than because of, the rules governing appointments." S. DE SMITH, *supra* note 72, at 137.

[112] AUSTRIAN CONSTITUTION, art. 87(1); CONSTITUTION OF THE FEDERAL REPUBLIC OF GERMANY, art. 97(1); ITALIAN CONSTITUTION, arts. 101 & 104. In slightly different phraseology, Article 64 of the French Constitution provides: "The President of the Republic is the guarantor of the independence of the judicial authority. . . . The judges have permanent tenure."

[113] The Conseil Supérieur de la Magistrature is instituted by the French Con-

Magistratura in Italy.[114] While the composition and powers of these bodies are not entirely identical, they effectively protect the judiciary against pressure through threats of removal from office, suspension, transfer, and the like.[115] To insure further the independence of the judiciary, these two bodies also participate in the promotion of judges.

In Austria and the Federal Republic of Germany, disciplinary powers over the judiciary are vested in the courts themselves.[116] In Germany, where a distinction must be drawn between "federal" and "state" judges, the German Constitutional Court (*Bundesverfassungsgericht*) is empowered to hear proceedings against federal judges alleged to have violated the German Constitution after indictment by the German Parliament (*Bundestag*).[117] In other cases a special panel of the German Supreme Court hears disciplinary matters.[118] Somewhat analogous provisions apply to judges in state (*Land*) service.[119] In the last few years the only real question as to the independence of the judiciary in Western Europe seems to have arisen in France in 1960–62, when special measures, including the establishment of emergency courts, were invoked to deal with the Algerian rebellion and with the French civilian and military officials

---

stitution, arts. 64 & 65. The basic law governing its operation is the Ordonnance No. 58–1271 of Dec. 22, 1958, [1958] J.O. 11556, [1959] B.L.D. 23.

[114] The Consiglio Superiore della Magistratura is instituted by the Italian Constitution, arts. 104 & 105. The basic law governing its operation is the Law of March 24, 1958, No. 195, *as amended* by Law of Dec. 18, 1967, No. 1198, *reprinted in* I CINQUE CODICI, CODICE DI PROCEDURA CIVILE 216 (Giuffrè 1968).

[115] Thus a French judge ordinarily may not be transferred to a different court against his will, even if this constitutes a promotion, except pursuant to a decision of the Conseil Supérieur de la Magistrature. Ordonnance No. 58–1270 of Dec. 22, 1958, [1958] J.O. 11551, [1959] B.L.D. 15, art. 4. Articles 43–58 of the same Ordonnance deal with disciplinary proceedings. For additional discussion see M. CAPPELLETTI, J. MERRYMAN & J. PERILLO, *supra* note 84, at 102–07; P. HERZOG, CIVIL PROCEDURE IN FRANCE 129–31 (1967).

[116] AUSTRIAN CONSTITUTION, art. 88(2); CONSTITUTION OF THE FEDERAL REPUBLIC OF GERMANY, art. 97(2).

[117] CONSTITUTION OF THE FEDERAL REPUBLIC OF GERMANY, art. 98(2); Law of Sept. 8, 1961 on the Judiciary, [1961] BGBl. 1665, *as amended* by Law of Aug. 18, 1965, [1965] BGBl. 891 § 25.

[118] *Id.* § 61.

[119] *Id.* § 77–84.

who opposed the government's policy of granting independence to Algeria.[120]

STRENGTHENING THE JUDICIAL SYSTEMS OF DEVELOPING COUNTRIES

Obviously, governments must learn not to ignore the health of their judicial systems. It will be of little value to people in a developing country if in the space of the next 20 or 30 years economic development programs will have accomplished their tasks and new standards of living are achieved, but at the cost of losing fundamental freedoms and human rights, which surely will disappear should the courts be systematically neglected. Such a prospect represents materialism gone mad, yet is quite possible in many countries where court budgets are far from adequate. To a degree, however, a protective factor exists in the increasing need for foreign technicians and private investment capital in order to attain expectations of economic viability in developing nations. Successful as public assistance schemes have been, it is recognized now that increasing responsibility must be borne by the private sectors of the developed nations through overseas investment and international trade. Without reasonable expectations of orderly investment or trading climates, protected by functioning legal systems providing remedial access to independent judicial or arbitral tribunals, business will not be inclined to venture in sizable quantities outside the favorable environments in which it now functions. Confidence will exist only when exporters and investors have some reasonable hope that in the

---

[120] Thus the High Military Tribunal, itself an emergency court created in 1961, was abolished in 1962 and replaced by another emergency-type court after it had failed to sentence the leader of the so-called O.A.S., General Salan, to death. This episode in French history came to an end in 1963, when a permanent court with jurisdiction over crimes against the State was created. Law No. 63–22 of Jan. 15, 1963, [1963] J.O. 507, [1963] D.L. 48. *Cf.* Canal, *supra* note 80 (voiding presidential decree [Ordonnance] having created special military tribunal). It should be noted that at least in France and Italy guarantees of permanent tenure apply only to the regular judiciary; the members of the bodies reviewing administrative action in certain circumstances (administrative tribunals, Conseil d'Etat, Consiglio di Stato) do not benefit from the formal guarantees mentioned. In practice, however, their position is entirely independent.

event of injury or loss their claims will be adjudicated promptly and fairly by local courts; when they, as aliens, will be able to seek and recover justice in the foreign court. In this way private investors, by demanding high legal standards, can influence development of legal institutions.

Legal systems do not evolve overnight. Should impatient governments allow the withering of the carefully nurtured traditions of excellence and impartiality often left in newly independent countries as legacies of colonial pasts, they will not soon be replaced. Even now, in many countries which have inherited the common law, competition among various ministries for scarce foreign exchange has left the judicial system badly in need. Funds are required to maintain law libraries dependent on foreign-published texts, journals, and digests; personnel is needed for the important support tasks of court stenography, law reporting, and administration; and, equally important, wise and experienced jurists must be attracted to the bench. In pre-independence days the British Colonial Office sponsored a judicial service which made judges available to all parts of the Empire. No similar institution has replaced it. In some countries— Nigeria is an example—the pressures of nationalism have not been permitted to oust expatriate members of the judiciary. Judicial competence remains the dominant criterion. Elsewhere on that continent, the members of the East African Common Services Organization (Kenya, Uganda, and Tanzania) subscribe to a single East African Court of Appeal, partly in order to utilize available judicial talent. Yet reason does not always prevail. The West African Court of Appeal is now defunct. A proposed regional court of appeal to serve all of the States of the Commonwealth Caribbean has not been launched. In many places expatriate judges are removed not because there are better-qualified national candidates but because chauvinism is all too often part of the pattern of independence.

There is no doubt that governments would prefer not to be accused either of interference with the judiciary or with supporting only incompetent legal institutions. Yet in the pressures of political life, when spending priorities must be fixed and when decisions often reflect the most urgent, rather than the most important, matters, government attitudes are not always what they should be. Only when courts achieve the stature in the public eye which they deserve will governments commit the necessary resources to them and to their supporting services. Perhaps only when alien investors—who already have been so influential in shaping world commercial and industrial practices—take an equally active interest in the effective operation of the courts in developing countries will governments assign to these institutions resources necessary for their proper operation. This result can only be achieved if these persons pursue their claims against both governments and individuals through local legal, as distinct from diplomatic, channels. The authors strongly advocate this practice.

In Latin America obstacles to the impartial and effective functioning of court systems also flow from the extremes of wealth and poverty found within the nations studied, and the general poverty of these nations and their resources as compared to wealthier capital-exporting States. There is no doubt that a person's political influence, relations, and riches will assure him better treatment while in custody and easier access to *amparo* and habeas corpus. In Brazil, for example, at least before the 1964 Revolution, university graduates detained for nonpolitical offenses automatically were accorded better food and sleeping accommodation than fellow prisoners. Affluent persons are, moreover, generally well-educated, aware of their rights, and better able to secure legal counsel. As a result, it is often inaccurate to speak of "equal" justice for all men. Ironically, as a result of their poverty, need for foreign investment, and history of unsettled border disputes with their neighbors, the less wealthy and weaker of the Latin American nations probably automatically, without consular intervention, accord better physical treatment and assure the expeditious handling of cases involving aliens from more powerful, richer non–Latin American nations. This fact is especially true where the alien is an individual, rather than a large company with an unfavorable image in local public opinion.

Moreover, the high cost of administering justice may price judicial relief outside the grasp of less affluent litigants. Latin American court systems generally are assigned small portions of the budget, so that funds are insufficient either to provide adequate physical facilities or to hire the administrative personnel required to process ever-increasing case loads. Indeed, funds are lacking even to recompense adequately present complements of secretaries, clerks, and

other court functionaries. Perhaps this state of affairs is but a residue of penny-pinching Spanish colonial policy, whereby minor
officials, after purchasing their offices, were to receive their
remuneration in fees from the public they were serving. "Hence . . .
the system of miscellaneous payments picturesquely known as
mordida. The standard fee for a document entitles the applicant to
nothing but the document in the official's good time. For extra help
and advice, for more expeditious service, he must expect to pay
extra."[121] For example, in Latin America, service of a complaint is
not effected by the plaintiff or his process server, but by a court
official, sometimes known as the *alguacil*. Once the court has decided
that a complaint has merit, it instructs the alguacil to serve the
defendant. To be sure that the defendant is served as quickly as
possible after court approval, plaintiffs' attorneys sometimes tip the
alguacil, who then may serve that defendant before any others he
may have on his list to be served that day. Armienta has written
of this phenomenon: "It is not unknown to ourselves, as Mexican
lawyers, the inveterate practice of tipping secretary-officials for carrying out certain procedural acts (service of process, executions,
attachments) their performance of which is made obligatory by their
mere acceptance of their positions. . . . [S]uch improper practice
promoted by ourselves and accepted with resignation by the judges
and magistrates, serves as a pretext for the unscrupulous lawyer,
for his own profit, to convince his client that the Secretary of
Court and even the Judge himself must be recompensed in the same
fashion."[122]

All these defects are aspects of instability, outcomes of new
patterns of social change and of the ferment of *uhuru* or *merdeka*
or *indépendance*. They do not serve to improve the quality or the
independence of either the judicial system or the judiciary. Nor, in
turn, do they inspire confidence on the part of litigants in the rule
of law or in the competent and impartial adjudication of disputes.

---

[121] J. PARRY, THE SPANISH SEABORNE EMPIRE 373 (1966).

[122] *La Onerosidad de Los Juicios* 5-6, CUARTO CONGRESO MEXICANO
DE DERECHO PROCESAL (1969). "But what makes the law slow, costly and discriminatory is its class character. Justice—even in the few countries where the
judiciary is really independent of the executive power—is a gentleman's justice
. . . which pays little attention to the problems of the common people." V. ALBA,
THE LATIN AMERICANS 346 (1969).

In the long run, of course, it is nationals and not aliens who suffer most from this shortsighted attitude, since they must rely much more upon their own courts than do outsiders.

Considering the weakness of even well-developed legal systems, on the basis of personal observation and interviews in a number of developing Commonwealth countries and elsewhere (and without intending to gloss over the many glaring deficiencies present), the authors are of the opinion that the heritage of an independent judiciary and, to a lesser extent, of the disciplined and dedicated bar, is present in many States.[123] Again and again in Africa and in Asia lawyers who represent numbers of expatriate and alien clients report that courts are so jealous of their reputations for fair dealing that there is a tendency for discriminatory results to appear *in favor* of the alien, simply to prove that the judges are not minions of the government which appointed them. This development is particularly true in the courts of superior jurisdiction where the standard of practice, the demeanor of counsel and the attitude of the judiciary reflect favorably on the exemplary English practice which is their model. The odd, unhappy incidents involving the integrity of courts of Commonwealth countries—that in Ghana in 1964 and that in Zambia in 1969—indicate both the tenacity of judges in the defense of their independence and the relatively few occasions on which that independence is challenged.

Even assuming political and economic stability, and judicial independence, the formal ability of aliens to gain access to courts and administrative tribunals in the countries where they are located is basic to the vindication of elementary substantive rights and to the successful operation of the Local Remedies Rule. To this problem the next Chapter turns.

---

[123] *See,* for example, the comments of Professor Gower: ". . . I am not very proud of the legal legacy which we have bequeathed to our colonies. But it must be admitted that this view would not be shared by most of the trained lawyers in those countries whose belief in the perfection of English law surpasses that of any Englishman, and who seem able to ignore most of the complications flowing from the duality of the English and customary laws." L. GOWER, INDEPENDENT AFRICA: THE CHALLENGE TO THE LEGAL PROFESSION 30 (1967). Professor Gower was speaking more specifically of its body of received English law than of legal institutions, but the two are not totally distinct.

CHAPTER V

Access by Aliens to Foreign Tribunals

Most nations allow aliens access to their tribunals on a basis of equality with nationals. Nevertheless, the differences in philosophies behind this granting of access, as well as the implementing legislation and treaties, warrant close examination. Even when access is assured, however, the credibility of such legislation may be diminished by requirements for posting excessive security bonds or by the inability of aliens to sue *in forma pauperis*.

Traditionally, four principal theories have determined the accessibility of local tribunals to aliens. In the first, that of extraterritoriality, aliens are governed by their own laws, even though abroad, and may be sued only in special courts in the host nation which apply that law. This system, once prevalent in the Middle and Far East, no longer exists. Under status-of-forces treaties today, even military personnel stationed abroad are subject to the jurisdiction of local courts for offenses not committed in the line of duty.

The second theory is that of reciprocity, according to which the rights of aliens depend upon corresponding rights being granted to citizens of the host country in the alien's nation. This reciprocity may be (a) diplomatic, where the alien has only those rights granted by treaty; (b) legislative, where the alien enjoys only those rights granted by legislation in his own country to citizens of his host State; or (c) reciprocity in fact, where the alien will enjoy those rights which are granted by law, by the courts, or by administrative practice in his own country to citizens of his host State.

The third theory determining the rights of aliens is the so-called restrictive system, pursuant to which equality between nationals and aliens, while proclaimed in theory, is subject to so many important exceptions, combined with official and unofficial hostility, arbitrariness, and suspicion, that any guarantees are meaningless.

The fourth theory is that of assimilation, or equal treatment, by which aliens are granted the same rights as nationals in the host State, with minor exceptions restricting political and commercial activity and concerning expulsion from the country.

The Commonwealth countries, the Latin American nations, and the United States of America adhere to the latter persuasion. None discriminates unreasonably against aliens; all grant them access to their tribunals equally with nationals. Nevertheless, the philosophies behind their apparently similar treatment of the alienage question are quite different, influenced primarily by historical experience.

In Commonwealth States, the alienage of a litigant is a wholly irrelevant factor should courts otherwise have jurisdiction. Indeed, there is no comprehensive statutory definition of the term "alien" in Great Britain. Nevertheless, the peculiar legal relationship between the Commonwealth countries complicates the question of alienage somewhat. While in large measure the individual is in no way affected by this legal fuzziness—which is largely historical in origin—and certainly is not affected in his right to be heard by the courts of Commonwealth countries, the issue may be of importance in the context of the Local Remedies Rule. That Rule, of course, is applied only when an alien interest is affected, as in the case of an American in the Congo or a Frenchman in Brazil. But what about a Canadian in Australia? Both Canada and Australia were former British colonies. However, once they attained independence and thereby gained international personality, problems arose concerning their legal relationship. What duties and responsibilities did international law require of them *inter se?* According to O'Connell, the answer

> was formulated in the doctrine that the Dominions and the United Kingdom *inter se* were bound by rules of constitutional and not of international law, or in some instances not bound by either. . . . It was considered that disputes between Commonwealth members should be settled either by the Privy Council, when this possessed jurisdiction, or through domestic channels. The reasoning behind this was never very clear, but the predominant factor seems to have been the importance of treating imperial matters as domestic, the Crown representing the unifying link. . . . To meet the need for arbitration between Commonwealth members it was proposed to

set up *ad hoc* tribunals of Commonwealth arbitrators who would have jurisdiction over justiciable disputes, but the proposal was never implemented.[1]

Following the Treaty of Versailles and the Imperial Conference of 1925, agreements between Commonwealth members still could not take the form of treaties, since such agreements are between heads of State and the theoretical indivisibility of the Crown prevented the acceptance of such a procedure. Therefore, the practice developed for Commonwealth members not to register inter se bilateral agreements, and to include in multilateral agreements with other nations reservations concerning their application inter se.

A more realistic attitude now exists regarding these agreements, but manifestations of earlier theories occasionally recur. For example, when in 1947 India invoked a 1927 agreement between itself and South Africa before the United Nations,[2] South Africa, relying on Article 2(7) of the United Nations Charter,[3] contended that the dispute was domestic, being inter se. Furthermore, the Declaration of Acceptance by Canada of the compulsory jurisdiction of the International Court of Justice contains a reservation with respect to disputes among Commonwealth members.[4] More recently, the legal position of the British subjects of Indian origin now suffering dis-

---

[1] 1 D. O'CONNELL, INTERNATIONAL LAW 391–92 (1965).

[2] The dispute was centered around the question of the treatment of people of Indian and Indo-Pakistani origin in the Union of South Africa. For a more detailed discussion of this and related incidents see Jennings, *The Commonwealth and International Law*, 30 BRIT. Y.B. INT'L L. 326–30 (1953).

[3] U.N. CHARTER art. 2(7): "Nothing contained in the present Charter shall authorize the United Nations to intervene in matters which are essentially within the domestic jurisdiction of any state or shall require the Members to submit such matters to settlement under the present Charter; but this principle shall not prejudice the application of enforcement measures under Chapter VII."

[4] The Declaration of Canada, dated September 20, 1929, and ratified July 28, 1930, contained a reservation with respect to "disputes with the government of any other Member of the League which is a Member of the British Commonwealth of Nations, all of which disputes shall be settled in such manner as the parties have agreed or shall agree . . . ." [1968–1969] I.C.J.Y.B. 46. Canada withdrew this acceptance on April 7, 1970, and replaced it with another. The new Declaration contains a similar reservation with respect to "disputes with the Government of any other country which is a member of the Commonwealth of Nations, all of which disputes shall be settled in such manner as the parties have agreed or shall agree." [1969–1970] I.C.J.Y.B. 55.

crimination in Kenya may be affected in some instances by the inter se doctrine.

For purposes of litigation, however, alienage generally is relevant in Commonwealth country courts only when the alien involved is an "alien enemy," which in Great Britain is a person whose sovereign or State is at war with that country.[5] The definition has been extended to include persons of whatever nationality, including British,[6] who carry on business or who reside voluntarily either in an enemy country[7] or in a country controlled by the enemy.[8] Generally speaking, an alien enemy may not sue in England except with special permission from the Crown.[9] If he does not reside in an enemy State and does not carry on business there, however, he may maintain a civil action in England.[10] Indeed, if the alien enemy is residing in England and has properly fulfilled registration requirements, he may sue in the English courts to protect his civil rights.[11]

Since 1870 alien friends have been able to sue in Great Britain and have been subject to suit in the same manner as British subjects.[12] This same rule applies generally to all Commonwealth countries. If a court otherwise has jurisdiction, the alienage of one or the other parties to a civil action is immaterial.[13] For this reason, special mention of aliens seldom is found in the constitutions or procedural laws of Commonwealth countries. In these instances, lack of reference is equivalent to lack of discrimination.

---

[5] Sylvester's Case, [1703] 7 Mod. Rep. 150. *See also In re* Merten's Patents, [1915] 1 K.B. 857, 867, where Lord Reading, C.J., says that the "natural" meaning of the term "alien enemy" is the one stated above.

[6] Scotland v. South African Territories (Ltd.), [1917] 33 T.L.R. 255; R. v. Kupfer, [1915] 2 K.B. 321.

[7] *In re* Merten's Patents, note 5 *supra;* Tingley v. Müller, [1917] 2 Ch. 144.

[8] Sovfracht (V/O) v. Van Udens Scheepvaart en Agentuur Maatschappij (N.V. Gebr.), [1943] A.C. 203; *In re* Anglo-International Bank, Ltd., [1943] Ch. 233.

[9] *In re* Merten's Patents, note 5 *supra.*

[10] *In re* Sutherland (Duchess), Bechoff, David, & Co. v. Bubna, [1915] 31 T.L.R. 248.

[11] Schaffenius v. Goldberg, [1916] 1 K.B. 284.

[12] *In re* Merten's Patents, note 5 *supra.*

[13] Jurisdiction of a superior court generally extends to all matters involving persons or property physically situated within the territorial limits of the court and to causes of action which arise therein.

By contrast, access to courts in Latin America is assured aliens by express stipulations in constitutions, in civil and procedural codes, in special legislation, and in treaties. These specific guarantees are the product of two trends in Latin American political and legal thought. The first, which was expressed in the immediate post-independence constitutions, was a desire to break completely with the Spanish colonial policy which had restricted trade with aliens and excluded them physically from the New World. Foreign investment and immigration were encouraged after independence by assuring aliens equal treatment with nationals. The philosophy of the Enlightenment pervades those early enactments, which promised sanctuary to all those fleeing the tyrannies of Europe.[14] Surprisingly, this trend still is evident, and according aliens the same treatment as nationals is considered a significant step forward in the expansion of human rights, rather than solely—as some persons in capital-exporting nations may believe—a repressive means of denying aliens their rights under international law. Thus the great Cuban jurist, Bustamante, wrote in 1943 that "civil equality between nationals and aliens represents a great victory of our times. Without it there would not have been possible the present development of human civilisation which is due to the constant interchange of individuals, products and ideas."[15]

The second, and more recently evolved trend, derives from desires to protect the State from alien domination or subversion, and reflects the philosophy of the Calvo Doctrine. By specifically according aliens, in constitutional and other legislation, equal access to court with nationals, restrictions are placed on the rights of aliens to invoke the diplomatic protection of their own States. In view of the history of alien invasion and economic dominance in Latin America, this trend is quite understandable. It is reflected further in general Latin American adherence to the principle of territorial sovereignty which, enshrined in Article 12 of the Charter of the Organization of American States, means that "jurisdiction of States within the

---

[14] The 1824 Constitution of the ill-fated Federal Republic of Central America proclaimed in Article 24 that "[t]he Republic is a sacred asylum for all foreigners and the fatherland of all those who wish to live within its territory."

[15] I DERECHO INTERNACIONAL PRIVADO 33 (1943).

limits of their national territory is exercised equally over all the inhabitants, whether nationals or aliens."[16]

Nevertheless, historical fears should not be permitted to obscure the fact that foreign investment is desperately required by Latin America, and that foreign investors and their governments are perhaps more disposed than ever before in history to play constructive roles in assisting national development. Therefore, while States are entitled to restrict alien conduct, Latin Americans should recall the advice of a Costa Rican commentator that "the internationalists have agreed to recognize that this freedom is not absolute, that States have the obligation to grant aliens a minimum of rights, those which are considered essential to personal development. The contrary—an unrestricted liberty—would be an abuse of sovereignty, and upon denying these rights the State which did so would merit the sanctions of international justice, since that minimum is recognised by International Law."[17] History records that when minimum rights were not assured to aliens, whatever the reason, either tribunals with extraterritorial jurisdiction evolved or aggressive intervention occurred. It is highly unlikely that current events would permit repetition of these phenomena, but it is without doubt in the economic interests of developing States neither to place unjustifiable burdens upon aliens, nor to rely unduly upon "national," as distinct from "minimum international," standards of treatment.

CONSTITUTIONAL GUARANTEES AND SPECIAL LEGISLATION

Inherent in the Local Remedies Rule are the two principles that an alien should have right of access to local courts *and* that no recourse to diplomatic protection should precede local litigation. The Calvo Doctrine, while emphasizing the first principle, has distorted the second by seeking to restrict unduly the right of diplomatic protection, either by denying the right altogether or by making it conditional upon a "denial of justice." As indicated earlier in this study, a "denial of justice" may be interpreted quite narrowly, and by local, rather than international, standards.

---

[16] CHARTER OF THE ORGANIZATION OF AMERICAN STATES, *reprinted in* H. P. DE VRIES & J. RODRIGUEZ-NOVAS, THE LAW OF THE AMERICAS 221 (1965).

[17] Runnebaum, *Condición Jurídica de los Extranjeros en Costa Rica*, 17 REVISTA DEL COLEGIO DE ABOGADOS 109, 117 (May–July 1961).

Constitutional provisions illustrate especially well the interconnection of the right of access to courts with the principle of territorial sovereignty, and with an obligation to use local courts exclusively. The Costa Rican Constitution provides that "foreigners have the same individual social rights and duties as Costa Ricans with such exceptions and limitations as this Constitution and the laws establish. They may not intervene in the political affairs of the country and are subject to the jurisdiction of the Courts of Justice and the authorities of the Republic, and may not resort to diplomatic intervention except as provided in international conventions."[18] Among rights guaranteed both Costa Ricans and foreigners is that of petition to any public or official body and the right to receive reparation "for injuries or damage to their persons, property, or moral interests through recourse to the laws. Justice must be prompt, thorough, without denial and in strict accordance with the laws."[19]

The Guatemalan Constitution declares: "Every person has free access to the courts for the purposes of exercising his rights of action in accordance with the law."[20] The context of the article indicates clearly that "persons" includes aliens as well as citizens. The same article, however, limits recourse to diplomatic protection: "Foreigners may have recourse to diplomatic channels only in the event of denial of justice. The mere fact that a decision may be adverse to their interests is not to be considered as such. In all cases, the legal recourse established by Guatemalan laws must have been exhausted."[21]

The Honduran Constitution, similar in nature, states that "in Honduras foreigners enjoy all the civil rights of Hondurans with such restrictions as may be established by laws for reasons of public security or national interest."[22] Aliens have the same rights and duties as Hondurans "with the exceptions and limitations that this Constitution and the laws provide."[23] Hondurans and, by inference, aliens, are guaranteed access to Honduran tribunals.[24] Nevertheless,

---

[18] Art. 19.
[19] Art. 41.
[20] Art. 74.
[21] *Id.*
[22] Art. 26.
[23] Art. 31.
[24] Art. 57 *et seq.*

the Constitution cautions, in language similar to that of Guatemala: "Aliens may not have recourse to diplomatic channels except in cases of a denial of justice. For these purposes denial of justice is not understood to mean a verdict which is unfavorable to the claimant."[25]

Peru's Constitution states that "[t]he Constitution and the laws afford protection to, and carry obligations equally for, all the inhabitants of the republic."[26] No distinction is drawn between alien or citizen "inhabitants." The "protection" referred to in the Constitution is illuminated by the 1963 *Ley Orgánica del Poder Judicial del Perú,* which states that "[t]he function of administering justice is the prerogative of the Judicial Power and is exercised by its competent courts and tribunals in accordance with the constitution and the law."[27] Litigants are guaranteed an inalienable right to a fair hearing in proceedings held in open court, the right to a judgment containing an exposition of the law and the reasons on which it is based, and assurance that cases once concluded will not be reopened.[28] Litigants also are assured the right to "compensation for judicial errors committed in criminal cases, after review as prescribed by law," and "the right of petition against the State for delicts committed by members of the Judiciary in the exercise of their duties, or by officers of other branches of government respecting the execution and compliance with judicial decisions and orders."[29] The executive branch is obliged, on pain of legal liability, to enforce judicial decisions and orders.[30] However, there is as well a general constitutional provision which, without reference to denial of justice, states: "Foreigners as regards property are in the same conditions as Peruvians without being able in any case to invoke an exceptional position in this respect or have recourse to diplomatic claims."[31] The Bolivian Constitution apparently denies all recourse to diplomatic remedies. Aliens are granted access to Bo-

---

[25] Art. 27.

[26] Art. 23.

[27] Decreto Ley No. 14605 de Julio de 1963; El Peruano, 26 July 1963, *as amended,* 19 August 1963, art. 1.

[28] Art. 3.

[29] Art. 3(f) & (g).

[30] Art. 3(h).

[31] Art. 32.

livian courts,[32] but "[f]oreign subjects and enterprises are subject to Bolivian laws and in no case may they invoke exceptional positions or have recourse to diplomatic claims."[33]

Other nations—Mexico, Venezuela, Argentina, Brazil—either do not supplement the right of access with constitutional obligations to utilize local tribunals or, as in Mexico and Venezuela, apply this requirement only in limited situations. The Argentine Constitution, for example, states that foreigners enjoy in the territory of the nation all of the civil rights of citizens, including the right to appear in court and to due process of law.[34] Similarly, the 1967 Brazilian Constitution guarantees resident foreigners the civil rights of Brazilians, including the rights of habeas corpus, to defend in court, to judicial assistance, and the right to "make representation to and to petition the public powers in defense of rights or against abuses of authority" without reference to limitations on diplomatic protection.[35] The Mexican Constitution promises aliens all civil rights granted Mexicans, including a broad right of access to the judicial process to prevent attacks on one's liberty or property.[36] The alien's right to invoke the protection of his government is expressly denied only in situations where he wishes to acquire land or mining concessions. If diplomatic protection is sought in such circumstances, the alien's interests shall be forfeit to the Mexican State.[37]

The Venezuelan Constitution provides that "foreigners have the same duties and rights as Venezuelans,"[38] and, furthermore, that "the courts will assist all inhabitants of the Republic in the enjoyment and exercise of the rights and guarantees which the Constitution establishes in conformity with the laws."[39] The procedure must be short and summary, and the competent judge will have the power to restore immediately *la situación jurídica infringida.*" The right of access is granted specifically without distinguishing between foreigners and nationals: "Everyone may use the organs of the ad-

---

[32] Art. 6(h).
[33] Art. 20.
[34] Arts. 18 & 20.
[35] Art. 150.
[36] Art. 33.
[37] Art. 27.
[38] Art. 45.
[39] Art. 49.

ministration of justice for the defense of his rights and interests, according to the terms and conditions established by the law, which will provide the norms to assure the exercise of this right to those who do not have sufficient means. The right to a fair hearing is an inviolable right at all stages and types of process."[40] The Constitution, pursuant to Article 127, only prohibits an alien's resort to diplomatic protection when a dispute has arisen out of a contract with the State or one of its agencies.

Various Latin American nations have special, supplementary legislation which further defines the rights and obligations of aliens within their territory. While these laws do not deny in all circumstances the rights of aliens to appeal to their own States for diplomatic assistance, the Venezuelan *Ley de Extranjeros*, for example, contains a Calvo-type restriction not found in the Constitution: "Neither domiciled aliens nor transients have the right to appeal to the diplomatic process, except when, after exhausting local remedies before competent authorities, it is evident that there has been a denial of justice after due proof of this fact."[41] The Honduran *Ley de Extranjería* in Article 26(2) accords aliens the right "to appeal to the protection of their country by diplomatic channels, in accordance with the provisions established by the Constitution."[42] This grant must be interpreted in the light of other stipulations, however, which provide that "aliens have in Honduras the same rights and obligations as Hondurans" and "aliens may not appeal to diplomatic channels except in cases of denial of justice. For this purpose, a denial of justice does not mean that a final judgment is unfavorable to the claimant."[43]

The Mexican *Ley de Nacionalidad y Naturalización* is marginally more severe. It repeats Article 33 of the Constitution, which guarantees aliens the same rights as Mexicans, but injects a prohibition on recourse to diplomatic remedies not found therein. After stating that aliens are obliged to pay duly authorized taxes of universal impact upon the general population, it provides: "Also, they [aliens]

---

[40] Art. 68.

[41] LEY DE EXTRANJEROS (La Torre ed.), art. 56

[42] Decreto No. 81 (1951), *reprinted in* I RECOPILACIÓN DE LEYES ADMINISTRATIVAS 808 (1965).

[43] Arts. 28 & 31.

are obliged to respect and obey the nation's institutions, laws and authorities, subjecting themselves to the decrees and judgments of its courts, without being able to invoke other procedures than those which the laws give to Mexicans. They can only appeal to the diplomatic channels in cases of denial of justice or in case of the voluntary and notoriously malicious delay in its administration."[44] The *Ley* also requires adding a clause to all contracts with local governments or federal authorities, renouncing diplomatic protection.[45] In practice, this clause is inserted in the charters of all Mexican corporations with alien equity ownership.

JUDICIAL CODES, TREATIES, AND INTERNATIONAL AGREEMENTS

The various Latin American civil, procedural, and commercial codes reflect the same concepts of territoriality and equality of treatment for aliens and nationals as do the constitutional provisions cited earlier. The result, when combined with a trend toward legal nationalism, channels aliens into local courts in their search for judicial relief. The existence of these codes reflects a difference with the Commonwealth countries. These latter are, on the whole, common law countries, in which comparatively less opportunity exists for formal written declarations. While Commonwealth countries have civil procedure codes, these codes are basically "rules of court" and by no means exhaustive. Moreover, they must be read against the background of the jurisprudence both of the country in question and of England. When this is done, it is found that silence favors the alien; that there is in most Commonwealth countries a complete absence of procedural discrimination. The alien friend stands before the courts equally with citizen or subject, his alienage an irrelevant factor.

By contrast, Latin American code articles indicating that the territorial ambit of the law applies to aliens and nationals alike are frequent. In Venezuela the Civil Code states that "the authority of the Law extends to all nationals and aliens who are found in the Republic," without distinguishing between alien residents or tran-

---

[44] Art. 32, *reprinted with all subsequent amendments in* R. DE PINA, ESTATUTO LEGAL DE LOS EXTRANJEROS 19 (3d ed. 1967).

[45] Art. 33.

sients.[46] The Honduran Civil Code simply provides that "the law is binding upon all the inhabitants of the Republic, including foreigners,"[47] while the Costa Rican Civil Code maintains that laws involving *orden público* bind "the inhabitants and even transients in the territory of Costa Rica."[48] Orden Público has been defined as referring to the laws determining the status, capacity, and family relations of an individual, but it is presumed also to include legislation designed to protect the internal organization and stability of the State. Hence the concept should be interpreted broadly. Mexico's Civil Code is more comprehensive: "[t]he laws of Mexico, *including* those which refer to the status and capacity of persons, are applicable to all the inhabitants of the Republic, be they nationals or aliens, whether they are domiciled in it or are transients."[49] The Mexican Commercial Code complements the Civil Code by requiring that foreign businessmen and companies operating in Mexico be subject to national laws and courts. This requirement parallels the Peruvian Commercial Code, which insists that foreign companies with branches in Peru appoint attorneys-in-fact "with powers to appear in court and to answer complaints,"[50] and Guatemala's Civil Code, which provides that foreign companies doing business therein are perforce subject to the jurisdiction of its courts.[51] The Costa Rican Commercial Code is similar.[52]

In Commonwealth countries a foreign company may be recognized, and usually is, as a legal person capable of suing and being sued. If it carries on business within the country, it is subject to certain requirements such as the registration of certain of its corporate documents, of the names and addresses of its directors and officers, and of the names and addresses of persons within the country authorized to accept service of legal process and other

---

[46] CÓDIGO CIVIL DE VENEZUELA DE 1942 (La Torre ed.), art. 8.

[47] CÓDIGO CIVIL DE 1906, art. 12.

[48] CÓDIGO CIVIL (Atilio Vicenzi ed. 1966), *as amended*, art. 2.

[49] CÓDIGO CIVIL PARA EL DISTRITO Y TERRITORIOS FEDERALES (Porrua ed. 1969), art. 12 (emphasis added).

[50] Nueva Ley de Sociedades Mercantiles (1966), art. 298.

[51] CÓDIGO PROCESAL, CIVIL Y MERCANTIL, 1968 RECOPILACIÓN DE LEYES 256 *et seq.*, art. 30.

[52] CÓDIGO DE COMERCIO Y SUS REFORMAS (Valle Peralta & Zurcher Acuña eds. 1967), art. 226. The code also requires the foreign branch "to renounce expressly the laws of its domicile." Art. 226(c).

documents on its behalf. Failure to comply with these requirements renders the company subject to certain penalties, often including disability to commence civil litigation.[53] While this latter penalty denies the foreign company access to courts, the intention of the legislation is not to discriminate against foreign companies but rather only to make them subject to the same obligations as domestic companies. The information contained in the documents to be registered is identical to that demanded of domestic companies, although often less extensive. The lack of discrimination is clearly observed in the case of a foreign company not carrying on business within the country, which is permitted to sue, without any conditions precedent, in precisely the same fashion as a legal person of non-alien character.

Interestingly, in Canada and Australia, which are both federal States, the constituent provinces or states have legal competence to incorporate companies. Such companies then are regarded as "foreign" for purposes of registration and deposit of information elsewhere in the same country equally as much as companies incorporated in foreign countries. Practice in the United States of America is similar. Thus, in Commonwealth countries alien companies, like alien individuals, are not regarded for litigation purposes as differing in any fundamental fashion from locally incorporated, or locally born, persons. Therefore, their rights as litigants are assured: no special bestowal of capacity by statute or regulation is necessary.

While the rules of court of Commonwealth countries generally are silent on the subject of aliens, in Latin America the concept of equal treatment of aliens and nationals permeates the codes of procedure. The Venezuelan Code of Civil Procedure states that the courts "are obliged to administer justice to nationals as well as foreigners,"[54] while admonishing courts to treat all parties equally, without showing any preference.[55] Argentina's Federal Code of Civil Procedure

---

[53] The detailed requirements are spelled out in the several companies acts or ordinances of the different countries. In Commonwealth countries the limited liability company in almost all instances is a creature of statute. The much older "charter" companies are rarely found except in Great Britain, where a number continue in existence from earlier times.

[54] CÓDIGO DE PROCEDIMIENTO CIVIL DE 1916 (La Torre ed.), art. 1.

[55] Art. 21.

similarly requires courts to treat parties alike,[56] while the Costa Rican Civil Code states that "the law does not recognize any difference between the Costa Rican and an alien with respect to the acquisition and enjoyment of civil rights."[57] Some provisions state specifically, as do the Venezuelan[58] and Honduran[59] Civil Codes, that aliens have the same civil rights as nationals, thus recognizing by implication their rights to initiate and defend lawsuits. This recognition is especially clear in the Peruvian Code of Civil Procedure, which entitles anyone in the enjoyment of his civil rights to sue either directly or through an attorney-in-fact.[60] Mexico's Code of Civil Procedure is similar, and proclaims that "[a]ll those who are in the full enjoyment of their civil rights may bring suit."[61] The Guatemalan Code of Civil Procedure is identical.[62]

By contrast, different historical experiences in the United States of America rendered unnecessary the evolution of doctrines similar to those expounded by Dr. Calvo and evidenced in Latin American constitutions and codes. Colonization at a later date than Latin America by people with a different world-view, relative religious tolerance, and a good measure of pre-independence self-government, combined with an unusually convenient and ample supply of mineral and other natural resources, produced political stability and economic prosperity within 50 years of independence. Unlike Latin America, foreign domination or conquest soon ceased to be a realistic menace. Moreover, the disorder which gave rise to demands by aliens in Latin America for diplomatic protection never existed to any comparable extent in the United States. There was, therefore, no political necessity to develop a conscious policy toward aliens.

Indeed, the United States by the 1830s clearly had begun to expand economically and geographically at the expense of its weaker neighbors to the south. There was, then, no interest in seeking

---

[56] Código Procesal, Civil y Comercial de la Nación, Ley No. 17,454 de 1967, art. 34(5)(c).

[57] Art. 21.

[58] Art. 26.

[59] Art. 49.

[60] Código de Procedimiento Civil, art. 1.

[61] Código de Procedimientos Civiles Para el Distrito y Territorios Federales (10th ed. 1964), art. 44.

[62] Art. 44.

limitations on the use of diplomatic protection, since it was often the United States citizen who was the complainant and therefore the beneficiary of this protection. Partly as a result of its dominating position, and partly due to the complexities of its federal political system which accords wide jurisdiction to state courts, the United States also has been reluctant to subscribe to hemispheric attempts, such as the Bustamante Code of Private International Law (hereinafter "the Bustamante Code") or the various resolutions of the Inter-American Committee of Jurists, to limit the procedural scope of its courts or of the protective role of the Department of State.

As a practical matter, federal and state courts soon recognized the common law rule, developed in England by the end of the sixteenth century,[63] that both resident and nonresident friendly aliens are entitled to sue and be sued as if they were citizens.[64] In the Civil Rights Act of 1870,[65] Congress codified this vestige of the common law by prohibiting states from denying to "any person" within their jurisdiction due process and the equal protection of the laws.

> All persons within the jurisdiction of the United States shall have the same right in every State and Territory to make and enforce contracts, to sue, be parties, give evidence, and to the full and equal benefit of all laws and proceedings for the security of persons and property as is enjoyed by white citizens, and shall be subject to like punishment, pains, penalties, taxes, licenses, and exactions of every kind, and to no other.[66]

[63] *See generally* 9 W. HOLDSWORTH, A HISTORY OF ENGLISH LAW 97 (7th ed. 1956). The Judiciary Act of 1789 specifically gave aliens access to the federal court system. Act of Sept. 24, 1789, ch. 20, § 11, 1 Stat. 78.

[64] Dunlop & Co. v. Ball, 6 U.S. (2 Cranch) 180 (1804) (British subject in diversity case held entitled to recover on bond given by defendant Virginia citizen before outbreak of American Revolution, it being noted that Virginia courts had reasserted the common law right of aliens generally to sue—and in particular of British subjects to sue since 1793). *See also* Taylor v. Carpenter, N.Y. Ch. (11 Paige) 292 (1844) (nonresident alien, a British subject, held entitled to maintain common law action for trademark infringement the same as a citizen). More recently, a Department of Justice Press Release of January 31, 1942, declared that "[n]o native, citizen, or subject of any nation with which the United States is at war and who is resident in the United States is prevented by federal statute or regulation from suing in federal or state courts." *Ex parte* Kawato, 317 U.S. 69, 77 n.13 (1942).

[65] Act of May 31, 1870, ch. 114, § 18, 16 Stat. 144.

[66] 42 U.S.C. § 1981 (1964).

Although primarily intended to protect negroes from discriminatory state legislation, this enactment has been held to oblige states to grant these same rights to aliens. It can be invoked by any aggrieved alien in an action against any state authority which discriminates against him. As early as 1886 the Supreme Court stated that "[t]he Fourteenth Amendment to the Constitution is not confined to the protection of citizens. . . . [Its] provisions are universal in their application, to all persons within the territorial jurisdiction, without regard to any differences of race, or color, or of nationality. . . ."[67] In 1948, granting the request of a resident Japanese national for a writ of mandamus to compel the California Fish and Game Commission to issue him a fishing license notwithstanding a state statute forbidding such issuance to any "person ineligible to citizenship," the Supreme Court held that the federal statute, "and the Fourteenth Amendment on which it rests in part protect 'all persons' against state legislation bearing unequally upon them either because of alienage or color."[68] So long as the alien is the citizen of a country with which the United States is not at war, his right to sue in all federal and state courts in the United States on common law causes of action is assured.

Aliens in the United States also are afforded access to courts on the same basis as citizens for statutory causes of action. Thus, nonresident aliens have been held entitled to maintain wrongful death actions under the New York version of Lord Campbell's Act,[69] when the court otherwise had jurisdiction over the defendant.[70]

---

[67] Yick Wo v. Hopkins, 118 U.S. 356 (1886).

[68] Takahashi v. Fish & Game Comm'n, 334 U.S. 410, 419–20 (1948).

[69] N.Y. ESTATES, POWERS AND TRUSTS LAW § 5–4.1 (McKinney 1967) provides: "The personal representative, duly appointed in this state or any other jurisdiction, of a decedent who is survived by distributees may maintain an action to recover damages for a wrongful act, neglect or default which caused the decedent's death against a person who would have been liable to the decedent by reason of such wrongful conduct if death had not ensued. Such an action must be commenced within two years after the decedent's death. When the distributees do not participate in the administration of the decedent's estate under a will appointing an executor who refuses to bring such action, the distributees are entitled to have an administrator appointed to prosecute the action for their benefit."

[70] Hamilton v. Erie R.R. Co., 219 N.Y. 343, 114 N.E. 399 (1916); Alfson v. Bush Co., 182 N.Y. 393, 75 N.E. 230 (1905). *See also* 3 AM. JUR.2d, *Aliens*

Similarly, nonresident alien dependents of workers injured within the scope of their occupation are entitled to the same workmen's compensation benefits as citizen dependents.[71] Aliens may maintain matrimonial actions for separation or divorce in New York so long as they satisfy the statutory requirement of residence within that state, although it has been held that a party cannot be deemed a "resident" of New York if he has only a temporary visitor's visa and has not acquired immigration papers.[72] Even this rule has been relaxed upon showing "unusual circumstances," particularly during wartime.[73] Aliens also may have access to federal courts on federally conferred actions. Thus, the Bankruptcy Act allows "any natural person" to become a bankrupt;[74] it has been held that a resident alien clearly can become a bankrupt,[75] and that a nonresident alien also may be adjudged a bankrupt if he has property located within the United States claimed by resident creditors.[76] In addition, alien seamen have been allowed to maintain statutory actions in admiralty to recover wages against foreign ships.[77]

---

and Citizens § 46 (1962); Annot., *Right to maintain action for wrongful death for benefit of nonresident aliens*, 138 A.L.R. 684, 686 (1942).

[71] *In re* Babb, 264 N.Y. 357, 191 N.E. 15 (1934). *See generally* N.Y. WORKMEN'S COMPENSATION LAW §§ 17, 25–b & 121–a (McKinney 1965) on the specific rights of aliens and nonresidents.

[72] Schwallbach v. Schwallbach, 84 N.Y.S.2d 345 (Sup. Ct. 1948), *aff'd*, 276 App. Div. 826, 93 N.Y.S.2d 716 (1st Dep't 1949).

[73] Townsend v. Townsend, 176 Misc. 19, 26 N.Y.S.2d 517 (Sup. Ct. 1941).

[74] Bankruptcy Act § 4, 30 Stat. 547 (1898), *as amended*, 11 U.S.C. § 22 (1964).

[75] *In re* Clisdell, 2 Am. Bankr. R. 424 (Ref. N.D.N.Y. 1899).

[76] *In re* Berthoud, 36 Am. Bankr. R. 555, 231 F. 529 (S.D.N.Y. 1916), *appeal dismissed*, 38 Am. Bankr. R. 440, 238 F. 797 (2d Cir. 1916).

[77] 46 U.S.C. § 597 (1964) provides:

"Every seaman on a vessel of the United States shall be entitled to receive on demand from the master of the vessel to which he belongs one-half part of the balance of his wages earned and remaining unpaid at the time when such demand is made at every port where such vessel, after the voyage has been commenced, shall load or deliver cargo before the voyage is ended, and all stipulations in the contract to the contrary shall be void: *Provided,* Such a demand shall not be made before the expiration of, nor oftener than once in five days nor more than once in the same harbor on the same entry. Any failure on the part of the master to comply with this demand shall release the seaman from his contract and he shall be entitled to full payment of wages earned. And when the voyage is ended every such seaman shall be entitled to the remainder of the wages which shall be then due him, as provided in section 596 of this title:

Alien plaintiffs sometimes are denied access to courts in the United States if the court in its discretion declines to exercise jurisdiction on the grounds of forum non conveniens. However, this doctrine is related not to the fact of alienage but to rules of equity and fair play. It is invoked equally against plaintiffs who are United States citizens but who are not residents of the forum. Courts have applied the doctrine primarily if one or, more generally, both parties are nonresidents of the forum, if the cause of action arose outside the jurisdiction, and if practical considerations such as ease of access to sources of proof and the cost of obtaining the attendance of witnesses justify dismissal of the action in order to compel the plaintiff to bring his action in an alternative and more "convenient" forum. Such exercise of judicial discretion has been held constitutional, whether the discretion is exercised on the judge's own motion[78] or is conferred by statute.[79] New York courts have limited the applicability of the doctrine in common law actions to cases where *both* parties are nonresidents of New York, and where the action arose outside New York State.[80]

Provided further, That notwithstanding any release signed by any seaman under section 644 of this title any court having jurisdiction may upon good cause shown set aside such release and take such action as justice shall require: *And provided further, That this section shall apply to seamen on foreign vessels while in harbors of the United States, and the courts of the United States shall be open to such seamen for its enforcement.* This section shall not apply to fishing or whaling vessels or yachts." (Emphasis added.)

[78] Gulf Oil Corp. v. Gilbert, 330 U.S. 501 (1947) (where Virginia resident sued a Pennsylvania corporation in a federal district court in New York for negligent destruction of plaintiff's warehouse in Virginia, and defendant corporation was licensed to do business in Virginia so that service of process could be obtained on it, dismissal of action by district court judge held not to constitute an abuse of discretion: the decision sets forth the major considerations in determining whether or not the forum is an "inconvenient" one).

[79] Douglas v. New Haven R.R. Co., 279 U.S. 377 (1929) (New York statute granting court discretion to dismiss actions brought by nonresidents against foreign corporations on foreign-based tort actions held not to violate the Privileges and Immunities Clause [Art. IV § 2] of the United States Constitution).

In De la Bouillerie v. de Vienne, 300 N.Y. 60, 89 N.E.2d 15 (1949), when an alien plaintiff sued an alien defendant for false imprisonment and conspiracy to defraud allegedly committed in France, and the plaintiff submitted an affidavit showing that the defendant was a resident of New York and had applied for citizenship papers, the dismissal of the action was reversed on the ground that New York Courts are bound to try an action for a foreign tort when either the plaintiff or the defendant is a resident of the state.

[80] For a discussion of New York tort cases generally, see Annot., *Discretion*

United States federal courts have allowed themselves considerably more discretion in declining jurisdiction for grounds of forum non conveniens, particularly in admiralty cases where both parties are aliens. The Ninth Circuit Court of Appeals has declared that "no alien has a constitutional right to sue in the United States courts," particularly where to allow an alien to bring a particular contract action would frustrate the intent of the contract and precipitate a deluge of cases which would clog even more seriously the already congested court calendars.[81] A federal court also has applied the doctrine where a nonresident French citizen sued a United States citizen for breach of a contract made in France on the grounds that the citizen defendant was actually resident in France and that the plaintiff could easily seek redress in French courts.[82]

In some situations an alien may be compelled to bring an action exclusively in either a federal or state court. Certain sections of the United States Judicial Code provide original federal jurisdiction where one or more aliens is a party and no federal question is involved. Thus, federal courts apparently have diversity jurisdiction in an action between an alien and a United States citizen, but not in an action between two aliens.[83] The Judicial Code, on

---

of court to refuse to entertain action for non-statutory tort occurring in another state or country, 48 A.L.R.2d 800, 831–36 (1956).

[81] Heine v. N.Y. Life Ins. Co., 50 F.2d 382 (9th Cir. 1931) (action brought by German citizen against New York corporation in Oregon on insurance policy issued and payable by its terms only in Germany held dismissed where action was brought to avoid anti-inflation measures in Germany and where to entertain action would result in innumerable similar actions being brought in American courts). The court cited Justice Holmes' opinion in Douglas v. New Haven R.R. Co. to the effect that "[t]here are manifest reasons for preferring residents in access to often overcrowded Courts, both in convenience and in the fact that broadly speaking it is they who pay for maintaining the Courts concerned." *Supra* note 79, at 387.

[82] De Sairigna v. Gould, 83 F. Supp. 270 (S.D.N.Y. 1949), citing the *Heine* case, note 81 *supra*. On application of the doctrine in contract actions see Annot., *Doctrine of forum non conveniens: assumption or denial of jurisdiction of contract action involving foreign elements*, 90 A.L.R.2d 1109 (1963).

[83] Unless a federal question is involved. 28 U.S.C. § 1332(a) (1964) on federal jurisdiction in diversity of citizenship cases provides:

The district courts shall have original jurisdiction of all civil actions where the matter in controversy exceeds the sum or value of $10,000, exclusive of interest and costs, and is between—
(1) citizens of different States;
(2) citizens of a State, *and foreign states or citizens or subjects thereof;* and

the other hand, confers upon federal courts exclusive jurisdiction of any action brought by an alien "for a tort only, committed in violation of the law of nations or a treaty of the United States";[84] this provision depriving state courts of jurisdiction has been strictly construed.[85] The Judicial Code also gives the Supreme Court of the United States original but not exclusive jurisdiction of any action brought by a state against an alien, although apparently no reported cases have arisen thereunder. Assuming the alien receives a fair and nondiscriminatory hearing of his claim or defense in the forum to which he is relegated by these provisions, his procedural rights are not seriously affected.

The venue provisions of the Judicial Code,[86] however, contain minor provisions which under certain circumstances might inconvenience alien litigants in federal courts. By case law an alien plaintiff in a federal diversity action may sue a citizen only where the citizen resides.[87] Nevertheless, Section 1391 (d) of the Judicial Code

---

(3) citizens of different States and *in which foreign states or citizens or subjects thereof are additional parties.* (Emphasis added.)
"An alien may select a federal court in which to sue a citizen of any state. . . ." *Ex parte* Edelstein, 30 F.2d 636, 638 (2d Cir. 1929). *Compare* Kavourgias v. Nicholaou Co., 148 F.2d 96 (9th Cir. 1945), where an action by a Greek citizen against a Greek corporation was dismissed.

[84] 28 U.S.C. § 1350 (1964).

[85] Khedivial Line, S.A.E. v. Seafarers' Int'l Union, 278 F.2d 49 (2d Cir. 1960) (the case was dismissed on the ground that the alleged tort under general maritime law did not constitute a tort in violation of a treaty or international law). In O'Reilly de Camara v. Brooke, 209 U.S. 45 (1908), the taking of a Spanish national's property by American military authorities in Cuba without compensation was held not to constitute a tort in violation of the law of nations where such taking had been ratified by the Congress and the President of the United States.

[86] 28 U.S.C. § 1391 (1964) on "Venue generally" provides:
(a) A civil action wherein jurisdiction is founded only on diversity of citizenship may, except as otherwise provided by law, be brought only in the judicial district where all plaintiffs or all defendants reside.
(b) A civil action wherein jurisdiction is not founded solely on diversity of citizenship may be brought only in the judicial district where all defendants reside, except as otherwise provided by law.
(c) A corporation may be sued in any judicial district in which it is incorporated or licensed to do business or is doing business, and such judicial district shall be regarded as the residence of such corporation for venue purposes.
(d) An alien may be sued in any district.

[87] In Prudencio v. Hanselmann, 178 F. Supp. 887 (D. Minn. 1959), plaintiff,

provides that an alien defendant in a diversity action "may be sued in any district."[88] It is unclear, however, whether or not an alien corporation whose officer is personally served within a particular jurisdiction also must be "doing business" within the jurisdiction for the court to retain the suit.[89] Furthermore, a court that otherwise may retain a suit against an alien may dismiss the action in its discretion on the grounds of forum non conveniens. It appears, therefore, that while aliens occasionally may be inconvenienced as concerns the federal judicial district where they may sue or be sued, their substantive rights are not affected by these provisions.

Unlike Latin America or the Commonwealth nations, European continental civil codes not infrequently provide that aliens shall enjoy only rights which are granted to nationals of the enacting

---

a Bolivian citizen residing in Minnesota, sued a North Dakota citizen in the District Court of Minnesota for injuries sustained in a motor accident in Minnesota. The court upheld defendant's motion to dismiss for lack of proper venue. The court reasoned that the action could not properly be brought where plaintiff resided under § 1391(a), because the phrase "diversity of citizenship" as used therein applied only to actions between United States citizens, notwithstanding that actions between a citizen and an alien were subsumed under the title "diversity of citizenship" in § 1332(a). The court followed a long line of cases holding that an alien is deemed not to reside in any district, and therefore may sue only in the district where the defendant resides. The decision cites extensive legislative history of the 1948 Judicial Code to support the holding.

[88] For a discussion of cases decided under this provision, see 1 J. MOORE, FEDERAL PRACTICE § 0.142[6] (1964). Before 1948 the rule was forged by court decisions based on interpretation of the predecessor of § 1391(b). Galveston & C. Ry. v. Gonzales, 151 U.S. 496 (1894); In re Hohorst, 150 U.S. 653 (1893); Lehigh Valley Coal Co. v. Washko, 231 F. 42 (2d Cir. 1916).

[89] Compare Paragon Oil Co. v. Panama Refining & Petrochemical Co., 192 F. Supp. 259 (S.D.N.Y. 1961), where an officer of a Panamanian corporation was served in New York, and the court looked to other contacts of the corporation with New York State so as to permit retention of jurisdiction under § 1391(c), with Japan Gas Lighter Ass'n v. Ronson Corp., 257 F. Supp. 219 (D.N.J. 1966), where the court stated that an alien corporation may be sued in any federal court subject only to the "protection with regard to the fairness of locale by the requirements of constitutional jurisdiction and service. . . ." (id. at 225)—a consideration which concerns only whether due process has been accorded by proper service under the fifth amendment. See, e.g., Seilon, Inc. v. Brema S.p.A., 271 F. Supp. 516 (N.D. Ohio 1967), where given the allegations of the complaint the court dismissed the action as to two of three defendants for lack of the requisite jurisdictional showing that the alien defendants could be served under the state "long-arm statute" by service of process on the Ohio Secretary of State.

State in the alien's home country.[90] The impact of these rules on the right of aliens to sue, however, is usually minimal. This fact is most clearly seen in Italy. Article 16 of the "Provisions on Law in General"[91] states that aliens, on condition of reciprocity, may enjoy the same rights as citizens. However, this reciprocity rule evidently must give way, as far as access to courts is concerned, before Article 24 of the Italian Constitution, according to which "[e]veryone may proceed at law for the protection of his rights and legitimate interests." Since the Italian Constitution utilizes the expression "everyone" when it wishes to confer rights independent of citizenship (otherwise, the expression "every citizen" is used), aliens have the same right of access to courts as Italian nationals.[92]

While in France Article 11 of the Civil Code makes an alien's exercise of "civil rights" (*droits civils*) dependent upon the existence of reciprocity guaranteed by treaty, this provision has received an increasingly narrow interpretation. Prevailing opinion is that Article 11 applies only where some other, more specific rule restricts the rights of aliens.[93] Consequently, aliens have access to courts even absent a specific treaty.[94] Where aliens sue French nationals this result, in fact, is required by Articles 14 and 15 of the French Civil

---

[90] ALLGEMEINES BUERGERLICHES GESETZBUCH § 33 (Manz ed. 1967) (Austrian General Civil Code); C. CIV., art. 11 (66th ed. Petits Codes Dalloz 1967); C. CIV. *Disposizioni Preliminari*, art. 16 (Hoepli 1968).

[91] *See* note 90 *supra*. The "Provisions on Law in General" (*Disposizioni sulla legge in generale*, more commonly known as *disposizioni preliminari*), which precede the Italian Civil Code, contain certain rules on the sources of law and conflict of law rules.

[92] M. CAPPELLETTI & J. PERILLO, CIVIL PROCEDURE IN ITALY 118–19 (1965); G. MORELLI, DRITTO PROCESSUALE CIVILE INTERNAZIONALE 76–77 (2d ed. 1954). *Cf.* COSTITUZIONE DELLA REPUBLICA ITALIANA, art. 10: "The Italian legal order shall conform to the generally recognized rules of international law. The legal condition of aliens is regulated by law in conformity with international norms and treaties. . . ."

[93] Lefait v. Société Galeries St.-Denis, July 27, 1948, [1948] D. Jur. 535 (Cass. Civ.). Most legal authors at first thought that the requirement of reciprocity applied to the exercise of all private rights, but other writers argued that the exercise of rights which they considered "natural" rights was not subject to any reciprocity. The current view is the one expressed in the case cited. *See* Maury & Lagarde, *Etranger*, in 1 DALLOZ, RÉPERTOIRE DE DROIT INTERNATIONAL at Nos. 105–128 (1968); H. BATIFFOL, TRAITÉ ELÉMENTAIRE DE DROIT INTERNATIONAL PRIVÉ 194–201 (4th ed. 1967).

[94] *See, e.g.*, Maury & Lagarde, *supra* note 93, at Nos. 217–218.

Code, which give French nationals the privilege of insisting on being sued in France.[95] Consequently, doubts as to the rights of aliens to sue in France arose in the past mainly when neither party had French nationality. Today, however, an alien can sue another alien in France provided one of the regular bases for jurisdiction, such as domicile, exists.[96] In determining the alien's capacity to sue, French courts ordinarily apply the law of the alien's nationality, usually in a quite liberal manner.[97]

The foregoing concerns only the alien's right of access viewed as an abstract proposition. Whenever rules of substantive law provide no remedy, or no right to judicial review, no proceedings can be brought. This situation obviously applies to both French and alien parties. However, there are some rules concerning judicial review of administrative acts of particular interest to aliens. Thus, as in Latin America, there is frequently no, or only a restricted right of, judicial review in connection with the denial or cancellation of residence permits and related measures intended to force aliens to leave the country.[98]

Reciprocity also is imposed by Article 33 of the Austrian Civil Code, the terms of which resemble provisions of the French and Italian Codes. Austrian commentators indicate that the article requires what they call "formal" reciprocity, namely, national treatment, not "material" reciprocity, or the existence of substantially similar rights and remedies. Existence of this reciprocity is generally tacitly assumed.[99] Problems concerning standing to sue are therefore rare, even in the absence of a treaty.[100]

General principles of international law, as well as treaties and

---

[95] In fact, absent a waiver, judgments by foreign courts against French nationals are not likely to be recognized in France. For a more detailed discussion see P. HERZOG, CIVIL PROCEDURE IN FRANCE 176–84 (1967).

[96] *Id.* at 179–80.

[97] *Id.* at 245. *Cf.* Taylor v. Bariquaund, 41 JOURNAL DU DROIT INTERNATIONAL 1278 (1914) (English partnership may sue under conditions of English Law in France).

[98] *See, e.g.,* Lagarde, *Cartes d'Identité,* in 1 DALLOZ, RÉPERTOIRE DE DROIT INTERNATIONAL at No. 11 (1968).

[99] I. SEIDL-HOHENVELDERN, AMERICAN-AUSTRIAN PRIVATE INTERNATIONAL LAW 38 (1963); H. KOEHLER, INTERNATIONALES PRIVATRECHT 29 (3d ed. 1966).

[100] *But see* Judgment of Oct. 25, 1961, 34 S.Z. 433 examining the existence of reciprocity.

other international agreements, incorporate the concept of equal treatment and guarantee aliens access to local courts.[101] The 1953 Argentine–United States Treaty of Friendship, Commerce and Navigation assures access to courts for nationals of both contracting parties,[102] as does the 1928 United States–Honduras Treaty of Friendship, Commerce and Consular Rights.[103] The latter states that "[t]he nationals of each High Contracting Party shall enjoy freedom of access to the courts of justice of the other on conforming to the local laws, as well for the prosecution as for the defense of their rights, and in all degrees of jurisdiction established by law."[104] The Treaty of Perpetual Friendship and Treatment of Nationals between France and Costa Rica[105] contains similar provisions, and the 1928 Convention on the Status of Aliens,[106] ratified by most Latin American nations, provides that "States should extend to foreigners, domiciled or in transit through their territory all individual guaranties extended to their own nationals, and the enjoyment of essential civil rights without detriment, as regards foreigners, to legal provisions governing the scope of and usages for the exercise of said rights and guaranties."[107] More recently, on December 15, 1959, the Peruvian Congress resolved to

---

[101] See Wilson, *Access-to-Courts Provisions in United States Commercial Treaties*, 47 AM. J. INT'L L. 20, 30–32 (1953). "Thus, when it acquired the Virgin Islands, the United States agreed that Danish subjects residing in the Islands should have the right to appear before the insular courts and to pursue the same course therein as citizens might." *Id.* at 32. Other treaties assure the inhabitants of newly acquired territories certain guarantees, such as the right to peaceful possession of their property, which implies the right of recourse to the courts. *See*, for example, Article 1 of the 1859 Wyke-Cruz Treaty between Great Britain and Honduras, relinquishing British control over the Bay Islands.

[102] 10 Stat. 1005, T.S. No. 4. The phraseology of this treaty, as well as treaties between the United States and Costa Rica (1851), Honduras (1864), and Nicaragua (1867), "seems to leave some doubt as to whether national treatment was specified for access to courts, or only for the right to employ counsel." Wilson, *supra* note 101, at 38 n.85.

[103] 45 Stat. 2618, T.S. No. 764.

[104] Art. I.

[105] *Cited in* Runnebaum, *Condición Jurídica de los Extranjeros en Costa Rica*, 17 REVISTA DEL COLEGIO DE ABOGADOS 109, 154 (No. 2, 1961).

[106] 46 Stat. 2753, T.S. No. 815, *reprinted as* Appendix II in W. GOLDSCHMIDT & J. RODRIGUEZ-NOVAS, AMERICAN-ARGENTINE PRIVATE INTERNATIONAL LAW (1966).

[107] Art. 5.

adopt the Universal Declaration of Human Rights,[108] Article 8 of which states: "Everyone has the right to an effective remedy by the competent national tribunals for acts violating the fundamental rights granted him by the constitution or by law."[109] On December 15, 1965, the Declaration was incorporated into the laws of the Republic,[110] thus supplementing guarantees of access and fair judicial treatment already theoretically available in Peruvian domestic law.[111]

The Bustamante Code in Article 1 also supports the equal treatment concept and provides that "foreigners who belong to any of the contracting States will enjoy in the territory of the others the same civil rights as nationals."[112] Nevertheless, the Code allows each contracting State "for reasons of orden público, to deny or to subordinate to special conditions the exercise of certain civil rights by nationals of the rest, and any of those States may, in such cases, deny or subordinate to special conditions the exercise of the same rights by nationals of the first."[113] Fortunately, national legislation assuring all aliens access exists to supplement the Code, because, as one author has commented, "the importance of the Bustamante Code is usually exaggerated outside of Latin America. In the first place, it is not binding in dealings with citizens of the United States, a country which has neither signed nor ratified it. Secondly, many Latin-American countries have ratified it only in homage to Bustamante

---

[108] Decreto Ley No. 13282 of December 9, 1959; 1959 NORMAS LEGALES Nos. 29–31 at 493.

[109] THE UNIVERSAL DECLARATION OF HUMAN RIGHTS, G.A. Res. 217, U.N. Doc. A/810 at 71 (1948).

[110] Order of December 15, 1965, *cited in* A. ARAMBURU MENCHACA, LA RECEPCIÓN DE LA DECLARACIÓN DE DERECHOS HUMANOS EN EL DERECHO PERUANO Y SUS EFECTOS INTERNACIONALES 5 (UNESCO/SS/HR/22).

[111] The authors are deeply indebted to Dr. Aramburu Menchaca for his excellent explanation of the Peruvian legal system in general, and of the reception of the Declaration of Human Rights in particular, during several personal interviews in Lima, Peru.

[112] Formally known as the CÓDIGO DE DERECHO INTERNACIONAL PRIVADO and adopted at the Sixth Pan American Conference in Havana in 1928. It is reprinted in J. MUCI ABRAHAM, LOS CONFLICTOS DE LEYES Y LA CODIFICACIÓN COLECTIVA EN AMERICA 49 (1955).

[113] *Id.* at art. 1, para. 2.

and will apply it only if it is in accordance with their own internal legislation."[114] Moreover, many signatories only ratified with substantial reservations. Venezuela, for instance, made reservations to 44 of 437 articles. The Code's deference to local law in so many instances perhaps accounts for its failure to indicate specifically rights which may legitimately be denied aliens. A review of domestic legislation, however, does not indicate that basic procedural rights relating to the initiation, defense and conduct of litigation by aliens are narrowly circumscribed.

European nations also have concluded numerous treaties containing access to court provisions. In particular, treaties of friendship, commerce, and navigation with the United States usually contain standard clauses securing to nationals of the contracting States easy access to courts.[115] In a somewhat similar vein, a multilateral convention among the member States of the European Economic Community has been drafted as regards the recognition of the legal personality of foreign corporations.[116]

---

[114] Schwind, *Derogation Clauses in Latin American Law,* 13 Am. J. Comp. L. 167, 172 (1964). Nine countries ratified with reservations: Bolivia, Brazil, Costa Rica, Chile, Ecuador, El Salvador, Haiti, the Dominican Republic, and Venezuela. Six countries ratified without reservations: Cuba, Guatemala, Honduras, Nicaragua, Panama, and Peru. Other Latin American conferences convened for similar purposes in Montevideo (1888 and 1939) and in Caracas (1911) were even less successful. No nation ratified the convention produced at Lima in 1878, and only a few ratified the Montevideo conventions. The 1911 so-called "Bolivarian" convention was attended by Bolivia, Ecuador, Peru, Colombia, and Venezuela. The end-product was really a series of treaties, ranging from such matters as reciprocity in recognition of academic degrees to agreements on patents and copyrights. They only minimally treated the procedural rights of aliens. *See* J. Muci Abraham, *supra* note 112, at 14–22.

[115] Treaty of Friendship, Commerce and Consular Rights with Austria, June 19, 1928, art. 1, 47 Stat. 1876, T.S. No. 838; Convention of Establishment with France, Nov. 25, 1959, art. III, [1960] 2 U.S.T. 2398, T.I.A.S. No. 4625; Treaty of Friendship, Commerce and Navigation with Germany, Oct. 29, 1954, art. IV, [1956] 2 U.S.T. 1839, T.I.A.S. No. 3593; Treaty of Friendship, Commerce and Navigation with Italy, Feb. 2, 1948, art. V(4), 63 Stat. 2255, T.I.A.S. No. 1965.

[116] *See, e.g.,* Goldman, *Le Projet de Convention entre les Etats Membres de la Communauté Economique Européenne sur la Reconaissance Mutuelle des Sociétés et Personnes Morales,* 31 Rabels Zeitschrift 201 (1967). The agreement is based on Article 220 of the Treaty establishing a European Economic Community, March 25, 1957, 298 U.N.T.S. 11, according to which the member States of the Community, insofar as necessary, shall enter into negotiations to

Most departures from equal or national treatment in Latin America would seem either to be in matters of substantive law, such as nationality requirements for the exercise of certain professions or with respect to the conduct of specific types of business, limitations on land ownership near frontiers or seacoasts, and prohibitions concerning participation in local politics. A historic variant, common to many Commonwealth countries but not found in Latin America, is the denial of the right to own a ship. Procedural restrictions or limitations, such as evidence that nationals also would be entitled to reciprocal rights in the alien's nation, are not a prerequisite to bringing suit in Latin America, as they sometimes are in continental European nations.

SECURITY FOR COSTS, SUITS IN FORMA PAUPERIS, AND LEGAL AID

A procedural hurdle which, generally speaking, faces nonresident plaintiffs more than others—and is therefore of great interest to aliens—is the practice in many courts of requiring deposits of security by plaintiffs for costs at the commencement of proceedings, generally following an application therefor by the defendant. Security for costs is a legitimate precaution, but one through which a court easily could block a nonresident's access by granting defendant's motion for an excessively high deposit. There is little, if any, evidence that this indirect denial of access is done in practice.

The present English rule departs from earlier procedures by which nonresident plaintiffs were invariably required to deposit security.[117] The court now is vested with discretion since "if, having regard to all the circumstances of the case, the Court thinks it just to do so, it may order the plaintiff to give such security for the defendant's costs of the action or other proceeding as it thinks just."[118] Security cannot

---

secure to their nationals national treatment as far as the protection of persons and the protection and enjoyment of rights are concerned, the elimination of double taxation, the mutual recognition of corporations and the simplification of formalities relating to the recognition of judgments.

[117] As a result, such former precedents as Crozat v. Brogden, [1894] 2 Q.B. 30, and In re Pretoria Pietersburg Rlwy. Co. (No. 2), [1904] 2 Ch. 359, are no longer applicable.

[118] RULES OF THE SUPREME COURT, 1965; Order 23, rule 1.

now be ordered as a matter of course from a nonresident plaintiff (who in most cases will be an alien) except where the court is satisfied that it will be just to do so. One factor which English courts consider in applications for security by defendants is the likelihood of success of the applicant's case. If there appears little chance that the defendant will prevail, the court will not likely order security. Indeed, it could be argued that it would be a denial of justice to order a plaintiff to pay security for the costs of a defendant with no defense to an action. Alternatively, if a defendant has admitted liability for as much of the plaintiff's claim as would equal the amount to which he is entitled as security, the court will not order security on the theory that it lies in the defendant's own hands to protect himself by paying this amount into court.[119] Where the defendant admits liability, security will not be ordered even where there is a counterclaim.[120]

English practice always has been that no order for security will be made if there are co-plaintiffs resident in England.[121] However, these persons must be genuine plaintiffs and not merely agents of the nonresident who have been named in an attempt to avoid security.[122] Naturally, if a plaintiff moves abroad permanently following commencement of proceedings, an order for security may be granted.[123] If, however, the nonresident plaintiff (or foreign company) has fixed assets within the jurisdiction, exceeding in value the amount reasonable for security, none will be ordered.[124] The English rules make clear that the court must identify the parties as the actual plaintiff and defendant no matter how they may be described in the pleadings. Thus the named defendant, if in the position of a plaintiff for purposes of the lawsuit, may be required to deposit security. Each case will be examined on its merits, and if a counterclaim is really in the nature of a cross-action, the defendant (if residing out of the jurisdiction) may be ordered to post security.[125] Security can-

---

[119] Hogan v. Hogan (No. 2), [1924] 2 Ir. R. 14.

[120] Winterfield v. Bradnum, [1878] 3 Q.B.D. 324.

[121] D'Hormusgée v. Grey, [1882] 10 Q.B.D. 13.

[122] Jones v. Gurney, 1913 W.N. 72.

[123] Massey v. Allen, [1879] 12 Ch. D. 807.

[124] Redfern v. Redfern, [1890] 63 L.T. 780; Re Appollinaris Co.'s Trade-Marks, [1891] 1 Ch. 1; Sacker v. Bessler & Co., [1887] 4 T.L.R. 17.

[125] Sykes v. Sacerdoti, [1885] 15 Q.B.D. 423; Mapleson v. Masini, [1879] 5 Q.B.D. 144; New Fenix Co. v. General Accident Corp., [1911] 2 K.B. 619.

not be required, though, from a nonresident defendant or person who has been compelled to engage in litigation and is simply exercising his right to take proceedings of a wholly defensive nature.[126] The amount of security, which in England is normally paid into court in cash but which in special cases may be by bond, is in the discretion of the court. English practice is not to fix the amount on a full indemnity basis, but to order a sum approximating two-thirds of estimated future costs.

In this area, as in so many regarding civil procedure, English practice is observed closely by courts in other Commonwealth countries, where it is followed if there appears to be no fundamental distinction in rules. The comments of the Court of Appeal for Eastern Africa are illustrative: "[T]hough some differences may arise consequent upon the wider powers conferred by the rules of this court, many of the principles laid down by English case law remain relevant to the judicial exercise of discretion by this court."[127] Interviews with lawyers in several African countries suggest that in some African courts, to avoid limiting access of nonresidents through heavy security requirements, judges tended to order very modest sums. This inclination has led to accusations that, far from discriminating against nonresident aliens, judicial practice was more likely to place residents in a disadvantageous position respecting outsiders.[128]

Additional security may be requested in the event of appeal. The principles to be followed were described by a Malayan court, and reflect again the procedural uniformity existing in Commonwealth courts:

> As to the principles upon which the Court should act, it appears to me that the discretion of the Court should be exercised according to the same principles as are followed by the Court of Appeal in England. . . . It is not necessary for me to review all the English authorities. The result of such authorities I take to be this: (1) The

---

[126] Naamlooze v. Bank of England, [1948] 1 All E.R. 465 (C.A.).

[127] Noormohamed Abdulla v. Patel, [1962] E. Afr. L.R. 447, 452 (Sir Trevor Gould).

[128] Two examples of the discretion exercised by Kenyan courts are found in Farrab Inc. v. Robson, [1957] E. Afr. L.R. 441, where £500 security was ordered of a plaintiff company incorporated in Tangier, and in V.H. Kapadia v. Thakersey Laxmidas, [1960] E. Afr. L.R. 852, where no security was ordered of a plaintiff ordinarily resident in Zanzibar.

probability that the appellant will be unable to pay the costs of the
appeal if unsuccessful as a special circumstance which will generally
entitle the respondent to an order for further security. (2) The fact
that there is a point of law reasonably fit to argue will be taken into
consideration in fixing the amount of the security, but will not in
itself be considered a sufficient ground for dispensing with security
altogether. (3) Where the insolvency of the appellant has been
brought about, or contributed to, by the wrongful act complained of
in the action, it would be a denial of justice to require security on
the ground of such insolvency. . . . (4) The application must be
prompt.[129]

Another factor considered by Commonwealth courts is whether the
courts of the State in which the plaintiff ordinarily resides would
enforce a judgment of the court in which the plaintiff is suing. This
factor sometimes is regarded as sufficient for refusing an order for
security. A Malayan court nevertheless granted an application on the
basis that registration in Singapore of a judgment of a court of the
Federation of Malaya is a judicial process and may be litigated.
Because registration was not automatic, security was ordered.[130]

Requirements concerning the posting of security in Europe appear
more burdensome than those in the Commonwealth, but the rules are
frequently so complex that it is not easy to assess their real impact.
In Austria, aliens must post security for costs in all cases except
matrimonial matters, actions on negotiable instruments, and other
proceedings of lesser importance.[131] No security need be posted in
proceedings before the Administrative Court.[132] Security is not

---

[129] Abu bin Mohamed v. Voo Fui Tong, [1938] M.L.J. 140, 141–42 (C.A.)
(Terrell, J.).

[130] Ng Hui Lip v. Chan Hwa Cheng, [1958] M.L.J. 57, followed by New
Malaya Co. v. Abu Bakar, [1961] M.L.J. 151. For an opposite decision, see
Coldham v. Raub Australian Gold Mining Co., [1940] M.L.J. 50; [1939]
F.M.S.L.R. 160.

[131] ZIVILPROZESSORDNUNG §§ 57, 60 (12th ed. Manz 1960) [hereinafter cited
as AUS. ZPO]. The posting of security is dispensed with, for instance, in the
case of claims brought under the law concerning liability for atomic accidents,
Atomhaftpflichtgesetz, April 29, 1964, [1964] BGBl. 758 § 32, and in actions
in which there are no real opposing parties. Judgment of April 11, 1958, 80
JURISTISCHE BLAETTER 474 (Aus. Sup. Ct.).

[132] The law concerning the Administrative court contains no such requirement.
Verwaltungsgerichtshofgesetz 1965, Nov. 17, 1964, [1965] BGBl. 289.

required from aliens exempted by treaty,[133] thus exempting nationals of signatories of the Hague Convention on Civil Procedure.[134] Nor is security required if the alien litigant's State does not require it from Austrian nationals. However, determination of reciprocity may be made by the court before which the action is pending only if the matter is very clear. Otherwise, the court must address an inqury to the Ministry of Justice and is bound by its answer.[135] The Ministry apparently bases such replies on information supplied by Austrian consular and diplomatic representatives abroad unless it finds sufficient data in its own files.

The amount of security depends on the expected cost of litigation, including fees of defendant's attorney.[136] Though attorneys' fees are regulated by an official schedule, the amount is nevertheless sometimes quite substantial.[137] Security usually must be posted in cash or by deposit of domestic securities. Sureties can be utilized only in very limited circumstances and are quite rare. The posting of security is unnecessary if the plaintiff owns sufficient real property, or rights secured by such property, in Austria.[138]

---

[133] The term "alien" includes all persons not having Austrian nationality, except refugees domiciled in Austria. In the case of corporations, the location of their "seat" (actual headquarters) controls. 2 H. FASCHING, KOMMENTAR ZU DEN ZIVILPROZESSGESETZEN 387, 388 (1962). The nationality of the defendant is immaterial. A defendant who is an American national can demand security from an American plaintiff. Judgment of Feb. 9, 1949, 22 S.Z. 49 (Aus. Sup. Ct.).

[134] Convention Relating to Civil Procedure, done March 1, 1954, art. 17, 286 U.N.T.S. 265. The Convention is in force among the following countries: Austria, Belgium, Czechoslovakia, Denmark, Finland, France, Germany (Federal Republic), Hungary, Italy, Luxembourg, The Netherlands, Norway, Poland, Portugal, Spain, Sweden, Switzerland, the U.S.S.R., the Vatican, and Yugoslavia. The Treaty of Friendship, Commerce and Consular Rights with Austria, June 19, 1928, 47 Stat. 1876, T.S. No. 838, does not cover security for costs, hence United States nationals must post security, even in the case of residents of States where security covers only court costs, not attorneys' fees. Judgment of Feb. 23, 1955, 11 OESTERREICHISCHE JURISTENZEITUNG 129 No. 70 (Aus. Sup. Ct.).

[135] Aus. ZPO § 57. The statement by the Ministry is unreviewable in any court. Cf. Judgment of Feb. 24, 1958, 13 OESTERREICHISCHE JURISTENZEITUNG 668 No. 41 (Aus. Admin. Ct.).

[136] Aus. ZPO §§ 57, 60.

[137] In substantial cases, a sum of Aus. schilling 10,000 (about $400) would not be unusual.

[138] Aus. ZPO §§ 56, 57.

The impact of these somewhat burdensome rules, however, is reduced by various factors. First, the requirement can be avoided by assigning a claim to an Austrian national.[139] Secondly, the defendant must demand security in *limine litis* or waive any rights thereto.[140] Finally, the plaintiff need not post security if he takes an oath before the court where the action is pending, or before a court at his residence, that he is financially unable to post security.[141] It has been held that an American national domiciled in New York sufficiently complies with this requirement if he so swears before a notary public.[142]

In France, security (usually called *cautio judicatum solvi*) likewise can be demanded from plaintiffs,[143] but the basis for calculating the amount differs. Security must cover expected court costs and the expected fee of defendant's litigation agent (*avoué*), but these costs are relatively small, the avoué's fee being strictly controlled by schedule. No security is due for the fee of defendant's attorney (*avocat*). On the other hand, security must include an amount to cover a possible judgment for defendant on a counterclaim for abusive procedure. Such counterclaims are almost a standard feature of defendants' pleadings in France, though rarely successful.[144] Since the value of the counterclaim is difficult to assess, security usually is fixed at an arbitrary amount, *e.g.*, 1,000F.

Before regular and commercial courts, security is required in all matters,[145] except in mere applications for provisional relief.[146] No

---

[139] Judgment of March 11, 1936, 13 EVIDENZBLATT DER RECHTSMITTELENT-SCHEIDUNGEN 132 No. 377 (Oberlandesgericht Vienna).

[140] Aus. ZPO § 59.

[141] *Id.* § 60. A grant of legal aid has the same effect. *Id.* § 64.

[142] Judgment of Sept. 2, 1953, 26 S.Z. 580 (Aus. Sup. Ct.). In the opinion of the Austrian Ministry of Justice, a citizen of the State of New York domiciled in Austria would not have to post security, since Austrian citizens domiciled in New York would not have to post security there.

[143] The procedural designation adopted by a party does not necessarily control, since the courts may look behind it. Additionally, security is due from intervenors. *Cf.* Maury & Lagarde, *Caution "Judicatum Solvi,"* in 1 RÉPERTOIRE DE DROIT INTERNATIONAL at Nos. 22–25 (1968).

[144] But the amount of security should not reflect the value of any other counterclaim.

[145] C. CIV. art. 16 (65th ed. Petits Codes Dalloz 1966); C. PRO. CIV. art. 166 (63d ed. Petits Codes Dalloz 1966).

security seems due for proceedings before the *Conseil d'Etat*, but the rule is different before the lower administrative courts, the *tribunaux administratifs*.[147] Security is due from all alien plaintiffs, unless they have the special status of "privileged residents,"[148] or enjoy treaty protection, such as the Hague Convention.[149] Reciprocity is immaterial unless guaranteed by treaty. There is some dispute whether the nationality of corporations should be determined on the basis of a control test, or on the basis of the location of their "seats" or actual headquarters (*siège social*).[150]

In France, the granting of legal aid (*assistance judiciaire*) does not operate to relieve a plaintiff from the obligation to post security.[151] However, if security is not demanded at the outset of a lawsuit, the defendant is deemed to have waived his right to claim it.[152] As in Latin America, further proceedings are stayed while the decision on security is pending. For this reason, defendants occasionally demand security primarily for dilatory purposes. Hence, the security requirement sometimes has been attacked by commentators. Reform proposals a few years ago suggested eliminating security deposits, or their restriction to nonresident alien plaintiffs.[153] However, they were not enacted into law. Nevertheless, the new Algerian Code of Civil Procedure adopts rules concerning

---

[146] *E.g.*, S.A.R.L. Thalia v. Vve Schlusnus, [1955] D. Jur. 492 (Cour d'appel, Paris).

[147] *See, e.g.*, Dlle Franszke, 89 JOURNAL DU DROIT INTERNATIONAL 426 (1962) (Tribunal Administratif de Bordeaux).

[148] Ordonnance No. 45–2658 of Nov. 2, 1945, [1945] J.O. 7225, [1946] D.L. 24, art. 17.

[149] As to the Hague Convention, see note 134 *supra*. France is a party to a large number of other bilateral and multilateral conventions relating to security for costs. For a listing see notes 188–191 *infra* and Maury & Lagarde, *supra* note 143, at Nos. 87–151. The Convention of Establishment with France, *supra* note 115, provides specifically in its Protocol No. 3 that the rules concerning security for costs remain unaffected by it. United States nationals therefore must post security in France. Barker Bros. v. Bussoz, [1961] D.J. 499 (Tribunal de Grande Instance de la Seine).

[150] Maury & Lagarde, *supra* note 143, at Nos. 10–12.

[151] *See* Barker Bros. v. Bussoz, note 149 *supra*.

[152] C. PRO. CIV. arts. 168, 192 (63d ed. Petits Codes Dalloz 1966).

[153] Herzog, *International Law, National Tribunals and the Rights of Aliens: The West European Experience*, 21 VAND. L. REV. 742, 747–48 (1968).

security for costs which follow the proposed French model quite closely.[154]

German rules on security are quite similar to the ones prevailing in Austria, though reciprocity must be determined by the court, not by an administrative agency.[155] Again, the deposit must provide for anticipated attorney's fees, which, as in Austria, are regulated by an official schedule.[156] The position of United States nationals in Germany, however, is slightly different from their position in Austria, since security is regulated by the Treaty of Friendship with Germany. According to that treaty, security need not be posted by individuals having their residence or a commercial establishment in the territory of the party where they bring suit.[157]

An entirely different situation prevails in Italy, which does not require aliens or nonresidents to post security. Nevertheless, Article 98 of the Italian Code of Civil Procedure authorizes the judge to order any plaintiff not granted legal aid to post security should there be justified grounds that a judgment for costs might remain unpaid.[158] This provision, however, was declared unconstitutional by the Italian Constitutional Court in 1960 on the ground that, by imposing more onerous provisions for bringing suit on poor than

---

[154] CODE DE PROCÉDURE CIVILE arts. 460–462 (Algeria 1966), *reprinted in* 56 REVUE CRITIQUE DE DROIT INTERNATIONAL PRIVÉ 626 (1967).

[155] ZPO §§ 110, 112 (C.H. Beck 1965); 1 B. WIECZOREK, ZIVILPROZESS-ORDNUNG UND NEBENGESETZE 845–79 (1957). No security need be given in suits arising out of rights recorded in the public land registers, in so-called documentary suits and in suits based on bills of exchange.

[156] Generally speaking, security is likely to be fixed at about three times a so-called basic fee. In a lawsuit involving an amount of $12,500, it thus might come to about $550.

[157] Treaty of Friendship, Commerce and Navigation with Germany, note 115 *supra*. There is a slight divergence between the English and German texts. According to the English text, the plaintiff's residence must be within the territory of the other contracting party, while under the German text it must be within the district of the court. A leading German commentator feels that in the case of suits by German nationals, it is enough if their residence is within the state of the United States where they bring their action, but a residence anywhere in the United States is sufficient for an action in the federal courts. In the case of United States nationals, a residence anywhere in Germany is sufficient. 1 A. BUELOW & H. ARNOLD, DER INTERNATIONALE RECHTSVERKEHR IN ZIVIL UND HANDELSSACHEN 391.5 n.16 (1954); M. DOMKE, AMERICAN-GERMAN PRIVATE LAW RELATIONS CASES 1945–1955, at 84 (1956).

[158] G. MORELLI, *supra* note 92, at 80–81.

on rich people, it violated Article 3 of the Italian Constitution providing for equality among all citizens, as well as Article 24 granting everyone the right to proceed at law for the defense of rights and "legitimate interests."[159] It follows that aliens in Italy cannot be required to post security.[160]

In Latin America, plaintiffs not domiciled in the State of the forum, or without sufficient property therein, may be required, under the device known as *arraigo*, to post a security bond as a condition precedent to bringing suit. Also, where the alien is the defendant, local procedure may allow preventive attachment of his property or posting a bond in lieu thereof. Known as *cautio judicatum solvi*, this device has been criticized by the Argentine commentator Goldschmidt as unconstitutional, since it violates the principle of equality between aliens and nationals.[161] Gowland, another Argentine writer, goes even further and condemns the arraigo concept as well.[162]

The necessity of the security bond in Latin America is connected with the court's power to require the losing party to pay all costs, sometimes including attorney's fees. As elsewhere, the theory is that the threat of a judgment for costs will discourage the presentation of unmeritorious or spurious claims or causes of action. The Mexican commentator Armienta, in a recent presentation at the Fourth Mexican Congress on Procedural Law, noted that "the permanent link between costs and the trial supports a development through which a judgment for costs becomes an effective means to diminish litigiousness (a grave procedural abuse) and to prevent improper use of

---

[159] Carabba v. Pres. Cons. Ministri, 16 RIVISTA DI DIRITTO PROCESSUALE 285 (1961) (Corte Costituzionale, Italy). *Cf.* Gualdino, *Cauzione per le Spese e Costituzione*, 15 RIVISTA TRIMESTRALE DI DIRITTO E PROCEDURA CIVILE 283 (1961).

[160] Judgment of Dec. 6, 1962, 1963 DIRITTO NEGLI SCAMBI INTERNAZIONALE 38 (Trib. Roma, Italy) (United States national). *But see* Gottardi, *Cauzione per le Spese nei Confronti dei Stranieri e Situazione di Reciprocitá, id.* at 39, who argues that the decision is wrong because the reciprocity requirement of Article 16, *Disposizioni Preliminari (see* note 91 *supra)* would demand the imposition of security for costs on nationals of countries which demand it from Italians even in the absence of a specific statute.

[161] W. GOLDSCHMIDT, 3 SISTEMA Y FILOSOPHIA DEL DERECHO INTERNACIONAL PRIVADO 90 (2d ed. 1940).

[162] N. Gowland, *La Excepción de Arraigo en Juicio en el Derecho Internacional*, 5 REVISTA DE DERECHO PROCESAL 121, 130–31 (1949).

those procedural devices which, designed to promote judicial certainty and to obtain a more just solution to the lawsuit, are otherwise distorted into obstacles which delay the trial. . . ."[163] Though this view represents the opinion of most Latin American nations, few have gone as far as the Mexican state of Morelos which, in its Code of Civil Procedure, punishes the "abuse of the right to litigate" with payment of costs and damages, and imposes a fine based upon the amount at issue.[164] The Mexican Federal Code of Civil Procedure also castigates defendants who unsuccessfully challenge the court's competence with costs and a fine of up to 3,000 pesos.[165] These penalties, however, are seldom enforced.

Some Latin American nations do not require security deposits. The Mexican Constitution provides in part that "the courts are ordered to administer justice in the terms and provisions established by law; their service will be free, with, consequently, judicial costs being prohibited."[166] This passage has been interpreted to mean that no security deposit is necessary, even by nondomiciled alien plaintiffs. Venezuela, however, provides in its Civil Code that a non-domiciliary plaintiff "must secure the payment of that to which he might be sentenced if he does not have sufficient property within the country, except as provided in special laws."[167] This deposit is only required for suits brought under the Civil Code; the Commercial Code states that "in commercial matters the nondomiciled plaintiff is not obliged to secure the payment of that to which he may be sentenced."[168]

The Venezuelan Code of Civil Procedure also enables a litigant to utilize his opponent's failure to provide a security bond as a basis for a preliminary objection.[169] The court on motion of a party may

---

[163] *La Onerosidad de los Juicios* 8-9 (1969).

[164] CÓDIGO DE PROCEDIMIENTOS CIVILES DEL ESTADO DE MORELOS, art. 10.

[165] Art. 263. The fine is payable to the other party and not into court.

[166] Art 17.

[167] Art. 36.

[168] CÓDIGO DE COMERCIO VENEZOLANO (La Torre ed. 1968), art. 1102. It could be argued, nevertheless, that an attachment could be obtained against a defendant's property even in commercial actions, since the same Commercial Code provides that "in anything else for which there is no special provision in this Title, the provisions of the Code of Civil Procedure will be observed." Art. 1119.

[169] Art. 248(8).

order attachment of property belonging either to a plaintiff or a defendant who is a transient or has disappeared, or when there is reason to believe he will try to flee the jurisdiction or hide this property, or will seek "to evade responsibilities."[170] If no property exists to satisfy the attachment order, "the proceedings may be halted at the request of the other party until the party against whom the attachment has been decreed provides sufficient security."[171]

This concern over absconding debtors (who usually form the bulk of "transcient defendants") also is expressed in the practice of some African Commonwealth countries. A rule usually provides that a defendant about to leave the jurisdiction, or who has disposed of his assets or removed them from the jurisdiction, may be required to post a bond if the plaintiff is able to satisfy the court that by reason of the defendant's acts the execution of any decree which may be made is likely to be obstructed or delayed.[172] The application is made by affidavit and can result in the defendant's arrest. He then must show cause why bail, or in lieu thereof imprisonment, should not be required. There is, of course, a likelihood that this rigorous rule could be abused by overly aggressive plaintiffs. This possibility is reduced, however, by the courts' normal reluctance to grant this order except in clear-cut cases. In addition, a plaintiff's zealousness is reduced by his knowledge that a common law action for false arrest may lie against him if he acts improperly.[173]

As in Venezuela, Argentina in its Federal Code of Civil and Commercial Procedure makes failure to post a security bond by a nondomiciled plaintiff without property in the country a ground for preliminary objection.[174] This security, known as the *tasa de justicia*, apparently is required whether or not the suit is brought under the federal civil or commercial codes.[175] The several Argen-

---

[170] Art. 376.

[171] Art. 377.

[172] *See* TANZANIAN CIVIL PROCEDURE CODE, Act No. 49, 1966, Order XXXVI, Rules 1–5.

[173] *Id.* The maximum period of detention is six months. A related but distinct deterrent to plaintiffs seeking to imprison debtor-defendants is found in the rules providing for detention of execution-debtors who evade payment of judgments. The execution-creditor must pay a subsistence allowance to maintain the prisoner. *See* TANZANIAN CIVIL PROCEDURE CODE, Order XXI, Rule 38.

[174] Art. 348.

[175] As in Venezuela, the property of a defendant debtor also may be attached if he is not domiciled in Argentina. Art. 209(1).

tine provinces have individual codes of civil procedure which, while not making failure to post security a ground for preliminary objection, nevertheless require a security deposit of any plaintiff, alien or national, not domiciled in the particular province. In Brazil, the Code of Civil Procedure states that nonresident plaintiffs, be they aliens or nationals, must, as in Austria, make a deposit for court costs if they do not possess sufficient real estate in Brazil to cover payment thereof.[176] The amount of security is largely within the discretion of the judge, as in Argentina, a fact which, at least in the opinion of some attorneys representing United States oil companies in Argentine courts, could permit discrimination against aliens in particular cases.

Costa Rica, although it departs from the conventional usage of terminology, has perhaps the most detailed provisions governing judicial security deposits. The Code of Civil Procedure provides for arraigo against the defendant, rather than against the plaintiff, before or after commencing suit "when it is feared that the person sued will absent himself or hide. . . . The security should be to the satisfaction of the judge and for the amount which he indicates to be prudent, and in no case less than twenty per cent of the complaint. . . ."[177] If the defendant leaves the country without appointing an attorney-in-fact to represent him in his absence, the deposit will be forfeited and judgment rendered against him for costs.[178] Still another provision enables defendants as well as plaintiffs to request that opponents post a guaranty (fianza) to assure payment of costs in the event they lose.[179] The Government and its entities are excepted from this requirement. This guaranty "will be twenty-five per cent of the value of the complaint." Nevertheless, in suits for over 5,000 colones (US $751) the judge may reduce the amount to a more realistic figure. Of course, if the plaintiff already has obtained a preventive attachment on the defendant's property, the judge may in his discretion dispense with, or reduce the amount of, the fianza.[180] If at any time a party believes the guaranty to have

---

[176] Art. 67.

[177] CÓDIGO DE PROCEDIMIENTOS CIVILES (A. Vicenzi ed. 1966), art. 139.

[178] Art. 142.

[179] Art. 192

[180] Arts. 172 & 192.

decreased in value, he may request the court to order its replenishment or substitution.[181]

The gap between theory and reality in Latin American procedural legislation is highlighted by the coexistence of requirements that aliens post security deposits with the provisions of the Bustamante Code, which requires equality of treatment for both aliens and nationals. The Code states that "no distinction will be made between nationals and foreigners in relation to posting a fianza in order to litigate,"[182] and provides as well that "aliens need not post security in order to bring complaints in private [criminal] actions in cases where it is not required of nationals."[183] It is interesting to note that Guatemala—which requires security deposits of aliens—ratified the Code without reservations, and that of the States which ratified with reservations, only Haiti specifically withheld approval of these two provisions. The possibility exists that an alien could allege the invalidity of a provision requiring fianza or arraigo of aliens only, on the grounds that treaty provisions ratified without reservation should take precedence over non-constitutional legislation. Indeed, such requirements could be deemed unconstitutional in that they

---

[181] Security provisions of varying detail also exist in Honduras and Peru. Article 223 of the Peruvian Code of Civil Procedure is similar to Article 270 of the Honduran Code: "A preventive attachment may be requested to secure the outcome of a suit which is to be, or has been, brought, whatever its state or nature." Nevertheless, Article 228 of the Peruvian Code indicates that the party seeking the attachment also must post a *fianza* or some other guaranty to the satisfaction of the court for possible costs, damages, and fines. If a party, after obtaining a preventive attachment before suit, does not file his complaint within either 10 days or the period fixed by the judge, the attachment will be lifted and the movant held responsible for costs and damages, and subject to a possible fine. A preventive attachment, according to Article 231, may not be granted if suit is brought outside of Peru, absent contrary treaty provisions. A guaranty of fianza, of course, may be given in lieu of attachment. CÓDIGO DE PROCEDIMIENTOS CIVILES (J. Fajardo ed. 1966).

Guatemalan *arraigo* legislation, by interjecting the element of reciprocity, differs markedly from that of other Latin American nations studied. Article 117 of the Code of Civil Procedure allows a defendant, as a preliminary objection, to require that plaintiffs who are transients or foreigners (which would seem to include even aliens domiciled in Guatemala) guarantee payment of legal costs, fines, and damages. However, this objection will not lie if the plaintiff proves that in his own country such a guaranty is not required of Guatemalans, or if the defendant is also a transient or a foreigner.

[182] Art. 383.

[183] Art. 385.

violated specific promises of equality contained in several constitutions. Bustamante probably would agree since, in his opinion, the Code rules out even preventive attachments placed on aliens' property for no other reason than that they were foreigners. Requirements of security bonds for aliens, he wrote, violated the principle of judicial equality of nationals and foreigners, and derive from "a spirit of hostility respecting those who do not belong to the forum state" and to fears that a local judgment against an alien could not be executed abroad.[184] While such apprehensions once may have been justified, they are much less relevant today, where ease of communication and increased familiarity with foreign legal systems should encourage courts to be more lenient regarding execution of foreign judgments.

It should be remembered as well that an increasing number of multilateral treaties designed to remove some of the legal difficulties encountered by the widespread movement across international boundaries of persons and goods contain provisions which expressly forbid requirements for security for nonresident litigants. These include the Carriage of Passengers by Rail Convention (Berne) 1952;[185] the Carriage of Goods by Rail Convention (Berne) 1952;[186] and the Carriage of Goods by Road Convention (Geneva) 1956.[187] Other multilateral conventions limiting security for costs are the Geneva Convention on Refugees, which grants refugees national treatment as to security for costs in the country in which they reside, and treatment analogous to that of nationals of their country of residence in the other signatory states,[188] the New York Convention on Stateless Persons, which extends to these persons the rules of the Geneva Convention on Refugees,[189] and the Convention on

---

[184] II DERECHO INTERNACIONAL PRIVADO 201 (1943 ed.).

[185] Convention Concerning the Carriage of Passengers and Luggage by Rail, Oct. 25, 1952, art. 55(4), 242 U.N.T.S. 355.

[186] Convention Concerning the Carriage of Goods by Rail, Oct. 25, 1952, art. 55(4), 241 U.N.T.S. 357.

[187] Convention on the Contract for the International Carriage of Goods by Road, May 19, 1956, art. 31(5), 399 U.N.T.S. 189.

[188] Convention Relating to the Status of Refugees, July 28, 1951, art. 16, 189 U.N.T.S. 150.

[189] Convention Relating to the Status of Stateless Persons, Sept. 28, 1954, art. 16, 360 U.N.T.S. 117.

the Recovery Abroad of Maintenance.[190] As mentioned previously, security for costs is likewise abolished by the Hague Convention on Civil Procedure.[191]

Still other conventions impliedly exclude security for costs as a result of the nondiscrimination clauses which they contain, including the Third Party Liability in the Field of Nuclear Energy Convention (Paris) 1960;[192] the Civil Liability for Nuclear Damage Convention (Vienna) 1963;[193] and the Convention on the Liability of Operators of Nuclear Ships (Brussels) 1962.[194] In contrast to this new, and welcome, attitude may be cited the 1929 Warsaw Convention on Carriage by Air, which impliedly permits security for costs in its provision that procedural matters are to be governed by the lex fori.[195]

The normal expense of litigation also may inhibit aliens and nationals alike from commencing or pursuing a lawsuit, thereby rendering less meaningful abstract guarantees of access or procedural due process. From time to time the high cost of litigation has been considered an effective device for coping with overcrowded courts, although this problem may not have been the one Socrates had in mind when, according to Plato, he stated that it was necessary to raise the cost of litigation in order to prevent people from filing law suits. Today, notwithstanding rising court costs, the growing complexity of modern life has meant an increase in litigation even in traditional societies where formalistic procedures remain geared to the leisurely lawsuits of another age.[196]

Fortunately, most States permit suits in forma pauperis. It is an

---

[190] Convention on the Recovery Abroad of Maintenance, June 20, 1956, art. 9, 268 U.N.T.S. 3.

[191] See note 134 supra.

[192] Third Party Liability in the Field of Nuclear Energy Convention, July 29, 1960, art. 14(a), reprinted in 55 AM. J. INT'L L. 1082 (1961).

[193] Convention on Civil Liability for Nuclear Damage, May 21, 1963, art. 13, reprinted in 2 INTERNATIONAL LEGAL MATERIALS 727 (1963).

[194] Convention on the Liability of Operators of Nuclear Ships, May 25, 1962, art. XII(3), reprinted in 57 AM. J. INT'L L. 268 (1963).

[195] Convention for the Unification of Certain Rules Relating to International Transportation by Air, Oct. 12, 1929, art. 28, 49 Stat. 3000, T.S. No. 876.

[196] It also has resulted in great strains being placed upon judicial machinery, resulting in congested court calendars and delays affecting both aliens and nationals alike.

important reflection of the attitudes of Latin American nations and Commonwealth countries that this procedure is available both to aliens and nationals, either as plaintiffs or defendants. Moreover, no showing of reciprocity is required where the petitioner is an alien. To be sure, practice generally requires that the alien reside in the particular country, but this requirement does not seem unreasonable. The right of poor persons to sue in forma pauperis, which is of very ancient origin in Britain,[197] gradually is being replaced in that country by a universal scheme of legal aid which makes the old device unnecessary. Wherever the new system is operative, suits in forma pauperis are not permitted.[198] The new form of assistance thus is replacing the old.

Requirements for security for costs, of course, can run counter to the intended benefit of suits in forma pauperis when nonresident aliens are involved. In the Canadian province of Alberta, for example, where aliens are entitled to sue in forma pauperis, this right proved of little help in one case to the alien plaintiff next-of-kin of a deceased. The widow involved was granted her application to sue in forma pauperis,[199] but was nevertheless required to deposit security for costs.[200] Manifesting the strange attitude exhibited so often by North American judges in the early years of this century in cases involving giant corporations, the learned appeal court judge felt it necessary to phrase his decision so as to minimize any further burden upon the defendant railway company which had, said the judge, "already been put to much costs" by the alien widow.[201]

The right to litigate in forma pauperis (also known as *beneficio de pobreza, declaración de pobreza,* or *beneficio de litigar sin gastos*) is provided in the codes of civil procedure of various Latin American countries. In addition, the constitutions of Venezuela, Honduras, and Mexico make specific reference to it as a matter of principle. The Venezuelan Constitution, without distinguishing between aliens and nationals, states that "everyone" is entitled to use the courts for the defense of his rights and interests, and that the law "will fix

---

[197] 11 Henry 7, c. 12 (1495).

[198] Legal Aid and Advice Act of 1949, 12, 13, & 14 Geo. 6, c. 51, § 2(1), at 625 (1949).

[199] Augustino v. Canadian Northwestern Ry. Co., [1927] 3 W.W.R. 321.

[200] [1928] 1 W.W.R. 481.

[201] *Id.* at 483.

the norms which will assure the exercise of this right to those who do not have sufficient means."[202] Honduras provides that "the writ of habeas corpus will be granted without costs,"[203] while Mexico states that the administration of justice is free, and that "judicial costs are prohibited."[204] Whether the litigant is rich or poor is irrelevant.

The procedural codes of several Latin American countries have certain features in common. To obtain the beneficio de pobreza in civil matters the petitioner must file a request in the court which is to hear, or is in the process of hearing, the case in question. Notice of the request is given to the opposing parties and, except in Argentina, to the Governmental Attorney so that they may, within periods varying from three to ten days, challenge the request and cross-examine any witnesses petitioner may present to support his request. Guatemala's Code is unique since in urgent cases it allows the judge, if the applicant is a person of "notorious poverty," to grant the beneficio provisionally for a period of two months.[205]

Mexico has carried legal assistance programs a step further. It is the only Latin American nation which has abolished judicial fees and that ubiquitous vestige of Spanish domination, the *papel sellado* or sealed paper. Hence, there is no need to include beneficio de pobreza provisions in either its federal or state procedural codes. Mexican practice in this respect is, to a degree, a modern revival of a much earlier pre-Columbian concept of free access to courts of justice in which rich and poor were treated alike. Nevertheless,

---

[202] Art. 68.

[203] Art. 68.

[204] Art. 17. Attorneys' fees still are borne by the parties.

[205] Art. 94. In general, the request for the beneficio itself need not be on sealed paper and any fees are waived for purposes of presentation. However, if the request is denied, the corresponding deferred costs must be paid. If the request is approved, petitioner's opponents, or the Government, at any stage of the trial may request that approval be withdrawn if it can be shown that petitioner's wealth has increased or that he had concealed his true financial status. In the latter event, Article 164 of the Costa Rican Code imposes a fine equivalent to 10 times the value of the costs and sealed paper from which he had been exempted. The Peruvian Code contains in Article 293 an unusual provision whereby the petitioner would be required to pay the costs from which he had been exempted if within three years after the termination of the suit his yearly income should exceed 50 pounds. In all countries, the grant of the beneficio is personal and nontransferable, and is valid only for the purposes of the case at bar, absent specific extensions to related litigation.

even under an apparently compassionate system as that now prevailing in Mexico, serious procedural and structural flaws exist which may enable a party to prevail over a less affluent opponent. These defects include meeting expenses occasioned by "tipping" and, perhaps, bribery, topics discussed previously.

A weakness which may destroy much of the value of the system has developed in Venezuela. There, opposing attorneys will challenge vigorously proof offered by impecunious plaintiffs attempting to acquire the beneficio. This challenge is made out of fear that applicants might, in a suit with little merit and without placing a security deposit, attach the property of a wealthy defendant. This attachment of course would be lifted only in return for a handsome out-of-court settlement. As a consequence, beneficio is granted infrequently and reluctantly.

Other factors in Latin America may prevent the beneficio from functioning as intended. Many of these nations have masses of citizens who participate but marginally in national life. In Venezuela, Honduras, and Argentina, the principal barriers they face are poverty and ignorance of their rights. In other countries such as Bolivia, Guatemala, and Peru, over half the population is of a basically aboriginal and non-European cultural orientation and little inclined to become involved in the formal national legal systems which, more often than not, are considered to be tools of their oppressors.[206] As a result, for example, legal provisions for suits in forma pauperis are not always invoked by persons who might qualify. The lower middle classes, on the other hand, may be either too proud to apply for the beneficio, or, while having enough property to disqualify them, may not be able to finance costly and prolonged litigation.[207] In some nations, therefore, the principal applicants seem to be aliens.[208]

---

[206] For a description of the treatment accorded the Guatemalan Indian populace since colonial times see Dawson, *Labor Legislation and Social Integration in Guatemala*, 1871–1944, 14 AM. J. COMP. L. 124 (1965). For a fictionalized portrayal of the Peruvian Indian's plight see C. ALGERIA, BROAD AND ALIEN IS THE WORLD (1941).

[207] This dilemma is not always confined to lesser-developed countries. *See* Norridge, *Are You too Rich for Legal Aid—But too Poor to go to Law?* Evening Standard (London), Feb. 3, 1970, at 13, col. 1.

[208] There still is disagreement as to whether a transient alien can obtain the

Whatever its defects, the beneficio is a prominent feature of all Latin American procedural codes. These nations have elevated their own statures by including a provision in the Bustamante Code, which in this respect was ratified without a single specific reservation, stating that: "The nationals of each contracting State will enjoy in each one of the others the beneficio de defensa por pobre, on the same terms as nationals."[209] Unlike the matter of security deposits, domestic legislation seems to follow this international standard.[210]

In the United States, aliens enjoy the same privilege as citizens to litigate in forma pauperis—as a poor person without the necessity of incurring costs and the expense of printing the stenographic record on appeal. Until its amendment in 1959, the applicable provision of the United States Judicial Code required that the applicant in a civil or criminal action also swear an affidavit of citizenship.[211] Therefore, the statute was held inapplicable to aliens.[212] The statute in its amended form, however, now applies to "any person," which includes aliens, and provides for court appointment of an attorney "to represent any such person unable to employ counsel."[213] Habeas corpus proceedings are free, as in Honduras, and the requirement of posting a security bond may be waived for impoverished defendants in the United States District Courts. The

---

beneficio as well as a domiciled alien. Also, controversy exists over whether the beneficio in the case of a nondomiciled alien should extend to exemption from security deposits. The old Argentine Código de Procesamiento Civil y Comercial in Article 601 exempted recipients of the beneficio from payment of security deposits. The new 1968 Code, however, simply exempts the litigant from costs, which might not include deposits. For a discussion of the relationship between the beneficio and security deposits see Goldschmidt, *Problemas de Derecho Internacional Procesal Hispano-Luso-Americano,* 1956 REVISTA DE DERECHO PROCESAL 269, 293–95.

[209] Art. 382.

[210] However, Bolivia, Costa Rica, Chile, Ecuador, and El Salvador ratified the Bustamante Code with general reservations. That is, on the condition that in the event of any conflict between domestic legislation and the Code, the former would prevail. This fact has led one commentator to opine that the Code is only truly in effect in those nations which ratified without reservations or only with reservations as to specific articles. J. MUCI ABRAHAM, *supra* note 112, at 37.

[211] 28 U.S.C. § 1915 (1964).

[212] *See, e.g.,* Elkins v. United States, 250 F.2d 145 (9th Cir. 1957).

[213] 28 U.S.C. § 1915(d) (1964).

New York Civil Practice Law and Rules grants substantially the same rights to all persons regardless of citizenship.[214]

Most European countries also have quite far-reaching provisions concerning legal aid (*armenrecht, assistance judiciaire*). A person granted legal aid by the appropriate authorities is freed, as in Latin America, from paying filing fees, stamp taxes, and the like and, in addition, becomes entitled to the free services of an attorney (including, in France, an avocat as well as an avoué, if both are necessary).[215] Unfortunately, unlike in Latin America, reciprocity requirements sometimes prevent aliens from taking advantage of these provisions.

In Austria, the legal aid situation is quite similar to that prevailing in the case of security for costs. Unless they are covered by a special treaty provision, aliens are entitled to legal aid only if reciprocity exists. Whenever there is doubt as to such reciprocity, an inquiry must be addressed to the Ministry of Justice, the decision of which is binding.[216] As to United States nationals in particular, the view seems to be that the generally less extensive character of the American legal aid system would not prevent the existence of reciprocity, but that American nationals not residing in Austria are not ordinarily entitled to it because in most states of the United States legal aid is available only for resident aliens.[217]

Whether aliens in France can benefit from legal aid in the absence of reciprocity is a somewhat controversial question. Some authors argue that the reciprocity rule of Article 11 of the Civil Code applies to the granting of legal aid, while other commentators feel that it does not. In practice, the legal aid *bureaux* charged with determining eligibility for legal assistance seem to be rather liberal as regards aliens; so-called privileged residents always are granted legal aid.[218]

---

[214] N.Y.C.P.L.R. §§ 1101 & 1102 (McKinney 1963).

[215] *See generally* Schweinburg, *Legal Assistance Abroad*, 17 U. CHI. L. REV. 270 (1949).

[216] AUS. ZPO §§ 63 & 64. The same rules apply to proceedings before the Verwaltungsgericht (Administrative Court): Verwaltungsgerichtshofgesetz, Nov. 17, 1964, [1965] BGBl. 289 § 61.

[217] 2 H. FASCHING, *supra* note 133, at 523–24; I. SEIDL-HOHENVELDERN, *supra* note 99, at 104.

[218] Lagarde, *Assistance Judiciaire*, in 1 DALLOZ, RÉPERTOIRE DE DROIT INTERNATIONAL at Nos. 2–8 (1968). In France, legal aid is not awarded by the courts

Furthermore, procedure before some courts is entirely gratuitous, and no professional assistance by attorneys is required. This situation, for instance, is true in the so-called social security courts,[219] a matter of some significance to the numerous foreign workers employed in France.

Legal aid of course must be granted to aliens when provided by treaty. France is a party to a number of treaties in this respect, including the Hague Convention on Civil Procedure.[220] The 1959 Convention of Establishment with France grants United States nationals in France and French nationals in the United States national treatment as far as legal aid is concerned.[221]

In Germany reciprocity also is a requirement for the granting of legal aid to aliens.[222] Unlike in Austria, it is up to the court before which a legal aid application is pending to decide if reciprocity exists. It may demand advice from the Ministry of Justice, but that body cannot make binding determinations. As in France, legal aid, of course, must be granted to aliens of a treaty so mandates. Germany is a signatory of the Hague Convention on Civil Procedure and the nationals of all the other signatories thus are entitled to legal aid.[223] The position of United States nationals is again peculiar. The Treaty of Friendship, Commerce and Navigation with Germany provides that German nationals are entitled to legal aid in proceedings before the Federal courts in the United States, while United States nationals suing in German courts must be granted legal aid if their action could have been brought in the United States Federal courts.[224] This lan-

---

directly, but by agencies (bureaux d'assistance judiciaire) composed of representatives of the bar and of various government departments.

[219] Decree No. 58–1291, Dec. 22, 1958, [1958] J.O. 11613, [1959] D.L. 49, art. 17 (parties may represent themselves or be represented by a fellow worker, or a representative of a trade union); art. 57 (procedure to be entirely free).

[220] Note 134 *supra,* arts. 20–24. Other treaties are listed by Lagarde, *supra* note 218, at Nos. 23–87.

[221] Convention of Establishment with France, *supra* note 115, art. III(1).

[222] Z.P.O. § 114 (C.H. Beck 1965). *Cf.* 1 B. WIECZOREK, *supra* note 155, at 898 (listing some exceptions to reciprocity rule).

[223] *See* note 220 *supra.*

[224] Treaty of Friendship, Commerce and Navigation with Germany, *supra* note 115, Protocol No. 7. For domestic political reasons, the United States was not willing to grant national treatment to German citizens before the state courts, while the German Federal Republic was unwilling to abandon completely the reciprocity rule unless legal aid would be guaranteed to its nationals before

guage seems to raise quite complex legal problems in cases where almost by definition the parties ought not to be unduly burdened.

Italy, where legal aid has a long history,[225] does not discriminate between citizens and aliens. The 1923 statute on which legal aid is based specifically included aliens,[226] and the right of aliens to legal aid was reinforced by Article 24(3) of the Italian Constitution, according to which "[d]estitute persons shall . . . be assured the means to plead, and to defend themselves before any judicial body." When the Italian Constitution wishes to restrict a right to citizens, it utilizes the words "every citizen"; hence, for constitutional reasons too, aliens are entitled to legal aid in Italy.

Unfortunately, not all Latin American nations have the well-developed legal aid systems of continental Europe. Venezuela[227] and Costa Rica[228] apparently have developed workable systems, although they are hampered by lack of funds. In Peru, the Lima Bar Association provides a wide range of services,[229] but the chances of

---

all courts in the United States. These facts explain the peculiar wording of the treaty.

[225] M. CAPPELLETTI, J. MERRYMAN & J. PERILLO, THE ITALIAN LEGAL SYSTEM 96–97 (1967). For a more critical view of legal aid in Italy see Denti, *I Poveri e la giustizia*, 16 RIVISTA DI DIRITTO PROCESSUALE 285 (1961).

[226] Royal Decree of Dec. 30, 1923, No. 3282, art. 14; G. MORELLI, *supra* note 92, at 81–82.

[227] In criminal matters, the *Ley Orgánica del Poder Judicial* provides for a Public Defender to represent the indigent, a system which seems to work well. Two eminent Venezuelan attorneys noted in a report to the International Commission of Jurists that "[w]e should also say that in our country the judicial representation and free legal assistance to the poor functions with a high degree of perfection, taking into account the practical difficulties which originate out of the growing volume of persons needing such assistance." R. DÍAZ & S. URBANEJA, EL IMPERIO DE LA LEY EN LA REPUBLICA DE VENEZUELA 91 (1965).

[228] The Costa Rican Código de Procedimientos Penales, art. 267, allows a judge to appoint a lawyer to defend persons whose income is less than 500 Colones a month. This lawyer may be a Public Defender, if there is one in the jurisdiction, or a private attorney. If an attorney should refuse such an appointment without good cause, the judge may subject him to "disciplinary action," states Article 270. This attorney is specifically allowed by Article 274 to see his client daily.

[229] Article 282 of the Peruvian Code provides for "free defense by the attorney for the poor which the judge appoints." The Lima Bar Association, reputedly the oldest such group in the Americas, maintains a special legal aid office "to give advice to and assume the defense of the indigent, the workers and in general of people with insufficient funds," and from which the judge may

assistance outside Lima do not appear good. In Mexico and in other nations with vigorous labor movements, unions often provide members with free legal assistance, especially in suits brought under labor legislation. Nevertheless, despite the sincere efforts of local bar associations, funds generally are lacking to assure systems of gratuitous, well-staffed legal defense on a par with the systems of European nations.

While the practice of free legal assistance to impecunious persons is spreading, it will be some time yet before persons involved in noncriminal actions will be able to assume always that aid is available. Both the United Nations International Covenant on Civil and Political Rights[230] and the European Convention for the Protection of Human Rights and Fundamental Freedoms[231] provide for legal assistance for a criminal accused when he has not sufficient means to pay for it and when "the interests of justice so require." Neither, however, provide free legal help in civil cases. A number of other conventions, however, some concluded under the auspices of the United Nations, do remove discrimination based upon nationality in the granting of legal aid.[232]

Even when access has been obtained, the alien often may find himself confronted with procedural machinery quite different from that to which he has been accustomed in his own nation. Moreover, jurisdictional requirements vary widely, and procedures appropriate for legal proceedings within the host State may be ill-suited for transnational litigation, where parties and their attorneys are separated not only by physical distances but also by distinct legal philosophies evolved over centuries of disparate historical experience.

---

choose an attorney. The Association's Code of Ethics states clearly that it is the lawyer's professional duty to defend the poor without payment, either if they request it or if it is so ordered by a court. CÓDIGO DE ETICA PROFESIONAL DEL COLEGIO DE ABOGADOS DE LIMA, art. 7 (1961).

[230] Art. 14(3)(d), G.A. Res. 2200, 21 U.N. GAOR, Supp. 16, at 52, U.N. Doc. A/6316 (1966).

[231] Nov. 4, 1950, art. 6(3)(c), 213 U.N.T.S. 221.

[232] See the conventions cited at notes 188–191 *supra*.

CHAPTER VI

Problems Encountered by Aliens in Litigation

Once access to a court or other tribunal has been gained, the alien and his counsel will be obliged to conduct the litigation under local procedural rules. If suit has been brought in a civil law jurisdiction, and the alien is a national of a country within the civil law system, these rules, although they may differ from country to country, will not necessarily seem strange or onerous. This situation also would be true if both the parties and the forum were located within common law countries, where similarity of procedural rules assures a basic legal familiarity despite great cultural or economic differences. However, if the alien or his counsel is from a common law nation, and the forum State is within the civil law system, certain aspects of local procedural rules may seem quite unfamiliar.

Although much descriptive and detailed material concerning civil law procedure already has been published, a few comments on courts and procedures may provide a useful general background against which to consider those special problems of jurisdiction, service of process, default judgments, and international legal assistance which may affect seriously the conduct of litigation abroad, and which may be aggravated by differences between civil and common law systems.[1]

---

[1] *See generally* H. CLAGETT, THE ADMINISTRATION OF JUSTICE IN LATIN AMERICA (1952); P. GARLAND, A BUSINESSMAN'S INTRODUCTION TO BRAZILIAN LAW AND PRACTICE 11–25 (1966); Eder, *Judicial Review in Latin America,* 21 OHIO STATE L.J. 570 (1960); Nebreda-Urbaneja & Berg, *Introduction to the Venezuelan Legal System—A Typical Civil Law System of Latin America,* 10 DE PAUL L. REV. 41 (1960); H. P. DE VRIES & J. RODRIGUEZ—NOVAS, THE LAW OF THE AMERICAS (1965); Dawson, *International Law, National Tribunals and the Rights of Aliens: The Latin-American Experience,* 21 VAND. L. REV. 712, 728–34 (1968). Especially extensive materials in English also are available concerning the basic aspects of European legal systems, their civil procedure, and international judicial cooperation as it affects these countries. For this rea-

GENERAL CIVIL LAW PROCEDURE: THE LATIN AMERICAN
EXAMPLE

The judicial power in Latin America functions within the traditional tripartite division of government into executive, legislative,
and judicial branches. In general, judges are appointed by one
branch with the approval of another, although in Brazil federal
legislation creates a career judiciary in which judges theoretically
retain great control over the selection of their colleagues and suc-
cessors.[2] The executive branch is considered the strongest and the
legislative branch the weakest, since the legislature formulates general legislation and the executive puts it into effect by *reglamentos* or
executive decrees. The power to issue reglamentos is very broad, and
until a reglamento appears a particular law may lack enforcement
provisions. The President, then, in effect has wide legislative powers,
and in times of emergency may legislate by decree, or pass so-called
decree-laws when the legislature is not in session or has been disbanded, as is presently the case in Argentina.[3]

Although the executive generally is prohibited by the constitution
from interfering in the exercise of judicial authority, it nevertheless
exerts great influence through the Ministry of Justice and the so-

---

son, the law in European countries is considered only occasionally in this
Chapter. For additional information concerning international judicial cooperation, see H. SMIT, INTERNATIONAL COOPERATION IN LITIGATION: EUROPE (1965)
(with individual country reports); concerning some international aspects of
Austrian law, see I. SEIDL-HOHENVELDERN, AMERICAN-AUSTRIAN PRIVATE IN-
TERNATIONAL LAW (1963); concerning German law in general, see E. COHN,
MANUAL OF GERMAN LAW (2d ed. 1968); concerning civil procedure in Ger-
many, see Kaplan, von Mehren & Schaefer, *Phases of German Civil Procedure*,
71 HARV. L. REV. 1193, 1443 (1958); on general aspects of French law, see R.
DAVID & H. P. DE VRIES, THE FRENCH LEGAL SYSTEM (1958); on some aspects
of French substantive law, see M. AMOS & F. WALTON, INTRODUCTION TO
FRENCH LAW (3d ed. 1967); as to French civil procedure, see P. HERZOG, CIVIL
PROCEDURE IN FRANCE (1967); concerning the general principles of Italian law,
see M. CAPPELLETTI, J. MERRYMAN & J. PERILLO, THE ITALIAN LEGAL SYSTEM
(1967); on civil procedure in Italy, see M. CAPPELLETTI & J. PERILLO, CIVIL
PROCEDURE IN ITALY (1965); on civil procedure in Sweden, see R. GINSBURG &
A. BRUZELIUS, CIVIL PROCEDURE IN SWEDEN (1965).

[2] Scheman, *Brazil's Career Judiciary*, 46 J. AM. JUD. SOC'Y 134 (1962).

[3] Article 54(3) of the 1967 Constitution of Brazil also provides that if the
President sends a bill to Congress which he deems "urgent," it automatically
becomes law if Congress does not act upon it within 40 days. CONSTITUTION OF
BRAZIL 1967 (Pan American Union ed. 1967).

called Government Attorney, a direct agent of the executive who represents the government in criminal cases, in civil cases involving expropriation and attachment of property, and in requests for the enforcement of foreign judgments. Further executive intervention into the judicial realm is illustrated by the coexistence of administrative courts with ordinary judicial organs and, as in Brazil, special executive courts in the labor, military and electoral areas.[4] Paradoxically, more effort is expended in preventing the judicial power from overlapping into the legislative and executive areas than vice versa. Thus, judicial precedent and stare decisis are given little weight, on the theory that if a judge rendered a decision which constituted binding precedent for future decisions he would be intruding upon the legislative or executive domains. This reluctance to permit legislation by judicial decree may be traced to Article 5 of the Code Napoleon, which, by prohibiting judges from prescribing general principles of law, sought to prevent a return to the abuses of rule-making powers which characterized pre-Revolutionary tribunals. Also relevant is the civil law precept that custom, and decisions interpreting it, cannot be sources of law. For example, Article 2 of the Honduran Civil Code states that "[c]ustom does not constitute a right except in those cases in which the law refers to it." The Argentine Civil Code in Article 1(17) states that "[u]sage, custom or practice cannot create rights except when the laws refer to them," while the Mexican Civil Code in Article 10 provides that neither disuse, custom, or contrary practice will excuse nonobservance of the law.

Although on the European continent the progenitors of today's civil law countries looked largely to written codes such as Justinian's *Corpus Juris Civilis* as sources of law,[5] in England customs, usages, and, eventually, court decisions interpreting and defining them came to be the primary source of law, an attitude adopted both in the Commonwealth and the United States.[6] The quite different outlook of the Latin American lawyer and judge has been described succinctly by Eder, an attorney with wide experience in Latin America:

---

[4] *Id.* arts. 120–135.

[5] *See generally* J. Vance, Sources of Latin American Law (1943); C. Walton, The Civil Law in Spain and Spanish-America (1900).

[6] P. Eder, A Comparative Survey of Anglo-American and Latin-American Law 4–6 (1950).

The Latin jurist is apt to carry the analogy of natural physical laws further than we care to. Just as there are natural laws governing the universe which it is within the province of the scientist to discover, so there are natural laws, he thinks, governing human relations which it is within the province of the jurist to ascertain. Within the framework of these natural laws, it is the duty of the legislator to lay down in advance the rules that shall govern human conduct and not leave the ascertainment of these rules to the haphazard decision of the courts when and if private litigants choose to thrash them out at their own risk and expense.[7]

As a result, Latin American judicial decisions generally cannot constitute, as they do in the common law system, binding precedent for future decisions.

The Civil Code of Chile, for example, states in Article 3 that "judicial decisions have no binding effect except in the cases in which they are pronounced." Article 17 of the Colombian Civil Code is almost identical. There are, however, limitations to this generalization, and the judge's power to interpret abstract code provisions, coupled with constant improvement in facilities for reporting decisions, as in Venezuela and Argentina, are eroding strict application. In Mexico, moreover, five consecutive decisions by the Supreme Court on the same constitutional point will bind all federal and state courts.[8] Also, as a practical matter, lower courts follow decisions of a superior court if they wish to avoid being overruled on appeal. It is interesting to note, however, that the 1949 Peron amendments to the Argentine Constitution, which provided that Supreme Court decisions interpreting the Constitution created judicial precedent binding on all other courts and judges in the country, did not survive the dictator's downfall.[9]

Latin American lawsuits commence with the presentation of the complaint (*demanda*) to the court. The judge then examines the complaint and, if it complies with formal requirements and is within his competence, will accept it (*admitir la demanda*) and order a copy served upon the defendant by a court official. Unlike practice in New

---

[7] *Id.* at 7.

[8] Ley de Amparo de 1936, arts. 192 & 193.

[9] For a brief comment discussing procedures to eradicate the Peron amendments ("the profanities of 1949") see Montaño, *The Constitutional Problem of the Argentine Republic*, 6 AM. J. COMP. L. 340, 344 (1957).

York State, for example, parties do not effect service themselves. The defendant then may file an answer with the court, interposing defenses, counterclaims, or raising preliminary and other objections.[10] Depending upon the country, a reply and a rejoinder also may be filed once objections have been settled by the court. At this point the judge may fix a period within which to present documentary proof and oral testimony.

There is little provision for the active, oral direct and cross-examination of parties and witnesses by opposing counsel so well known in common law jurisdictions. The testimony of witnesses normally is not taken in open court, but before a judge's secretary or clerk, and then only as to factual matters and upon written interrogatories supplied by the parties. The clerk, who need not be a lawyer, reads the questions to the witness and either records the answers in longhand or on a typewriter. If the answer is lengthy, the clerk in some jurisdictions composes a summary. The 1967 Argentine Code is an exception, and in Article 126 allows a party to request the Court's permission to use shorthand stenographers and even tape recorders.[11] While attorneys representing the opposing parties may be present, generally they may not question witnesses directly, but must use the clerk as an intermediary. In special circumstances the judge's presence may be requested, but this step usually is not taken. Most codes also allow using interpreters if a witness or party does not speak Spanish. The written answers then are placed in the case file, which the judge reads before rendering his decision.[12] There are, of course, variants from this central theme. The Peruvian Code of Civil Procedure allows a litigant or his attorney to question the other party directly and orally,[13] as does the Venezuelan Code.[14]

---

[10] Including, in some nations, a demand that nonresident plaintiffs post security bonds. *See generally* text at notes 117–195 of Chapter V.

[11] CÓDIGO PROCESAL CIVIL Y COMERCIAL DE LA NACIÓN, Ley No. 17,454, Boletín Oficial, Nov. 7, 1967. Tape-recording also is permitted in England, Australia, South Africa, Canada, and in some of the United States of America. For a discussion of the technical problems of introducing this system into a small nation see Gershoni, *The Development of Tape-Recorded Procedures in Israel,* 53 J. AM. JUD. SOC'Y 330 (1970).

[12] *See* comparison of trials in the United States and Latin America in P. EDER, *supra* note 6, at 37–38.

[13] CÓDIGO DE PROCEDIMIENTOS CIVILES (J. Fajardo ed. 1965), art. 366.

[14] CÓDIGO DE PROCEDIMIENTO CIVIL (La Torre ed. 1968), arts. 296–299.

The jury trial never has attained the importance in Latin America which it enjoys in England and elsewhere. Although various constitutions mention the right to trial by jury, it is nearly always in connection with criminal actions rather than civil cases, and in several countries its use is restricted further to libel actions. In some nations constitutional provisions for jury trials never have been implemented, even in the criminal area. Latin Americans claim that promptness and certainty in the administration of justice would be imperiled if juries were utilized. Since in many civil law nations judges are career officials, experience and training supposedly leave them better qualified to interpret both the facts and the procedural codes' evidentiary provisions. The real explanation, however, may have more sociological overtones: juries may ill suit societies which are not homogeneous, and which are composed of supreme individualists segregated from each other by visible hierarchal distinctions based upon wealth, power, social status, culture, and education.[15]

In the absence of a jury system the rules of evidence, which in Latin America are included within the procedural codes, did not develop, as in England and the United States, through accumulation of judicial precedents designed to prevent juries from being prejudiced or misled. Therefore complicated judge-made precepts such as those surrounding the hearsay rule and its exceptions are unknown. Instead, the tendency is to admit as much evidence, as possible, leav-

---

[15] For an interesting profile of the highly individualistic Argentine national character, with its decidedly European orientation, see T. FILLOL, SOCIAL FACTORS IN ECONOMIC DEVELOPMENT: THE ARGENTINE CASE 5–39 (1961). Tannenbaum, referring to Guatemala, with its large Indian populace which participates only marginally in national economic and political life, writes "there can be no national leadership because culturally there is no nation." F. TANNENBAUM, TEN KEYS TO LATIN AMERICA 116 (1960). Guatemala is in effect a nonnational state. Dawson, *Labor Legislation and Social Integration in Guatemala: 1871–1944*, 14 AM. J. COMP. L. 124, 127–38 (1965). The same may be said of Peru, Ecuador, and Bolivia, which clearly are divided culturally between majorities of a primarily aboriginal, non-European orientation, and minorities who consider themselves part of the twentieth-century Western world. SOCIAL CHANGE IN LATIN AMERICA TODAY: ITS IMPLICATIONS FOR UNITED STATES POLICY 68–176 (Council on Foreign Relations ed. 1960). In 1920, an attempt to introduce the jury system "as a permanent institution produced one of the most bitter disputes in Peru's legal history." Cooper, *The Administration of Justice in Peru*, 53 J. AM. JUD. SOC'Y 338 (1970).

ing the weighing thereof to the court.[16] Nevertheless, Latin American codes restrict more narrowly than common law countries those persons who can testify in court. Article 450 of the Peruvian Code of Civil Procedure disqualifies as witnesses persons under 18 years of age, the insane, persons deprived of the use of reason by drunkenness or some other cause at the time the deed occurred about which they are to testify, deaf-mutes who cannot read or write, persons considered unworthy of belief due to notorious bad habits or vagrancy, perjurors, and persons sentenced to prison. However, according to Article 480 of the Peruvian Code, a witness who does not speak Spanish may be examined through an interpreter appointed by the judge, and Article 491 provides for expert testimony upon "points which demand special knowledge in some science or art."

The Argentine Code is not as restrictive, although Article 427 excludes spouses and persons in direct line of descent from the parties, as does Article 453 of the Peruvian Code, with certain limitations. Under Article 443 of the Argentine Code, questions asked witnesses must relate only to facts, while Article 446 states that anyone who interrupts a witness's testimony may be fined. No party without court permission can summon more that 12 witnesses.[17] The Venezuelan Code in Article 287 states that an "honest woman" may not be compelled to testify, and excludes deaf or mute persons who can neither read nor write.[18] It is one of the least restrictive of the codes examined and does not limit the number of witnesses who may be called.

While unfamiliarity with local procedures—which even within the same legal system may vary widely from country to country—does not justify allegations of denials of justice, it underlines emphatically the necessity of intelligent selection of local counsel. However, local counsel's legal background, training and outlook may differ markedly from that of the alien's common law–trained attorney, and may

---

[16] This approach accords with progressive thinking in the United States, as demonstrated by the liberal admissibility requirements of the MODEL CODE OF EVIDENCE rules 501–531 (1942).

[17] Art. 430. Article 237 of the Brazilian CÓDIGO DE PROCESSO CIVIL limits witnesses to 10 per party.

[18] Art. 286.

pose special problems of communication and coordination.[19] The common law attorney is taught by the case method to analyze facts and details in order to arrive, by inductive reasoning, at principles necessary to solve legal problems. He is inclined, moreover, to take an interest in the purely commercial side of his client's business, since he has been schooled to appreciate the importance of avoiding future legal problems by suggesting the form or course of business practices. If he is house counsel to a large corporation, this willingness to intervene in commercial matters may be even more pronounced and eventually lead to his assuming a basically nonlegal leadership role within the corporate hierarchy.

The civil law–trained attorney, especially in Latin America, conceives of his function in entirely different terms. His training has placed greater emphasis on the study of doctrine, theory, the codes, and legal history. His reasoning tends to be deductive, theorizing from a set of broad general code precepts in order to discover answers to particular problems. He tends to regard himself as a professional man, which, especially in Latin America, conveys a certain prestige not always enjoyed by the businessman. He is, therefore, except in more sophisticated jurisdictions, perhaps less inclined to concern himself with a client's business affairs or their potential ability to create future legal difficulties. The concept of permanent house counsel is relatively new in Latin America, except in banks and the larger enterprises, and the attorney seldom envisages himself assuming a nonlegal managerial position with a corporate client. Moreover, unless the Latin American attorney is from a nation with a federal system of government, or is associated with a large law firm with international clients, he probably has not had extensive experience with conflict-of-laws problems. Due to the primarily domestic or purely export orientation of most Latin American commercial activity, he also is unlikely to possess extensive knowledge of the laws of other nations, although this lack of familiarity is gradually disappearing with common market developments in Central and South America. His United States co-counsel, however, who must live and work in a nation with fifty different legal systems, is more

---

[19] Dawson, *Professional Interchange Among Lawyers in the Americas,* 53 A.B.A.J. 903, 905 (1967).

accustomed to considering the conflicting impact in one legal system of a contract entered into or performed in another.

Unless these differences in background and outlook are recognized quite early in a relationship, serious communications problems may develop between common law and civil law co-counsel, with the one never quite understanding why the other is advising him to take a certain course of action to protect the interests of their mutual client. One potential area of misunderstanding, especially in Latin America, is in the drafting of briefs and other documents.[20] Latin American court documents tend to be closely typed, without the separate paragraphing and spacing which United States lawyers utilize to emphasize certain points. What is involved, however, is more than a question of style. Very often local rules and practice require that documents must be typed on sheets of special, stamped paper, upon which, in order to prevent subsequent alterations or insertions, no blank spaces may be left in the text of the document itself.

Documents, even in complicated cases, tend to be shorter and terser than their United States counterparts, albeit more numerous. Certainly the exhaustive "Brandeis brief" is unknown in Latin America. Instead, if a code section is cited it is not always quoted in full, and little or no mention will be made of cases, except perhaps when rendered by the Supreme Court. This laconic treatment often is related to the relatively low value placed upon case law as precedent for future decision. There is a tendency to mention, but not to cite copiously from, commentators who in the past have suggested how code provisions should be interpreted. These writers probably have greater influence upon the process of decision than case law. Also, the civil law–trained judge, who frequently is a career official, is expected to know the law and its interpretations and not to require more than minimal assistance from counsel.

The lack of good reporting and indexing systems in Latin America presents further problems, making it difficult to locate relevant cases, laws, and their amendments.[21] Frequently only Supreme Court

---

[20] For an interesting discussion of the problems of communication see Lalive, *Negotiations with American Lawyers—A Foreign Lawyer's View,* and Brudno, *Negotiations with Foreign Lawyers—An American Lawyer's View,* in NEGOTIATION AND DRAFTING INTERNATIONAL COMMERCIAL CONTRACTS 1 & 23 (Southwestern Legal Foundation ed. 1966).

[21] Problems in finding the law in Latin America are discussed in Cooper &

decisions are published in a particular country, although now reporting systems, even of lower court decisions, are available in Argentina, Brazil, Mexico, and Venezuela. The reporters, however, often merely summarize a decision. Each country publishes new laws and regulations in an official gazette, but often no official index to the gazette exists, so that attorneys must compile their own. Venezuela is exceptional, for it recently has published an excellent comprehensive legislative index which could be emulated by the other nations of the area.[22] Ironically, the best up-to-date, comprehensive, index for all the Latin American gazettes is found in a New York City law firm.

Finally, a very real problem is presented by court congestion, which may not only increase the length of time necessary to obtain a requisite hearing, but which necessarily decreases the time that public defenders, where they exist, can devote to a particular case. This congestion ultimately relates not only to the same increased complexities and problems of urban life which beset courts in the United States of America, but also to waves of internal migration as country dwellers flock to the cities to escape the hopeless poverty of rural life. They eke out existence in hovels built from packing cases, cardboard, and mud bricks in the *favelas* in Rio de Janiero, the *barriadas of Lima,* and the *villas de miseria* of Buenos Aires. Their presence has created grave political, social, and health dilemmas, as well as bitter problems of social maladjustment, crime and law enforcement.

One of the most frequently heard complaints among aliens living and working in Latin America is that, while court procedures are generally fair, an inordinately long time elapses before decisions are rendered. There is, of course, no doubt that justice delayed is justice denied, and dilatory administration of justice on more than one occasion has inspired complaints of denial of justice. The American Law Institute's *Restatement of the Foreign Relations Law of the United States* includes among factors to be considered in determining if an alien has had a fair trial whether he has had the benefit of "reason-

---

Furnish, *Latin America: A Challenge to the Common Lawyer*, 21 J. LEGAL ED. 435 (1969).

[22] Ministro de Justicia, INDICE DE LEGISLACIÓN VIGENTE (Hasta 31-12-1968) (1969).

able dispatch by the tribunal or administrative authority in reaching a determination."[23] Courts in Brazil and Mexico nevertheless are so congested that they cannot pass promptly upon applications for *mandados da segurança* and *amparo,* which were designed to assure swift relief from governmental violations of basic civil rights.[24] A member of the Brazilian Bar writes:

> [G]iven the relative lack of expeditious handling of civil cases by the judicial system plus the relative unavailability of emergency remedies, plus traditionally low awards, it is desirable to conduct one's affairs in such a manner that if it is necessary to resort to court, the most rapid and best protected remedy is available. Generally speaking, this would involve an executory or summary proceeding, which in turn generally presupposes an obligation which is "liquid and certain," such as a negotiable instrument or a secured credit (by mortgage, pledge, etc.), which normally does not include a suit upon a contract.[25]

Before casting the first stone, however, one might consider that until 1968 in New York State there had been no addition to the Manhattan and the Bronx Supreme Courts in 43 years. In the supreme courts there were delays of over 6 months in tort jury cases in some 15 counties, ranging as high as 54 months in Suffolk County and 50 months in Duchess and Rockland Counties. Pending cases in 1968 totalled over 67,500 for the New York Supreme Court, and 140,000 for New York City's Civil Court.[26] Fortunately, this problem is one with which governments, bar associations, and organized public opinion increasingly are becoming concerned, and a consensus exists that solutions must be found in the near future. The 1967 Argentine federal procedural code suggests a unique approach, providing in great detail in Articles 167 and 168 for disciplinary action against judges who do not decide cases within time limits established by the code.

Against this general background, an examination of the special

---

[23] RESTATEMENT, FOREIGN RELATIONS LAW OF THE UNITED STATES § 181(h) (1965).

[24] P. EDER, *supra* note 1, at 584.

[25] P. GARLAND, *supra* note 1, at 23.

[26] Fuld, *The Gordian Knot: Congestion and Delay in our Courts,* 39 N.Y.S.B.A.J. 488, 489 (1967).

problems presented to aliens by procedural rules concerning jurisdiction, service of process, and the time periods within which to
present and answer pleadings may prove useful.

JURISDICTION, SERVICE OF PROCESS, TIME PERIODS, AND DEFAULT JUDGMENTS

In civil law nations the domicile of either the plaintiff or the
defendant is normally the appropriate place in which to bring suit.
Some codes of civil procedure may require aliens wishing to sue to
designate a domicile in those countries, while related provisions
in commercial codes may demand that foreign companies doing
business in the country appoint attorneys-in-fact with the power to
commence and defend lawsuits.

Moreover, through "long-arm" provisions in the codes, an alien
not domiciled in the nation wherein suit is brought may be sued and
a valid judgment obtained even if he or a representative does not
appear to defend. Article 35 of the Venezuelan Civil Code provides:
"Even persons not domiciled in Venezuela may be sued therein by
reason of obligations assumed in the Republic or which are to be
performed in Venezuela." Article 88 of the Venezuelan Code of Civil
Procedure supplements the Civil Code by permitting nondomiciliaries not within Venezuela to be sued in actions involving real estate
located in Venezuela and on obligations arising out of contracts or
acts performed in Venezuela. Article 89 allows suit against transients
not only in the causes of action enumerated in Article 88, but in "all
types of personal actions in which execution may be demanded in
any place." Mexico's Civil Code in Article 13 also provides that
"the legal effects of acts and contracts signed abroad to be executed
in the territory of the Republic will be governed by the provisions
of this Code."

Although Latin American legislation has contained "long-arm"
provisions for many years, it is only comparatively recently, in
attempts to obtain personal jurisdiction over out-of-state motorists,
that this device has been adopted in various jurisdictions in the
United States. Thus, the New York Civil Practice Law and Rules
enables a court to acquire personal jurisdiction over any nondomiciliary when the cause of action has arisen out of any business

transacted, or tort committed, within the state. The requisite contact by the defendant with the state need not be extensive or prolonged, or even of the type which would be equivalent to "doing business" within New York.[27]

By contrast, inclusion of nonresidents in the jurisdiction of courts is an old, well-established practice in England and in all Commonwealth countries whose courts have based their civil procedure on the English model. Leave of the court always is required for service outside the jurisdiction (*ex juris*). It may be granted, normally, in a range of circumstances including suits involving land located within the jurisdiction, when relief is sought against persons domiciled in the jurisdiction at time of death, and in actions arising out of torts or breaches of contract committed within the jurisdiction. Additionally, grounds for "long-arm" jurisdiction exist in the case of a party out of the jurisdiction who is a necessary or proper party to an action properly brought against some other person duly served within the jurisdiction.[28]

The power of a court to grant leave to serve its process outside of

---

[27] Section 302(a) of the N.Y.C.P.L.R. (McKinney Supp. 1970) provides: "As to a cause of action arising from any of the acts enumerated in this section, a court may exercise personal jurisdiction over any nondomiciliary, or his executor or administrator, who in person or through an agent: 1. transacts any business within the state; or 2. commits a tortious act within the state, except as to a cause of action for defamation of character arising from the act; or 3. commits a tortious act without the state causing injury to person or property within the state, except as to a cause of action for defamation of character arising from the act, if he (i) regularly does or solicits business, or engages in any other persistent course of conduct, or derives substantial revenue from goods used or consumed or services rendered, in the state, or (ii) expects or should reasonably expect the act to have consequences in the state and derives substantial revenue from interstate or international commerce; or 4. owns, uses or possesses any real property situated within the state."

[28] The requirement that the action be one "properly brought" is to protect the person outside the jurisdiction. The court will not consider whether the action is bound to succeed, but will need to be satisfied that there is a real issue between the plaintiff and the party within the jurisdiction. *See* in this respect Ellinger v. Guinness, Mahon & Co., [1939] 4 All E.R. 16, and Tyne Improvement Commissioners v. Armement Anversois S/A, [1949] A.C. 326, [1949] 1 All E.R. 294 (H.L.). It is not sufficient if the action against the defendants within the jurisdiction is merely subsidiary to that against the person without, against whom the order for service ex juris is sought. *See Re* Schintz, Schintz v. Warr, [1926] Ch. 710 (C.A.).

its own jurisdiction is a discretionary matter, however, and this discretion, in England and elsewhere in the Commonwealth, is exercised judicially and with great care.[29] Especially is this the case when the person sought to be served is an alien owing no allegiance to the courts of England.[30] Care should be taken before putting "a foreigner, who owes no allegiance here, to the inconvenience and annoyance of being brought to contest his rights in this country. . . ."[31] The most important consideration is "the comparative advantage in furtherance of justice to all parties. . . ."[32] For these reasons the court always will pay heed, in its consideration of an application for an order for service ex juris, to the forum conveniens.[33]

Generally, attempts by alien defendants to oust the jurisdiction of Latin American courts by including derogation clauses in contracts are not effective if the place of performance or the domicile of one of the parties is the Latin American nation in which suit is brought. There are, to be sure, provisions in several Latin American codes indicating that parties may select a tribunal in which to air their grievances to the exclusion of courts which would otherwise be competent to hear the case.[34] Thus Mexico's Commercial Code in Article 1104 states that "no matter what the nature of the suit, there will be preferred to any other judge: I. He of the place which the debtor has designated for suit for payment; II. He of the place

---

[29] Williams v. Cartwright, [1895] 1 Q.B. 142 (C.A.); Bowling v. Cox, [1926] A.C. 751.

[30] Tyne Improvement Commissioners v. Armement Anversois S/A, *supra* note 28, at 338, 350.

[31] Société Générale de Paris v. Dreyfus Bros., [1885] 29 Ch.D. 239, 243 (Pearson, J.). *See also* John Russell & Co. v. Cayzer, Irvine & Co., [1916] 2 A.C. 298, 304 (H.L.).

[32] The Hagen, [1908] P. 189, 204 (Kennedy, L.J.).

[33] The procedures which must be followed to serve documents in a foreign jurisdiction through the local courts or by use of consular officers are considerably less difficult among Commonwealth countries than among States generally, apart from treaty arrangements in the form of bilateral civil procedure conventions or the 1964 Hague Convention on the Service Abroad of Judicial and Extrajudicial Documents in Civil or Commercial Matters, *reprinted in* 60 AM. J. INT'L L. 464 (1966).

[34] Article 40 of Peru's Code of Civil Procedure states that the court with competence to hear a case is the one to which the parties have submitted, either expressly or tacitly, and Article 151 of the Mexican Code is similar.

designated in the contract for performance of the obligation."[35]
Guatemala's Code of Civil Procedure is more ambiguous, and in
Articles 3 and 14 suggests that suit may be brought either at the
place designated by the parties or at the defendant's elected domicile. Moreover, Article 17 states that a plaintiff in any personal
action has the right to sue in the court of the defendant's domicile
"notwithstanding any waiver or submission." Attempts to oust the
jurisdiction of Latin American courts by exclusive submission to the
courts of another State never have been successful when, as according to Article 12, Section 1 of Brazil's Introductory Law to the Civil
Code, the object of the dispute is real estate, or when the litigation
involves laws recognized as within the exclusive competence of national courts, such as penal or labor legislation.

There is also a prevalent theory in Latin America, derived from
an 1894 decision of the Supreme Court of Spain, that domestic rules
of competence may not be applied when the dispute is transnational
in nature.[36] Thus, while procedural codes may contain general provisions allowing parties to a contract to elect a special forum within
the country in which each is domiciled, the same general provisions
might not be deemed to permit submission to the jurisdiction of a
tribunal abroad. This trend toward legal nationalism has been
especially apparent in Argentina and Brazil, where courts have
shown increasing reluctance, beginning with derogation clauses in
adhesion contracts and proceeding to contracts where there was
more equal bargaining power between the parties, to honor ouster
of jurisdiction (prorogation) clauses.[37] Finally, in 1967, the new
Argentine Federal Code of Civil and Commercial Procedure provided in Article 1 that "the competence of the national courts cannot
be ousted," a provision some Argentine attorneys interpret as placing
severe obstacles to Latin American economic integration.[38] The trend
is understandable, however, in light of rising Latin American economic and political nationalism, of the tradition of equal treatment

---

[35] CÓDIGO DE COMERCIO (Porrua ed. 1968).
[36] Ortala v. Hoyas, 76 JURISPRUDENCIA CIVIL 376, *discussed in* Schwind,
Derogation Clauses in Latin American Law, 13 AM. J. COMP. L. 167, 168
(1969).
[37] *Id.* at 168–71.
[38] Personal interviews in Buenos Aires in 1968.

of foreigners and nationals, and of the fear that nationals might be disadvantaged by being compelled to bring suits in other legal systems. Even agreements and treaties between the Latin American nations, which in theory may replace domestic legislation on the same matter, apparently leave the question of competence to local law. The 1940 Montevideo Treaty on International Law permits ouster only upon the defendant's consent. While Article 318 of the Bustamante Code provides that suits should be brought before the court to which the parties have submitted, it concludes with the proviso that at least one of the parties should be a citizen or domiciliary of the forum, and that submission should not be prohibited by local law. Experienced international counsel therefore customarily explain to clients that mere inclusion in contracts of a derogation clause or of a provision for arbitration in another country is no guarantee that litigation in Latin American courts will be avoided.

This legal nationalism also is evidenced by requirements in most Latin American nations, excepting Argentina and Brazil, that all public contracts between aliens and either the government of the host country or one of its ministries or agencies contain a so-called Calvo Clause, in which the alien agrees to submit all disputes growing out of the contractual relationship to local courts, and to eschew any appeals to the diplomatic protection of his government. For example, Article 17 of the Peruvian Constitution provides: "Mercantile companies, national or foreign, are subject, without restrictions, to the laws of the Republic. In every State contract with foreigners, or in the concessions in the latter's favour, it must be expressly stated that they must submit to the laws and tribunals of the Republic and renounce all diplomatic claims."[39] These requirements differ from unilateral attempts to impose the Calvo Doctrine through municipal or constitutional law, as discussed earlier, since the alien specifically contracts to waive his rights to diplomatic protection. The voluntary nature of this waiver is, however, sometimes open to question, since aliens may be forced to subscribe to such clauses as the price of doing business in foreign jurisdictions. A typical Calvo Clause which Mexican practice requires be inserted in the charters of corporations having foreign shareholders provides:

---

[39] CONSTITUTION OF THE REPUBLIC OF PERU 1933 (Pan American Union ed. 1967).

"Every alien who at the time of formation of a company, or at any time thereafter, acquires or may acquire an interest or participation in said company shall be considered by that simple fact as a Mexican in connection thereof, and it shall be understood that he agrees not to invoke the protection of his government under the penalty in case of breach of this agreement, of losing his interest or participation to the Mexican Nation."[40]

Nevertheless, if the contractual Calvo Clause allows appeals to diplomatic protection upon denial of justice, it may be considered as merely declarative of general international principles, and thus superfluous but proper. If drawn broadly enough to exclude denials of justice from diplomatic recourse, the clause becomes more controversial. In such cases protecting governments maintain, on the Vatelian theory that any injury to the alien also vicariously injures his own State, that the State has an independent right of action which the individual cannot waive. However, the United States does not consider insertion of Calvo Clauses in contracts as improper, and refuses to advise citizens not to make such commitments. Moreover, the United States is not uninfluenced, in deciding whether or not to espouse a claim, by the execution of such a renunciation, and regards it as binding on the individual, insofar as what is waived is not the right of protection belonging to his State but his own power "to request the exercise of that right in his favour."[41] Also, as a matter of policy, the United States Department of State does not espouse contract claims of citizens against other States absent a breach of substantive international law, such as a gross denial of justice.

Doctrinal arguments aside, arbitral awards beginning in the nineteenth century exhibit marked tendencies to uphold the validity of contractual Calvo Clauses, although they also indicate that they do

---

[40] The Venezuelan Constitution in Article 127 states: "In the contracts with a public interest . . . there will be considered as incorporated, even though not expressly, a clause according to which the doubts and disputes which may arise therefrom and which are not resolved amicably by the contracting parties will be decided by the competent courts of the Republic, in accordance with its laws, since for no reason or cause may they give rise to foreign claims." This clause is included by Venezuelan attorneys when drafting contracts between aliens and governmental entities.

[41] MANUAL OF PUBLIC INTERNATIONAL LAW 591 (M. Sorensen ed. 1968).

not preclude appeals to diplomatic remedies if aliens are denied justice in the local tribunals to which they have submitted themselves. Such a claim would not arise out of the contract, and therefore would not violate the alien's undertaking therein. The decisions also indicate that waiver ceases to be binding if the host government has declared the contract null and void, or has otherwise obviously violated it, on the equitable "clean-hands" theory "that a party cannot take advantage of a clause in a contract when it is at the same time in breach of it or denying its legal validity."[42]

Alien defendants also may be inconvenienced by procedural restrictions. For example, if the alien is defendant in a civil or commercial action and is not present or residing in the forum State or has not appointed a representative or attorney-in-fact to accept process in his name, he may not receive notice of the action against him in time to defend. If the defendant's address abroad is known to the plaintiff, he is required by legislation in Costa Rica, Honduras, Guatemala, and Peru to give this information to the court. The latter, in order to avoid unfairness, will notify the defendant direct of the proceedings. In Costa Rica, according to Article 98 of the Code of Civil Procedure, unless a treaty provides the contrary the court will request the Ministry of Foreign Affairs to transmit the notice to the Costa Rican consulate in the alien's nation. The consul then invites the alien to the consulate and delivers the complaint to him. The Honduran system governing service of court orders abroad is more intricate and involves issuance of the notice by the Supreme Court, which in turn transmits it to the Ministry of Justice which then delivers it to the Ministry of Foreign Affairs for service abroad.[43] The Code does not state specifically who will serve the process abroad, or how it will be accomplished, leaving this matter to guidelines set, in the absence of treaty, by general governmental policy. Guatemala's Code of Civil Procedure also requires notification via a request or letters rogatory issued by the Supreme Court to a court in the defendant's State,[44] while Peru gives the plaintiff the option of designating whether notification should be made through the courts of the country wherein the defendant resides or

---

[42] *Id.* at 593.

[43] CÓDIGO DE PROCEDIMIENTOS, art. 117.

[44] Art. 73.

through the local Peruvian consulate.[45] The Brazilian Code of Civil Procedure simply states that defendants abroad may be served by letters rogatory.[46] While the Argentine and Mexican codes do not state specifically the means by which process may be served upon defendants with known addresses abroad, related provisions indicate that direct notice is contemplated.[47]

If direct, personal notice cannot be achieved, an alien may suffer a default judgment. Nevertheless, in order to avoid unfairness all Latin American nations examined provide for notice by publication when the defendant is not to be found within the jurisdiction and his address is unknown. The Venezuelan Code of Civil Procedure, however, in Article 137 makes it quite clear that valid notice may be given by publication not only to a defendant whose address abroad is unknown, but also "when it is proven that a defendant is not within the Republic. . . ." Notice is published in the official newspaper and in two others, and the court fixes a time within which the defendant must appear to answer. Once the term expires and no answer is received, the court will appoint a "defender" and serve the notice on this person. This same procedure, in contrast to the other nations studied, even may be utilized to notify defendants with known addresses abroad but who are not in the country. Whether a default judgment rendered on this basis against a defendant with a known address should be enforced abroad may be seriously questioned.

Other Latin American nations providing for notification by publication require that all efforts to serve the defendant personally have been attempted in vain. Article 122 of the Mexican Federal Code of Civil Procedure prescribes publication in the *Boletín Judicial* and in two other newspapers "of major circulation" for three consecutive days, advising the defendant that he must appear within a period of not less than 15, nor more than 60, days. Peru requires publication

---

[45] Art. 157.

[46] Art. 175.

[47] For example, Article 340 of the Argentine Federal Code of Civil Procedure provides for issuing letters requisitorial to the judge of the place where a defendant who is not within the jurisdiction may be found. While the article would seem to be designed for application within Argentina, it could be interpreted as applicable to service abroad as well.

for 20 days "in the capital of the republic,"[48] while Costa Rica requires two publications in the *Boletín Judicial*, with an eight-day interval.[49] The time to answer begins to run from the last day of publication in Costa Rica, although an extension is allowed in Peru. The Honduran Code of Civil Procedure provisions on publication merely require posting the citation at the court, rather than newspaper publication, which does not seem well calculated to provide effective notice to parties abroad.[50] Corresponding Guatemalan provisions are quite vague and suggest that, where the defendant's address abroad is unknown, the court may decide on the best manner in which to give notice.[51] By contrast, Argentina's Federal Procedural Code is certainly the most innovative, since not only does it require publication in the *Boletín Oficial* and in a newspaper of major circulation at the defendant's last known domicile,[52] but also authorizes notice by official radio broadcasts.[53]

It should be emphasized that, with the exception of Venezuela, these methods of service by publication may be invoked only if the defendant's address is unknown and only once all attempts at personal service (which could include unsuccessful efforts to serve through commissions or letters rogatory) have failed. The possibility that an alien corporate defendant's address abroad is unknown or unascertainable is slight. Unless the foreign company defendant has only marginal contacts with the forum State, it usually must appoint an agent or attorney-in-fact for purposes of legal notifications as a prerequisite for doing business. Moreover, even service by publication in Latin America contrasts favorably with the system of notification *au parquet* once utilized in France and in some continental nations. Until recently, service of process in France upon an alien defendant with a known address abroad could be made by delivery of the summons to the *procureur* attached to the local French Court. Though he then had an obligation to transmit the summons to the

---

[48] Código de Procedimientos Civiles, art. 160.

[49] Código de Procedimientos Civiles, art. 103.

[50] Art. 100.

[51] Código Procesal, Civil y Mercantil, art. 74.

[52] Art. 146. Presumably, this notice could include publication at the defendant's last known residence abroad as well as in Argentina.

[53] Art. 148. It is doubtful, however, if this procedure would apply to service abroad.

defendant by diplomatic channels, service was considered complete as of the moment the procureur had been served, with time to appear beginning to run at once. As a result, default judgments could be obtained in France before effective notice reached the defendant. However, since 1965 a copy of the summons must be mailed to the defendant on the same day the procureur has been served, and a default judgment will not ordinarily be entered unless the defendant received actual notice.[54]

Of major concern to alien defendants residing outside the forum State are the periods of time provided in procedural codes for answering pleadings or appealing adverse decisions. These periods seem rather brief today when litigation between parties located continents apart is such a distinct possibility. For example, the time allowed in various Latin American Codes of Civil Procedure to answer or raise objections to a complaint ranges from 6 to 30 days;[55] counterclaims must be answered within 6 to 15 days.[56] The time periods within which appeals from adverse judgments must be filed will vary from 3 to 15 days, depending upon the country involved.[57] If the appeal is from an interlocutory judgment, the periods may be even shorter.[58] Such curtailed periods are not entirely inexplicable. Often procedural codes were adopted a number of years ago, as was the 1906 Honduran Code, before international litigation became the distinct possibility it is today. Or, as with the new Argentine Code, the draftsmen thought that short time periods would accelerate court procedures and minimize delay in the administration of justice.

---

[54] C. Pro. Civ. arts. 69(10), 1033–3 (Petits Codes Dalloz 63d ed. 1966). *See* P. Herzog, *supra* note 1, at 611–18. Similar legislation is found in Belgium, Greece, and The Netherlands.

[55] In Honduras 6 days are allowed (art. 264); between 15 and 30 days in Costa Rica (art. 209); 15 days in Argentina (art. 338); 9 days in Mexico (art. 256); and 10 days in Brazil, Peru, and Venezuela (arts. 292, 320, and 244, respectively).

[56] In Honduras and Peru 6 days are permitted (arts. 297 and 329, respectively); 6 days in Mexico (art. 272); 10 days in Venezuela (art. 268); 5 days in Brazil (art. 193); 9 to 15 days in Costa Rica (art. 226); and 15 days in Argentina (art. 355).

[57] In Honduras and Guatemala appeals from ordinary judgments must be filed in 3 days (arts. 203 and 209, respectively); 5 days in Costa Rica, Argentina, Mexico, and Peru (arts. 863, 244, 691 and 1093, respectively); 5 days also in Venezuela (arts. 176, 177 and 181); and 15 days in Brazil (art. 823).

[58] In Peru a party has only 3 days to appeal from an interlocutory judgment, as opposed to 5 days for appeals from a final judgment. Art. 1093.

These periods, however, generally do not begin to run until the day after the defendant receives actual delivery of the notice or summons. Where the defendant is notified by publication, the time may begin to run on the last day of publication. Hence the periods are not really as short as they at first might seem. Moreover, the time periods for service and notification generally may be extended if the defendant, be he alien or national, is not within the jurisdiction. Thus, while the Argentine Code ordinarily allows 15 days in which to answer complaints, it permits extensions of 1 day for every 2 kilometers between a defendant who is still within the country and the court where suit was brought.[59] If the defendant is outside Argentina, Article 342, in language almost identical to corresponding provisions in the Honduran[60] and Mexican Codes,[61] allows the judge to fix the time in which to answer, "taking account of the distances and of the greater or lesser ease of communications." Venezuela, however, does not differentiate between a defendant abroad and a defendant still in the country but out of the jurisdiction. Extensions of the time to answer and to appeal are both permitted pursuant to Article 157, which allows an extra day for every 30 kilometers. The Peruvian Code is less explicit but allows extensions for reasons of distance according to a schedule which the Supreme Court must prepare every 5 years.[62] Evidently there is no formal code provision for extensions in Guatemala. Practice suggests, however, that in the event a defendant were served abroad, the period would start to run only upon his actual receipt of notice.

The extensions granted in Costa Rica vary with the part of the world in which the defendant is found. Article 210, while allowing up to 30 days for defendants still in Costa Rica but not residing within the forum, permits the same extensions of time for defendants abroad as are permitted for obtaining evidence abroad. Thus, defendants in Central America, Panama, Cuba, Puerto Rico, or the United States of America have 50 days to answer; defendants in Colombia, Venezuela, Mexico, and the Antilles have 70; defendants in Great Britain, France, Spain, Portugal, Belgium, or Holland have 90; and

---

[59] Art. 158.
[60] Art. 266.
[61] Art. 134.
[62] Art. 181.

defendants elsewhere have 120.[63] These periods may be increased by 50 percent if the judge believes that due to communications difficulties they may be inadequate.[64]

Apparently, except in Venezuela, no formal provisions govern extensions for purposes of appeal, but this lacuna is not necessarily unfair if an appellant has been present or represented in the proceedings below, since in that event he can petition for an extension. Moreover, no discrimination exists between aliens and nationals as to rights to appeal. If an alien has been granted access to the lower court he will be granted, under the doctrine of national treatment, the same rights to appeal available to nationals. An extension of time in which to reply to a counterclaim also could be requested on the argument that since a counterclaim should be regarded as a complaint the alien plaintiff, now converted into a defendant, should be allowed the extensions normally permitted alien defendants abroad. However, since in order to bring the action in the first place the alien plaintiff would have had to appoint an attorney-in-fact to file the complaint, a court might reasonably deny such a request, finding that the plaintiff-defendant, be he alien or national, already was represented by counsel and, in effect, "present" in the jurisdiction.

If, despite time extensions and efforts to effect service personally or by publication, a defendant does not answer or object within the designated period, Latin American procedural codes permit plaintiffs to request that the defendant be declared in *rebeldía* or default.

---

[63] Art. 234.

[64] Venezuela and Mexico, upon application, also allow special extensions of the time normally designated for taking evidence where documents or witnesses are to be found at some distance from the forum. In Venezuela, Article 283 of the Code of Civil Procedure states that such extensions cannot exceed 6 months for any part of Europe or America, while Mexico's Federal Code of Civil Procedure in Article 303 allows no more than 100 days for North America, Central America and the Antilles, nor more than 120 days for any other part of the world. The geographical distinctions are thus less elaborate than in Costa Rica. Peru, in Article 353 of its Code of Civil Procedure, also permits extensions of the normal 15- to 50-day period for presenting evidence, but the length of the extension is based upon the schedule issued by the Supreme Court pursuant to Article 181. Unlike the Costa Rican Code, the Venezuelan and Mexican Codes do not relate the extensions granted for obtaining evidence abroad to the time to answer complaints.

This declaration does not excuse plaintiffs from presenting evidence to support their claims, although it generally will permit attachment of defendant's property within the jurisdiction. Unlike United States practice, defendants in Latin American nations may not always have a clearly defined right to reopen default judgments. Costa Rica and Mexico are exceptional, since their procedural codes provide special appellate machinery to assist litigants who have not been notified in sufficient time to appear and defend. In Costa Rica, if the defendant has not appeared and has been declared in default, a special appeal (*recurso de revisión*) will lie to the Supreme Court if he can show he was prevented from appearing by *force majeure* or because he was out of the country from the beginning of the action.[65] This special appeal must be filed within three months of the termination of the impediment which prevented his appearing, or within three months of his return, or of the moment when, while absent, he learned of the suit against him.[66] Mexico also enables defendants to seek relief in the Supreme Court by means of the *apelación extra-ordinaria*: "The appeal will be admissible within the three months which follow the day of the notification of judgment . . . when the defendant has been cited by publication (*edictos*) and the judgment has been given in default."[67] Where notification of the default judgment was by publication, execution may not be obtained, unless the plaintiff posts a bond, until three months after the last day of publication in the *Boletín Judicial* or other appropriate newspaper.[68] A defendant in default also may reenter the lawsuit at any time and offer evidence in his own favor.[69] Moreover, Article 648 of the Mexican Federal Code of Civil Procedure provides for lifting any attachment if a defendant can show that his appearance was prevented by *fuerza mayor insuperable*. However, the defaulting defendant who has been served personally may only appeal a default judgment pursuant to the usual rules, which require filing notice within five days of final judgment.

---

[65] Código de Procedimientos Civiles, art. 933.

[66] Art. 934.

[67] Código de Procedimientos Civiles Para el Distrito y Territorios Federales, art. 717.

[68] Art. 644.

[69] Arts. 645 & 646.

Unfortunately not all procedural codes are as clear as those of Costa Rica or Mexico. The Guatemalan Code allows a defendant to challenge a default judgment and an attachment made pursuant thereto if he can prove that he was prevented from appearing by fuerza mayor insuperable.[70] The applicable article does not indicate a time period in which to bring the appeal, nor distinguish, as does Mexico, between defendants served personally and those served by publication. Peru, like Mexico, allows a defendant to reenter the case at any time, supplying evidence in his own behalf, provided that he pays any fines which may have been levied during his delinquency.[71] Once judgment has been rendered, however, the only recourse apparently lies through normal appellate procedure, which requires filing appeals within five days after judgment. Venezuela's code might permit appeal from a default judgment under Article 421(3), which allows appeal to Cassation (the highest court in Venezuela) from a judgment rendered in such a way so as to deprive a defendant of an opportunity to defend. The usual appeal period of five days would seem to apply, unless the court allows an extension.[72]

While the European nations are equally diverse respecting the rules for reopening default judgments, the 1965 Hague Convention on the Service Abroad of Judicial and Extrajudicial Documents in Civil and Commercial Matters seeks to provide a certain uniformity and minimize any unfairness to aliens not resident in the forum State.[73]

International Legal Assistance

An alien who brings suit in his host State may have to serve the defendant with process abroad or to obtain testimony abroad for use in the forum State. However, the jurisdiction of the courts of any State is confined to the national territory, and consequently courts do not have the power to perform procedural acts abroad. Instead, they must request assistance from appropriate judicial or

---

[70] Art. 114.

[71] Código de Procedimientos Civiles, arts. 195–201.

[72] Personal interviews in Caracas in 1970.

[73] See text at notes 85–88 infra.

comparable authorities in other nations. Unfortunately, absent a convention, treaty, or specific internal legislation, the authorities in one State cannot be compelled to assist their counterparts in another except on grounds of international comity. This procedure contrasts with constitutional obligations of courts in different parts or provinces of the same nation to assist one another as, for example, in Mexico and the United States of America.

Assistance requested between the courts of two sovereign States is known as "international legal assistance," and normally encompasses at least two separate problems which may be treated differently in applicable treaties and legislation: first, the service of writs, summonses and notifications; and, second, the obtaining of written and oral testimony for use as evidence in the forum State. While this topic has been treated extensively elsewhere, new treaty developments and the increasing frequency of litigation involving parties and witnesses located in different countries indicate that at least the most salient points should be reviewed again.[74]

With few exceptions, provisions in national codes of civil procedure governing international judicial assistance are imprecise and unsatisfactory. However, in the United States the 1964 amendments to the Federal Rules of Civil Procedure and to the United States Code established broad and liberal procedures to be followed in federal courts regarding transmitting and receiving requests for judicial assistance. The fact that the initiator of the request might be an alien is irrelevant, and no reciprocity is required. Pursuant to Section 1781 of Title 28 of the United States Code, the Department of State now is empowered to receive a letter rogatory seeking testimony from a foreign or international tribunal and to transmit it to the domestic court or agency to which it is addressed. Once the letter rogatory is received, the district court of the district in which the deponent resides or is found may order him to give his testimony or produce the document sought in the foreign request.[75] The court's order may prescribe the practice and procedure to be followed, "which may be in whole or part the practice and procedure of the

---

[74] See generally H. SMIT, note 1 supra.

[75] 28 U.S.C. § 1782 (1964), discussed in Amram, Public Law No. 88–619 of October 3, 1964—New Developments in International Judicial Assistance in the United States of America, 32 J. BAR ASS'N OF DIST. OF COLUM. 24 (1965).

foreign country or the international tribunal."[76] This practice assures the validity of the testimony under the law of the forum abroad where the suit has been brought. The only limitation is that a person may not be compelled to testify or produce a document "in violation of any legally applicable privilege." By the same token the Department of State also will transmit requests and letters rogatory from United States courts to courts or agencies abroad. This procedure does not preclude direct transmittal abroad of requests or letters rogatory by courts themselves without intervention of the Department of State, nor invalidate a request for assistance made by a foreign or international court direct to a United States court. Testimony taken abroad may be used in the federal courts even if not obtained in a manner which conforms strictly with the formalities of domestic rules of evidence.

The 1964 amendments also authorized United States courts to issue subpoenas requesting the personal appearance as witnesses before them of nationals or residents of the United States who might be found in foreign countries. Service of the subpoena is effected in the same fashion that process is served upon parties abroad. According to Rule 4(i) of the Federal Rules of Civil Procedure, service abroad may be made pursuant to laws of the foreign country, among other methods.[77] Section 1696 of Title 28 of the United States Code

---

[76] *Id.*

[77] FED. R. CIV. P. 4 provides, *inter alia:*

. . . (i) Alternative Provisions for Service in a Foreign Country

(1) Manner. When the federal or state law referred to in subdivision (e) of this rule authorizes service upon a party not an inhabitant of or found within the state in which the district court is held, and service is to be effected upon the party in a foreign country, it is also sufficient if service of the summons and complaint is made: (A) in the manner prescribed by the law of the foreign country for service in that country in an action in any of its courts of general jurisdiction; or (B) as directed by the foreign authority in response to a letter rogatory, when service in either case is reasonably calculated to give actual notice; or (C) upon an individual, by delivery to him personally, and upon a corporation or partnership or association, by delivery to an officer, a managing or general agent; or (D) by any form of mail, requiring a signed receipt, to be addressed and dispatched by the clerk of the court to the party to be served; or (E) as directed by order of the court. Service under (C) or (E) above may be made by any person who is not a party and is not less than 18 years of age or who is designated by order of the district court or by the foreign court. On request, the clerk shall deliver the summons to the plaintiff for transmission to the person or the foreign court or officer who will make the service.

also provides that the district court of the district in which a person resides or is found may order service upon him "of any document issued in connection with a foreign or international tribunal," thus indicating a corresponding willingness to assist foreign courts in proceedings directed against parties within the United States. There is no restriction on the court's power to assist, and the district judge may act either in response to a letter or request from a foreign court, or upon the direct application of any interested person. The same section enables service of the foreign process to be effected in the United States by an interested person, even without court order or permission.

The procedural legislation of other nations, however, is not as comprehensive or unrestricted. For example, the extent to which Brazilian courts may honor requests for international assistance is unclear and apparently is left to the discretion of the Supreme Court. Case law suggests that requests for service of process are less likely to be honored than requests for information or the taking of testimony.[78] By contrast, both Peru and Venezuela in Articles 1167 and 755 of their respective Codes of Civil Procedure state clearly that requests for service and for the taking of testimony will be honored.[79] Venezuela's Procedural Code provisions are more detailed and indicate specifically, as the Peruvian Code does indirectly, that, unlike Brazil, intervention by the Supreme Court is not required. Instead, the local judge of first instance is authorized to comply with the request from abroad.[80] Where service of process is requested from abroad, Venezuelan judges will use the procedures provided in the

---

(2) Return. Proof of service may be made as prescribed by subdivision (g) of this rule, or by the law of the foreign country, or by order of the court. When service is made pursuant to subparagraph (1)(D) of this subdivision, proof of service shall include a receipt signed by the addressee or other evidence of delivery to the addressee satisfactory to the court.

[78] P. GARLAND, AMERICAN-BRAZILIAN PRIVATE INTERNATIONAL LAW 98 (1959). Article 797 of the Código de Processo Civil states: "Letters rogatory from foreign authorities do not require homologation and shall be executed, following the grant of exequatur by the Chief Justice, by the judge of the district in which the requested acts are to be carried out."

[79] The Peruvian Code of Civil Procedure provides for commissioning Peruvian diplomatic and consular personnel to take testimony abroad for use in domestic legislation. Art. 377,

[80] Art. 755,

Code of Civil Procedure for domestic litigation unless the requesting authority specifies another method of service compatible with domestic legislation.[81] Venezuela apparently will accept requests transmitted directly from a foreign court with proper consular authentication, as well as requests transmitted through traditional diplomatic means.

Costa Rican procedure illustrates the need for unification in this area, since the Code of Civil Procedure, while indicating a willingness to comply with requests both for service of process and information, first requires the *exequatur*, or approval, of the Supreme Court.[82] This requirement theoretically would enable requests to be rejected for reasons of public policy, a result contrary to the spirit of the Bustamante Code, which in Articles 388–393 seeks to provide certainty and uniformity. However, Costa Rica, Bolivia, Chile, Ecuador, and El Salvador ratified the Code with a general reservation as to any provisions which might run contrary to domestic legislation at the time of ratification or in the future. The other nations examined—with the exceptions of Mexico and Argentina, which did not ratify the Code at all—made neither general nor specific reservations as to those articles dealing with international judicial assistance.

Not surprisingly, recent reports of the Inter-American Juridical Committee manifest an interest both in revising those articles of the Bustamante Code relating to international judicial assistance and in obtaining the specific adherence thereto of the signatory nations, since the Code's provisions are too vague to be truly useful.[83] For example, Article 388 endorses the use of diplomatic channels— at best a cumbersome device—for transmittal of process or other requests, although the contracting States may agree among themselves upon other methods. This provision would seem little more than a restatement of traditional practice with its lack of uniformity. The receiving judge, under Article 390, may decide, with no ap-

---

[81] A. Hernandez-Breton, Código de Procedimiento Civil Venezolano 421 n.1 (1966).

[82] Art. 1024. Normally, exequatur is a process required only when enforcement of a foreign judgment is requested.

[83] *See* Nadelmann, *The Question of Revision of the Bustamante Code,* 57 Am. J. Int'l L. 384, 386 (1963).

parent guidelines, whether he will give effect to the foreign request. Article 391 requires without exception that the law of the place of receipt be applied in executing requests.[84] Thus, local procedures and rules governing the taking of testimony would be utilized, rather than methods normally followed in the requesting State. Such a requirement is not especially harmful as long as the rules of evidence are basically identical in the two States, as would be true, for instance, if Honduras and Guatemala were involved. However, if the States belonged to two different legal systems the results could be unfortunate. In civil law systems oral evidence often is taken before the secretary of the court, who may make a résumé of the testimony rather than transcribe it verbatim. This summarized testimony may be of little value or even inadmissible in a forum State which adheres to the common law system. Therefore the Bustamante Code as now drafted would not seem the best basis upon which to design a uniform program of international judicial assistance.

Greater progress toward a more workable, uniform system, however, was achieved in Europe when The Hague Conference on Private International Law drafted the 1965 Convention on the Service Abroad of Judicial and Extrajudicial Documents in Civil or Commercial Matters (hereinafter called the "Service Convention")[85] and the 1968 Convention on the Taking of Evidence Abroad in Civil or Commercial Matters (hereinafter called the "Evidence Convention").[86]

The Service Convention, which is a revision of Chapter I of the 1954 Hague Convention on Civil Procedure, has been ratified by the United States and is now in force. The drafters, it is said, were influenced by the 1964 amendments to Title 28 of the United States Code, which were distributed by the United States delegates at The

---

[84] The less comprehensive 1911 Bolivarian Treaty on Foreign Acts ratified by Bolivia, Colombia, Ecuador, Peru, and Venezuela similarly provides in Article 11 that requests for judicial assistance "will be processed according to the laws of the country where execution is sought." II TRATADOS PÚBLICOS Y ACUERDOS INTERNACIONALES DE VENEZUELA: 1910–1920, at 475, 477 (1950).

[85] [1969] 1 U.S.T. 361, T.I.A.S. No. 6638 (effective Feb. 10, 1968), *reprinted in* 22 THE RECORD 296 (1967). *See also* Amram, *United States Ratification of the Hague Convention on Service of Documents Abroad*, 61 AM. J. INT'L L. 1019 (1967).

[86] *Reprinted in* 8 INTERNATIONAL LEGAL MATERIALS 37 (1969).

Hague to their foreign colleagues. Perhaps as a result, the Convention requires no basic changes in United States practice or amendments to existing legislation. Article 2 requires each State to designate a Central Authority to receive requests for service. This Central Authority of the addressee State, according to Article 5, will serve the document itself or have it served "by an appropriate agency" either pursuant to procedures used in domestic litigation or by the method designated by the applicant, provided this method is not inconsistent with local law. This procedure contrasts most favorably with the Bustamante Code, which permits execution or service only pursuant to local procedures. Use of the Central Authority is not obligatory, and the Convention, as does United States law, permits alternate methods of service—including direct personal service or by mail—provided the host State has no objection. Service by consular or diplomatic officers also is permitted, but this procedure is considered only as one of several secondary alternatives and not, as in the Bustamante Code, a primary means of service. Evidence of service is supplied by a simple certificate of performance for which elaborate authentication procedures are not required. Article 13 limits the grounds for refusing requests for service of process to situations where compliance would infringe upon the executing State's "sovereignty or security." A vague public policy defense for noncompliance would be insufficient. Under the Bustamante Code, standards for rejection are left to the discretion of the judge.

In addition to simplifying the procedures for obtaining judicial assistance, the Convention seeks to minimize the possibly unfair impact of certain continental procedural rules concerning service of process and default judgments. As already noted, in several civil law countries plaintiffs may serve process upon nondomiciliaries with known addresses abroad by service upon the district attorney at the forum court, with time to answer beginning to run from the moment of delivery of the process upon that official. As a result, default judgments with no notice sometimes have been possible against nonresident aliens.[87] Under Article 15 of the Convention,

---

[87] Note 54 *supra*. However, recent reforms in French procedural law, largely in response to France's accession to the Convention, while retaining parquet service, now require proof of actual notification and extend the time to appear and answer up to three months before a default judgment will be given.

however, a default judgment may not be entered until it can be established either that service was effected by the methods prescribed by local law for suits against defendants found within the nation, or that actual delivery of the document was made to the defendant by a method authorized by the Convention. In either event, the defendant must have had sufficient time to appear and defend. Article 16 authorizes the reopening of a default judgment if the defendant was not notified in time to defend or appeal, or "has disclosed a *prima facie* defence to the action on the merits." A number of members of the Hague Conference traditionally have regarded service of foreign legal documents within their territory as a violation of sovereignty unless made through diplomatic channels. The Convention now allows other means of service, although, except for service through the Central Authority, it "does not guarantee to United States litigants the same freedom to serve legal papers in other contracting States . . . as is available to foreign litigants in the United States. . . ."[88]

The Evidence Convention, which has not yet come into force, complements the Service Convention not only by seeking a degree of uniformity, but also by attempting to compromise differences between civil and common law techniques in obtaining evidence. One salient difference, which has been the source of much confusion, is that common law countries customarily seek to obtain testimony abroad by stipulation or through commissions to consuls or commissioners. The United States federal courts even will appoint as commissioner a foreign judge who may come to the United States and examine witnesses directly, using the rules of procedure of the foreign State in which the action is pending. Applications for both the issuance of letters rogatory for use abroad, and compliance with ones emanating from civil law countries, met with comparatively little success in federal courts prior to 1964. Civil law countries, however, have been reluctant to rely upon or permit testimony to be taken except by the written interrogatory technique of

---

[88] Committee on International Law of the Association of the Bar of the City of New York, *The Hague Convention on the Service Abroad of Judicial and Extrajudicial Documents in Civil or Commercial Matters*, 22 THE RECORD 280, 284 (1967). For example, an addressee State may object to a particular method of service as "incompatible" with its internal law. Article 5(h). This standard seems rather vague.

letters rogatory or letters of request. Consequently, evidence obtained abroad might not always be admissible in the forum State.

The Convention spans the gap between the two systems since, in the words of a long-time United States Delegate to The Hague Conferences on Private International Law, it "is drawn on the basic principle that any system of obtaining evidence or securing the performance of other judicial acts internationally must be 'tolerable' in the state of execution and 'utilizable' in the forum of the state of origin where the action is pending."[89] Moreover, although the Convention in Article 1 establishes the Letter of Request as the primary means of soliciting and obtaining testimony or documentary evidence abroad, it also allows contracting States to obtain evidence by the use of consular authorities as commissioners.[90] The Letter of Request, however, is clearly the principal instrument intended for use by the drafters, since States are allowed to make reservations to that chapter in the Convention permitting the use of consuls and commissioners. Nonetheless, a definite concession has been made by the civil law countries, since commissioners may be utilized and consuls are allowed to take testimony of their own nationals abroad without soliciting the permission of the host State unless required to do so by specific declaration.[91]

Like the Service Convention, the Evidence Convention provides for designation in each country of a Central Authority to receive Letters of Request and to transmit them to the court or body competent to execute them. The requesting authority then is informed of the time and place for which the examination is scheduled and, states Article 8, may be permitted to send "judicial personnel" to be present. There is no indication, however, that the foreign "judicial personnel" would be allowed, as in the United States, to participate in the examinations themselves. The judicial authority conducting the examination will apply its own procedural law unless the requesting authority desires that some other method be utilized which is not "incompatible with the internal law of the State of execution or is impossible of performance by reason of its internal practice and

[89] Amram, *The Proposed Convention on the Taking of Evidence Abroad,* 55 A.B.A.J. 651, 652 (1969).

[90] Art. 15.

[91] Art. 15.

procedure or by reason of practical difficulties."[92] Recalcitrant witnesses may be compelled to appear by the same "measures of compulsion" used to obtain compliance in domestic proceedings.[93]

In a fashion similar to the Service Convention, the Evidence Convention provides that refusal of judicial assistance may not be based solely "on the ground that under its internal law the State of execution claims exclusive jurisdiction over the subject-matter of the action or that its internal law would not admit a right of action on it."[94] Refusal may be justified only to the extent that execution does not fall within the functions of the local judiciary or if execution would prejudice the sovereignty or security of the addressee State. The Bustamante Code, it will be recalled, leaves the decision to refuse execution entirely to the discretion of the judge in the requested State.

The Service and Evidence Conventions indicate that an apparently workable system of international judicial cooperation acceptable to both civil and common law countries can be devised by which litigation with transnational aspects, both as to parties and to witnesses, may be conducted fairly and efficiently. To date, only a relatively few nations have chosen to be bound by the terms of the Service Convention, while the Evidence Convention has yet to receive the requisite number of ratifications. Fortunately, both Conventions have liberal accession clauses permitting adherence even by States which are not members of The Hague Conference, so that it is conceivable that more of the lesser-developed nations of both civil and common law backgrounds will accept their terms. Also, it may be hoped that the methods employed in the Conventions may serve as inspiration to the Inter-American Juridical Committee in their deliberations on revising the inadequate Bustamante Code.

The structural procedural problems discussed in this Chapter and in its predecessors, although in general not unduly or deliberately unfair or discriminatory as far as concerns aliens, may become increasingly complicated when an alien seeks to bring suit against his host government, or in some other way enjoin State action which threatens to impinge upon his personal and economic rights.

---

[92] Art. 9.

[93] Art. 10.

[94] Art. 12.

Chapter VII

Protection Against Governmental Action

An alien should be especially interested in the conditions under which suits may be brought against his host government, or its officials and agencies, since it is that government which, under traditional international law, is obliged to assure him a minimum standard of fair treatment. Moreover, it is where litigation involving governments is contemplated that the economic and political environment in the host State may impinge most severely upon the alien's enjoyment of the full benefit of the judicial process.

Litigation against governmental units generally falls into three broad categories: suits to enforce personal rights (such as proceedings to review the lawfulness of a detention), suits to vindicate property rights (such as actions to obtain compensation for property taken by eminent domain or nationalization), and, lastly, proceedings to review the legality or the constitutionality of administrative action (such as the denial of a building permit or the like). Unfortunately, procedures in these various cases overlap a great deal in many countries, so that these distinctions sometimes remain somewhat theoretical.

Governmental Liability to Suit and Review of Administrative Activity

Inherent in the phrase "the rule of law" is the understanding that no person is above the law, that all persons are tried in the same courts under the same laws irrespective of position. It does not follow, however, that the source of those laws—the government, and its officers and agents—is vulnerable to suit. Indeed in many countries, England included, the doctrine of absolute sovereign immunity held sway for many years. Hand in hand with the phrase "rule of law" went its apparently inconsistent companion "the sovereign can do no wrong."[1] Only comparatively recently has the concept of government responsibility been incorporated into Crown proceedings statutes. These statutes have virtually erased the distinction between sovereign and subject and eliminated the old "petition of right," hitherto the form of action necessary to commence suit against the government in England and in the Commonwealth countries, but which required governmental consent as a condition precedent.

Even so, wide variations exist from State to State in the rights of a person aggrieved against the government in his country of residence. In some States suit may be brought as of right, in others only by leave; many States distinguish between actions in tort and actions in contract; still another distinction is sometimes drawn between citizens and aliens, or between resident and nonresident aliens.

In England, the general common law rule was that no legal proceeding could be brought against the sovereign, for the courts were the King's courts and therefore possessed no jurisdiction over him. The principal way in which redress could be sought for grievances was by petition of right, which required royal consent. It was through this process that damages or property were recoverable from the Crown on both legal and equitable grounds. "A petition of right is merely an amicable litigation taken by the consent of the Crown against the Crown itself."[2] It was well established at common law that a petition of right lay both for liquidated sums due under a contract[3] and for unliquidated damages for breach of contract.[4] A petition of right did not lie, however, for damages for torts allegedly committed either by the Crown or by a servant of the Crown acting within the scope of his authority.[5] A second form of procedure was available for redress of grievances through a suit against the Attorney General for a declaratory judgment. This

---

[1] The inconsistency in theory is apparent, not real. "The sovereign can do no wrong" does not mean that "anything the sovereign does is proper." It means, or originally meant, that the sovereign is incapable of wrongdoing.

[2] Hollinshead v. Hazleton, [1916] 1 A.C. 428, 450 (Lord Atkinson).

[3] Thames Iron Works & Ship Building Co. v. R., [1869] 10 B. & S. 33 (Q.B.).

[4] Thomas v. The Queen, [1874] L.R. 10 Q.B. 31.

[5] Viscount Canterbury v. Attorney General, [1843] 1 Ph. 306 (Ch.).

proceeding required no governmental consent, but was limited in application.[6]

Modern English practice commenced with the enactment of the 1947 Crown Proceedings Act,[7] which abolished the special forms of procedure for suit against and by the Crown. As a result, suits against the government are generally now governed by the same rules as proceedings between subjects. While the Crown Proceedings Act is largely concerned with procedural reforms, it makes one important substantive alteration: it erases the old legal fiction that the sovereign can do no wrong and subjects the Crown to liability in tort in much the same way as if it were a private person.[8] There are, as would be expected, certain saving provisions as regards acts of the Crown done under its prerogative and in exercise of statutory powers.[9] Additionally, two exceptions exist to the type of relief a court may order against the Crown. An order or injunction for specific performance will not be granted; instead, a declaratory order will issue.[10] Second, an order for recovery of land or delivery of property will not lie against the Crown; once again, a declaratory order will be given.[11] Although the Crown is immune from normal methods of enforcing judgments, the Act provides means of execution.[12]

All the developing Commonwealth countries involved in this study attained independence either coincidental with or subsequent to the coming into force in 1947 of modern English practice. Nevertheless, the influence of the English statute is widespread. In some instances the principle of government liability is stated in the simplest of terms, as in the Republic of Singapore, where the Constitution states "[t]he Government may sue and be sued."[13] This statement, coupled

---

[6] *See* Dyson v. Attorney General, [1911] 1 K.B. 410 (C.A.); Dyson v. Attorney General, [1912] 1 Ch. 158 (C.A.); Esquimalt & Nanaimo Ry. Co. v. Wilson, [1920] A.C. 358.

[7] 10 & 11 Geo. 6, c. 44.

[8] *Id.* § 2.

[9] *Id.* § 11(1). It should be noted as well that the Act does not apply to proceedings involving Her Majesty in her private capacity, which still must be pursued by way of petition of right. *See* § 40(1).

[10] *Id.* § 21(1).

[11] *Id.*

[12] *Id.* § 27.

[13] CONSTITUTION OF THE REPUBLIC OF SINGAPORE, § 21(2).

with the 1956 Government Proceedings Ordinance,[14] subjects the Republic to liability both in contract and in tort by procedures similar to those procedures governing suits between subjects. The same Ordinance is applicable in the Federation of Malaysia.

Elsewhere in Asia the situation differs. In Pakistan, for example, the concept of sovereign immunity, by virtue of its peculiar history, never took root and thus no procedure for petition of right became imbedded in Pakistani law.[15] Not surprisingly, therefore, the concept of equality under the law is firmly recognized by the courts. The Supreme Court of Pakistan has expressed itself as follows: "Public power is now exercised in Pakistan under the Constitution of 1962, of which Article 2 requires that every citizen shall be dealt with strictly in accordance with law."[16] Continuing in that case, the Chief Justice distinguished an earlier English case[17] in which the House of Lords held that, where a Crown minister is authorized to act when he has "reasonable cause to believe" in the existence of certain facts, the courts neither will inquire into the grounds for his belief nor consider whether grounds existed on which such belief could reasonably be based.[18] The court concluded that seemingly discre-

---

[14] Federation of Malaya, Government Proceedings Ordinance, No. 58 of 1956.

[15] What is now Pakistan was until 1758 under the rule of the Moghul Emperors. At that time it passed under control of the East India Company and remained in that position until 1858, when it became subservient to the British Crown. Pakistan gained independence in 1947.

[16] Ghulam Jilani v. Government of West Pakistan, Pakistan Legal Decisions [1967] S.C. 373, 389 (Cornelius, C.J.).

[17] Liversidge v. Anderson, [1942] A.C. 206.

[18] "Under the Constitution of Pakistan a wholly different state of affairs prevails. Power is expressly given by Article 98 to the Superior Court to probe into the exercise of public power by executive authorities, howhighsoever, to determine whether they have acted with lawful authority. The judicial power is reduced to a nullity if laws are so worded or interpreted that the executive authorities may make what statutory rules they please thereunder and may use this freedom to make themselves the final Judges of their own 'satisfaction' for imposing restraints on the enjoyment of the fundamenal rights of citizens. Article 2 of the Constitution could be deprived of all its content through this process and the Courts would cease to be guardians of the nation's liberties." *Supra* note 16, at 392–93. This case was approved and followed by the Supreme Court in Abdul Baqi Baluch v. Government of Pakistan, Pakistan Legal Decisions [1968] S.C. 313, where the court made clear that a judicial review was not in the nature of an appeal against the decision of an executive authority or the substitution of the discretion of the court for that of officials, but rather to ensure that the authority had acted properly and not in an unlawful manner.

tionary acts of officials were subject to judicial review; that public power must be exercised within the bounds of the Constitution and not arbitrarily or perversely; that ascertainment of "reasonable grounds" for governmental action is a quasi-judicial function; and that the government, as any person, must subject its acts to review by the courts to ensure that they are lawful.

In Ceylon, on the other hand, where the Crown traditionally has not been liable in tort, a bill to make it responsible for delicts under common law and for failure to comply with statutory duties was introduced into each of the two Houses of Parliament by government ministers during the parliamentary sessions of 1967–1968 and 1968–1969, but on each occasion failed to be enacted into law.[19] Clearly, however, the Ceylonese Government regards this reform as necessary.

In Africa, both Tanzania[20] and Kenya[21] provide for government liability in contract as well as in tort. The nature of the relief available against the Tanzanian Government is almost identical, word for word, to provisions contained in the English statute.[22] Ghana, which for some 12 years following independence circumscribed the rights of persons to commence proceedings against the Government,[23] recently removed all barriers, thus making its practice consistent with that of most Commonwealth countries.[24] The previous requirement of consent by the Attorney General was removed for all causes of action arising on or after May 1, 1969; the only requirement remaining now is service upon the Attorney General of one month's written notice of intention to commence proceedings.[25] Moreover, action may be brought against the governments

---

[19] The Crown (Liability in Delict) Bill, 1967–68: The Senate, Bill 16, Jan. 9, 1968; The House of Representatives, Bill 52, Jan. 27, 1968; The Senate, Bill 3, July 26, 1968; The House of Representatives, Bill 20, Aug. 10, 1968.
[20] Government Proceedings Act, 1967 (Act No. 16 of 1967).
[21] Government Proceedings Ordinance, Cap. 40 of The Laws of Kenya, *as amended*, Act No. 21 of 1966. For limitations periods against the government see A.G. Kenya v. Hayter, [1958] E. Afr. L.R. 393, where it was held that the Crown could rely on the limitations in the Public Officers Protection Ordinance to the same extent that an individual officer could.
[22] *Supra* note 20, § 11. *See also* note 7 *supra.*
[23] State Proceedings Act, 1961 (Act 51).
[24] State Proceedings Act (Amendment) Decree, 1969 (N.L.C.D. 352).
[25] *Id.* § 1(2).

of the two eldest members of the Commonwealth, Canada and Australia, by citizens and aliens alike in both tort and contract.[26]

In the Commonwealth, the traditional technique for judicial review of activities by the executive or judicial branch alleged to conflict with principles of natural justice is through the use of the prerogative writs.[27] In England and in most Commonwealth countries it is by this means that executive acts and proceedings of inferior courts are examined in superior courts to assure observance of basic legal rights. The writs most often used are mandamus, prohibition, and certiorari. In England since 1938,[28] and in many other countries, the writs themselves no longer issue as such. Instead, orders are made having the same effect, thus avoiding some of the complicated technicalities previously encountered. The degree of control a superior court is able to exercise through these orders is limited, but it is sufficient to ensure that the inferior court or

---

[26] Canada: Crown Liability Act, CAN. REV. STAT. c. 30 (1952–1953). Australia: See §§ 75(iii) and 78 of the Constitution, and §§ 56 and 64 of the Judiciary Act, 1903–1966. See also Asiatic Steam Navigation Co. v. The Commonwealth, 96 Commw. L.R. 397 (1955).

[27] There are no constitutional requirements of due process in Great Britain. Instead, a not entirely dissimilar, and in some respects equally vague and elusive, concept is employed to ensure fair play. It is called "natural justice" and is normally used by courts of law, but not without difficulty, to evaluate the procedures of administrative tribunals. Said Lord Shaw: "In so far as the term 'natural justice' means that a result or process should be just, it is a harmless though it may be a high-sounding expression; in so far as it attempts to reflect the old jus naturale it is a confused and unwarranted transfer into the ethical sphere of a term employed for other distinctions; and, in so far as it is resorted to for other purposes, it is vacuous." Local Gov't Bd. v. Arlidge, [1915] A.C. 120, 138.

Whatever natural justice is, however, there is no doubt that it is deeply embedded in the British character and for that reason has been introduced repeatedly into the former colonies. A British Government Committee spoke of the term in this fashion in 1932: "Although 'natural justice' does not fall within those definite and well-recognized rules of law which English Courts of law enforce, we think it is beyond doubt that there are certain canons of judicial conduct to which all tribunals and persons who have to give judicial or quasi-judicial decisions ought to conform. The principles on which they rest are, we think, implicit in the rule of law. Their observance is demanded by our national sense of justice. . . ." COMMITTEE ON MINISTERS' POWERS, REPORT, CD. No. 4060, at 76 (1932).

[28] See Administration of Justice (Miscellaneous Provisions) Act of 1938, 1 & 2 Geo. 6, c. 63.

tribunal remains within its jurisdiction and does not disobey dictates of natural justice. Indeed, the two instances may be regarded as analogous.[29]

The prerogative writs have long been known to courts throughout the Commonwealth, being first introduced into India in 1733 when supreme courts were established in the Presidency towns of Calcutta, Bombay, and Madras. The territorial scope of the writ powers was limited at that time to the area of original jurisdiction of these courts, and personally limited to all servants of the East India Company. The jurisdiction of the High Court to issue prerogative writs later was extended throughout India by the Government of India Act, 1935.[30] Following partition in 1947, both India and Pakistan accorded their superior courts similar jurisdiction. These provisions are important because each country's constitution identifies certain fundamental rights which are protected in many instances through prerogative writs.[31] Moreover, in Pakistan it is clear that the remedial jurisdiction of the Supreme Court and of the High Courts to issue prerogative writs continues in certain instances, notwithstanding the abrogation of the Constitution on October 7, 1958, and the continuing state of emergency since that date.[32] This fact is remarkable evidence of the strength of Pakistani judicial institutions and the resiliency of the country's legal fabric.

The prerogative writs also have been continued in the courts of other newly independent Commonwealth countries. In Nigeria, the Federal Supreme Court has discussed the use of certiorari in the event inferior courts fail to observe principles of natural justice.[33]

---

[29] According to Lord Caldecote, C.J., in R. v. Wandsworth Justices, *ex parte* Read, [1942] 1 K.B. 281, 283.

[30] 26 Geo. 5 & 1 Edw. 8, c. 2.

[31] CONSTITUTION OF INDIA, pt. III, arts. 12–35. CONSTITUTION OF PAKISTAN, pt. II, c. i (*as amended*); pt. III, art. 21; pt. VII, art. 170.

[32] *See* the Laws (Continuance in Force) Order, dated Oct. 10, 1958, §§ 2(4–7). Recent Pakistani decisions dealing with this and similar problems are Mahboob Ali Malik v. Province of W. Pakistan, Pakistan Legal Decisions [1963] Lah. 575; Shaukat Ali v. Comm'r, Pakistan Legal Decisions [1963] Lah. 127; Muhammad Khan v. Additional Comm'r, Pakistan Legal Decisions [1964] Lah. 401; Muhammad Khan v. Border Allotment Comm'n, Pakistan Legal Decisions [1965] S.C. 623; Jamal Shah v. The Member Election Comm'n, Pakistan Legal Decisions [1966] S.C. 1.

[33] Queen v. Lieut. Governor of the E. Region; *Ex parte* Okafor Chiagbana, (1957) 2 Selected Judgments of the Fed. Supreme Court of Nigeria 46.

On another occasion the same court questioned whether, even where certiorari has been abrogated by statute, it might not still issue to quash an order on the grounds of manifest lack of jurisdiction in the tribunal or in the person who issued the order, or of manifest fraud by the party procuring it.[34] In Ghana, applications for prerogative writs are heard by the High Court.[35] The Court of Appeal of Ghana now has jurisdiction to entertain appeals from applications for prerogative writs refused by the Court, although this possibility has not always existed.[36]

In Tanzania, the High Court has been called upon to consider the now obsolescent "writ" and the "order" which has replaced it for certiorari, mandamus, and the other prerogative writs. The court stated that there was a historical difference between the two forms of remedy, the procedure by writ being ancient and that by order being modern, but that the distinction was not fundamental and involved little more than terminology. The court added that it will always look, unless precluded by law, to substance and reality rather than to form and phraseology.[37] The Supreme Court of Kenya has

---

[34] Babatunde v. Governor of the W. Region, (1960) 5 Selected Judgments of the Fed. Supreme Court of Nigeria 59.

[35] "The High Court shall have: (a) original jurisdiction in all matters": The Courts Decree, 1966, (N.L.C.D. 84) § 26; previously in force as § 29 of the Courts Act, 1960, (C.A.9). For mandamus generally in Ghana see Comptroller of Customs & Excise v. Akam, (1955) 1 W. Afr. L.R. 56 and Mould v. de Vine, [1962] 1 Ghana L.R. 533; for certiorari see Quansah v. Tagoe, (1956) 2 W. Afr. L.R. 90.

[36] Until 1960 the Court of Appeal, under its then ordinance (The Court of Appeal Ordinance, 1957) was without jurisdiction in this respect. On two occasions early in 1960 it had refused to hear such appeals, and on each occasion commented on its dissatisfaction with this limitation. "We cannot . . . amend the law any more than we exact it; this is entirely for the legislature, and we may hope it will be a matter to receive consideration." *In re* Okine, 1960 Ghana L.R. 84, 88 (van Lare, J.A.). "We repeat the hope expressed that provision in our law for a right of appeal in a case such as this will receive the consideration of the legislature." *In re* Amponsah, 1960 Ghana L.R. 140, 146 (Korsah, C.J.). The legislature was responsive and by The Courts Act, 1960 (C.A.9), gave to the Court of Appeal—then called the Supreme Court—the additional jurisdiction in Section 8(1)(c) over "appeals from any decision given by the High Court in any other matter whatsoever." Section 13 states: "Notwithstanding anything to the contrary in any other provision of this Act, the Supreme Court may entertain any appeal from any Court on any terms which it may think just." Jurisdiction in habeas corpus is now spelled out specifically in The Habeas Corpus Act, 1964 (Act 244) § 5.

[37] *Re* an Application by Fazal Kassam (Mills) Ltd., [1960] E. Afr. L.R. 1002.

cautioned, however, that the prerogative jurisdiction of the court cannot ordinarily be involved so long as a statutory remedy by way of appeal is available.[38]

The superior courts of Ceylon have jurisdiction to issue prerogative writs by virtue of the provisions of The Courts Ordinance,[39] and they enjoy wide powers to review executive orders affecting the liberties of individuals, including aliens.[40] Even where, as in Malaysia, local rules contain no special provisions for entertaining applications for prerogative writs, a source of authority often is available in English practice. "The procedure in applying for an order of certiorari is well settled in the United Kingdom. Unfortunately, no provisions exist in our Rules of the Supreme Court to entertain such an application. However, Order 1 Rule 2 . . . permits us to resort to the procedure adopted in the High Court of Justice in England."[41] Therefore, the basic principles underlying the prerogative writs are well known in Malaysia and have been the object of judicial scrutiny.[42] The Judicial Committee of the Privy Council recently dealt with two appeals involving the use of prerogative writs in the courts of the Commonwealth, one from Ceylon and the other from Hong Kong, further evidence of the ubiquitous nature of this effective remedy.[43]

In theory, problems of sovereign immunity and reciprocity generally should not arise in Latin America when an alien seeks to sue his host State. South of the Rio Grande, States are considered juridical persons with rights and obligations at private law. Hence,

---

[38] Re an Application by the Atty. Gen. of Tanganyika, [1958] E. Afr. L.R. 482. This application was for mandamus. For a discussion of the Kenya practice with respect to certiorari, see Farmers Bus Service v. The Transp. Licensing Appeal Tribunal, [1959] E. Afr. L.R. 779.

[39] Cap. 6, Legis. Enactments Ceylon, Vol. 1, § 45.

[40] See In re Bracegirdle, 39 New Law Rep. 193 (1937).

[41] Gnanasundram v. Public Serv. Comm'n, [1966] 1 MALAYAN L.J. 157, 157–58 (Raja Azlan Shah, J.). For a discussion of the procedure of applications for certiorari see Yegappan v. District Council Cent., Province Wellesley, [1964] MALAYAN L.J. 328.

[42] See Re Chiew Siew Khim, [1964] MALAYAN L.J. 414, referred to and followed in Re Ijot Binti Beliku, [1966] 1 MALAYAN L.J. 22.

[43] Bd. of Trustees of the Maradana Mosque v. Badiuddin Mahmud, [1967] 1 A.C. 13 (1966) (on appeal from the Supreme Court of Ceylon, where certiorari had been refused, judgment reversed); Re Chien Sing-Shou, [1967] 2 All E.R. 1228 (on appeal from the Supreme Court of Hong Kong, where certiorari had been refused, appeal dismissed).

a State can be summoned to account for its actions in open court when it infringes rights guaranteed both aliens and nationals by the Constitution, by private contracts, and by the doctrine of equal treatment. Nevertheless, the practical availability of remedies may be conditioned upon the extralegal factors discussed earlier, which may distort the climate of justice.

At least one country, Venezuela, has special legislation specifically enabling aliens to sue the Government. The *Ley de Extranjeros* states that aliens wishing to sue the State for damages, for expropriation, or for the seizure of goods by national employees or by the State in time of civil war or disturbance of peace may only do so pursuant to the provisions of that law.[44] No recourse to diplomatic remedies by domiciled or transient aliens will be permitted except after all appeals have been exhausted and a denial of justice "has been proved."[45] Actions must be brought either by lodging an administrative claim with the Ministry of Foreign Relations or by filing a complaint in the Supreme Court of Cassation, Venezuela's highest court.[46]

Other nations enable the foreigner to sue the State in the ordinary court system, so that suits by aliens frequently are entertained by the lower courts, often with favorable results. Even when the administration of Argentina's President Ilia in 1963 cancelled petroleum concession contracts executed by the predecessor Frondizi government, the oil companies, most of which were foreign, sought to obtain court orders restraining Yacimientos Petroliferos Fiscales, the government oil monopoly, from occupying the fields in question.[47] A January 13, 1966 decision by the Peruvian Supreme Court also should be noted. Until recently the sale of matches in Peru was a government monopoly. The Government imported matches from the Swedish Match Company, reselling them in boxes under a colorful trademark depicting a Peruvian llama which had been registered in Peru in the name of the Swedish Match Company since 1924. In 1954 the monopoly was abolished, and 9 years later

---

[44] LEY DE EXTRANJEROS, art. 55 (La Torre ed. 1968).

[45] Art. 56.

[46] Arts. 60 & 62.

[47] For an analysis of the background of the cancellation see Luce, *Argentina and the Hickenlooper Amendment*, 54 CALIF. L. REV. 2078 (1966).

a private firm in Lima entered into an agreement with the Swedish Match Company to import matches and sell them under the llama trademark. Legislators in Congress then alleged that the Swedish company was using the trademark improperly, since it had become State property through use by the Government monopoly for over 40 years. Accordingly, on September 30, 1964, the executive branch ordered the mark reregistered as state property. The Swedish company sued, receiving a favorable decision in first instance, losing in second instance, and then winning a final victory in the Supreme Court, which ordered the Government to reregister the trademark in the plaintiff's name.[48]

The constitutions of some States with especially long histories of revolution seek, like Guatemala, to put the world on notice that their responsibility is limited: "Neither Guatemalans nor aliens may claim indemnification from the State for damages caused by armed movements or civil disturbances."[49] No distinction is drawn between resident and transient aliens. In a similar vein, the Venezuelan Ley de Extranjeros does not permit aliens to sue the Government for damages caused by revolutionaries.[50] In addition, the Venezuelan Constitution states that in no case may nationals or foreigners claim indemnification from the Government except where the injury was caused by "legitimate authorities in the exercise of their public function."[51]

To protect private rights from abuse by the State or its functionaries, Latin Americans, fully aware of their turbulent political heritage, have devised several procedural safeguards which may be invoked by both aliens and nationals in the regular courts of justice. The effectiveness of these remedies may be inversely proportional to the strength of the regime in power, and, very often, related to the wealth, education, and influence of the person invoking them. Moreover, the declaration of a state of siege may prevent their invocation. Nevertheless, these procedures, which include the well-

---

[48] BOLETÍN INFORMATIVO DEL MINISTRO DE RELACIONES EXTERIORES No. 1443, Lima, Feb. 15, 1966.

[49] CONSTITUCIÓN DE LA REPÚBLICA DE GUATEMALA 1965, art. 148 (Ministerio de Gobernación 3d ed. 1965).

[50] *Supra* note 44, art. 59.

[51] CONSTITUCIÓN DE LA REPÚBLICA DE VENEZUELA 1961, art. 47 (La Torre ed. 1969).

known Mexican *amparo* and its variants, habeas corpus, the Brazilian *mandado de segurança,* and the action for unconstitutionality, do provide a minimal assurance that basic rights will be protected. The Mexican Hector Fix Zamudio has written that all Latin American Constitutions have guaranteed basic rights for some time, but it has become increasingly apparent that "the simple elevation of certain human rights to the level of constitutional precepts was not enough to guarantee their effectiveness, as the tragic and tormented history of our Latin American nations has repeatedly demonstrated."[52] Thus, it becomes necessary to examine the procedures by which the guarantees are "guaranteed."

The amparo relief developed in Mexico is available to nationals and aliens alike; it has proven an effective technique by which the constitutionality of legislative, executive, and judicial action can be tested.[53] It enjoins government actions relating to a wide range of topics by extending the habeas corpus concept, which in theory applies only to restrictions on personal movement, to all constitutional guarantees. However, it is available only in federal courts, since only they can declare statutes unconstitutional. Moreover, the action can be directed only against an act of public authority—be it legislative, administrative, or judicial—and not against private parties. Proof is required of direct personal injury, although this need not be financial. Due to historical reasons, until relatively recently amparo actions could be brought of right in the Supreme Court, which had no discretion similar to that of the United States Supreme Court respecting certiorari petitions to reject applications. The result was an immense backlog of cases until a system of "collegiate" circuit courts of appeal was created in 1951 to assist the Supreme Court in amparo decisions. In 1967 the jurisdiction of these courts was expanded, and provision made for creating additional courts. The decisions are final, and the case load is apportioned

---

[52] Zamudio, *La Protección Procesal de las Garantias Individuales en America Latina,* 9 REVISTA DE LA COMISIÓN INTERNACIONAL DE JURISTAS 69, 72 (Dec. 1968).

[53] *See* Camargo, *The Claim of "Amparo" in Mexico: Constitutional Protection of Human Rights,* 6 CALIF. WESTERN L. REV. 201 (1970). *See generally* H. CLAGETT, THE ADMINISTRATION OF JUSTICE IN LATIN AMERICA 133–39 (1952), and the discussion in Eder, *Judicial Review in Latin America,* 21 OHIO STATE L.J. 570, 599–604 (1960).

so that the Supreme Court reviews only the most important amparos, usually those involving serious constitutional problems.[54]

Amparo to protect civil rights, however, should be distinguished from an amparo action to review the constitutionality of statutes and the decisions of state courts and administrative agencies. If the matter at issue involves imprisonment or violation of basic civil rights, the restitution of which is of immediate importance, a much less complicated procedure may be utilized to obtain relief. A simple petition to the district court is theoretically sufficient. The petition should describe the act against which amparo is sought and the constitutional provisions deemed violated. There is no need even to commence an action or retain a lawyer. If the judge finds just cause, he may order the official responsible to cease and desist pending a hearing.[55] The procedure is supposed to be summary and rapid, although some Mexican attorneys complain that during the student rioting preceding the 1968 Olympic Games prisoners were transferred from one precinct house to another in order to prevent their relatives, attorneys, and the judges before whom amparo had been filed from knowing where they were and obtaining the habeas corpus type of relief provided by amparo.[56]

There are other limitiations on amparo, since in general it cannot enjoin the violation of government contracts or expropriations for

---

[54] Most amparo proceedings based on unconstitutionality of statutes seem to be suits attacking tax legislation as unfair and inequitable. Each person affected must bring his own suit, because a decision against unconstitutionality is not valid erga omnes. Procedure in these cases is much slower than were basic civil rights are threatened.

[55] See generally L. CABRERA, EL PODER JUDICIAL FEDERAL MEXICANO Y EL CONSTITUYENTE DE 1917 (1968).

[56] Interviews during 1969 in Mexico City. Also, through the Ley de Disolución Social, which forms part of the Mexican Penal Code, "subversives" may be jailed and imprisoned. Article 145 states: "A prison term of two to twelve years and a fine of from one thousand to ten thousand pesos [US $160 to US $800] shall be applied to any foreigner or Mexican who in speech or writing, or by any other means, carries on political propaganda among foreigners or Mexican nationals, spreading ideas, programs or forms of action of any foreign government which disturb the public order or affect the sovereignty of the Mexican State." The constitutionality of this law has been debated in Mexico, but its conflict with amparo principles and constitutional guarantees never has been satisfactorily resolved. See Stevens, Legality and Extra-Legality in Mexico, 12 J. INTER-AM. STUDIES AND WORLD AFFAIRS 62 (1970).

the public benefit. Thus, Mexican courts held that amparo did not lie against decrees nationalizing foreign oil properties because the community interest was involved.[57] Furthermore, decisions of unconstitutionality apply only to the case at bar, and precedent binding on lower courts is created only when the Supreme Court renders five identical amparo decisions on the same constitutional point.[58] Otherwise, Article 76 of the *Ley de Amparo* specifically provides that decisions will only affect the parties who have sought it, "without making a general declaration with respect to the law or act which motivated the action."[59] This provision is not surprising, since it reflects general Latin American reluctance to permit legislation by judicial decree, to them an impermissive intrusion of the judiciary into the legislative domain.

The amparo concept has proven readily exportable. It has been introduced into the legislation of almost all the other Latin American nations, although none except Honduras and, in theory at least, Nicaragua, has accorded it the breadth of application it enjoys in Mexico.[60] The Honduran Constitution, for instance, guarantees an individual's right of amparo "in order to make effective the exercise of all the guarantees which this Constitution establishes when he is unjustly prevented from enjoying them by laws or acts of any public authority, agent or official."[61] It also assures habeas corpus to prevent unlawful restraints on movement.[62] A 1936 law, however, unites, as does Mexico, these two types of relief under the rubric of amparo, establishing procedures to enforce both habeas corpus and amparo and authorizing the Supreme Court, through the amparo

---

[57] Eder, *supra* note 53, at 601–02.

[58] Nueva Ley de Amparo, arts. 192 & 193, *Diario Official*, Jan. 10, 1936, *as amended, Diario Official*, April 30, 1968.

[59] Art. 76.

[60] On the international level, the Mexican Delegation at the 1948 Bogotá Conference proposed a resolution which subsequently became Article 28 of the American Declaration of the Rights and Duties of Man: "Every person may resort to the courts to ensure respect for his legal rights. There should likewise be available to him a simple and brief procedure whereby the courts will protect him from acts of authority which, to his prejudice, violate any fundamental constitutional rights." Zamudio, *supra* note 52, at 104.

[61] *Supra* note 49, art. 67.

[62] Art. 68.

procedure, to declare laws unconstitutional.[63] The court may order the temporary suspension of the offending act or order until final decision.[64] Amparo is not available in purely civil actions, that is, when the parties are private persons, or to attack final judgments in criminal actions.[65] Moreover, the impact of a decision is, as in Mexico, limited to the parties, and it may not be considered of universal application or as nullifying the law in question.[66]

In some nations, liberty from unlawful detention is assured by separate incorporation of habeas corpus into constitutions and other legislation. Relief from unconstitutional laws, administrative action, and court decisions is available separately either by special court procedures or by truncated versions of amparo. The Costa Rican Constitution, for example, guarantees habeas corpus to anyone deprived of personal liberty, giving the Supreme Court exclusive jurisdiction over such cases.[67] The 1932 Costa Rican *Ley de Habeas Corpus,* designed to supplement the Constitution, indicates clearly its sole intent to prevent unlawful detention and illegal restrictions on freedom of movement.[68] The Constitution also guarantees access to amparo in such other courts as the law may provide "to maintain or establish the enjoyment of *other* rights conferred by this Constitution."[69] The 1950 *Ley de Amparo* again supplements the Constitution by providing the procedural machinery for amparo, but it excludes from amparo legislative acts and court decisions, suggesting that it may only be invoked against administrative decisions.[70] The constitutionality of legislation and lower court decisions may be tested only in the Supreme Court pursuant to the Code of Civil

---

[63] Ley de Amparo, arts. 1 & 5, *as amended, La Gaceta,* Oct. 30, 1967.

[64] Art. 26.

[65] Art. 36.

[66] Arts. 41 & 47.

[67] CONSTITUTION OF THE REPUBLIC OF COSTA RICA 1949, art. 48 (Pan American Union ed. 1965).

[68] Ley No. 35, Nov. 24, 1932, art. 1, LEYES USUALES 2 (A. Vicenzi ed. 1966).

[69] *Supra* note 67, art. 48 (emphasis added).

[70] Ley No. 1161, June 2, 1950, arts. 1 & 3, LEYES USUALES 5 (A. Vicenzi ed. 1966). If the defendant is the President, his ministers, a governor, or the chief of the Guardia Civil, the action must be brought before the Supreme Court en banc. In all other cases the local criminal court of the district where the violation transpired has competence. Art. 6.

Procedure and not through amparo.[71] As in Mexico and Honduras, a decision of unconstitutionality in Costa Rica affects only the parties, the Constitution specifically providing that "a law does not become abrogated or repealed except by a subsequent law, and disuse, custom, or contrary practice cannot be claimed against its enforcement."[72]

Guatemalan legislation, like Costa Rican, distinguishes between habeas corpus and amparo, restricting the first to restraints on movement, but it differs in that Article 260 of the Constitution establishes a *Tribunal Extraordinario de Amparo* to hear appeals against the Supreme Court, Congress, and the Council of State for "acts and resolutions not purely legislative." While the Constitution allows amparo to attack a law for unconstitutionality in ordinary courts, it also provides a special Court of Constitutionality of 12 members, composed of the President and 4 Justices of the Supreme Court and 7 judges from lower appellate courts.[73] A "concrete case" is needed for an appeal to lie, but unlike Costa Rica, Honduras, and Mexico, a decision against constitutionality will have a general effect erga omnes; a successful attack on constitutionality through amparo in the lower courts apparently will bind only the parties.[74] The Guatemalan system of a special tribunal for constitutional appeals is unusual in Latin America, and resembles more the so-called "Austrian" or "European" system which deprives ordinary courts of jurisdiction in such matters.[75]

The Guatemalan system also contrasts with the so-called "popular action" provided in the Colombian Constitution, by which private citizens may challenge the constitutionality of laws and decrees before the Supreme Court without showing either an actual controversy or imminent damage to constitutional rights.[76] Moreover, it "permits challenge of statutes dealing with purely administrative matters not likely to become the subject of private litigation and thus integrates

---

[71] Art. 962.

[72] *Supra* note 67, art. 129.

[73] *Supra* note 49, art. 262.

[74] Arts. 80, 246, & 265.

[75] The norm in Latin America is to empower the ordinary court system to rule on the constitutionality of legislation and administrative actions.

[76] CONSTITUTION OF THE REPUBLIC OF COLOMBIA 1886, art. 214 (Pan American Union ed. 1962).

the duty of the Supreme Court to act as guardian of the whole Constitution and not merely of the Bill of Rights."[77] It has been utilized to hold confiscation of enemy alien property unconstitutional,[78] and to invalidate legislation expropriating private property for public use without compensation, interfering with freedom of speech, and granting special privileges conflicting with the principle of equality before the law.[79] Unlike in Mexico, a decision against constitutionality in Colombia renders the law null and void, not only as to the parties but also in general. Such a decision, however, is not retroactive.

The amparo concept, following its introduction in 1921 in the Constitution of the Province of Santa Fé, was adopted rapidly by the constitutions and supplementary legislation of most Argentine provinces, many of which also have separate provisions regarding habeas corpus.[80] On the national or federal level, the right of amparo is not guaranteed by the Argentine Constitution but by judicial precedent. In 1957 the Supreme Court, in a case involving the arbitrary closing of a newspaper, departed from a prior trend of decision to uphold rights hitherto not protected by habeas corpus. In finding an infringement of constitutional freedoms of the press and of industry, the Court stated:

> In consideration of the character and hierarchy of the principle
> of the Fundamental Charter relating to individual rights, this Supreme Court, with its present composition and on the first opportunity to make a pronouncement on the point, departs from the
> doctrine traditionally declared by the court to the extent that it
> relegated to the course of ordinary procedures, administrative or
> judicial, the protection of rights not strictly comprised in habeas

---

[77] Eder, *supra* note 53, at 592.

[78] Eder, *Confiscation of Enemy Alien Property Held Unconstitutional by Colombian Supreme Court,* 54 Am. J. Int'l L. 159 (1960).

[79] Grant, *Judicial Control of the Constitutionality of Statutes and Administrative Legislation in Colombia: Nature and Evolution of the Present System,* 23 S. Cal. L. Rev. 484 (1950).

[80] Zamudio, *supra* note 52, at 91. At least two provinces, however—Chaco and Nequen—have only habeas corpus provisions in their constitutions. These provisions, nevertheless, are sufficiently broad to provide judicial relief for violations of other constitutional guarantees. This procedure contrasts with the practice in other Latin American nations of protecting both freedom of movement and all other constitutional guarantees by amparo.

corpus. . . . The constitutional precepts as well as the institutional experience of the country jointly demand the full enjoyment and exercise of individual guarantees for the effective vigor of the State of Law and impose the duty on the Judges to assure them. . . . The record is returned to the court below to serve notice on the police authorities to desist from the restrictions, etc.[81]

Since 1957 the Argentine Supreme Court has granted amparo relief on several other occasions. In 1966, Law No. 16986 consolidated decisions in this area. Issued under the military government of General Carlos Ongania, the law has been criticized as overly restrictive because it not only denies amparo against court decisions, but also against measures taken pursuant to the Law of National Defense which, to protect the nation from subversion, authorizes suspension of constitutional guarantees.[82] The Law states explicitly that amparo will not be allowed when "judicial intervention will directly or indirectly compromise the regular performance, with dignity and efficiency, of a public service, or with the carrying out of the activities of the State."[83]

In Argentina, relief against unconstitutional legislation is available not through amparo or habeas corpus, but through the *recurso extraordinario* brought before the Supreme Court. This device is somewhat analogous to the former writ of error in the United States. As in the United States and Guatemala, but unlike Colombia, a concrete case or controversy is required; that is, a party can only attack a law's constitutionality in a federal or provincial court if his

---

[81] *Discussed and quoted in* Eder, *Habeas Corpus Disembodied: The Latin American Experience,* in XXTH CENTURY COMPARATIVE AND CONFLICTS LAW 463, 471–72 (K. Nadelmann, A. von Mehren & J. Hazard eds. 1961). The Argentine Federal Constitution does not specifically grant the right of habeas corpus either, although some writers believe it is implicit in Article 18. The 1863 Judiciary Law, however, does provide the equivalent of habeas corpus, although the term itself is not employed. Provincial constitutions provide specifically for habeas corpus, as does the Federal Code of Civil Procedure, but in many provincial jurisdictions it is used interchangeably, and confusingly, with the term *amparo de libertad* and its scope extended beyond mere protection from unlawful detention.

[82] *Discussed in* Zamudio, *supra* note 52, at 94.

[83] *Discussed and quoted in* Vescovi, *La Protección Procesal de las Garantias Individuales en America Latina,* 1967 REVISTA IBEROAMERICANA DE DERECHO PROCESAL 471, 480 (No. 3).

economic interests or legal rights have been violated by enforcement of the measure in question. The writ lies against court decisions, but not against administrative acts except where an administrative official was exercising judicial or quasi-judicial function. Perhaps originally conceived as a defense against unconstitutional provincial legislation, in 1887 the recurso was invoked to declare an act of the Federal Congress unconstitutional—a prerogative the Supreme Court has exercised ever since.[84]

Like Costa Rica, Guatemala, and Argentina, in Venezuela habeas corpus and amparo constitute two distinct remedies, devised, respectively, to prevent unlawful detention and to assure freedom of other constitutional guarantees from arbitrary governmental action. Both remedies are available to resident aliens and nationals, since Article 49 of the Constitution states that "the Courts will give relief (*ampararán*) to all inhabitants of the Republic in the enjoyment and exercise of the rights and guarantees established by the Constitution in accord with the law." The same article concludes by stating that procedures must be brief and summary, and that the court has the power "to restore immediately" the status quo ante.[85] No specific procedure has yet been established in supplementary legislation by which amparo may be requested. However, citing Article 50 of the Constitution, which warns that the absence of laws regulating the exercise of guaranteed rights may not prevent the exercise of the same, Venezuelan courts have utilized the habeas corpus procedure set forth in the Constitution to grant amparo against administrative actions.[86] In both types of proceedings, complainants must petition the Criminal Judge of First Instance of the place where the offending act was committed, or of the place where the petitioner is to be found. This judge then must seek confirmation of his decision by the appropriate Superior Appellate Court, which must affirm or reject the lower court's decision within 72 hours.[87]

The Venezuelan Constitution enumerates among the powers of the

---

[84] *Discussed in* Eder, *supra* note 53, at 575–78, and generally in J. VANOSSI, ASPECTOS DEL RECURSO EXTRAORDINARIO DE INCONSTITUCIONALIDAD (1966).

[85] *Supra* note 51, art. 49.

[86] R. ZERPA, RECURSO DE AMPARO CONTRA ARBITRARIEDAD DE FUNCIONARIO PÚBLICO 4 (1968).

[87] *Supra* note 51, Transitory Provisions, § 5.

Supreme Court that of declaring the total or partial nullity of both federal and state laws, of municipal ordinances, and of acts of other deliberative bodies which conflict with the Constitution.[88] The Court must hear petitions on constitutionality en banc, although it can also refer the matter to a special tribunal composed of the President of the Court and various other justices.[89] A declaration of unconstitutionality, as in Colombia, extends beyond the parties and, unlike Mexico, nullifies the measure in question erga omnes.

Peru and Brazil depart somewhat from patterns examined in other Latin American nations. The Peruvian Constitution seeks to protect all guarantees by habeas corpus, rather than amparo, including freedom from arrest without a warrant, the right of public assembly, and protection from unauthorized searches and seizures.[90] However, although the Constitution in theory authorizes a "popular action" to test the constitutionality of legislation,[91] the Supreme Court in 1947 and 1948 rejected three petitions attacking executive decrees, holding that procedural legislation to implement the "popular action" had not been passed by Congress.[92] The President of the Supreme Court stated in an address that "[i]t is for the Congress to provide the proper solution. Its attributes and wisdom will determine whether it will grant to the Judicial Power, and in what amplitude, a function of such significance and at the same time will enact the procedural rules for its exercise."[93] Finally, in 1963, Congress passed the *Ley Orgánica de Poder Judicial* which, while it does not specifically give courts the power to declare laws null and void or unconstitutional erga omnes, states that in case of a conflict between a law and the Constitution the latter should prevail. Also, "the judges and Courts shall not apply the decrees and regulations of the

---

[88] Art. 215.

[89] Art. 216. No concrete case or controversy is required. Moreover, a private citizen may challenge the constitutionality of an Act of Congress, as occurred in 1969 when an action was brought seeking judicial review of the law establishing a new method for the selection of judges in Venezuela.

[90] CONSTITUTION OF THE REPUBLIC OF PERU 1933, art. 69 (Pan American Union ed. 1967).

[91] Art. 133.

[92] Eder, *supra* note 53, at 606.

[93] *Quoted id.* at 607.

Executive Power or of any other authority which are contrary to the Constitution."[94]

Brazil was the first Latin American nation to adopt habeas corpus. The 1830 Penal Code made it a criminal offense for judges to refuse or delay issuance of the writ, which in 1871 was specifically extended to aliens.[95] While initially designed to prevent restraints upon movement, the writ eventually was extended to threats to personal freedoms even where no detention had occurred. Thus, the first Brazilian Republican constitution in 1891 provided that habeas corpus should be "given whenever an individual suffers or is in imminent danger of suffering violence or coercion by reason of illegality or abuse of power."[96] Since illegality was considered to include unconstitutionality, the writ was expanded to assure judicial review of legislative and executive acts.

In 1926 a Constitutional amendment limited habeas corpus to its original purpose—protection against unjustifiable restrictions on freedom of movement.[97] In order to fill the gap thus created, the 1934 Brazilian Constitution incorporated the mandado de segurança, or Writ of Security, to prevent abuse of rights other than freedom of movement. The 1967 Constitution preserves the writ: "A writ of security shall be granted to protect a clear and certain right of an individual not protected by habeas corpus, regardless of what authority may be responsible for the illegality or abuse of power."[98] Like the Mexican amparo, the writ of security is a broad concept which has been expanded as the need arose. Moreover, it empowers courts to enjoin administrative actions which would impair any of the constitutional rights except those protected by habeas corpus. Although opinions differ, the writ also may be used to attack the

---

[94] Ley Orgánica de Poder Judicial del Perú, art. 8; Decreto Ley No. 14605 de 25 de Julio de 1963; *El Peruano;* July 26, 1963, *as amended,* Aug. 19, 1963. It is discussed in Zamudio, *La Protección Procesal de las Garantias Individuales en America Latina,* 1967 REVISTA IBEROAMERICANA DE DERECHO PROCESAL 393, 431–32 (No. 3).

[95] Eder, *supra* note 81, at 465–67.

[96] *Id.* at 467.

[97] Eder, *supra* note 53, at 581.

[98] CONSTITUTION OF BRAZIL 1967, art. 150(21) (Pan American Union ed. 1967).

constitutionality of legislation provided injury can be shown. It cannot be invoked, however, to test constitutionality in the abstract, nor will it lie against judicial decisions except where no procedural remedy is available to compel suspension of the offending decision, without which irreparable damage would result. As with the Mexican amparo, but unlike in Argentina, the writ never lies against private parties unless they exercise powers delegated by the government.[99] A commonly invoked procedure, its great value lies in preventing government action before it occurs, thus avoiding the necessity of subsequent recourse to administrative or judicial claim procedures to recover damages arising from the illegal action. The writ must be filed in the Supreme Court when directed against the President of the Republic, and in the Federal Court of Appeals when cabinet ministers are its target. Since it is considered a "summary action," it is, in theory at least, adjudicated expeditiously.[100] Unfortunately, court congestion occasions delays which may impair its effectiveness.[101]

Obviously, rights to amparo, habeas corpus, and the mandado de segurança may be seriously infringed—as indeed are the rights which these writs are designed to protect—wherever the judiciary may be intimidated by the executive branch, or where general constitutional guarantees have been suspended. Experience indicates, however, that except in the genuinely revolutionary situations such as arose in Cuba, aliens from wealthier, more powerful nations are more likely to fare better than nationals. Even if aggressive self-help is no longer a viable policy, the memory of it persists. Moreover, the desire to obtain economic aid and foreign investment, as seems evident after the recent Bolivian coup with its initial anti-*Yanqui* overtones, eventually may enable cooler heads to prevail in the councils of government.[102]

[99] *Discussed in* Clagett, *supra* note 53, at 141–42; Eder, *supra* note 53, at 582–84; Eder, *supra* note 81, at 468–69.

[100] *But see* Eder, *supra* note 53, at 584.

[101] In the Federal District between 1950 and 1958 approximately 22,000 mandados were filed as against a total of 9,942 other types of actions brought against the government. H. P. DE VRIES & J. RODRIGUEZ-NOVAS, THE LAW OF THE AMERICAS 196 (1965).

[102] In addition to ordinary courts, some Latin American nations, such as Colombia, Costa Rica, and Guatemala, have special administrative courts independent of the judicial power, the function of which is to adjudicate com-

In contrast to Latin America, in the United States the theoretical capacity of nationals and aliens to sue both Federal and state governments has been hindered by the concept of sovereign immunity. Consequently, rights to sue the government are accorded by special statute, rather than by general procedural legislation. Thus, in 1797 the Federal government agreed to submit, in suits against citizens, to all counterclaims that defendants might present up to the amount of the government's claim.[103] Establishment of the Court of Claims in 1855 permitted citizens to sue the government directly in contract,[104] while the passage in 1946 of the Federal Tort Claims Act permitted suit against the Federal government in tort.[105] These Acts permit suits by aliens.

If the plaintiff is an alien, however, he must show in the Court of Claims that a United States citizen would be entitled to sue the government in the courts of the alien's country. "Citizens or subjects of any foreign government which accords to citizens of the United States the right to prosecute claims against their government in its courts may sue the United States in the Court of Claims if the subject matter of the suit is otherwise within such court's jurisdiction."[106] A similar rule governs in personam libels brought in admiralty for salvage and for damage caused by public vessels: "No suit may be brought . . . by a national of any foreign government unless it shall appear to the satisfaction of the court in which suit is brought that said government, under similar circumstances, allows nationals of the United States to sue in its courts."[107] The former statute has been interpreted liberally, however, and it is not necessary to show that a right to sue exists abroad: it is sufficient to show

---

plaints against the application of administrative law. The type of litigation and procedure is generally known as "lo contencioso—administrativo." In Argentina, Brazil, Peru, Venezuela, and Honduras, however, these complaints are handled in the ordinary courts, often through the *amparo, mandado de segurança,* or *recurso da inconstitucionalidad.* The special administrative courts in the other nations have their own jurisdiction and procedure to which aliens have equal access with nationals; both must first exhaust administrative remedies.

[103] Act of March 3, 1797, 1 Stat. 514–15.

[104] 10 Stat. 612 (1855), *as amended,* 28 U.S.C. § 1491 (1964).

[105] 60 Stat. 842 (1946), *as amended,* 28 U.S.C. § 2671 (Supp. V, 1965–1969).

[106] 62 Stat. 976 (1948), *as amended,* 28 U.S.C. § 2502(a) (Supp. V, 1965–1969).

[107] 43 Stat. 1113 (1925), 46 U.S.C. § 785 (1964).

that citizens of the alien's government are not permitted greater rights on the particular kind of claim than would be allowed United States citizens in those courts.[108] The latter statute apparently has been interpreted more restrictively.[109]

Federal courts also have construed bilateral treaties giving nationals of each contracting party access to the courts of the other (though not necessarily in suits against each other's governments) as implying that reciprocity exists.[110] The Court of Claims has held a reciprocity limitation inapplicable, moreover, when friendly aliens sue under the Fifth Amendment for "just compensation" for the taking of property.[111] Since the 1948 Judicial Code revisions, proof of foreign law under the statute, and hence proof of reciprocity where required by statute, has been deemed a question of fact to be pled and proven by the litigant, but Federal courts may take judicial notice of foreign laws on their own motion if they are matters of common knowledge.[112] With the adoption in 1966 of Federal Rule 44.1, proof of foreign law has been made considerably easier.[113]

Of course, both aliens and nationals in the United States may challenge the constitutionality of state or Federal legislation or of

---

[108] *See, e.g.*, Marcos v. United States, 102 F. Supp. 547, 551 (Ct. Cl. 1952).

[109] "Libellants' right to sue thus depends on whether the United States court is satisfied that the Greek courts would entertain an action by a United States national for salvage services to a vessel of the Royal Hellenic Navy." Vernicos Shipping Co. v. United States, 349 F.2d 465, 467 (2d Cir. 1965).

[110] Zalcmanis v. United States, 173 F. Supp. 355, 146 Ct. Cl. 254 (1959), *cert. denied*, 362 U.S. 917 (1960). The Latvian–United States Treaty of 1928 was found sufficient by its terms to satisfy the reciprocity requirement as long as it remained in force by virtue of United States failure to recognize Soviet occupation of Latvia. For a general discussion of access-to-courts provisions in such bilateral treaties, see Wilson, *Access-to-Courts Provisions in United States Commercial Treaties*, 47 AM. J. INT'L L. 20 (1953).

[111] Russian Volunteer Fleet v. United States, 282 U.S. 481, 491–92 (1931).

[112] 2B W. BARRON & A. HOLTZOFF, FEDERAL PRACTICE AND PROCEDURE § 963, at 225–26 (1961). Furthermore, since 1959 proof of foreign law and reciprocity has been somewhat less burdensome due to a Department of State circular separating into different categories States which permit suit by United States citizens and States which do not. 8 M. WHITEMAN, DIGEST OF INTERNATIONAL LAW 411–13 (1967).

[113] FED. R. CIV. P. 44.1. *See generally* Miller, *Federal Rule 44.1 and the "Fact" Approach to Determining Foreign Law: Death Knell for a Die-Hard Doctrine*, 65 MICH. L. REV. 613 (1967).

administrative action depriving them of guarantees afforded by the Constitution and its amendments. However, they must have standing to sue and a genuine "case or controversy" must exist. Courts may not, as in Austria, France, and Guatemala, render constitutional or advisory decisions in the abstract. A Supreme Court decision on the constitutionality of a particular law or action binds all state and lower Federal courts, and the law or act in question, or the particular portion thereof declared unconstitutional, has no further practical force or effect. The remedy of habeas corpus is available in all state and Federal courts to aliens and nationals alike.[114]

The protection of individuals against arbitrary governmental action has quite different procedural aspects in continental Europe than in common law nations. Despite common historical and legal origins, there also are substantial dissimilarities with procedures prevailing in Latin American countries. This peculiar European development seems due to French historical experience, since French public law furnished a model more or less closely copied in other countries.

In pre-revolutionary France, powerful appellate tribunals, *Parlements,* staffed with quasi-hereditary judges, exercised far-reaching powers. Established in Paris and several other important cities, they frequently attempted to oversee the administration of the province in which they were sitting, dealing with problems ranging from food shortages to press censorship, as well as what one today would call police brutality. In addition, they sometimes enacted new rules of substantive law through *arrêts de règlement.* Furthermore, they asserted the right to prevent registration of new royal legislation in the clerks' offices of their courts—according to French theory a precondition for the validity of legislation—if they considered such legislation unwise or conflicting with traditional legal principles. In this way they exercised a type of constitutional review long before *Marbury v. Madison*[115] established the principle in the United States. These activities, however, often hindered needed reforms. Consequently, the revolutionary legislators who created a new French

---

[114] Nishimura Ekiu v. United States, 142 U.S. 651 (1891).
[115] 5 U.S. (1 Cranch) 137 (1803).

judicial structure in 1790 provided that the courts in no way could interfere with executive (administrative) or legislative functions.[116] No French court even today may review the constitutionality of legislation, nor, with minor exceptions, are regular courts empowered to review administrative acts. While at various periods since 1790 special bodies have been created to review the constitutionality of legislation, their roles were usually insignificant. The present French Constitution, enacted in 1958, provides a Constitutional Council with certain review powers. At the request of high government officials it may, and sometimes must, review the constitutionality of legislation before promulgation by the President of the Republic. A statute declared unconstitutional may not be promulgated and hence never comes into effect.[117] However, a duly promulgated statute cannot be subjected to the scrutiny of the Constitutional Council, nor can private individuals obtain standing to attack it.

The review of administrative action presented a graver problem. In the course of time it fell to a special section of the Council of State, a body formally within the executive branch and hence not affected by the legislative prohibition against judicial interference in executive matters, to review administrative acts. In this way the Council of State, while maintaining its former role as legal adviser to the executive, became in fact, though not in theory, a court for reviewing administrative action.[118] Its role in counteracting arbitrary action has been most significant, and it frequently has imposed standards analogous to those of "natural justice" or "due process" on French administrative agencies.[119] The Council of State, however,

---

[116] See, e.g., J. BRISSAUD, A HISTORY OF FRENCH PUBLIC LAW 442, 445–51, 563 (1915). The law of July 16–24, 1790, which prohibits judges from interfering in any way with the legislature or executive function and from summoning administrative officials before them, is reprinted in current editions of collections of French statutes relating to public law. See CODE ADMINISTRATIF at 212 (9th ed. Petits Codes Dalloz 1966).

[117] CONSTITUTION DE LA RÉPUBLIQUE FRANCAISE, arts. 56–63. See generally Engel, Judicial Review and Political Preview of Legislation in Post-War France, 6 INTER-AM. L. REV. 53 (1964); Waline, The Constitutional Council of the French Republic, 12 AM. J. COMP. L. 483 (1963).

[118] See, e.g., M. WALINE, DROIT ADMINISTRATIF 28–33 (9th ed. 1963). See also B. SCHWARTZ, FRENCH ADMINISTRATIVE LAW AND THE COMMON-LAW WORLD (1954); L. BROWN & J. GARNER, FRENCH ADMINISTRATIVE LAW (1967).

[119] M. WALINE, supra note 118, at 465–68. The basis of these rules sometimes must be sought more in concepts of natural justice than in precise constitutional

never has asserted a right to review the constitutionality of legislation. When faced with a duly promulgated statute, it must abide by it. Nevertheless, the Council is not precluded from investigating whether subordinate legislation, such as regulations issued by the executive, is in conformity with law and, indeed, has done so quite frequently.[120] After the end of World War II, the Council's case load became so crushing that it was necessary to transfer most of its review power to regional administrative tribunals. The Council is now primarily an appellate body for the regional administrative tribunals, although it retains some original jurisdiction.[121]

Generally, all French administrative acts are reviewable by the administrative tribunals or the Council of State, except for cases involving matters of high executive policy or *actes de gouvernement*.[122] However, a statute may specifically exclude review, although such exclusion will not lightly be inferred. The bases on which review of administrative action may be demanded are quite technical. In substance, review is possible if the applicant alleges either a lack of jurisdiction by the administrative body, illegality of a substantive or procedural nature, or the exercise of administrative powers for improper purposes.[123] The review procedure itself is largely written and fairly flexible, and no special procedural hurdles prevent aliens from seeking relief.[124] Nevertheless, as noted earlier,

---

or statutory provision. For practical examples *see, e.g.,* Téry, June 20, 1913, [1913] Rec. Cons. d'Et. 736, [1920] S. Jur. III. 13 (disciplinary measure against teacher requires granting him due hearing); Barel, May 28, 1954, [1954] D. Jur. 594, [1954] S. Jur. III. 97 (Conseil d'Etat) (executive branch may not exclude otherwise qualified candidate from training school for higher civil servants merely because of his political views).

[120] *Cf.* Syndicat Général des Ingénieurs Conseils, June 26, 1959, [1959] D. Jur. 541, [1959] S. Jur. I. 202 (Conseil d'Etat).

[121] The administrative tribunals and their predecessor bodies go back to the time of the French Revolution, but until 1953 their jurisdiction was relatively limited. B. SCHWARTZ, *supra* note 118, at 45–50; Decree No. 53–934 of Sept. 30, 1953, [1953] J.O. 8593, [1953] D.L. 376.

[122] M. WALINE, *supra* note 118, at 216–25. The *acte de gouvernement* exception applies particularly, but not exclusively, to cases involving French foreign relations. *Cf.* Prince Napoleon, Feb. 19, 1875, [1875] Rec. Con. d'Et. 155, [1875] D.P. III. 18; Radiodiffusion Francaise, [1950] S. Jur. III. 73, [1950] Sem. Jur. II. 5542 (Tribunal des Conflits).

[123] M. WALINE, *supra* note 118, at 449–88.

[124] The standard text is J. AUBY & R. DRAGO, TRAITE DE CONTENTIEUX ADMINISTRATIF (1962).

rules of substantive administrative law may limit or exclude judicial review in certain matters affecting aliens, such as expulsion, residence permits, and related problems.[125] A wider availability of the protection available through the Council of State and its subordinate tribunals therefore would seem desirable.

French law has not accepted the traditional Anglo-American doctrine of governmental immunity against suit for money damages. Nevertheless, as a general rule suits against local or the national government cannot be brought in ordinary courts; they must be brought in the Council of State or administrative tribunals. Governmental units will be liable for acts of their servants if they are in some way service-connected.[126] In elaborating through case law the principles of governmental liability, the Council of State has not always followed rules of private law. Sometimes it has been a trailblazer for developments in private law, as in the creation of rules of absolute tort liability,[127] other times it has been somewhat more restrictive than private law, as in the case of nonpecuniary losses in torts.[128] The rule that damage claims against the French government may not be pursued before the ordinary courts is statutory and hence subject to modification by statute and, indeed, by case law. For example, since 1957, all automobile accident claims must be brought before regular courts, which also will hear certain claims relating to indirect taxes, claims based on blatantly illegal governmental acts, such as arbitrary arrests or destruction of property, and claims by students for injuries in public schools.[129] No special restrictions, except for security for costs, seem to prevent aliens in France from asserting their right to damages against the government.

---

[125] As to the need to post security for costs before the administrative tribunals but not before the Council of State, see text at notes 143–154 of Chapter V.

[126] The ordinary courts will not be competent if a "public service" function (rather than a purely proprietary one) is involved. See generally M. WALINE, supra note 118, at 793–813; Blanco, Feb. 8, 1873, [1873] D.P. III. 17, [1873] S. Jur. III. 53 (Tribunal des Conflits); Soc. "Le Béton," Oct. 19, 1956, [1956] D. Jur. 681, [1957] Sem. Jur. II. 9765 (Conseil d'Etat).

[127] See, e.g., Regnault-Desroziers, March 28, 1919, [1920] D.P. III. 1, [1918–1919] S. Jur. III. 25 (Conseil d'Etat).

[128] But see Ministre des Travaux Publics v. Consorts Letisserand, Nov. 24, 1961, [1962] D. Jur. 34, [1962] S. Jur. I. 82 (Conseil d'Etat) (damages [dommage moral] awarded to father for loss of his married son).

[129] M. WALINE, supra note 118, at 808–17.

The solutions found in France for the protection of individuals against illegal or arbitrary governmental action were widely imitated, since they apparently provided adequate protection to individuals without subjecting the executive to undue interference from the judiciary. The absence of judicial review of the constitutionality of statutes was not a very substantial problem in the case of France, since in the prevailing view the main document embodying the catalogue of French civil liberties, the Declaration of the Rights of Man and of the Citizen of 1789—which is incorporated into the Preamble of the present French Constitution—is a guideline for State policy, not an instrument with direct and immediate legal consequences, particularly in the face of a duly promulgated statute.[130] Legislation in other countries nevertheless manifested a greater interest in protecting individuals against encroachment of constitutional rights through a more expansive judicial review.

A solution which achieves this result without sacrificing the principle that regular courts should not interfere with executive or legislative functions was incorporated in the Austrian Constitution of 1920/1929, and is known as the "Austrian System."[131] The protection of individuals against unlawful or unconstitutional governmental action is confided to the Constitutional Court and the

---

[130] The *Conseil d'Etat* has utilized the Declaration of the Rights of Man and other materials contained in the Preamble to the French Constitution to elaborate basic principles of proper administrative action which it has enforced where there was no statute directly in point, despite the fact that such principles are not exclusively based on the Preamble. *See* note 119 *supra*. It does not apply such principles, however, where a statute specifically provides otherwise. M. Long, P. Weil & G. Braibant, Les Grand Arrêts de la Jurisprudence Administrative 470–71 (4th rev. ed. 1965) (with extensive citations concerning this problem). The draftsmen of the early Latin American constitutions and codes were influenced by the French example, especially in their reluctance to allow "judge-made" law or precedent to supersede or to have equal status with legislative acts. Nevertheless, post-1850 Latin American constitutions and codes, influenced by United States practice, deviated from the French example sufficiently to incorporate provisions for judicial review.

[131] For a theoretical discussion contrasting the "Austrian System" with the "American System" which enables all courts to rule on the constitutionality of legislation, *see* M. Cappelletti, Il Controllo Giudiziaro di Costituzionalitá delle Leggi nel Diritto Comparato 49 (1968). *See also* Cappelletti & Adams, *Judicial Review of Legislation: European Antecedents and Adaptations,* 79 Harv. L. Rev. 1207 (1966). The Austrian System has been copied in Guatemala. *See* text accompanying notes 73–75 *supra*.

Administrative Court, both of which exist outside the ordinary civil and criminal court hierarchies, culminating in the Austrian Supreme Court. Requests for review of administrative decisions must be addressed to the Administrative Court, and review is possible only after exhaustion of administrative remedies.[132] Reciprocity rules governing legal aid in civil cases apply,[133] but otherwise apparently no procedural obstacles restrict aliens' rights to obtain review of administrative decisions.

When an administrative decision directly affects a person's constitutional rights, review must be sought—after the exhaustion of all administrative remedies—within the wider jurisdiction of the Constitutional, not the Administrative, Court.[134] At the request of the Austrian Federal Government, the Court may rule in a declaratory judgment procedure on the constitutionality of provincial statutes; at the request of a provincial government, it may assess the constitutionality of a Federal statute. Regular Austrian courts may not rule on the constitutionality of statutes, nor even on the legality of administrative regulations. However, any Austrian court which doubts the validity of an administrative regulation involved in a pending case may stay proceedings and request a ruling from the Constitutional Court. Lower courts may not do so when the constitutionality of a statute is at issue; but, if doubts as to a statute's constitutionality arise in the American Supreme or Administrative Court, they may stay proceedings and request a guiding decision from the Constitutional Court.[135] Nevertheless, the parties cannot

---

[132] The basic statute governing the Administrative Court is the Law of Nov. 17, 1965 concerning the Administrative Court, [1965] BGBl. 289 (Aus.). As to reviewability of administrative decisions see L. ADAMOVICH, HANDBUCH DES OESTERREICHISCHEN VERWALTUNGSRECHTS 294 (5th ed. 1957); Baeck, *Postwar Judicial Review of Legislative Acts: Austria*, 26 TUL. L. REV. 70 (1951); Baeck, *Judicial Review of Administrative Decisions in Foreign Countries—Austria*, [1959] ABA INTERNATIONAL AND COMPARATIVE LAW SECTION PROCEEDINGS 173. *Cf.* Parker, *Administrative Law through Foreign Glasses: The Austrian Experience*, 15 RUTGERS L. REV. 551 (1961).

[133] Law of Nov. 17, 1964 concerning the Administrative Court, [1965] BGBl. 289, § 61 (Aus.).

[134] BUNDESVERFASSUNGSGESETZ, art. 144 (Aus.). *See* I. SEIDL-HOHENVELDERN, AMERICAN-AUSTRIAN PRIVATE INTERNATIONAL LAW 95 (1963). *See generally* F. ERMACORA, DER VERFASSUNGSGERICHTSHOF (1956).

[135] BUNDESVERFASSUNGSGESETZ, arts. 139 & 140 (Aus.). The Constitutional Court has jurisdiction in a number of other areas. *See generally* Melichar, *Die*

compel a court unwilling to transfer a case to the Constitutional Court to do so.

The Austrian Constitution contains few direct provisions dealing with civil rights. However, a Bill of Rights enacted in 1867 was incorporated by reference. Guarantees of individual liberties contained in various other instruments, such as the Peace Treaty of St. Germain and the Austrian State Treaty of 1955, also are considered part of the Constitution and applied by the Constitutional Court.[136] Since the end of World War II, protection of individual rights and freedoms through the Constitutional Court seems to have worked fairly well, despite the seeming procedural clumsiness. Two factors, however, reduce somewhat the significance of the guarantees thereby assured. First, some of the constitutional guarantees limit only executive action; they do not always preclude legislative invasion of rights. Second, the Constitution can be amended by a two-thirds vote of Parliament.[137] Theoretically, at least, this provision could make impairment of civil rights possible by a legislative coalition of the two major parties.

No particular procedural problems prevent aliens from asserting rights before the Constitutional Court, although the normal reciprocity rules in legal aid petitions apply.[138] However, all the substantive Constitutional guarantees do not necessarily apply to aliens. If the provision speaks of "every person," aliens are included; if reference is to "every citizen," the right does not benefit aliens.[139]

Verfassungsgerichtsbarkeit in Oesterreich, in CONSTITUTIONAL REVIEW IN THE WORLD TODAY 449–79 (1962).

[136] The 1867 Bill of Rights is officially the Basic Law on the general rights of citizens. Dec. 21, 1867, [1867] RGB2. No. 142. The number of different instruments which contain civil rights provisions considered part of the Constitution is quite large. Substantial problems of inclusion, exclusion, and coordination arise. *See* I. SEIDL-HOHENVELDERN, *supra* note 134, at 35–36; Schaeffer, *Legal Restraints on Personal Liberties in Austria,* in 19 OESTERREICHISCHE ZEITSCHRIFT FUER OEFFENTLICHES RECHT 37 (1969).

[137] BUNDESVERFASSUNGSGESETZ, art. 44 (Aus.).

[138] L. WERNER & H. KLECATSKY, DAS OESTERREICHISCHE BUNDESVERFASSUNGSRECHT § 17, at 729 n.1 (1961). As to the rule in civil cases see text at notes 99–100 of Chapter V.

[139] *See, e.g.,* F. ERMACORA, HANDBUCH DER GRUNFREIHEITEN UND MENSCHENRECHTE 25 (1963). Applicable to everybody: freedom from arbitrary arrest, freedom from searches, and freedom of petition. Applicable to Austrian

A decision of the Austrian Constitutional Court declaring a statute unconstitutional is immediately effective as to the parties. It becomes binding generally, and in effect results in a repeal of the statutory provision involved, only after publication in the Official Gazette.[140]

Regarding government liability, Austrian law makes a distinction between proprietary and governmental functions somewhat similar to that long recognized in the United States law of municipal liability.[141] The distinction may be hard to draw. Issuance of an administrative decision obviously involves a "governmental" function. Treatment of a patient in a governmental medical institution is a "proprietary" function, yet giving a vaccination pursuant to the vaccination law is "governmental."[142] For "proprietary" functions, ordinary private law rules traditionally have been applicable, including normal rules of civil procedure.[143] Aliens have the same rights as in civil suits generally. Sovereign immunity has not been a problem. As to "governmental" functions, liability is essentially based on the *Amtshaftungsgesetz* or Governmental Liability Law of 1948.[144] In many respects the law is quite liberal, since there is no exception for discretionary functions. In claims based on administrative or judicial decisions, though, it is not sufficient to show that an erroneous legal theory was applied; there must be either an abuse of discretion or gross negligence.[145]

Both "governmental" and "proprietary" claims must be brought in the ordinary courts, which, if the validity of an administrative decision is at issue, must obtain a ruling from the Administrative Court. Claims under the Amtshaftungsgesetz for "governmental"

---

nationals only: access to public positions, freedom of assembly, and freedom of establishment.

[140] BUNDESVERFASSUNGSGESETZ, art. 140(3) (Aus.).

[141] The expressions usually used in Austria are *Privatwirtschaftsverwaltung* and *Hoheitsverwaltung*. See L. ADAMOVICH, *supra* note 132, at 8–12.

[142] E. LOEBENSTEIN & G. KANIAK, KOMMENTAR ZUM AMTSHAFTUNGSGESETZ 44–47 (1951) and 13 (Supp. 1957); Spanner, *Haftung des Staates fuer rechtswiedriges Verhalten seiner Organe*, in LIABILITY OF THE STATE FOR ILLEGAL CONDUCT OF ITS ORGANS 505, at 515–20 (H. Mosler ed. 1967).

[143] L. ADAMOVICH, *supra* note 132, at 285 n.1.

[144] Dec. 8, 1948, [1949] BGBl. 49 (Aus.).

[145] Spanner, *supra* note 142, at 515–17, 524–26, 529–30. No liability can be imposed on account of decisions of the Constitutional Court, Administrative Court, and Supreme Court. Harm which could have been avoided through appeal to the Administrative Court is likewise not compensable.

liability can be brought by aliens only if reciprocity is shown. Here, reciprocity implies not merely national treatment, but existence of rights substantially similar to ones available in Austria. To determine reciprocity, the court may rely only on treaties or on declarations previously published in the Official Gazette. In all other cases the court must request information from the Federal Chancery.[146] Since the Chancery seems to apply a rather strict standard, the requirement has been justly criticized.[147]

The "Austrian System" for protecting constitutional rights exists in the German Federal Republic with significant variations; in particular, the German Constitutional Court has somewhat wider jurisdiction than its Austrian counterpart. It may review not only administrative acts which allegedly violate constitutional rights, but judicial decisions as well. Furthermore, the power to request the Constitutional Court for a declaratory judgment on a statute's constitutionality is not limited to Federal and Provincial government; it also can be exercised by one-third of the members of Parliament. Regular courts cannot declare laws unconstitutional, but must stay proceedings and refer the matter to the Constitutional Court. Unlike in Austria, this right is not limited to cases in the Supreme Court; nor is there a need for a stay and transfer if a court resolves issues in favor of constitutionality. Furthermore, individuals can petition the Constitutional Court to declare a statute unconstitutional if it directly affects their civil rights.[148] No particular procedural hurdles prevent aliens from utilizing these constitutional review procedures, provided they assert violation of a constitutional right not limited to German citizens.

---

[146] The Chancery's reply is binding. Governmental Liability Law, *supra* note 144, at § 7. Judgment of Feb. 24, 1958, 13 OESTERREICHISCHE JURISTENZEITUNG 668, No. 41 (Aus. Adm. Ct.) (no review of Chancery decision by Administrative Court). The Federal Chancery (*Bundeskanzleramt*) conducts Austrian foreign affairs.

[147] Spanner, *supra* note 142, at 521–22.

[148] GRUNDGESETZ, arts. 93 & 100 (Ger.). The Constitutional Court also has a number of functions not listed here. *See* E. McWHINNEY, CONSTITUTIONALISM IN GERMANY AND THE FEDERAL CONSTITUTIONAL COURT (1962); Dietz, *Judicial Review in Europe*, 55 MICH. L. REV. 539 (1957); Rupp, *Judicial Review in the Federal Republic of Germany*, 9 AM. J. COMP. L. 29 (1960). The basic law governing the Constitutional Court is the Law of March 12, 1951, [1951] BGBl. 243.

The Constitution of the German Federal Republic contains a detailed catalogue of human rights binding upon the executive, judicial, and legislative branches.[149] The Austrian pattern has been followed in their application to aliens: articles concerning rights intended to protect everybody without regard to nationality usually are phrased "everybody may" or "everybody is entitled to"; rights available only to German nationals use the phrase "every German."[150] Although limitation of civil rights by legislation is permitted in only a few areas,[151] the German Constitution, like its Austrian counterpart, also can be amended easily; a two-thirds vote of both houses of Parliament is sufficient.[152]

For review of administrative action, Germany has created much more complex machinery than Austria. For instance, administrative courts exist in each state, from which appeals are possible to appellate administrative courts. Some states possess a third appellate level. If violations of Federal rather than state law are involved, further review by the Federal Administrative Court is sometimes possible. Until 1945, it was a general principle of German public law that judicial review was available only in those cases specifically provided by law. At present, all administrative decisions generally are reviewable.[153]

---

[149] GRUNDGESETZ, art. 1(3) (Ger.).

[150] K. BRINKMANN, GRUNDRECHTS-KOMMENTAR ZUM GRUNDGESETZ art. 1 No. I(7)(a) (1967). Available to everybody: rights guaranteeing personal freedom, equality before the law, and freedom of religion. Available to Germans only: the right to peaceful assembly, to form associations, to free movement upon the territory of the State, and to choose a trade or profession. By contrast, Latin American constitutional guarantees are all generally applicable to aliens, with exceptions as to political activity.

[151] In addition, GRUNDGESETZ, art. 19 (Ger.) provides that such a statute must be of general applicability and in no event infringe the essential nature of a right.

[152] GRUNDGESETZ, art. 79 (Ger.).

[153] See generally C. ULE, VERWALTUNGSPROZESSRECHT (4th ed. 1966); Bachof, German Administrative Law with Special Reference to the Latest Developments in the System of Legal Protection, 2 INT'L & COMP. L.Q. 368 (1953). Organization and procedure of the administrative courts is governed by the Law on Administrative Courts of Jan. 21, 1960, [1960] BGBl. 17. Organization and procedure of the tax courts is governed by the Law on Tax Courts of Oct. 6, 1965, [1965] BGBl. 1477. The following court systems exist in the German Federal Republic: the regular courts for ordinary civil and criminal cases (culminating in the Supreme [Federal] Court), the administrative courts, the

In Germany, as in Austria, government liability for "proprietary" functions is governed by the general—including procedural—rules concerning tort actions. In addition, the rules establishing nonfault liability in certain cases of high risk, such as the operation of railroads or automobiles, or electric power transmission, are applicable. In such actions aliens are in exactly the same position as if they were suing a private individual. Sovereign immunity is no obstacle.[154] The German Civil Code of 1900 established a far-reaching liability of individual governmental officials for true "governmental" functions.[155] Liability of governmental units themselves was governed by somewhat restrictive Federal and provincial statutes. The Bonn Constitution of 1949 (following the pattern of the Weimar Constitution) establishes wide liability of governmental units—federal and provincial—for "governmental" acts.[156] The extent to which this constitutional provision overrides earlier restrictive statutes is not always easily ascertainable, and such statutes have not become completely unconstitutional.[157] Unfortunately, the statute governing Federal liability and most provincial statutes require

---

tax courts, the labor courts, and the social security courts. Apart from these tribunals is the Federal Constitutional Court. There are provincial constitutional courts in all provinces except Schleswig-Holstein and Berlin.

[154] 2 T. Soergel & W. Siebert, Buergerliches Gesetzbuch 1358–59 (9th ed. 1962); Jaenicke, *Haftung des Staates fuer rechtswidriges Verhalten seiner Organe*, in Liability of the State for Illegal Conduct of Its Organs 69, at 86 (H. Mosler ed. 1967). For a somewhat dated English translation of the statutes governing liability for aircraft, automobiles, and railroads, see A. von Mehren, The Civil Law System 416–52 (1957). Except for the cases covered by the statutes mentioned, the scope of the rule of *respondeat superior* is more restricted in German (and also Austrian) law than in Anglo-American law. BGB § 831 (C.H. Beck 1967).

[155] This provision is still in force. BGB § 839 (C.H. Beck 1967). The distinction between "governmental" and "proprietary" functions has given rise to much controversy. It is not, of course, drawn in the same way as in American law. For an extensive discussion see 2 T. Soergel & W. Siebert, *supra* note 154, at 1329–50.

[156] Grundgesetz, art. 34 (Ger).

[157] Judgments of May 10, 1954, 13 BGHZ 241; Oct. 1, 1956, 9 Neue Juristische Wochenschrift 1836 (Ger. Sup. Ct.); July 13, 1961, 17 Juristenzeitung 100. As to the German Federal Government, see the Law on the Liability of the Reich for its Employees of May 22, 1910, [1910] RBGl. 798 § 7. As to provincial legislation see Frowein, *Staatshaftung gegenueber Auslaendern*, 19 Juristenzeitung 358–60 (1964).

reciprocity in suits by aliens. This reciprocity, absent a treaty, ordinarily must be shown by a Government declaration published in the Official Gazette. Declarations have been issued as to Belgium, France, Greece, Japan, and The Netherlands, among others. Where an alien is unable to sue because of the reciprocity rule, the individual Civil Code liability of the governmental officer offers another, but not necessarily satisfactory, avenue of relief.[158] Actions to assert governmental liability, whatever their legal basis, must be brought in the regular courts.

A third variant of the "Austrian System" of constitutional review appears in Italy, where a Constitutional Court was provided in the postwar Constitution. The Court may rule on the constitutionality of legislation in proceedings brought especially for that purpose, as at the request of the central government to test a regional statute.[159] Although private individuals have no right to bring a case directly before the Constitutional Court, they may raise a constitutional issue in any case pending before some other court. If that court, which also may act on its own motion, finds that resolution of the constitutional issue is necessary to its decision, it stays proceedings and requests a ruling from the Constitutional Court. Unlike in the United States, regular courts cannot declare a law unconstitutional.[160] A decision of unconstitutionality is binding erga omnes

---

[158] 2 T. SOERGEL & S. SIEBERT, *supra* note 154, at 1357.

[159] COSTITUZIONE DELLA REPUBBLICA ITALIANA, arts. 127, 134 & 135. An analogous right rests with the regional governments.

[160] LEGGE COSTITUZIONALE of Feb. 9, 1948, No. 1, art. 1. If the court before which the issue of constitutionality has been raised refuses to request a ruling from the Constitutional Court, such a demand can be made again on appeal. However, if a court decides not to request a ruling from the Constitutional Court, that ruling itself cannot be reviewed by the Constitutional Court. As to the procedural details, see Law on the Organization and Functioning of the Constitutional Court, March 11, 1953, No. 87, arts. 23–36, in I CINQUE CODICI lxxix, lxxxiii–lxxxvi (Giuffrè 1968).
Article 177 of the 1957 Treaty of Rome establishing the European Economic Community permits a somewhat analogous procedure. If litigants in national courts allege a violation of a Treaty provision, the national court may refer the question to the Court of Justice of the European Communities. The Court, however, cannot rule on conflicts between the Treaty and municipal law; it can only interpret the Treaty and define Community norms, leaving their application in particular cases to national tribunals. The case of Costa v. ENEL, 10 Rec. 1195, 2 CCH Com. Mkt. Rep. ¶8023 (EEC 1964) is especially interesting

from the day following its publication.[161] The Italian Constitutional Court has played a significant role in giving life to the demands of the Italian Constitution, in spite of perceptible hesitancy by some regular judges to refer cases.[162] It should be noted that Italian Law knows no procedure analogous to the *Verfassungsbeschwerde* in Germany, through which an individual administrative or judicial decision is reviewable directly by the Constitutional Court.[163] As in the Federal Republic of Germany, a bill of rights forms an intrinsic part of the Italian Constitution. There is also a basic similarity in the types of rights available to citizens only, and to all persons generally.[164]

Review of administrative action, extending occasionally beyond examination of legality to questions of desirability, is widely available. Traditional Italian concepts distinguish between administrative acts interfering with "rights" and acts interfering with "legitimate interests."[165] In the former, relief through money damages is avail-

---

because it combined referrals by a lower court in Milan both to the Italian Constitutional Court and to the Court of Justice of the European Communities. Claimant argued that the law nationalizing the privately owned electrical industry, which placed ENEL in a monopoly position, violated not only the Italian Constitution, but also provisions in the Treaty of Rome relating to freedom of establishment. The case is discussed in Angulo & Dawson, *Access by Natural and Legal Persons to the Court of Justice of the European Communities,* 36 U. Cinn. L. Rev. 583, 644–47 (1967), and in Stein, *Toward Supremacy of Treaty-Constitution by Judicial Fiat: On the Margin of the Costa Case,* 63 Mich. L. Rev. 491 (1965).

[161] *Supra* note 159, art. 136.

[162] M. Cappelletti, J. Merryman & J. Perillo, The Italian Legal System 75–79 (1967). *See also* Adams & Barile, *The Italian Constitutional Court in Its First Two Years of Activity,* 7 Buffalo L. Rev. 250 (1958); Cassandro, *The Constitutional Court of Italy,* 8 Am. J. Comp. L. 1 (1959); Treves, *Judicial Review of Legislation in Italy,* 7 J. Pub. L. 345 (1958). The Constitutional Court has functions not described here, such as the conduct of what one might call impeachment trials.

[163] A. Sandulli, Rapporti tra Giustizia Comune e Giustizia Costituzionale in Italia 25 (1968).

[164] *Supra* note 159, arts. 13–54. *Cf.* note 150 *supra.*

[165] The unauthorized tearing down of a building would be an example of a violation of a right of the owner. The use of improper bidding procedures to the detriment of a particular bidder would not violate that person's rights, since the rules as to public contracts are designed for the protection of the public in general, but it would violate a legitimate interest of the unsuccessful bidder. *See* M. Cappelletti, J. Merryman & J. Perillo, *supra* note 162, at 81–82.

230 INT'L LAW, NAT'L TRIBUNALS, RIGHTS OF ALIENS

able in regular courts. When interference with "legitimate interests" is alleged, revocation or modification of administrative acts may be obtained in administrative courts, or, if acts of the central government are involved, in the Council of State.[166] While in Italy a proprietary-governmental dichotomy was used at one time to determine when suit could be brought, as in Austria and Germany, this approach eventually was abandoned. At present, the Italian Constitution recognizes governmental liability quite broadly.[167] There are, however, some exceptions. The government apparently is not liable for political acts of a discretionary nature, and liability based on defects in highways seems to arise only if the defect constituted a trap.[168]

The Italian Constitution provides that everybody may proceed at law for the protection of his rights and legitimate interests.[169] When the Italian Constitution uses the term "everybody," it means to include aliens as well as citizens. It follows that aliens and citizens alike may sue the Republic or its subdivisions for damages, seek review of administrative action before appropriate bodies, or raise constitutional issues in pending cases and request a transfer of the case to the Constitutional Court, although in the latter case obviously only if the constitutional right claimed is available to aliens. Since the right to proceed at law is guaranteed by the Italian Constitution, the reciprocity requirement of the Preliminary Dispositions of the Civil Code does not seem applicable.[170]

In conclusion, whatever the differences in procedural detail, all the countries examined permit suit against the governments and their agencies in contract, in tort, and for violation of fundamental

---

[166] *Id.* at 83–84. There are separate bodies to review administrative acts of the provinces and regions, from which an appeal lies to the Council of State and some other special tribunals.

[167] *Supra* note 159, art. 28. *See,* in particular, Law of March 20, 1865, No. 2248, Annex E (granting jurisdiction to the regular courts for suits arising out of violations by executive agencies of individual rights). Galeotti, *La responsabilité de l'Etat pour le comportement illégal de ses organes,* in LIABILITY OF THE STATE FOR ILLEGAL CONDUCT OF ITS ORGANS 295, at 306 (H. Mosler ed. 1967).

[168] *Id.* at 319, 326.

[169] *Supra* note 159, art. 24.

[170] Art. 6. This view is the general, but not quite unanimous, one. It is supported by the theory that the constitutional guarantees take priority over legislative enactments such as codes.

rights. The principal formal limitation in continental Europe and, in theory at least, in the United States, is a showing of reciprocity. Special procedures nevertheless may govern the manner in which private litigants, including aliens, may challenge a government's taking of private property for a public purpose. Since this area is one of great concern, and since both the frequency and scope of these takings have increased notably since World War II, the topic merits special consideration.

GOVERNMENTAL LIABILITY TO SUIT FOR ACTIONS INFRINGING UPON PROPERTY RIGHTS

It is unlikely that even the most devoted disciple of the free-enterprise system would regard public expropriation of private property as totally unethical and wholly inappropriate under all circumstances. Certainly concepts of "eminent domain" in the United States and "public interest" in the Commonwealth are well rooted and accepted. In developed countries it is only in the application of these principles that differences of opinion arise: notice, terms of compensation, rights of appeal, or recourse to independent tribunals. Sometimes, however, it may appear that in developing nations the principle of compensation itself is in doubt. Nevertheless, if remedies available are examined coincidentally with nationalization announcements and speeches, not only may some of the irrational heat be removed from the protestations of investors but, and equally important, the distinction between act and relief may result in pressures being brought to bear upon all countries to introduce adequate compensatory features into their legislation.

Nationalization fervor may have passed its zenith in Asia, where increasing political attention now is being devoted quite properly to the more fundamental social issue of land reform. In Africa, however, pressures for nationalization of foreign-owned industry are gaining momentum. Following the compulsory acquisition by the Government of Zambia of a controlling interest in large copper mining companies in August, 1969, *The Times* of London commented editorially:

> [T]he fact should be faced that behind the popularity of the nationalization move lie two strong African motives, extending

throughout the continent. The first is the feeling that African wealth should be owned (as was tribal land) by the black inhabitants, not by expatriates. The second is the growing African ambition to manage commercial and mining enterprises, not just to work for white managements. As African graduates flow back from the world's universities in growing numbers the conviction hardens among Africans that they now have the needed skills to manage and control, and serve on boards. It would be a grave mistake to underrate this sentiment or reject it as "extremism." It would be equally foolish to assume that African-owned enterprises cannot work successfully or employ white experts. The nationalization of the Katanga mines disproved such white business prejudice (for which the African term is "neo-colonialist mentality"), if the Suez Canal had left it in any doubt. What must be faced, therefore, is that with every successful African seizure of control the demand for nationalization will grow in other African countries.[171]

The compensatory steps taken by the Zambian Government invite the suggestion that if as much public attention had been paid to the Tanzanian Foreign Investment (Protection) Act of 1963[172] as was paid to the 1967 Arusha Declaration, the outcry following the latter would have been less shrill and better balanced. The remedy offered by the statute is extrajudicial, but it nevertheless exists and so certainly falls within the category of one that must be exhausted. The act enables any alien to apply to the Tanzanian Government for certification that his enterprise will "further the economic development of, or benefit" Tanzania.[173] If at any time an approved enterprise, or property belonging to an approved enterprise, is nationalized or expropriated, "the full and fair value of such enterprise or property shall be ascertained" and the holder compen-

---

[171] The Times (London), Aug. 19, 1969, at 5, cols. 1–3. The Zambian government announced on November 17, 1969, that it would pay some $294 million for the 51 percent controlling interest of the Zambian operation of the two companies, Anglo American Corp. of South Africa and Roan Selection Trust Ltd. of Lusaka. The figure was based on an estimated valuation as at December 31, 1969, and is to be paid by 6 percent government-guaranteed bonds issued by the Zambian Industrial Development Corporation. Payments will be in semi-annual installments over 8 years for Roan Selection and over 12 years for Anglo American. There is provision for accelerated payments.

[172] Tanganyika, Act No. 40 of 1963.

[173] *Id.* § 3(2).

sated.[174] Should the compulsory acquisition be of company shares, their "full and fair value" shall be paid.[175] Compensation is made in the foreign currency and may be transferred abroad at prevailing official exchange rates. The remedy is provided by Section 6(3) of the Act:

> If any question arises between the Government and the holder of a certificate as to the value of any enterprise, property, stock, or share, the question shall be referred to and determined by arbitration, and at any arbitration each party shall appoint one arbitrator, who shall jointly appoint a third.

Pursuant to President Nyerere's Arusha Declaration, the Tanzanian Parliament in February 1967 passed five expropriation statutes, carefully inserting in each a clause stating: "Nothing in this Act shall be construed so as to affect in any way the rights of the holder of a certificate issued under the Foreign Investments (Protection) Act of 1963."[176] The five statutes dealt with banks,[177] trading firms,[178] agricultural firms,[179] insurance companies,[180] and industrial concerns.[181] In each case a State corporation assumed ownership and management of the scheduled entities. A uniform section appears in each of the five acts: "The United Republic shall pay full and fair compensation, . . . provided that the said amount of compensation shall be payable in such manner and in such installments as the Minister of Finance, after consultation with the person entitled, shall determine."[182] Should the person entitled to receive compensation not be satisfied with the manner and the installments, he most

---

[174] *Id.* § 6(1).

[175] *Id.* § 6(2).

[176] *See, e.g.,* The State Trading Corporation (Establishment and Vesting of Interests) Act (1967), Tanzania, Act No. 2 of 1967.

[177] The National Bank of Commerce (Establishment and Vesting of Assets and Liabilities) Act (1967), Tanzania, Act No. 1 of 1967.

[178] *See* note 176 *supra.*

[179] The National Agricultural Products Board (Vesting of Interests) Act (1967), Tanzania, Act No. 3 of 1967.

[180] The Insurance (Vesting of Interests and Regulation) Act (1967), Tanzania, Act No. 4 of 1967.

[181] The Industrial Shares (Acquisition) Act (1967), Tanzania, Act No. 5 of 1967.

[182] Act No. 1, § 10; Act No. 2, § 12; Act No. 3, § 7; Act No. 4, § 6; Act No. No. 5, § 4.

likely will turn to the Government Proceedings Act of 1967,[183] which subjects the Government to liability in contract, tort, and "in other respects to which it would be subject if it were a private person of full age and capacity,"[184] and which further provides that money decrees shall apply against the Government as they do against private persons.[185]

In Kenya, foreign investment is protected by the Foreign Investments Protection Act of 1964,[186] which is almost identical to the Tanzanian statute after which it was modeled. There is, however, a major variation. The Kenya act makes illegal compulsory acquisition of any property without full and prompt payment of compensation as required by the Constitution.[187] Article 19, which applies to citizens and aliens, provides that no property shall be taken compulsorily except where (1) the taking is in the public interest; (2) the necessity affords reasonable justification for the causing of any hardship that may result to the property owner; and (3) there is prompt payment of full compensation.[188] In addition, any person who has a right or interest in any property which has been acquired or possessed compulsorily shall have "a right of direct access to the Supreme Court" for the determination of (1) his interest, (2) the legality of the taking, and (3) the amount of compensation to which he is entitled, as well as for obtaining prompt payment of that compensation.[189] No alien entitled to compensation may be prevented from remitting that compensation free from any charge or tax.[190]

On the African west coast, Ghana in 1963 proclaimed the Capital Investments Act.[191] No investment under the terms of the Act "shall be subject to expropriation . . . . Where, however, in exceptional

---

[183] *See* note 20 *supra*.
[184] *Id.* § 3(1).
[185] *Id.* § 14(1).
[186] Cap. 518, THE REVISED LAWS OF KENYA, 1967.
[187] Found as a schedule to the Kenya Independence Order in Council, 1963, (STAT. INSTR. No. 1968 of 1963). For a discussion of amendments to the Constitution see Njonjo, *Recent Constitutional Changes in Kenya*, 1 E. AFR. L.J. 98 (1965). Mr. Njonjo is the Attorney General of Kenya.
[188] Art. 19, § 2.
[189] *Id.*
[190] *Id.* § 4.
[191] Ghana, Act No. 172 of 1963.

circumstances, an approved project is taken over in the public interest, the Government shall pay fair compensation" in the currency in which the investment was originally made.[192] Disputes over compensation are referred to an arbitrator appointed by the parties or, failing such appointment, to arbitration through the International Bank for Reconstruction and Development.[193]

In Ceylon, where nationalization of assets of certain foreign-owned oil companies in 1962 precipitated the suspension of United States foreign aid, statutory authority exists both for expropriation and payment of compensation. The Ceylon Petroleum Corporation Act[194] created a body corporate vested with exclusive rights of import, export, sale, exploration, and exploitation of petroleum and petroleum products. Provision was made for the compulsory acquisition of, and payment for, property required by the Corporation. Part IV of the statute is devoted to the terms, quantum, and method of payment of compensation, and Part V establishes a special Compensation Tribunal to handle valuation questions. The basis of compensation appears exceedingly narrow and unsophisticated, but the principle of payment is nevertheless part of the law of Ceylon.[195] The failure of this machinery to resolve the impasse with the oil companies is made evident in the passage of the 1967 Ceylon Petroleum (Foreign Claims) Compensation Act,[196] which gives effect to the agreements made between the Government of Ceylon and the several oil companies respecting payment for expropriated assets.[197]

---

[192] *Id.* § 8(1)(2).

[193] *Id.* § 8(3).

[194] Act No. 28 of 1961, Legis. Enactments of Ceylon (1967), Vol. II, p. 779.

[195] *See, e.g.,* Section 47(1): "The amount of compensation to be paid under this Act in respect of any property vested on any date in the Corporation shall be the actual price paid by the owner for the purchase of such property and an additional sum which is equal to the reasonable value of any additions and improvements made to such property by any person who was interested, or if such purchase price is not ascertainable, be an amount equal to the price which such property would have fetched if it had been sold in the open market on the day on which the property was vested in the Corporation." The subsection continues to state that the compensation to be awarded for movables shall be subject to a deduction for depreciation. There is no provision for payment on the basis of a business as a going concern, only on the market value of the severable parts.

[196] Act No. 19 of 1965, Legis. Enactments of Ceylon (1967), Vol. II, p. 1606.

[197] For an official statement on the attitude of Ceylon toward foreign invest-

A new international standard of compensation procedure may have been established by Canada with the introduction into Parliament in 1969 of a Bill containing innovative procedures respecting valuation and payment. Compensation will be paid on the basis of market value, but if the property is used as a residence, and the value is less than that of reasonably equivalent property to which the owner must relocate, a sum sufficient to acquire the latter shall be paid. Additionally, and most important, the Government must compensate the owner within a given period whether or not valuation is contested.[198] No longer can a powerful government withhold payment from an expropriated landowner while endless rounds of valuation contests and appeals take place.

Constitutions in Latin American republics guarantee citizens and aliens alike the right to own private property, subject to the State's right to take property for public necessity or utility upon payment of compensation. The Argentine Constitution establishes that "property is inviolable and no inhabitant of the nation can be deprived thereof except by virtue of a sentence founded on law. Expropriation for reasons of public utility must be authorized by law and previously compensated,"[199] while the Peruvian Constitution states that "property is inviolable, whether it be material, intellectual, literary, or artistic. No one may be deprived of his own property except for reasons of public utility legally proven and after appraised compensation."[200] Similar constitutional provisions are found in Honduras, Brazil, Venezuela, and Guatemala.[201] The procedures

---

ment, see the pamphlet entitled "Government Policy on Private Foreign Investment" issued by the Ministry of Planning and Economic Affairs, Colombo, June 1967.

[198] An Act Respecting the Expropriation of Land, Bill C–136, 2d Session, 28th Parliament.

[199] CONSTITUTION OF THE REPUBLIC OF ARGENTINA 1853, art. 17 (Pan American Union ed. 1963).

[200] *Supra* note 90, art. 29.

[201] Article 154 of the Honduran Constitution states that "the State recognizes, promotes and guarantees private property." Article 156 provides that "the expropriation of property on grounds of public need or necessity must be accomplished through a law or a judgment based on law, and shall not take place without prior compensation." CONSTITUTION OF THE REPUBLIC OF HONDURAS 1965, arts. 154 & 156 (Pan American Union ed. 1966).

Article 150(22) of the Constitution of Brazil is similar and declares that "the right to own property shall be guaranteed, except in cases of expropriation for

followed in eminent domain cases are set forth subsequently in special legislation.

The right to own land and to receive compensation for its taking also is accorded aliens in Latin America, either specifically or implicitly through the equal treatment doctrine. The Peruvian Constitution provides that "[f]oreigners, as regards property, are in the same condition as Peruvians, without being able in any case to invoke an exceptional position in this respect or have recourse to diplomatic claims."[202] The Brazilian Constitution in Article 150 "insures to Brazilians and to foreigners residing in the country the inviolability of rights concerning life, liberty, security and property," while the Honduran Constitution provides "inhabitants of Honduras" with "the right to be protected without any discrimination, and the enjoyment of their life, security, honor, liberty, work and property."[203] Nevertheless, many countries limit the substantive rights of aliens to own real estate along national frontiers or the seacoasts. Thus, Mexico forbids any foreigner from owning land within the *faja prohibida* along frontiers or coastlines. The Honduran Constitution limits to natural-born Hondurans ownership of land "located in zones adjacent to the boundaries with neighboring states, land located along the shores of the two oceans, to a width of forty kilometers," and land on islands and reefs off the coast,[204] while the Peruvian Constitution forbids aliens to acquire or possess land, waters, mines, or fuel within 50 kilometers of the frontiers.[205] Any alien unwise enough to acquire land in these areas may have little grounds for appeal in the event of confiscation.

---

public necessity or utility or social interest, with previous and fair compensation in money," although in certain situations rural land may be expropriated for purposes of agrarian reform through payment of compensation in public bonds. A. PEREIRA, A CONSTITUIÇÃO DO BRASIL (1967).

Article 101 of the Venezuelan Constitution provides that "only for reasons of public utility or social interest, by a final judgment and payment of just indemnification may the expropriation of any type of property be declared." In cases of expropriation of land for purposes of agrarian reform, the Article continues, payment may be deferred or paid partially in bonds. *Supra* note 51, art. 101. *See also supra* note 49, art. 71.

[202] *Supra* note 90, art. 32.

[203] In both countries these guarantees apparently are not specifically assured to transient aliens.

[204] *Supra* note 61, art. 159.

[205] *Supra* note 90, art. 36.

Despite limitations on the location and scope of ownership, aliens in the Latin American nations studied enjoy the same rights as nationals to contest deprivations of their property pursuant to the special legislation governing agrarian reform and eminent domain. These actions may be brought either in special tribunals or in national or state courts, coupled with demands for injunctive relief. Two examples are illustrative.

The general Argentine law governing expropriations provides that all goods necessary or needed for purposes of public utility, whatever their juridical nature, whether or not they are being used in commerce, and whether or not they are tangible or intangible, may be the object of expropriation, including the property of provincial and municipal governments.[206] If the expropriating authority is unable to negotiate appropriate compensation with the owner, it may begin proceedings in the Federal Court of First Instance of the appropriate district, which, in summary proceedings, will determine compensation based on an opinion requested from the permanent Assessment Tribunal in Buenos Aires. The Tribunal must reach a decision within 30 days. The judge also must notify the owner of the request so that he will have sufficient time to appoint a representative to participate in the Tribunal's deliberations.

When there is no agreement between the parties, and the matter involves real property, the expropriating authority may obtain immediate possession by depositing with the local Federal Court the assessed tax value of the land plus 30 percent. Decisions of the Federal Court may be appealed through the Federal appellate process, and the Argentine Supreme Court even has held that it is possible to deviate from the conclusions of the Assessment Tribunal when there are sufficiently well-grounded reasons. The Argentine legal process also provides injunctive relief under which expropriation proceedings can be suspended and requests for evaluation attacked. The State's judgment of the public utility of the taking, however, cannot be challenged. If the taking involves personalty, the Court of First Instance may appoint an expert to value the goods in lieu of referral to the Assessment Tribunal. Various Argentine provinces have their own expropriation laws, and real property may

---

[206] Ley No. 13.264, Sept. 22, 1948.

also be taken by the Federal Government pursuant to Law No. 14.392 of 1955, the purpose of which is to promote rural settlement and land reform.[207]

Under Brazil's Constitution, property also may be taken pursuant to eminent domain, but the procedure must be exercised within the state court system, even if the expropriating authority is the Federal Government.[208] Unlike Argentina, Brazil does not, except on the appellate level, possess a federal court structure paralleling the state courts. As in Argentina, the expropriating authority must notify an owner that his property has been decreed of public utility and must offer compensation. At that point the property owner may approach the local office of the expropriating agent and seek an amicable settlement. Unless the owner settles with the expropriating authority, the latter, within five years after the declaration of taking, must seek an order entitling it to possession of the land. Otherwise the declaration of public utility becomes ineffective and a second declaration must be obtained. After the application for the possession order is filed, the court designates an appraiser. The attorneys for the deprived owner and for the expropriating agency may appoint experts

---

[207] In Venezuela, as in Argentina, property may be taken by the State pursuant to a general *Ley de Expropiación por Causa de Utilidad Pública o Social,* or by the *Ley de Reforma Agraria.* Under the Ley de Expropiación, the expropriating authority (generally a Government entity if the land is to be taken for roads, railways, sewers, schools, fortifications, or airfields) publishes an expropriating decree. The owners are notified and offered compensation. If the offer is refused, a special Valuation Commission composed of the Judge of the local Court of First Instance, a person designated by the expropriating authority and a person designated by the owners will be convened. If agreement is still impossible, the expropriating authority must file a request for expropriation before a Court of First Instance, which then will notify the owners, who can oppose the taking only if they can show a violation of law, or that the entire property rather than a portion thereof should be taken. A cognizable violation of the law, apparently, could be only a procedural violation, such as lack of proper notice or of a declaration by a competent public authority that the taking was necessary for public purposes, or by a showing that the taking was not required by public utility. An appeal will also lie to the Court of Second Instance. After final judgment, the judge will supervise the appointment of valuation experts if the parties cannot agree on a price.

[208] Brazilian expropriation procedure is discussed in detail in H. P. DE VRIES & J. RODRIGUEZ-NOVAS, *supra* note 101, at 150–57. The basic expropriation law is Decree Law No. 3365 of June 21, 1941, *as amended,* Law No. 2786 of March 21, 1956. The Code of Civil Procedure applies where the basic law is silent.

to assist the appraiser. If the expropriating agency can show urgency, the judge may grant provisional possession ex parte if the agency deposits into court "the price offered and such offer is at least twenty times the rental value of the property subject to real estate tax or if the amount corresponds to the assessed value of the immovables as determined in the preceding fiscal year."[209] The owner must be served with notice of the proceeding; notice may be by publication if he is not in the country.

If the parties agree on compensation, the court enters a decree approving the agreement. If the parties cannot come to terms, the judge, after considering the appraiser's report and hearing the arguments of both parties, will decide on the correct amount of compensation and, once payment has been tendered, order the owner to relinquish possession and title. Payment must be in cash, not bonds, and must precede the actual taking. As in Argentina, the judge's order is sufficient to obtain passage of title. The expropriating agency simply takes a copy of the decree to the Registrar of Real Properties, who then records the transfer. The only defenses which can be raised during these proceedings are to challenge either the improper nature of the procedure, e.g., that notification was not received, or to allege that compensation was inadequate. The court's decision on these points may be appealed. One must commence a separate action to repossess or to obtain a restraining order or mandado de segurança through which the declaration of public utility can be challenged and damages sought.

In the United States, Article I, Section 10 of the Federal Constitution declares: "No State shall . . . pass any . . . Law impairing the Obligation of Contract," while the Fifth Amendment provides "nor shall private property be taken for public use, without just compensation." It cannot be said, unfortunately, that these precepts never have been breached. Following the Panic of 1837, the States of Mississippi, Louisiana, Maryland, Pennsylvania, Indiana, and Michigan either stopped interest payments on, or repudiated, the bonds which they had sold to foreign investors (mostly British) in order to finance a canal construction boom. Nevertheless, courts in the United States almost consistently have provided relief to na-

---

[209] H. P. DE VRIES & J. RODRIGUEZ-NOVAS, *supra* note 101, at 152.

tionals and aliens whose property rights were menaced by improper state or Federal action.[210] Even if the plaintiff is an alien corporation existing under the laws of a country with which the United States has no diplomatic relations, it has been held that suit may be brought against the United States for payment of "just compensation" for private property taken for public use.[211]

European constitutions, in contrast to constitutions of Latin American countries and the United States, do not always provide assurance against uncompensated expropriation or nationalization, although expropriation statutes usually provide for fair compensation. Since treaties frequently grant additional protection to aliens, their position may be more favorable than that of nationals.

In France, the 1789 Declaration of the Rights of Man provides that property is a sacred and inviolable right of which nobody may be deprived except in cases of evident public necessity and subject to payment of just, prior compensation.[212] The Declaration has been incorporated into the Preamble of the 1958 French Constitution but, as noted, this incorporation does not give the Declaration's principles the effect of a rule of law overriding subsequent legislation.[213] Expropriation is thus entirely a statutory matter governed principally by a law enacted in 1958.[214] Expropriation requires an administrative declaration that the project is for a public use, and a subsequent court decision transferring title.[215] If no agreement between the parties as to valuation is reached, the matter is brought before a special part of the regular court of first instance composed of a single judge and dealing exclusively with expropriation matters. The procedure is fairly expeditious and adapted to the subject matter. The indemnity awarded must cover the entire direct financial

[210] For a discussion of the leading cases in the United States in this area see McAllister, *United States Constitutional Law and Its Relation to a Contract Between a State and a Foreign National*, in THE RIGHTS AND DUTIES OF PRIVATE INVESTORS ABROAD 213 (Southwestern Legal Foundation ed. 1965).

[211] Russian Volunteer Fleet v. United States, 282 U.S. 481 (1931).

[212] *Reprinted in* CODE ADMINISTRATIF 210, 212 (9th ed. Petits Codes Dalloz 1966). *Accord,* C. CIV. art. 545 (66th ed. Petits Codes Dalloz 1966).

[213] *See* notes 120–128 *supra.*

[214] Ordonnance No. 58–997 of Oct. 23, 1958, [1958] J.O. 9654, [1958] D.L. 355.

[215] *Id.* arts. 1, 2, 6, 7.

loss caused by the expropriation and, in practice, is based on the value of the property taken, augmented by a sum intended to cover the expenses of reinvestment. Interestingly, tenants in certain cases must be relocated in low-rent housing instead of being given a cash indemnity. Certain speculative increases in value, however, are disregarded in determining the indemnity.[216] The present French law seems to work well and to afford adequate protection to all concerned.[217]

Without binding constitutional provisions, the enactment of statutes providing less than adequate compensation is not impossible. Substantial nationalizations occurred in France immediately after World War II affecting the Renault automobile works, an aircraft engine factory, the entire gas and electric industry, the coal mining industry, and a substantial part of banking and insurance. In some instances, since nationalizations were designed to penalize owners who had collaborated with German authorities, no compensation was given. In the case of the coal, gas, and electric industries, compensation was provided through long-term bonds bearing relatively low interest rates. Few international complications arose except in the electric industry, where special arrangements were made with Switzerland to afford more ample compensation to Swiss shareholders.[218] The provisions of Article IV of the 1959 Convention of Establishment between the United States and France, which requires prompt, just, adequate, and nondiscriminatory compensation,[219] may be useful should further nationalizations occur.

The extent to which the Austrian Constitution prevents expropriation without compensation is somewhat uncertain. Article 5 of the 1867 Bill of Rights declares merely that expropriation can occur only

---

[216] *Id.* arts. 10–23.

[217] In case of de facto appropriation, the French Government (or other de facto appropriator) may be sued in the regular courts for compensation. The same is true in the case of temporary requisitions. M. WALINE, *supra* note 118, at 92–93.

[218] For a detailed discussion see De Vries & Hoeniger, *Post-Liberation Nationalizations in France,* 50 COLUM. L. REV. 629 (1950).

[219] Convention of Establishment with France, Nov. 25, 1959, art. IV, [1960] 2 U.S.T. 2398, T.I.A.S. No. 4625 (effective Dec. 21, 1960). Point 5 of the Annexed Protocol makes this Convention applicable to nationalizations, and Point 6 to interests held directly or indirectly.

pursuant to law. The Austrian Civil Code requires adequate compensation,[220] but, since it is only a statute, it has been held that no compensation is required constitutionally if the taking legislation excludes it.[221] However, Austria has ratified the European Convention on Human Rights,[222] so that it could be argued that the provisions of the Convention have acquired constitutional status and hence that compensation for aliens now is required. Aliens also may be in a better position than Austrian citizens because public international law is considered part of Austrian law and requires compensation to aliens for expropriation. However, that rule does not have a constitutional character and could be superseded by a statute to the contrary.[223] Fortunately, pursuant to the Civil Code[224] and to the statute presently governing expropriation,[225] full compensation must be paid, and the elements of valuation are fairly similar to ones used in the United States and other common law countries.

The Constitution of the German Federal Republic contains more detailed provisions concerning expropriation than does the Austrian Constitution. Article 14 permits condemnation only for a public use and pursuant to a law providing for compensation based upon a just consideration of the interests of the general public and of the affected parties. Article 15 authorizes nationalizations and related measures, but it refers back to Article 14 for compensation principles.[226] The

---

[220] ALLGEMEINES BUERGERLICHES GESETZBUCH § 365 (28th ed. Manz 1967).

[221] See, e.g., Judgment of Oct. 10, 1953 (Verfassungsgerichtshof), in 9 OESTERREICHISCHE JURISTENZEITUNG 76 (Aus. 1954).

[222] European Treaty Series No. 5, 1 EUROPEAN YEARBOOK 317 (1955).

[223] F. ERMACORA, supra note 139, at 159–79; I. SEIDL-HOHENVELDERN, supra note 134, at 42–44.

[224] See note 220 supra.

[225] The procedure in most expropriation cases is governed by the law concerning condemnation for railroad purposes of February 18, 1878, [1878] RGBl. No. 30, republished in [1954] BGBl. Nr. 71, which is applicable when there is no other specific statute in point. According to Section 4, the condemnor must compensate for all economic losses caused by the expropriation. United States nationals receive additional protection through Article I of the Treaty of Friendship, Commerce and Consular Rights with Austria, June 19, 1928, 47 Stat. 1876, T.S. No. 838 (effective May 27, 1931).

[226] GRUNDGESETZ, arts. 14(3), 15 (Ger.). There has been a substantial amount of condemnation in the Federal Republic of Germany, but the authorization for nationalizations in Article 15 has remained largely unused. Indeed, there has been a tendency to return certain government-owned enterprises to the private sector.

phrase "compensation in the light of a just consideration of the interests of the affected parties" has provoked dispute. It has been argued both that this standard means "just compensation," in other words, payment of full value, and that even token compensation would satisfy the Constitution.[227] Expropriation legislation in the German Federal Republic is largely found in provinces,[228] although federal expropriation laws also exist. Consequently, as in Argentina, the number of applicable statutes is quite large. In practice, full market value ordinarily will be awarded,[229] but there are some cases, e.g., in connection with legislation concerning the clearing of bomb sites, in which some elements of value are excluded by statute and less than full market value has been awarded.[230] Since, however, the Treaty of Friendship, Commerce and Navigation between the United States and Germany provides that nationals of the contracting parties may not be deprived of property without just compensation,[231] the German Supreme Court held that a United States national was entitled to full compensation even in a bomb site case.[232] Disputes concerning compensation are brought before the regular courts rather than before special tribunals.[233]

In most countries, if the taking of property is not an isolated occurrence motivated by conventional reasons of public utility, such as highway or railroad construction, but instead by purposes of restructuring the economic order, experience indicates that special nationalization legislation will be decreed. Constitutional guarantees of fair or prepaid compensation often will be ignored, as in recent Cuban nationalization decrees. There, compensation for seized alien

---

[227] K. BRINKMANN, *supra* note 150, at art. 19, No. I(7)(a) (citing various views).

[228] *See* EGBGB art. 109 (C. H. Beck 1964).

[229] *See* cases cited by K. BRINKMANN, note 150 *supra*.

[230] Judgment of April 3, 1956 (Kammergericht, Berlin), in 9 NEUE JURISTISCHE WOCHENSCHRIFT 1358 (1956) (statutory exclusion of increase in value occurring after 1936 due to municipal planning activity found constitutional).

[231] October 29, 1954, [1956] 2 U.S.T. 1839, T.I.A.S. No. 3593, art. V(4) (effective July 14, 1956) ("[J]ust compensation . . . shall represent the equivalent of the property taken . . . in an effectively realizable form and without unnecessary delay.")

[232] Judgment of Dec. 19, 1957, 26 BGHZ 200, 11 NEUE JURISTISCHE WOCHENSCHRIFT 463 (1958).

[233] This procedure is guaranteed by the Constitution. GRUNDGESETZ, art. 14(3) (Ger.). *See* K. BRINKMANN, *supra* note 150, at art. 14, No. I(8)(b).

property was to be provided from a fund derived from the income resulting from sugar sales to the United States at historically unrealistic prices, and at a time when Cuba's share of the United States sugar quota had been suspended.[234] Where compensation promised by the nationalizing legislation is so illusory, and when no appeal to duly constituted courts is permitted, local remedies need not be exhausted and aliens should be entitled to request espousal by their own States in the absence of an international appellate mechanism.[235]

Despite the apparent inability of capital-exporting and importing States to reconcile their differing substantive concepts concerning the proper use, control, and ownership of wealth, the International Bank for Reconstruction and Development, while not an institution primarily concerned with the formulation of new legal precedent or doctrine, has made a substantial procedural contribution to the pacific settlement of disputes in this area. In 1965 the Executive Directors of the Bank submitted to member governments the Convention on the Settlement of Investment Disputes between States and Nationals of Other States.[236] The Convention is posited on the theory that arbitration and conciliation are alternatives generally more preferable to alien investors than either exclusive reliance on the tribunals of host States or on the uncertainty of diplomatic representations. It thus is a product of the post–World War II events which undermined faith in both the Local Remedies Rule and in protecting States' ability and willingness to invoke self-help devices to protect nationals. On balance, if the Bank's system functions properly, it may be, at least for the time being, the most effective device for obtaining prompt, impartial decisions politically more acceptable to both host and protecting States.

---

[234] *See* discussion in Dawson & Weston, *Banco Nacional de Cuba v. Sabbatino: New Wine in Old Bottles*, 31 U. Chi. L. Rev. 63 (1963).

[235] This reasoning was the thrust of a bulletin issued by the United States Department of State stating that it would be presumed that local remedies in Cuba were nonexistent, and that therefore they need not be exhausted prior to filing claims with the Department. *See* 56 Am. J. Int'l L. 167 (1962).

[236] The convention, which came into force in 1966, is reprinted in 60 Am. J. Int'l L. 892 (1966). It is discussed in Szasz, *Arbitration Under the Auspices of the World Bank*, 3 Int'l Lawyer 312 (1969). *See also* G. Schwarzenberger, Foreign Investments and International Law 135–52 (1969).

In brief, the Convention establishes the International Centre for Settlement of Investment Disputes, at which panels of conciliators and arbitrators designated by the contracting States are maintained. The function of a conciliation commission is to clarify the issues in dispute and to suggest settlement on mutually acceptable terms. Their recommendations are not obligatory upon the parties. Arbitral tribunals, however, can render binding decisions. The tribunal will apply the rules of law agreed upon by the parties or, absent agreement, will apply the law of the Contracting State party, as well as those rules of international law deemed applicable. If the parties consent, the tribunal may also decide the dispute *ex aequo et bono*.

Both parties must agree in writing to submit disputes to the Centre. This agreement may take the form of a clause in a contract between an alien investor and his host State to cover certain (or all) disputes during the course of their relationship, *e.g.*, during the construction of a particular project. Consent may also be established by a specific submission, signed by both parties after a dispute has arisen. Once the parties consent to arbitration, a protecting State is precluded from offering diplomatic espousal to its citizen or from interposing an international claim. Of course, should a host State refuse to honor a decision against it, this restriction would no longer apply. Contracting States consent to treat awards as if they were final judgments of domestic courts, and must take the necessary steps to execute the award within their own legal systems.[237] However, submission of a dispute does not affect any immunity from execution the State may enjoy under national or international law, a definite weakness in the procedure provided by the Centre.

While a State's consent to the Centre's jurisdiction may be evidenced in a private agreement with an alien investor, investment legislation, as in Afghanistan and Ghana, may provide for submission to the Centre of disputes arising out of that legislation. Bilateral treaties, moreover, such as the 1968 Agreement for Economic Cooperation between the Netherlands and Indonesia "will allow either

---

[237] Special legislation in the United States, passed upon its acceptance of the Convention, gives federal district courts exclusive jurisdiction over the enforcement of awards rendered pursuant to the Convention regardless of the amount in controversy. The award is considered to be a claim arising under a treaty and gives aliens access to the federal court system to obtain enforcement. 22 U.S.C. 1650 (a) (Supp. V, 1965–1969).

the host Government or an investor having the nationality of the other party to require the submission to the Centre of any dispute arising out of an investment covered by the Agreement."[238]

To date, the Convention has been ratified by 57 capital-importing and exporting nations. They include a number of the new African and Asian nations, such as Cameroon, Central African Republic, Ceylon, Gabon, Ghana, Kenya, Korea, Morocco, Nigeria, Somalia, and others. The United Kingdom, France, and the United States also have ratified the Convention, but no Latin American nation has yet joined this impressive and extensive list. This lack of Latin American interest is doubly unfortunate since, in addition to the other benefits provided, the World Bank's Convention represents a significant step in the gradual recognition of individuals as subjects of international law, enabling private persons to bring sovereign States before international tribunals.

Presuming that an affirmative judgment can be obtained by an alien, either against a person or a government in local courts, special factors which may or may not depend upon the victor's alien status can hinder enforcement. Some of these factors are discussed at length in the following Chapter.

---

[238] International Centre for Settlement of Investment Disputes, Annual Report 1967/1968 at 5.

Chapter VIII

Special Problems Encountered by Aliens in Enforcing Foreign Remedies

Even if an alien successfully obtains access to a court abroad, surmounts the procedural obstacles of a foreign legal system, and obtains a judgment on the merits, he still may confront barriers which can prevent enjoyment of the fruits of victory. In addition to the normal procedural problems of executing upon a defendant's property in order to satisfy a judgment, foreign exchange regulations may make it difficult or impossible for the alien to remit to his home country any amounts obtained. Alternatively, the plaintiff may have to enforce his judgment in still another country where the defendant has property. Therefore no discussion of an alien's procedural rights would be complete without reviewing both the hurdles imposed by exchange controls and by rules concerning enforcement of foreign judicial and arbitral awards.[1]

EXCHANGE CONTROLS

In today's economically interdependent world, States must guard the value of their currencies with the same fervor once reserved only for frontiers. Yet the attacks to which monetary systems are susceptible are much more varied, and therefore much more difficult to defend against, than armed invasion over State borders. Foremost among the difficulties is identifying the attacker, for he may be acting on the purest of motives and only incidentally affecting the financial structure of the State. To meet these difficulties, exchange

---

[1] Thus the Committee on Foreign Law of the Association of the Bar of the City of New York concluded in 1955 "that in view of the exchange control and the difficulty of coping with procedural requirements, it is rarely advisable, under the present state of the law, to attempt to enforce an American judgment in the Argentine." Committee on Foreign Law, *American Judgments Abroad— Argentine Republic*, 11 THE RECORD 147, 150 (1956).

control legislation generally is broadly worded, phrased in the negative, and aimed at all persons. Frequently, it does not distinguish between citizens and aliens as such, prohibiting or regulating instead transactions between "residents" and "nonresidents." Obviously, however, a significant number of those people affected are foreigners. An alien who seeks to repatriate invested capital, to remit profits of a business venture or the fruits of a victorious lawsuit, to reorganize the capital structure of a company, to borrow money, and in some places even to invest in a going concern or to organize a new business, will find himself involved more often than not with exchange controls.[2] Nor should one assume that these restrictions are symptoms of ailing economies and encountered only in developing countries. At present, of the 140-plus independent States in the world, only a handful are completely free of currency or exchange controls. In all other places, transactions in one or more of such items as local currency, foreign currency, gold, securities, imports, exports, property transfers, travel, and a long list of activities affecting in one way or another the balance-of-payments position of the State and the value of its currency in the international market place, are subject to regulations and restrictions of widely varying complexity, severity, and wisdom.

Perhaps nothing is more inhibiting to prospective investors or businessmen than confronting in some developing countries seemingly unending lines of government employees, the greater number of whom have not the slightest comprehension of the intent of the regulations they are implementing, presiding over lengthy questionnaires in multiple copies. There is little doubt that citizens and aliens are aggrieved equally by these conditions, since bureaucracy run rampant seldom distinguishes among its victims. However, the effect of exchange controls, as distinct from their application, unquestionably is felt more by aliens, and particularly by nonresident aliens, than by citizens. An alien litigant in a country with severe balance-of-payment difficulties and consequent comprehensive exchange controls may discover that he is unable to remove from the jurisdiction

---

[2] In Colombia, in order to be assured that foreign exchange will be available for repayment of loans granted by foreign entities, the loan itself must be registered with, and approved by, the Banco de la Republica. Similar requirements exist in Brazil.

the money judgment obtained in a successful lawsuit. An alien businessman whose enterprise has been nationalized may find the compensation funds to be in local currency and incapable of conversion into, say, dollars, sterling, or deutsche marks. A shareholder in a profitable foreign venture may be informed that government decrees require that all dividends be paid into a local, blocked account. A creditor may be told that government regulations at the situs of the debt do not permit repayments of the indebtedness to leave the country. Exchange laws thus demand careful attention by aliens planning to invest or live abroad, not only due to their potential adverse impact, but also because of the relative facility and frequency with which they may be changed.

One example of a comprehensive exchange control law is that of the Republic of Singapore.[3] That law, by virtue of the very active commercial policies of the Singapore Government, the highly qualified civil service, and the general vitality of the Singapore business and banking communities, is one of the most efficiently and wisely administered exchange laws found anywhere. The legislation provides that no person, alien or citizen, shall perform any of the following acts in Singapore respecting currency payments except with permission of the Controller of Foreign Exchange:

> (a) make any payment to or for the credit of a person resident in the scheduled territories [*i.e.*, Singapore] by order or on behalf of a person resident outside the scheduled territories; or
> (b) place any sum to the credit of any person outside the scheduled territories [except on the receipt of satisfaction of a debt].[4]

The same ordinance prohibits any act "which involves, is in association with, or is preparatory to, the making of any payment outside

---

[3] The Exchange Control Ordinance, 1953 (Malayan Ordinance 57 of 1953), as extended to Singapore and modified by the Modification of Laws (Exchange Control) Order, 1964 (L.N. 238 of 1964) and the Modification of Laws (Exchange Control) Order, 1965 (G.N. Sp. No. S223 of 1965). Acts of other Commonwealth countries almost identical in wording are: *Ghana*—Exchange Control Act, 1961 (Act 71); *see also* Currency Act, 1964 (Act 242) and amendments; *Kenya*—Exchange Control Act, Cap. 113 REV. LAWS OF KENYA, 1967; *Tanzania*—Exchange Control Ordinance, Cap. 294 REV. LAWS OF TANZANIA. For a recent study of investment in Singapore see FOREIGN INVESTMENT & INDUSTRIALISATION IN SINGAPORE (H. Hughes & Y. Seng eds. 1969).

[4] *Id.* § 8.

Singapore, to or for the credit of a person resident outside the scheduled territories."[5] Nor can any payment be made to persons resident anywhere which will have the effect of transferring to or creating in favor of a person a right to receive a payment or to acquire property outside of the scheduled territories.[6] All such rights are included, be they present, future, vested, or contingent.

The ordinance provides, respecting money judgments, that there shall be implied in every such judgment or order or in any award given under Singapore law "that any sum required to be paid . . . [whether as a debt, damages, or otherwise] shall not be paid except with the permission of the Controller."[7] Provision is made for full discharge of any judgment debtor by payment into court of any judgments against him, which it would be unlawful for exchange reasons to pay direct. Execution is varied accordingly as well. There is ample evidence, however, of the willingness of the Controller to permit foreign exchange resulting from litigation to leave the jurisdiction.

Elsewhere the situation varies. However, the Reserve Bank of India, which is responsible for the administration of the 1948 Foreign Exchange Regulations Act of that country, claims to be cooperative in granting approval for remittances of foreign exchange. In Ceylon, the complexities and the incentive ingredients of the law may cause more difficulties. Foreign Exchange Entitlement Certificates (FEEC's) are offered for sale by tender in Ceylon in a somewhat similar fashion to treasury bills in some Western countries.[8]

Alien claimants, of course, may encounter difficulties much more sophisticated than simple bars to removal of judgment funds. An example may be found in a somewhat disturbing judgment of the Supreme Court of India, refusing to interfere with an order of the High Court of Calcutta staying the effect of an arbitration agreement. This agreement provided for settlement in New York of disputes arising out of a sales contract for manganese ore by an Indian firm to a New York company.[9] The New York concern had

---

[5] *Id.* § 9.

[6] *Id.* § 10.

[7] *Id.*, Fourth Schedule, § 1.

[8] *See* Exchange Control Act, No. 24 of 1953, *as amended,* Cap. 423 LEG. ENACTMENTS OF CEYLON, Vol. XII.

[9] Michael Golodetz v. Serajuddin & Co., [1963] ALL INDIA RPTR. 1044.

commenced proceedings in India to enforce the agreement and to proceed with arbitration in New York. The Indian firm defended and asked for a stay, one of the grounds being its inability under Indian foreign exchange laws to move the necessary witnesses out of the country. Speaking for the Supreme Court, Shah, J., stated:

> It must be observed that having regard to the severe restrictions imposed in the matter of providing foreign exchange to individual citizens it would be impossible for the respondents to take their witnesses to New York and to attend before the arbitrators at the arbitration proceeding to defend the case against them and the proceeding before the arbitrators would in effect be ex parte. That would result in injustice to the respondents. Undoubtedly the appellants would be put to some inconvenience if they are required to defend the suit filed against them in India, but the High Court has considered the balance of inconvenience and the other circumstances and has come to the conclusion, and in our judgment that conclusion is right, that the facts established make out "sufficient reason" for not granting stay.[10]

The above judgment illustrates the wide-ranging impact of exchange controls. A subsequent decision of the High Court of Calcutta fortunately appears to offer some hope that exchange controls cannot block the effect of all arbitration agreements providing for hearings outside of India.[11] Counsel for the United States company involved in this latter case suggested that the difficulties of the earlier case could be overcome, and the arbitration take place in the United States as agreed, if the Court accepted three concessions which his client was willing to make: first, if the Indian firm was not in a position to produce its witnesses outside India, it would be at liberty to apply to the Court for a variation of the existing order staying a lawsuit commenced by the Indian firm in India in defiance of the arbitral clause; second, that in the event the Indian firm was prejudiced in calling its witnesses owing to foreign exchange restrictions, it could apply for examination of them in India and the United States company would not object; third, if the Indian firm "experiences difficulties in the conduct of its case in any manner whatsoever

---

[10] Id. at 1047.

[11] B.P. Khemka Private Ltd. v. M. Golodetz & Co. (unreported judgment of the High Court at Calcutta, Aug. 10, 1966).

due to foreign exchange control or restrictions" it would be at liberty to apply for variations in the Order to Stay. The High Court of Calcutta concluded that in consideration of these concessions it would not be proper to refuse the stay of proceedings on grounds of foreign exchange restrictions.

Even where the specter of exchange controls does not succeed in disrupting the course of litigation itself, investors require assurance that they will be able to remit any monetary awards in their favor. This need is especially apparent where compensation for nationalized property may be immobilized within the taking State pursuant to currency control regulations. Remittance of fair compensation for nationalized interests is a legitimate objective of an alien investor yet one which, prima facie, is inconsistent with exchange controls. Special concern for this interest nevertheless appears in a number of developing countries. Protection is best provided in Kenya, where the Constitution declares that compensation shall be paid in all compulsory acquisitions and that persons entitled thereto shall not be prevented from remitting it out of Kenya free from any charge or tax.[12] In Ghana, furthermore, legislation protects approved investments from expropriation except on payment of fair compensation in the currency in which the investment originally was made.[13]

Because exchange controls are the rule, rather than the exception, they also are found in several developed States. In Australia, for example, controls are likely to affect more often the alien investor than the alien litigant. The Australian Government requires the Reserve Bank to be consulted before overseas companies, or Australian companies in which there is a substantial overseas shareholding, complete plans to borrow in Australia. The general aim is to prevent foreign interests from absorbing too great a portion of locally available financing. The Australian Government considers that undue reliance by subsidiaries or branches of overseas companies upon

---

[12] Art. XIX. Such legislation assuring the remittance of compensation would seem of great importance. Otherwise, a deprived alien's efforts to remove his award or his investment from the country could be met with a defense of sovereign immunity or the Act of State Doctrine. *See* French v. Banco Nacional de Cuba, 23 N.Y.2d 46, 242 N.E. 29 704, 295 N.Y.S. 2d 433 (1968), *discussed in* Lillich, *International Law, 1969 Survey of N.Y. Law,* 21 SYRACUSE L. REV. 451, 470–74 (1970).

[13] Capital Investments Act, 1963 (Act No. 172), § 8.

local capital sources would add excessively to demands on "a diminished supply of investible resources" and reduce the availability of capital to local companies. The result, of course, could be an adverse affect upon the balance of payments.[14]

Exchange control in Australia is administered so as to encourage foreign investment. All remittances abroad require exchange control approval, but in practice no restrictions are imposed upon current transactions. Moreover, Australian trading banks are authorized to deal with the majority of transactions as agents of the Reserve Bank. All current net income, after tax, accruing to overseas investors may be remitted without restriction. Approval is required but normally granted for repatriation of capital by overseas residents. While commitments to permit repatriation are not made in advance, as they are for instance in Colombia, approval is withheld only in exceptional circumstances once an actual application is submitted. The Australian Government has declared that Australia values its past record of fair treatment of repatriation applications and would not lightly damage the reputation earned in this field.

In most European countries, exchange controls have existed since before World War II, but current administrative interpretation is usually quite liberal. In Austria, transfers of funds between residents and nonresidents are illegal unless licensed by the Austrian National Bank.[15] However, since Austria has enjoyed adequate foreign exchange reserves in recent years, the Austrian National Bank has issued a number of "blanket" licenses making it unnecessary to apply for individual authorizations. The Austrian schilling is fully convertible for nonresidents.[16] Similar situations prevail in other European countries, at least as to current transactions, but this state of affairs is obviously dependent on continued favorable economic conditions. France is an example in point. Late in 1966, a statute abrogated existing exchange controls, though the Government was authorized to enact exchange control measures by decree.[17] Pursuant

---

[14] Similar restrictions are found in Peru and Venezuela.

[15] The basic statute is the Exchange Control Act of July 25, 1946, [1946] BGBl. No. 162 (Aus.).

[16] I. SEIDL-HOHENVELDERN, AMERICAN-AUSTRIAN PRIVATE INTERNATIONAL LAW 55 (1963).

[17] Law No. 66–1008 of Dec. 28, 1966, [1966] J.O. 11621, [1967] D.L. 30.

to that authorization, rules regulating capital transactions were adopted,[18] essentially as a means of regulating the capital market rather than to prevent foreign exchange outflow. But when the economy experienced serious difficulties following the strikes of May 1968, exchange controls were immediately imposed for current transactions as well.[19] Their abrogation a few months later was of short duration, since economic difficulties persisted.[20] At present, exchange controls are in effect in France for current as well as capital transactions.[21] Again, however, aliens are in a somewhat better position than French nationals.

These and similar regulations, owing to chronic global economic instability, will be with us for some time. Since regulations usually are administrative in nature, as is the case in France, they are subject to frequent change. Therefore their current status should be reviewed periodically by alien residents and investors.

The Recognition and Enforcement of Foreign Judgments

The alien litigant may have occasion to ask more of the courts of another country than mere service of process on his adversaries or the interrogation of witnesses. He may wish, if he is a defendant, to interpose as a defense of res judicata a decision in his favor on the same facts in the court of another State. Or he may seek, after being victorious in one country, execution on property located in yet another nation.

In each of these cases he must request the local court to honor decisions rendered in another jurisdiction. Sometimes such a request will be denied on public policy grounds, as when a court in State *A*

---

[18] Decree No. 67-78 of Jan. 27, 1967, [1967] J.O. 1073, [1967] D.L. 81, 56 REVUE CRITIQUE DE DROIT INTERNATIONAL PRIVÉ [REV. CRIT. D.I.P.] 400 (1967), *as amended* by Decree No. 69-264 of March 21, 1969, J.O. March 27, 1969, 96 JOURNAL DU DROIT INTERNATIONAL [CLUNET] 774 (1969) (regulating French direct investments abroad, foreign investments in France, the sale of foreign securities in France, and foreign loans).

[19] Decree No. 68-481 of May 29, 1968, [1968] J.O. 5308, [1968] D.L. 204.

[20] Decree No. 68-788 of Sept. 4, 1968, [1968] J.O. 8513, [1968] D.L. 271.

[21] Decree No. 68-1021 of Nov. 24, 1968, [1968] J.O. 11081, 96 JOURNAL DU DROIT INTERNATIONAL [CLUNET] 207 (1969).

refuses to order execution of a court or administrative decision in State B purporting to confiscate property located in State A.[22] However, most nations are willing to place their local legal processes at the disposal of alien plaintiffs who have been successful abroad, provided certain requisites are met. These requirements, as might be expected, vary considerably from nation to nation, even within a legal suborder such as exists in Latin America. Unfortunately, the ideal of automatic recognition of foreign judgments is far from attained, since international agreements assuring rapid recognition by the contracting parties of each other's judicial decisions are not very frequent between common law and civil law countries.[23]

The earliest basis upon which English law accorded recognition to foreign judgments undoubtedly was comity—the theory that the law of nations required the courts of one State to assist those of another. For this reason, jurisdiction for enforcement within England of foreign judgments first fell to the High Court of Admiralty without heed to the subject matter of the action, for it was this court which was charged with administering the law of nations. However, foreign judgments today generally are recognized by the ordinary courts on the assumption that a vested right is created when the judicial process has worked properly elsewhere. A key ingredient in the validity of any judgment, of course, is the jurisdiction of the original court. Accordingly, lack of jurisdiction of the foreign court is one of the principal grounds upon which enforcement of foreign judgments is denied.

Lack of jurisdiction assumes various forms. English courts, for example, will deny enforcement of a foreign judgment which purports to attach a person who, under international law, is entitled to immunity.[24] Jurisdictional failure occurs again when a foreign

---

[22] See, e.g., Republic of Iraq v. First Nat'l City Bank, 353 F.2d 47 (2d Cir. 1965), cert. denied, 382 U.S. 1027 (1966).

[23] Concerning treaties relating to the recognition of foreign judgments, see text at notes 144–152 infra. For a more detailed discussion of the recognition and enforcement of foreign country judgments, see, e.g., I. SZÁSZY, INTERNATIONAL CIVIL PROCEDURE 523–601 (1967); Smit, International Res Judicata and Collateral Estoppel in the United States, 9 U.C.L.A. L. REV. 44 (1962); von Mehren & Trautman, Recognition of Foreign Adjudications: A Survey and a Suggested Approach, 81 HARV. L. REV. 1601 (1968).

[24] The Foreign Judgments (Reciprocal Enforcement) Act, 1933, 23 & 24 Geo. 5, c. 13, § 4(3)(c).

court purports to affect immovable property located outside of its territory.[25] Another ground upon which enforcement of foreign judgments is opposed in England is the failure to observe the requirement that the defendant in the foreign proceedings be notified of the action in sufficient time to enable him to appear and defend.[26] This particular ground, only related indirectly to jurisdiction, is rooted in concepts of natural justice. Still another category of foreign judgments refused recognition or enforcement under the English law of conflicts concerns judgments which, if recognized or enforced in England, would contravene public policy. Examples include attempts to enforce foreign penal or revenue laws.[27] A claim for foreign taxes will not lie in English courts.[28]

Foreign judgments formerly were recognized or enforced at common law in accordance with the above principles. Now, in England and in most Commonwealth countries, the existence of statutory procedures makes enforcement much less cumbersome. The foreign judgment need not be sued upon. Instead, a simple process of registration qualifies it for execution, giving it the same quality as a judgment of a local court. These statutory provisions generally operate on a basis of reciprocity, and also include requirements that the foreign judgment be final and unsatisfied. Occasionally, a provision that no appeals are pending is included; if not, this ground is one which a foreign judgment debtor may raise in opposing registration. In England, the old common law requirements respecting due notice and public policy also have been given legislative effect. The English statutes in this area once again illustrate distinctions between Commonwealth and "foreign" countries. The earliest English statute of this variety which was applicable outside the United Kingdom was the Administration of Justice Act, 1920, which ex-

---

[25] *Id.* § 4(3)(a). This failure is a corollary of the principle that English courts have no jurisdiction to determine the title to, or the right to the possession of, any immovable situate outside England.

[26] Baker v. Wadsworth, [1896] 67 L.J.Q.B. 301. *See also* Jacobson v. Frachon, [1927] 44 T.L.R. 103, 105 (Atkin, L.J.).

[27] Huntington v. Attrill, [1893] A.C. 150 (penal laws); Sydney Municipal Council v. Bull, [1909] 1 K.B. 7; *Re* Visser, Queen of Holland v. Drukker, [1928] 1 Ch. 877 (revenue laws).

[28] Government of India v. Taylor, [1955] A.C. 491. Nor does an extraprovincial tax claim lie in another Canadian province: City of Regina v. McVey, [1922] 23 Ont. W.N. 32.

tended only to Commonwealth countries. It was followed in 1933 by the Foreign Judgments (Reciprocal Enforcement) Act, which extends both to Commonwealth and non-Commonwealth countries. Under this act and statutes in many Commonwealth countries modeled upon it, registration of foreign judgments may obtain upon ex parte applications. However, the local court normally retains the same discretion over execution of foreign judgments as it does with respect to its own judgments.

The wording of many enforcement-of-foreign-judgment statutes of Commonwealth countries is almost identical. Required for registration is evidence that reciprocity exists, that the judgment is final, and that it is for a sum of money, not taxes. Registration may be set aside if it can be shown to have been obtained improperly, if the judgment was of a court without jurisdiction, if the defendant had insufficient notice and did not appear, if the judgment was obtained by fraud or would contravene public policy in the registering State, or if the rights under the judgment are not vested in the applicant.[29] Interestingly, the Canadian province of Alberta adds an additional ground: if "the judgment debtor would have a good defence if an action were brought on the original judgment."[30]

Foreign judgments, of course, may be pleaded as defenses to actions for the same subject matter and will be recognized if the judgment was in favor of the defendant or, if in favor of the plaintiff, has been fully satisfied. The onus generally lies upon defendants to show that the foreign judgment concerns the same matter at issue in the local court.

The process by which a tribunal decides to concede extraterritorial effect to judgments rendered in other nations is known as

---

[29] *See* in these respects: *Ceylon*—The Enforcement of Foreign Judgments Act, c. 93, LEG. ENACTMENTS OF CEYLON, 1956, and The Reciprocal Enforcement of Judgments Act, c. 94, LEG. ENACTMENTS OF CEYLON, 1956 (the latter applying only to judgments of United Kingdom courts); *Ghana*—The Judgments (International Enforcement) Act, 1960 (Act 20); *Kenya*—The Foreign Judgments Enforcement Ordinance, c. 43, REV. LAWS OF KENYA; *Singapore*—*Foreign Judgments* (Reciprocal Enforcement) Ordinance, No. 29 of 1959; *Tanzania*—Foreign Judgments (Reciprocal Enforcement) Act, c. 8 of the REV. LAWS OF TANZANIA.

[30] The Reciprocal Enforcement of Judgments Act, STAT. ALBERTA 1958, c. 33, § 3(6)(g). The conditions in the Alberta Act appear not as grounds for deregistering but as bars to registration.

homologation in Brazil and *exequatur* in the other Latin American States. The intensity with which the foreign judgment is examined for conformity with national law and public policy varies considerably, but in none of these States does there exist the simple registration system prevailing in the Commonwealth. However, if the judgment passes the tests prescribed by local procedural codes, exequatur or homologation will be granted. The effect of this grant, according to the Spanish commentator Sanchez-Apellaniz, is "the incorporation of the foreign judgment into the national juridical order, . . . the naturalization . . . of the foreign decision . . . making the foreign judgment the same as a national judgment."[31] The exequatur decision then may be utilized to interpose a defense of res judicata, or to serve as a basis for an order of execution upon a defendant's property. Execution itself is, however, a separate process, and is conducted according to the norms established for national judgments.

Latin American procedural code provisions regulating recognition and execution of foreign judgments demonstrate a greater diversity than articles in the same codes dealing with suits in forma pauperis and security bonds. Attempts to achieve uniformity have been unsuccessful, even though this area would seem ripe for codification due to the great increases in regional trade inspired by the Latin American Free Trade Association and the Central American Common Market. For example, the Bustamante Code in Articles 423–433 seeks to allow recognition and execution without requiring reciprocity. However, Venezuela specifically made reservations to these articles, and many Latin American nations require evidence that judgments of their courts would be recognized in the courts of the nation which issued the judgment for which exequatur was requested. Treaties between the United States and Nicaragua,[32] Honduras,[33] and Argentina,[34] respectively, are silent as concerns foreign judg-

---

[31] *Reconocimiento y Ejecución de Sentencias Extranjeras en Derecho Hispano-Americano*, 1956 REVISTA DE DERECHO PROCESAL 61, 90 (No. 2).

[32] Treaty of Friendship, Commerce and Navigation between the United States and Nicaragua, 9 U.S.T. 449, T.I.A.S. No. 4024, 367 U.N.T.S. 3 (effective May 24, 1958).

[33] Treaty of Friendship, Commerce and Consular Rights with Honduras, Dec. 7, 1927, 45 Stat. 2618 (1929), T.S. No. 764 (effective July 23, 1928).

[34] Treaty of Friendship, Commerce and Navigation with Argentina, 10 Stat. 1005 (1855), T.S. No. 4 (effective Dec. 20, 1854).

ments, although each agreement assures citizens of each contracting party access to the courts of the other.

There is, unfortunately, no international full faith and credit for foreign judgments such as exists among the states of the United States and among the provinces of Argentina. Nevertheless, Latin American courts do not review the merits of foreign decisions, but only consider whether they meet local criteria.[35] Thus, Article 608 of the Mexican Federal Code of Civil Procedure states that the court "may not examine or decide concerning the justice or injustice of the judgment, nor on the foundations of fact or law upon which it rests, being confined only to examining its authenticity, and if it should or should not be executed according to Mexican law."[36] Case law in Brazil is to the same effect, and Brazilian courts will not reexamine the jurisdiction of the foreign court except in instances of blatant denials of procedural due process, as where the defendant's consent to the jurisdiction of the foreign courts had been coerced or derived from an adhesion contract. Also, foreign judgments on matters pending before a Brazilian court, regardless of which action was filed first, will not be homologated.[37]

In the absence of treaty, Brazil, Costa Rica, and Argentina do not demand reciprocity as a condition precedent to exequatur.[38] Venezuelan,[39] Peruvian,[40] Guatemalan,[41] and Honduran[42] courts will request documentary proof, however, usually in the form of a consular affidavit (the codes are not specific on this point), that courts of the nation in which the judgment was rendered would execute final judgments issued by courts in the nation where exequatur is

---

[35] Sanchez-Apellaniz, *supra* note 31, at 95–96.

[36] CÓDIGO DE PROCEDIMIENTOS CIVILES PARA EL DISTRITO Y TERRITORIOS FEDERALES (M. Andrade ed. 1964).

[37] P. GARLAND, AMERICAN-BRAZILIAN PRIVATE INTERNATIONAL LAW 93–95 (1959).

[38] For a discussion of the enforcement of foreign judgments in Argentina see Gowland, *Ejecución de Sentencias Extranjeras*, 1956 REVISTA DE DERECHO PROCESAL 321 (No. 3).

[39] CÓDIGO DE PROCEDIMIENTO CIVIL VENEZOLANO, art. 747 (A. Hernandez-Breton ed. 1966).

[40] CÓDIGO DE PROCEDIMIENTOS CIVILES, arts. 1155, 1156 & 1157 (J. Fajardo ed. 1965).

[41] CÓDIGO PROCESAL, CIVIL Y MERCANTIL, art. 344, 1968 RECOPILACIÓN DE LEYES 256.

[42] CÓDIGO DE PROCEDIMIENTOS, art. 237.

solicited.[43] Venezuela, moreover, requires evidence that foreign courts do not review cases on the merits.[44] Guatemala's reciprocity requirement is phrased somewhat differently, with Article 344 of the Code of Civil Procedure according foreign judgments "the value which the legislation or decisions of the country of origin assign to the judgments issued by Guatemalan courts." The Peruvian Code of Civil Procedure is similar.[45] In Honduras, all is not lost if reciprocity cannot be proven, since a foreign judgment still may be executed if the judgment has been granted in a "personal" action, if the defendant was not in default, and if the obligation is legal in Honduras.[46] In Venezuela, Guatemala, and Peru, however, no such "second chance" is offered applicants who cannot demonstrate reciprocity. Mexico's Federal Code of Civil Procedure introduces a unique concept when it states that, in the absence of a treaty, foreign judgments will have the effect established by "international reciprocity."[47]

Frequently, applications for homologation or exequatur must be presented to the nation's highest court, as in Brazil,[48] Venezuela,[49] Costa Rica,[50] and Honduras.[51] The procedural codes of Guatemala,[52]

---

[43] In Venezuela, an affidavit signed by two practicing attorneys in the foreign state asserting that reciprocal treatment will be granted may suffice for nations within the Western Hemisphere, including the United States. Unfortunately, neither the United States nor the Latin American nations have procedures, as does Austria, whereby certifications of reciprocity may be obtained from administrative authorities in the nation where exequatur is requested. See Herzog, *International Law, National Tribunals and the Rights of Aliens: The West European Experience*, 21 VAND. L. REV. 742, 750–57 (1968).

[44] Art. 747.

[45] Art. 1156.

[46] Art. 238.

[47] Art. 604. A rather unclear expression, to be sure, the constitutionality of such provisions has been challenged, perhaps since it violates the principle of equal treatment of aliens and nationals. See discussion in Nadelmann, *Non-Recognition of American Money Judgments Abroad and What To Do About It*, 42 IOWA L. REV. 236, 250–51 (1957).

[48] CÓDIGO DE PROCESO CIVIL, art. 785 (V. Sabino ed. 1969).

[49] CÓDIGO DE PROCEDIMIENTO CIVIL VENEZOLANO, art. 746.

[50] CÓDIGO DE PROCEDIMIENTOS CIVILES, art. 1024 (A. Vicenzi ed. 1966).

[51] Art. 239.

[52] Art. 346.

Argentina,[53] Mexico,[54] and Peru,[55] and practice in the United States, however, require that application be made to the court (usually of first instance) that would have had competence if the suit had originally been brought in that country. This requirement would mean, of course, the court of the defendant's domicile if he is a national of the host State. This latter method seems the more sensible, since once the Supreme Court of Costa Rica, for example, grants exequatur, it then must refer the matter, for purposes of execution and according to Article 1025 of the Code of Civil Procedure, to a lower court at the defendant's domicile. This extra step can be time-consuming and costly.

If the foreign judgment affects real, and sometimes movable, property in the Latin American nation (as distinguished from a "personal action"), it may not receive exequatur even where reciprocity requirements have been met. Venezuela's Code of Civil Procedure forbids granting exequatur to suits affecting Venezuelan real estate,[56] as does the Peruvian Code, which, alone among the codes studied, also denies exequatur to foreign judgments relating to ships flying the Peruvian flag, to civil actions arising out of torts perpetrated in Peru, and actions affecting the inheritance rights of Peruvians or aliens domiciled in Peru.[57] The Argentine Federal Code of Civil Procedure requires that the foreign judgment be in a "personal action," which can be interpreted to mean that exequatur will not be granted in cases involving Argentine real estate.[58] Mexico's Code of Civil Procedure in Article 605 (II) also requires that the foreign judgment be obtained in a "personal action," as does the Guatemalan Code.[59] Other Latin American codes are silent concerning foreign judgments on local real property, but the principle

[53] Código Procesal Civil y Comercial de la Nación, art. 518, Ley No. 17454, *Boletín Oficial*, Nov. 7, 1967.

[54] Art. 606.

[55] Art. 1161.

[56] Art. 748(1).

[57] Art. 1160. Article 1158 denies recognition to foreign judgments seeking to determine the civil status, personal capacity or family relations of Peruvians or of foreigners domiciled in Peru. Article 1159 empowers Peruvian courts to deny exequatur to foreign judgments which are "contrary to morals, good customs or against the laws of the Republic."

[58] Art. 517(1).

[59] Art. 345(1).

of territoriality and other expressions in the codes on competence of local tribunals over domestic real estate would not seem to augur well for enforcement of foreign judgments in this area. There may be some doubt even as to the enforceability of foreign judgments purporting to affect movable property. Article 517 of the Argentine Code permits exequatur for foreign judgments concerning personal property only if the property was brought to Argentina during or after the foreign litigation.

Any attempt to affect local property also could be denied exequatur under procedural codes denying execution to obligations which are against public policy (*orden público*), as in Costa Rica,[60] Argentina,[61] and Brazil;[62] or which are not legal (*licito*) in the nation where execution is sought, as in Guatemala,[63] Mexico,[64] Honduras,[65] and Venezuela;[66] or which, as in Peru, "are contrary to morals, good customs or prohibited by the laws of the Republic."[67] A similar public policy justification is sometimes utilized by courts in the United States to deny enforcement to foreign decrees purporting to confiscate real or personal property located within the United States.[68] Argentina's Federal Code in Article 517 (6) also demands that the foreign judgment "not be incompatible with another [judgment] rendered, prior thereto or simultaneously, by an Argentine court." A distinguished Argentine commentator has written that a reply to a questionnaire prepared for the 1925 Hague Conference stated that in such a case "a real conflict of jurisdictional sovereignty would be produced, which could only be adequately resolved by diplomatic means."[69] No other Latin American procedural code examined contains this requirement.

---

[60] Art. 1022(4).

[61] Arts. 517(3)(4).

[62] Art. 792.

[63] Art. 345(3).

[64] Art. 605(III).

[65] Art. 238(3).

[66] Art. 748(4).

[67] Art. 1159.

[68] "[W]hen property confiscated is within the United States at the time of the attempted confiscation our courts will give effect to acts of state 'only if they are consistent with the policy and law of the United States.' " Republic of Iraq v. First Nat'l City Bank, *supra* note 22, at 51, *citing* RESTATEMENT, FOREIGN RELATIONS LAW OF THE UNITED STATES § 46 (Proposed Official Draft 1962).

[69] 3 W. GOLDSCHMIDT, DERECHIO INTERNACIONAL PRIVADO 215 (1954).

All Latin American nations agree that the court which issued the foreign judgment must have had "competence" to do so (a combination of proper venue and adequate jurisdiction over subject matter and litigants), and that the judgment should be translated into Spanish (Portuguese in Brazil) and a copy authenticated abroad by consular authorities in the forum State. The Brazilian Code of Civil Procedure also requires an authenticated "Letter of Sentence," writes a Brazilian lawyer, which "is an official court document embodying the judgment which is available in Brazil and Portugal and some other continental systems."[70] In practice the Brazilian Supreme Court has not demanded this document where foreign jurisdictions do not issue them. Other nations, such as Peru, require only authenticated copies of the judgments and proof of notification to defendants,[71] although Venezuela[72] and Mexico[73] also demand presentation of the *ejecutoria,* which is akin to the Brazilian "Letter of Sentence" or, in the United States, to an order of execution.

While the Honduran, Costa Rican, Guatemalan, and Mexican codes do not specify the documentation which must accompany exequatur applications, it may be safely presumed that as a minimum they will require a translated, authenticated version of the final judgment, together with a certificate from a consular or court official in the forum that the judgment is final and may not be appealed, and certified copies of negotiable instruments, agreements, and other documents relating to the transaction which gave rise to the litigation.

Most Latin American nations require that the defendant receive personal notice of the action against him, although Brazilian courts will be satisfied if every effort is made to give notice. "Normally, the standards of the foreign jurisdiction are automatically accepted but if they are so inadequate as to suggest basic unfairness, Brazilian courts will not recognize the resulting judgment."[74] Peru[75] and

---

[70] P. GARLAND, *supra* note 37, at 95–96.

[71] CÓDIGO DE PROCEDIMIENTOS CIVILES, art. 1161.

[72] CÓDIGO DE PROCEDIMIENTO CIVIL VENEZOLANO, art. 749.

[73] CÓDIGO DE PROCEDIMIENTOS CIVILES PARA EL DISTRITO Y TERRITORIOS FEDERALES, art. 607.

[74] P. GARLAND, *supra* note 37, at 95.

[75] CÓDIGO DE PROCEDIMIENTO CIVIL, art. 1159.

Venezuela[76] require that defendants be notified (*citado*) according to the laws of the foreign jurisdiction, although Venezuela demands in addition that defendants be notified sufficiently in advance so that they will have time to appear and defend.[77] The Argentine Code, while not mentioning the laws concerning notification in the foreign State, requires that notice be given personally if the losing party resides in Argentina.[78]

Most Latin American nations honor default judgments if notification and reciprocity requirements have been met. Honduras, however, will not grant exequatur to default judgments absent a treaty or reciprocity, although, as already indicated, it will honor judgments in which a defendant appeared.[79] The Guatemalan Procedural Code grants exequatur to foreign judgments "which have not been granted in default or against an allegedly absent person who is domiciled in Guatemala."[80] This article is almost identical to Article 559 (2) of the old Argentine Federal Code of Civil and Commercial Procedure, discarded when the 1967 code came into effect. It would seem to apply whether or not the defendant is an alien, since the determining factor is one of domicile and not nationality.[81]

Various codes also differ concerning opportunities to oppose exequatur petitions. The Mexican Federal Procedural Code, which permits a challenge to the translation of the supporting documents, also requires the presence of a government representative at the

---

[76] Art. 748(3).

[77] Mexico, in Article 605(IV) of its procedural code, merely requires personal notice so he can defend.

[78] Código Procesal Civil y Comercial de la Nación, art. 517(2).

[79] Código de Procedimientos, art. 238.

[80] Art. 345(2).

[81] The Argentine commentator Gowland, citing case law concerning old Article 559(2), stated that it "does not refer only to Argentines, but also to foreigners. Thus, he who is sued in the country of his origin, but who is domiciled in Argentina, may oppose the execution. But the defendant must have had his domicile in the Republic at the moment suit was commenced; if he is domiciled abroad, although not in the country where the judgment is issued, and later comes to the Republic, he cannot invoke this provision, since in that manner he could evade compliance with his obligation." *Ejecución de Sentencias Extranjeras*, 1956 Revista de Derecho Procesal 321, 329 (No. 3). *See also* Goldschmidt, *Reconocimiento y Ejecución de Resoluciones Judiciales Extranjeras en la República Argentina*, 7 Revista de Derecho Procesal 215 (1951).

hearing,[82] as does the Honduran Code.[83] The Costa Rican, Honduran, Argentine, and Venezuelan codes seem to assume service of the application upon the opposing party, who must answer within a period of time which may be as short as 3 days in Honduras.[84] Peru grants defendants 10 days in which to answer,[85] and, in the absence of treaty, the burden of showing the force accorded Peruvian judgments abroad is placed upon the plaintiff.[86] The Guatemalan Code does not indicate the existence of any right to oppose exequatur and in Brazil homologation "is almost exclusively a formal review of the documents."[87] Countries which allow opposition to exequatur will grant the decree in default if the defendant does not appear to contest the application within the requisite time period.

Where, however, the foreign judgment determines status, as in divorce or adoption proceedings, commentators differ as to whether exequatur is required. In Brazil, the Law of Introduction to the Code of Civil Procedure states that homologation is not required for decisions determining status, but the courts are divided, some contending that divorce decrees were meant to be included in the provisions concerning homologation.[88] To eliminate uncertainty, one Brazilian attorney suggests "that all foreign decisions be presented to the Supreme Court for its homologation inasmuch as it appears willing to homologate all sentences meeting the formal requirements. . . ."[89] The Venezuelan Code of Civil Procedure requires exequatur for decisions concerning "emancipation, adoption and other matters of a non-contentious nature," but dispenses with application to the Court of Cassation, requiring only presentation of the request to the lower or superior court of the district where the decision will be invoked.[90] However, since in Venezuela divorce actions are considered adversary proceedings, exequatur and a showing of reciprocity are required.[91] The Mexican, Guatemalan,

---

[82] Arts. 607 & 330.

[83] Art. 240.

[84] Art. 240.

[85] Art. 1163.

[86] Art. 1162.

[87] P. GARLAND, *supra* note 37, at 93.

[88] *Id.*

[89] *Id.* at 97.

[90] Art. 754.

[91] Also, the grounds for divorce should be substantially the same as would be

Argentine, Peruvian, Costa Rican, and Honduran codes are silent on this point, but nevertheless, to be safe, attorneys often advise their clients to seek exequatur even for decisions determining status. Argentina's Code requires that foreign judgments also meet regular exequatur requirements when pleaded as authority in another case.[92] This requirement might be considered to apply to recognition of foreign determinations of status where no execution is sought, as well as to use of the judgment as res judicata or for purposes of proving foreign law. Foreign divorce decrees also may present special problems, since if both parties are not represented adequately in the foreign tribunal exequatur may be denied on grounds of public policy, especially in Brazil and Argentina where final divorces cannot be obtained locally.

In at least one nation, Costa Rica, the procedural code specifically allows exequatur applicants to obtain a preventive attachment upon property, provided a security deposit is made.[93] Argentina also requires, even in exequatur proceedings, payment of the "justice tax" discussed earlier, based upon the amount claimed.[94] Presumably the *beneficio de pobreza* could be obtained by an impecunious exequatur applicant, although the relevant Argentine and Peruvian code provisions speak of the beneficio in relation to the presentation or answering of a complaint (*demanda*). The Costa Rican Code states that the beneficio "may only be requested for a specific lawsuit" (*Juicio*),[95] but Venezuela grants the beneficio both for adversary litigation and "to vindicate some right in a non-contentious manner," which might be interpreted to include exequatur applica-

---

permitted in Venezuela. However, exequatur will not be granted to a divorce obtained abroad by a Venezuelan and an alien who had lived as man and wife in Venezuela, and where the events which justified the actions for divorce had occurred in Venezuela. Such a case could be considered an attempt to usurp or oust the jurisdiction of the Venezuelan courts, thereby violating Article 748(2) of the Code of Civil Procedure which refuses exequatur to a judgment of a court which has assumed jurisdiction which rightfully belonged to a Venezuelan court.

[92] Art. 519.

[93] Art. 1026. Goldschmidt writes that in Argentina a preventive attachment could be requested at the moment the exequatur petition is presented. *Supra* note 81, at 263.

[94] Committee on Foreign Law, note 1 *supra*.

[95] Art. 157.

tions.[96] In practice, however, if an applicant had sufficient funds to win a suit in another country, he probably has enough to finance an exequatur. An injustice would more likely occur where an impoverished alien defendant who already had obtained the beneficio sought to interpose a foreign judgment as a res judicata defense but could not obtain extension of the beneficio to the costs of obtaining exequatur.

In France, Austria, Germany, and Italy, a variety of rules also can make enforcement or recognition of foreign judgments difficult. As elsewhere, these rules are not specifically designed to discriminate against aliens. Nevertheless, in their practical application they necessarily have a greater impact upon aliens than upon nationals, especially since the foreign judgment will not be recognized if, as in Latin America and in the United States, it conflicts with local public policy.

In France, enforcement of foreign judgments is, absent an applicable treaty, largely a matter of case law.[97] Nonmatrimonial judgments may neither be given a res judicata effect nor be enforced until they have been granted exequatur in an ordinary civil action before the court of first instance (*tribunal de grande instance*) which is otherwise competent. A judgment creditor must prove first that the foreign court had jurisdiction under French concepts, unlike in Latin America where the relevant jurisdictional standards are those of the nation where the judgment was first obtained. This requirement creates a substantial problem for aliens because, under Articles 14 and 15 of the French Civil Code, French courts always have jurisdiction in actions between aliens and French nationals (or between two French nationals), regardless of the domicile or residence of the parties, provided the action does not involve land abroad or enforcement of foreign judgments. These rules have been construed as rules of exclusive jurisdiction; foreign judgments rendered against French nationals are therefore unlikely to be recog-

---

[96] CÓDIGO DE PROCEDIMIENTO CIVIL VENEZOLANO, art. 32.

[97] The only statutory rules are C. CIV. art. 2123 (Petits Codes Dalloz 66th ed. 1966) and C. PRO. CIV. art. 546 (Petits Codes Dalloz 63d ed. 1966). The recognition of foreign judgments in France has been extensively discussed in English-language publications. *See, e.g.*, P. HERZOG, CIVIL PROCEDURE IN FRANCE 587–608 (1967) and authorities there cited. Consequently, only a few recent authorities not listed there will be cited here.

nized in France unless the French national has waived Articles 14 and 15. A written waiver will be effective, but waiver also can be implied from the defendant's conduct, such as participation in the lawsuit abroad. In recent years, courts have been increasingly liberal in finding that waivers exist.[98]

For some time it was questionable whether the French court had to reexamine the procedural correctness of the foreign judgment under foreign law, or whether compliance with minimum standards of procedural fairness, as in Brazil, was sufficient. A recent decision makes it clear that only the latter requirement must be fulfilled; thus, the French court will check only whether the defendant was given an adequate opportunity to appear and be heard.[99] Specifically French rules of procedure not related to minimum standards of fairness, such as the rule requiring an opinion in every case, are also unlikely to be imposed upon foreign tribunals.[100] More burdensome on its face is the requirement that foreign courts use the same choice-of-law rules French courts would have used. However, this requirement may be disregarded if such rules would not have produced a different result. Finally, exequatur, as in Latin American countries, must be refused if the foreign judgment violates French public policy (*ordre public*). However, in recent years courts have interpreted this requirement quite liberally in favor of applicants.

At one time, French courts did not necessarily grant exequatur to foreign judgments even if all the above conditions were fulfilled. If the judgment debtor, who has the burden of proof, could demonstrate that the foreign judgment was wrong on the law or on the facts, exequatur might be refused. This review of foreign judgments on the merits (*révision aux fonds*) precipitated the United States Supreme Court's famous decision in *Hilton v. Guyot*,[101] denying effect to a French judgment. It was definitely abandoned in 1964.[102]

[98] Bachir v. Dame Bachir, Oct. 4, 1967, 57 REV. CRIT. D.I.P. 98 (1968) (Cass. Civ. 1re); Hochapfel v. Chebali, Oct. 25, 1966, 56 REV. CRIT. D.I.P. 557 (1967) (Cass. Civ. 1re).
[99] Bachir v Dame Bachir, note 98 *supra*.
[100] *See* Gerstlé v. Soc. Merry Hull, Nov. 22, 1966, 56 REV. CRIT. D.I.P. 372 (1967) (arbitration case).
[101] 159 U.S. 113 (1895). The case is discussed in the text accompanying notes 135–138 *infra*.
[102] Munzer v. Dame Jacoby-Munzer, Jan. 7, 1964, 91 JOURNAL DU DROIT

Divorce and other matrimonial judgments have res judicata effect in France without exequatur, except if they are to be used as a basis for "constraint upon person or property," such as the enforcement of support or custody awards. When exequatur is sought for a matrimonial judgment, or when such a judgment is used as res judicata and the other side challenges its validity, it must meet the same exequatur tests as a nonmatrimonial judgment. The rule requiring the use of French choice-of-law rules is applied somewhat more stringently to matrimonial judgments. Consequently, Mexican divorces of residents of states of the United States often are denied recognition in France, even though such divorces may be valid in the state where the parties reside.[103] Reciprocity is not required for the recognition of a foreign judgment in France, whether or not a matrimonial judgment is involved.

In Austria, foreign judgments may be enforced or recognized in nonmatrimonial matters only if reciprocity is insured by treaty or by an official declaration of the Austrian Government published in the Austrian Official Gazette (*Bundesgesetzblatt*).[104] Such declarations have been issued as to Germany, Hungary, Italy, and Rumania.[105] United States judgments, however, are covered neither by treaty nor by Governmental declaration. In addition to reciprocity, applicants must show that the foreign court had jurisdiction in accordance with Austrian concepts and that the defendant was either served in person abroad or through official judicial cooperation. This requirement

---

INTERNATIONAL [CLUNET] 302 (1964), [1964] J.C.P. II, 13590 (Cass. Civ. 1re). For a comment on the case see Nadelmann, *French Courts Recognize Foreign Money-Judgments: One Down and More to Go*, 13 AM. J. COMP. L. 72 (1964).

[103] De Gunzburg v. Dame Schrey, June 18, 1964, 56 REV. CRIT. D.I.P. 340 (1967) (Cour d'Appel, Paris); Freed, *Recognition of Mexican Divorces—France*, 1 INT'L LAWYER 55 (1966).

[104] EXECUTIONSORDNUNG §§ 79, 84 (10th ed. Manz 1961) (Aus.). The sections deal only with the enforcement of foreign judgments but are also applied to recognition. Judgment of Dec. 14, 1949, 22 S.Z. 454 (Oberster Gerichtshof, Aus.). The declaration mentioned in the text should not be confused with the administrative determination of reciprocity made in cases involving security for costs and legal aid. The notice in the Official Gazette is not an individual determination, but more in the nature of an administrative regulation.

[105] *See* Hoyer, *Bemerkungen zur Geschichte der Vollstreckung auslaendischer Entscheidungen in Oesterreich im 19. Jahrhundert*, 5 ZEITSCHRIFT FUER RECHTS-VERGLEICHUNG 94, 102 (1964).

would create an additional obstacle to enforcing United States judgments. The defendant also must have had a chance to participate in the proceedings.[106]

Recognition of divorce and other matrimonial judgments in Austria is governed by a wartime German decree.[107] Judgments rendered by the national court of both spouses may be recognized without further proceedings. In all other cases, a foreign matrimonial judgment is effective for any purpose, including remarriage, only after administrative approval by the Austrian Ministry of Justice, which determines whether the foreign court had jurisdiction in accordance with Austrian jurisdictional concepts. Thus, a judgment will not be recognized if the husband is an Austrian national who has resided in Austria during the suit. If against an Austrian national who failed to appear, the judgment may be recognized only if process was served upon the defendant in person in the foreign country or elsewhere by international judicial cooperation.[108] Proceedings before the Ministry of Justice are informal, rapid, and inexpensive. Review can be sought before the Administrative Court,[109] but the number of appeals is extremely small.[110]

German law also distinguishes between the effectiveness of foreign matrimonial and nonmatrimonial judgments. In the latter, reciprocity generally is required. It must be determined by the court, which may seek assistance from the executive branch.[111] A leading, but fairly old, case denied that reciprocity existed as to California, in spite of that state's liberal legislation concerning foreign judg-

---

[106] EXECUTIONSORDNUNG §§ 80, 81 (10th ed. Manz 1961) (Aus.). *See also* 3 H. FASCHING, KOMMENTAR ZU DEN ZIVILPROZESSGESETZEN 699–700 (1962).

[107] Fourth Implementing Decree concerning the Marriage Law, Oct. 25, 1941, [1941] RGBl. 654 § 24. In the Federal Republic of Germany the decree has been replaced by new legislation. *See* note 115 *infra*.

[108] This result follows from the interplay of the Fourth Implementing Decree, *supra* note 107, Section 328 of the German Code of Civil Procedure (Zivilprozessordnung) to which the decree refers for the substantive conditions of recognition, and the Austrian Law on Jurisdiction, Aug. 1, 1895, [1895] Aus. RGBl. No. 111, § 76.

[109] H. KOEHLER, INTERNATIONALES PRIVATRECHT 68 (3d ed. 1966).

[110] Since 1945 there were probably about 10,000 administrative procedures for the recognition of foreign divorces; the number of cases in which review was sought is probably not much in excess of 15.

[111] ZPO § 328 (C.H. Beck 1968).

ments.[112] This much-criticized decision has at times, but not univer-sally, been followed for judgments from other states.[113] In addition, foreign default judgments rendered against German nationals may be recognized only if the German national was either personally served within the foreign court's jurisdiction or through formal judicial cooperation.[114]

Divorce and other matrimonial judgments are effective in Germany only if officially recognized by the Department of Justice of the competent province (*Land*).[115] The procedure is largely within the discretion of the administrative agency. Review by the territorially competent intermediate appellate tribunal (*Oberlandesgericht*) is possible.[116] Reciprocity is not required for recognition of matrimonial judgments in Germany.[117] In other respects, the rules applicable to nonmatrimonial judgments must be used. Recognition will be denied if the foreign court applied substantive rules less favorable to the German party than those indicated by German choice of law rules.[118] Matrimonial judgments granted by courts of the country of which both spouses are nationals are effective without administrative recognition.

Italian rules concerning the recognition of foreign judgments are largely statutory and differ substantially from French and German provisions. In order to be enforced, or to have general res judicata effect, a foreign judgment must receive judicial approval in a proceeding known as *delibazione*.[119] This proceeding must be brought not before the ordinary court of first instance, but before the intermediate appellate court, the *Corte di Appello*.[120] It is possible to

---

[112] C. v. Rh. & M. Feuerversicherungsaktiengesellschaft, March 26, 1909, 70 RGZ 434 (the *San Francisco Earthquake Case*). The case interpreted CAL. LAWS 1907, ch. 178.
[113] L. RAAPE, INTERNATIONALES PRIVATRECHT 137 (5th ed. 1961); Felber, *Die Vollstreckbarkeit von Urteilen Amerikanischer Gerichte in Deutschland*, 60 JURISTISCHE WOCHENSCHRIFT 112 (1931); Nadelmann, *supra* note 47, at 252.
[114] ZPO § 328 (C.H. Beck 1968).
[115] Law Modifying Rules of Family Law, Aug. 11, 1961, [1961] BGBl. 1221, art. 7. The law replaced the decree mentioned in note 107 *supra*.
[116] Review beyond this level is not possible.
[117] Law of Aug. 11, 1961, *supra* note 115, art. 7, § 1(1).
[118] ZPO § 606(a) (C.H. Beck 1968); L. RAAPE, *supra* note 113, at 308.
[119] Law of Aug. 11, 1961, *supra* note 115, art. 7, § 1(1).
[120] C. PRO. CIV., art. 796 (Giuffrè 1968).

utilize a foreign judgment in a pending proceeding without a prior delibazione procedure; the judge before whom the action is pending, however, must subject the foreign judgment to the same scrutiny as required in delibazione. Absent a formal delibazione, the foreign judgment has, however, no effect outside the action in which utilized.[121] A judgment approved in delibazione is for all practical purposes treated as an Italian judgment.[122]

To be approved, a foreign judgment must have been rendered by a court having jurisdiction pursuant to Italian rules of international competence.[123] The criteria for jurisdiction are fairly liberal, and include domicile, residence, the location of property, or of an obligation (such as a tort or contract).[124] As in Latin American nations, a contractual grant of jurisdiction to a foreign court by an Italian national residing in Italy may not be recognized.[125] The procedural regularity of the foreign judgment is tested only to a limited extent: process must have been served in accordance with foreign law, the defendant must have had a reasonable time to appear, and judgment must be final. Approval may not be granted if the foreign judgment contradicts an Italian judgment rendered between the same parties on the same subject matter or contravenes Italian public policy.[126]

Ordinarily, as in Latin America, Italian courts may not reexamine the merits. However, in a few instances where there may be reason to doubt the fairness of the foreign judgment, reexamination of the merits is possible in the delibazione procedure. These instances include default judgments and judgments rendered in circumstances in which a final judgment of an Italian court could be reopened. The court may act only at the request of the party against whom recognition is sought.[127] If reexamination of the merits is requested while

---

[121] C. PRO. CIV., art. 799 (Giuffrè 1968).

[122] M. CAPPELLETTI & J. PERILLO, CIVIL PROCEDURE IN ITALY 367–69 (1965). The recognition is considered as retroactively effective as of the date of the original judgment.

[123] C. PRO. CIV., art. 797(1) (Giuffrè 1968).

[124] C. PRO. CIV., art. 4 (Giuffrè 1968); M. CAPPELLETTI & J. PERILLO, *supra* note 122, at 85–90, 373–76.

[125] C. PRO. CIV., art. 2 (Giuffrè 1968).

[126] C. PRO. CIV., arts. 797(2)–(7) (Giuffrè 1968).

[127] C. PRO. CIV., art. 798 (Giuffrè 1968). According to C. PRO. CIV., arts. 395(1)–(4), (6), to which Article 798 refers, an Italian judgment is subject to reopening in the following cases: fraud by a party, the use of means of proof

the validity of a foreign judgment is at issue in a court of first instance, the proceedings must be stayed and the matter transferred to the competent Corte di Appello.[128] In cases where the merits are reexamined, the court may either render its own judgment or recognize the foreign judgment.[129]

The Italian Code of Civil Procedure does not distinguish between recognition of foreign matrimonial and nonmatrimonial judgments. However, rules of substantive law create additional obstacles to the recognition of foreign divorce decrees. Since divorce was not legal in Italy until late 1970,[130] Italian courts have considered foreign divorce judgments in which both parties were Italian nationals, and sometimes even judgments in which only one party was an Italian national, as violating Italian public policy, and hence have refused recognition. The same was true of annulments rendered on grounds not available in Italy. While these rules were independent of the religion of the parties, in addition, through the Lateran Treaties, Italy had granted exclusive jurisdiction over marriages concluded in Italy in the Roman Catholic Church to the Church.[131] Consequently, foreign annulments or divorces generally were not recognized, regardless of the parties' nationality, if the marriage had been celebrated in Italy in the Church.[132] Several years must pass before the effect of the 1970 divorce law on the recognition of foreign matrimonial judgments can be ascertained.

---

declared false after the judgment, discovery after the judgment of decisive documents which could not have been used because of an act of God or of the opposing party, substantial error by the court as to a fact not actually litigated, and fraud by the court if established by judgment. Application of these rules to proceedings before a common law court obviously would be difficult.

[128] C. Pro. Civ., art. 799 (Giuffrè 1968).

[129] For a detailed discussion see Carbone, 1 *Giudizio di Riesame del Merito*, [1968] Rivista di Diritto Internazionale Privato e Processuale 510.

[130] C. Civ., art. 149 (Hoepli 1968): "Marriage is dissolved only by the death of one of the spouses." The first divorce law in Italy since 1815 took effect on December 18, 1970. N.Y. Times, Dec. 19, 1970, at 2, col. 4.

[131] C. Civ., art. 82 (Hoepli 1968): "A marriage celebrated before a catholic priest is governed by the Concordat with the Holy See and by the special laws relating to that matter." Concordat between the Holy See and Italy, Feb. 11, 1929, art. 34, [1929] Gaz. Uff. No. 130.

[132] M. Cappelletti & J. Perillo, *supra* note 122, at 378–80. For a more detailed discussion (with extensive case citations) of the validity of foreign matrimonial judgments in Italy, see R. Monaco, L'Efficacia della Legge nello Spazio 194–210 (2d ed. 1964).

In the United States, foreign judgments are not entitled to unqualified recognition and enforcement because the so-called full faith and credit clause of the Constitution requires enforcement (assuming jurisdiction of the rendering court) only if rendered by a court of another state of the federal union.[133] Judgments rendered abroad are enforceable only for reasons of "comity," provided they emanate from "courts which fulfilled the jurisdictional requirements."[134] The United States Supreme Court, in its 1895 decision in *Hilton v. Guyot*,[135] not only adopted this view, but declared in addition that, as a matter of federal judicial policy, foreign judgments should be enforceable without an inquiry de novo into the merits only if the foreign court in question also recognized United States judgments as fully enforceable without such inquiry. In *Hilton*, the Court found that courts in France, where the judgment had been rendered, did not accord full recognition to American judgments without examining the merits; as a result, the French judgment was only "prima facie evidence of the justice of the plaintiff's claim,"[136] and not fully enforceable.

However, the reciprocity requirement presumably established in *Hilton* does not bind state courts, which "have not followed the decision."[137] Moreover, due to a 1938 United States Supreme Court decision, lower federal courts must apply the substantive law of the states within which they sit.[138] This substantive law includes conflicts principles as determined by decisions of the courts of the state in question. New York State courts recognize foreign judgments as fully enforceable as sister-state judgments, regardless of whether

---

[133] Article IV, section 1 of the United States Constitution provides that "Full Faith and Credit shall be given in each State to the public Acts, Records, and judicial Proceedings of every other State. And the Congress may by general Laws prescribe the Manner in which such Acts, Records and Proceedings shall be proved, and the Effect thereof."

[134] *See* discussion in Nadelmann, *supra* note 47, at 240.

[135] 159 U.S. 113 (1895).

[136] *Id.* at 227.

[137] Nadelmann, *supra* note 47, at 241. "At present it is generally assumed that state law determines the recognition [and enforcement] due to foreign nation judgments." Ginsburg, *Recognition and Enforcement of Foreign Civil Judgments: A Summary View of the Situation in the United States*, 4 INT'L LAWYER 720, 721 (1970).

[138] Erie R.R. v. Tompkins, 304 U.S. 64 (1938).

courts of the rendering country accord reciprocity to American judgments or reexamine the merits of the case.[139] Consequently, a federal court sitting in New York or in most other states of the Federal union would apply that state's laws respecting enforcement of foreign judgments rather than be guided by *Hilton*.

Nevertheless, great misunderstanding exists abroad regarding the enforceability of foreign judments in the United States. Consequently, civil law nations such as Germany, which require reciprocity, are reluctant to enforce the judgments of courts in the United States. Indeed, the 1953 edition of a commentary on the German Code of Civil Procedure lists the United States as not meeting the German Code's reciprocity requirements, since courts in the United States allegedly may reexamine the merits of cases before them.[140] Similar doubts persist in Latin America, where attorneys have complained to the authors that in order to obtain recognition of a foreign judgment in New York it is virtually necessary to begin suit de novo. Such attitudes seem incredible, since New York and other states have recognition principles embodied in their case law and in the Uniform Foreign Money Judgments Recognition Act[141] at least as liberal as those found in multilateral Latin American agreements. These misapprehensions are, it is feared, largely due to lack of statutory provisions stating that reciprocity is not necessary, as well

---

[139] Provided, of course, that New York public policy is not violated. *See* Cowans v. Ticonderoga Pulp & Paper Co., 219 App. Div. 120, 219 N.Y.S. 284 (3d Dep't 1927) (Judgment from province of Quebec held enforceable like a sister-state judgment even though Quebec Code of Civil Procedure permitted examination into the merits of judgments rendered outside Quebec and sought to be enforced there); Johnston v. Compagnie Générale Transatlantique, 242 N.Y. 381, 152 N.E. 121 (1926) (French judgment held enforceable like a sister-state judgment notwithstanding lack of reciprocity; the New York Court of Appeals also expressly held that the decision of *Hilton v. Guyot* was not binding on New York State courts). *See also* Nepronay v. Kir, 5 App. Div. 2d 238, 173 N.Y.S.2d 146 (1st Dep't 1958). Examples in other jurisdictions of the tendency to treat foreign-nation judgments as if they were judgments of sister states include: Cherum v. Frishman, 236 F. Supp. 292 (D.D.C. 1964); Adamsen v. Adamsen, 195 A.2d 418 (Conn. 1963).

[140] Nadelmann, *supra* note 47, at 254–55.

[141] *See* 9B U.L.A. 64 (1966). As of 1968 the Act was in force in California, Illinois, Maryland, Massachusetts (with a reciprocity clause added), New York, Michigan, and Oklahoma. *See* Kulzer, *Recognition of Foreign Country Judgments in New York: The Uniform Foreign Money Judgments Recognition Act*, 18 BUFFALO L. REV. 1 (1968), and Ginsburg, *supra* note 137, at 732–36.

as to unfamiliarity in civil law jurisdictions with case reporting systems in the United States.[142]

INTERNATIONAL AGREEMENTS AND THE ENFORCEMENT OF FOREIGN JUDICIAL AND ARBITRAL AWARDS

The complexity of the rules concerning the recognition and enforcement of foreign judgments has induced many countries to conclude bilateral agreements dealing with the topic. Such treaties usually simplify formalities, sometimes eliminate the need for special procedures entirely when recognition of the res judicata effect of a foreign judgment rather than its enforcement is concerned, and usually indicate the conditions which a foreign judgment must fulfill in order to be recognized or enforced. Some agreements go further, and regulate judicial jurisdiction in relations between two States apart from the recognition and enforcement of foreign judgments.[143]

Unfortunately, multilateral agreements concerning the enforcement of judgments are sometimes narrowly circumscribed by the subject matter to which they apply, such as the support of dependents,[144] the transportation of passengers and goods by rail,[145] or navigation on the Rhine.[146] The treaties instituting the European Communities provide for the quasi-automatic recognition of judg-

---

[142] "Generally speaking, the task of proving our law in the foreign court is not easy. The reciprocity states are code countries and its courts are unfamiliar with the principle of stare decisis. Few of our states have a statutory provision and in many states recent decisions on the subject are lacking. As far as proof of the law is concerned, codification would ameliorate conditions." Nadelmann, *supra* note 47, at 252.

[143] *See generally* Weser, *Jugement Etranger*, in 2 DALLOZ, RÉPERTOIRE DE DROIT INTERNATIONAL at Nos. 263–68 (1969). Treaties containing jurisdictional bases for the recognition of foreign judgments without concerning themselves with the internal jurisdiction of the country where the judgment was rendered are said to provide indirect rules of jurisdiction; treaties concerning the internal jurisdiction of the country in which the judgment was rendered are said to contain rules of direct jurisdiction. *Cf.* Smit, *The Terms Jurisdiction and Competence in Comparative Law*, 10 AM. J. COMP. L. 64 (1964).

[144] Convention on the Recovery Abroad of Maintenance, June 20, 1956, 268 U.N.T.S. 3 (Preamble). The Convention provides for procedures somewhat analogous to those of the Uniform Support of Dependents Act in the United States.

[145] *See* notes 185 & 186 of Chapter V.

[146] Revised Convention for the Navigation of the Rhine, Oct. 17, 1868, art. 40, 2 EUROPEAN YEARBOOK 258 (1956).

ments of the Court of Justice of the European Communities in all member States.[147] In addition, the member States of these Communities have signed a treaty concerning jurisdiction of courts and the recognition and enforcement of judgments.[148] That treaty does not cover matrimonial matters; a treaty concerning bankruptcy has been drafted but not yet signed.[149] Once the judgments treaty has become effective, it should facilitate materially the recognition and enforcement of judgments among the "Six."

The Hague Conference on Private International Law repeatedly has studied the recognition and enforcement of foreign judgments. The widely adopted 1954 Convention concerning civil procedure contains a provision for the almost automatic enforcement of judgments for costs.[150] Of more general scope is the Convention on the Recognition and Enforcement of Foreign Judgments prepared in 1966 by an Extraordinary Session of the Hague Conference. However, signature and ratification of this convention will not suffice to make it effective; it applies only between those States signing special implementing agreements.[151] A second agreement developed

---

[147] Treaty Establishing the European Coal and Steel Community, April 18, 1951, arts. 44 & 92, 261 U.N.T.S. 140; Treaty Establishing the European Economic Community, March 25, 1957, arts. 187 & 192, 298 U.N.T.S. 11; Treaty Establishing the European Atomic Energy Community, March 25, 1957, arts. 159 & 164, 298 U.N.T.S. 167.

[148] Convention concerning Judicial Jurisdiction and Recognition and Enforcement of Judgments in Civil and Commercial Matters, Sept. 17, 1968, CCH Com. Mkt. Rep. 6003. *Cf.* Hay, *The Common Market Preliminary Draft Convention on the Recognition and Enforcement of Judgments—Some Considerations of Policy and Interpretation*, 16 AM. J. COMP. L. 149 (1968); Nadelmann, *Jurisdictionally Improper Fora in Treaties on Recognition of Judgments: The Common Market Draft*, 67 COLUM. L. REV. 995 (1967); Weser, *Some Reflections on the Draft Treaty on Execution of Judgments in the E.E.C.*, [1965] U. ILL. L.F. 771.

[149] Weser, *supra* note 143, at No. 318.

[150] Convention relating to Civil Procedure, March 1, 1954, arts. 18 & 19, 286 U.N.T.S. 265.

[151] Convention on the Recognition and Enforcement of Foreign Judgments in Civil and Commercial Matters, and Supplementary Protocol. Official text in Conférence de la Haye de Droit Internationale Privé, RECUEIL DES CONVENTIONS DE LA HAYE 106, 124 (1966), *reprinted in* 15 AM. J. COMP. L. 362 (1967). For comments see Nadelmann & von Mehren, *The Extraordinary Session of the Hague Conference on Private International Law*, 60 AM. J. INT'L L. 803 (1966), and Nadelmann, *The Common Market Judgments Convention and a Hague Conference Recommendation: What Steps Next?* 82 HARV. L. REV. 1282 (1969).

by the Hague Conference on Private International Law and finally adopted at its Eleventh Session in 1968 deals with the recognition of divorce judgments, but is not yet in force.[152]

Already in effect, however, are certain Latin American agreements concerning foreign judgments. As already indicated, the intent of the principal such convention, the Bustamante Code, may be thwarted in practice by reservations permitting requirements of reciprocity and other conflicting provisions in national procedural codes. For example, in the Bustamante Code execution of the foreign judgment is left to local law, which may vary greatly. Of perhaps greater efficacy, since it involves fewer parties, is the 1940 Montevideo Treaty of International Procedural Law, which was ratified by Uruguay, Argentina, and Paraguay in 1942, 1956, and 1958, respectively.[153] While the treaty does not assure automatic recognition of final judgments and arbitral awards, it establishes simplified recognition requirements: (a) the judgment or award must be issued by competent authority; (b) it must be final or res judicata where issued; (c) the defendant must have been legally notified, have appeared or been declared in default pursuant to the laws of the forum; and (d) enforcement of the judgment must not be against public policy. The exequatur application must be accompanied by a copy of the complete judgment; by affidavits to indicate compliance with (c) above; and by an authenticated copy of the writ of execution or a document showing it to be res judicata, together with a copy of the law pursuant to which the judgment was issued. Unlike the Bustamante Code, recognition and execution is left to the courts which would

---

[152] Von Mehren, *The Draft Convention on the Recognition of Divorces and Legal Separations*, 16 AM. J. COMP. L. 590 (1968) (with text of convention); Foster & Freed, *The Hague Draft Convention on Recognition of Foreign Divorces and Separations*, 1 FAMILY L.Q. 83 (1968); Nadelmann, *Habitual Residence and Nationality as Tests at The Hague: The 1968 Convention on Recognition of Divorces*, 47 TEXAS L. REV. 766 (1969). *See also* Amram, *Report on the 11th Session of the Hague Conference on Private International Law*, 63 AM. J. INT'L L. 521 (1969).

[153] *Discussed in* Goldschmidt, *El Tratado de Derecho Procesal Internacional de Montevideo de 1940*, 1957 REVISTA DE DERECHO PROCESAL 99 (No. 3), and in Bidart, *Planteamiento Procesal del Tema de la Sentencia Extranjera*, 1959 REVISTA DE DERECHO PROCESAL 3 (No. 1). The Treaty also seeks to establish bases for a simplified system of international judicial assistance. Bolivia, Brazil, Chile, Colombia, and Peru participated in the Conference but did not ratify.

ordinarily have original jurisdiction or competence in such matters, thus establishing a certain uniformity. No reciprocity is required, and preventive attachments may be requested.

The 1940 Treaty was a definite improvement upon its predecessor, the Montevideo Treaty of 1889.[154] The latter agreement was sufficiently ambiguous to be interpreted by Argentine courts as disallowing preventive attachments in exequatur proceedings, although Uruguayan courts had been granting attachments under local procedural rules.[155] Moreover, while the 1889 Treaty in Article 5 accorded foreign judgments and arbitral awards "the same force that they have in the country where they have been rendered" provided they did not contravene "laws of orden público in the country of their execution," it did not provide specifically, as does its 1940 successor, for the procedures to enable the foreign judgment to be invoked as res judicata. The other important Latin American treaty in this area now in force is the so-called Bolivarian Treaty of 1911 on the Execution of Foreign Acts. Ratified by Colombia, Ecuador, Peru, Bolivia, and Venezuela, it reiterates the provisions of the 1889 Montevideo Treaty and similarly rejects reciprocity as a precondition for recognition and enforcement.[156]

Unfortunately, problems of achieving uniformity in the recognition and enforcement of foreign arbitral awards have been even less satisfactorily resolved. Much of the difficulty stems from the original freedom of the parties to decide which law should govern their agreement to submit disputes to arbitration. Their choice of law and legal systems may or may not coincide with the law of the place where the arbitration is to occur. Nor, of course, need the law to be applied to the submission be the same as that which applies to the contract in dispute. It is entirely possible that the submission provides that certain of the possible contractual disputes be settled by the law of one country and others by the law of another. This makes it difficult, on occasion, to determine the proper law of the submission agreement in the event of disputes respecting its enforcement.

---

[154] The parties thereto are Argentina, Uruguay, Bolivia, Paraguay, Peru, and Colombia. Goldschmidt, *supra* note 153, at 100. The 1889 Treaty is still in force between Colombia, Bolivia, and Peru.

[155] *Id.* at 108.

[156] II Tratados Públicos y Acuerdos Internacionales en Venezuela: 1910–1920, at 475 (1950).

However, an arbitral award must be consistent with the law of the country where arbitration is held. It is this law, for example, which will govern the regularity of the proceedings. Thus, in enforcement proceedings elsewhere, defenses likely will be based upon alleged irregularities in the application of the law of the country where the arbitration took place. In England, however, additional defenses, similar to those available against foreign judgments, may be raised on grounds of fraud or public policy. Elsewhere, statutory provisions similar to those employed for foreign judgments provide for registration. In Alberta, the definition of "foreign judgment" in the Reciprocal Enforcement of Judgments Act[157] includes "an award in an arbitration proceeding if the award, under the law in force in the jurisdiction where it was made, has become enforceable in the same manner as a judgment given by a court in that jurisdiction."

The 1927 Geneva Convention on the Execution of Foreign Arbitral Awards[158] attempts to identify the ingredients necessary for enforcement. The Convention, which was not ratified by any Latin American nation, requires the award to have been made by the arbitral tribunal provided for in the submission or constituted in the manner agreed upon by the parties. It must also conform with the law governing the arbitration procedure.

Basically, the difficulty which arises in enforcing foreign arbitral, as distinct from judicial, awards is that the former arise out of contract, whereas the latter involve no voluntary element. Thus, where the foreign award has not been reduced to a foreign judgment, the theory persists that the award must be pursued in local courts as a claim in contract. This could entail bringing suit de novo. If, of course, the foreign award has been reduced to a foreign judgment, it is most likely that it will be the latter which the victorious party will seek to enforce. Lest one presume, however, that to proceed this way is foolproof, it must be remembered that submission to arbitration in a foreign country does not necessarily presume submission as well to the jurisdiction of the courts of that country for purposes of enforcing the arbitral award.[159]

---

[157] *Supra* note 30, § 2(1)(a).

[158] Convention on the Execution of Foreign Arbitral Awards, Sept. 26, 1927, [1930] Gr. Brit. T.S. No. 28 (CMD. 3655), 92 L.N.T.S. 301.

[159] In this respect see Domke, *On the Enforcement Abroad of American Arbitration Awards*, 17 LAW & CONTEMP. PROB. 545 (1952).

It may well be that proof of only three factors is required in order to enforce a foreign arbitral award, as an English court has stated:[160] (i) the submission, (ii) that the arbitration was conducted in accordance with the terms of the submission, and (iii) that the award is valid according to the law of the country where it was made. In Australia, however, the requirements are more sophisticated. It must be shown that:

(a) The award was made in accordance with an arbitration agreement valid under the law applicable to the agreement;

(b) The award is final in the country in which it was made;

(c) It was made in respect of a matter which may be lawfully referred to arbitration under Australian law and the enforcement of the award would not be contrary to Australian public policy or Australian law;

(d) The award has not been annulled in the country in which it was made;

(e) The party against whom the award was made was given sufficient notice of the arbitration proceedings or, if he was under a legal incapacity, he must have been properly represented; and

(f) The award must deal with all of the questions referred to the arbitrator and must not contain decisions on matters beyond the scope of the arbitration agreement.[161]

Enforcement problems arise not because an alien is one of the parties, but rather because of the interjection of second or third legal systems and bodies of law. Elements of discrimination and actions which could be regarded on the international level as denials of justice are unlikely to occur. There is a great need, however, for more multilateral cooperation in order to ensure uniform, simplified enforcement and recognition procedures for arbitral awards. Such conventions would permit easy examination of allegations of failure to exhaust local remedies in pursuing locally a foreign award.

Enforcement of foreign arbitration awards in Latin America is not specifically provided for in the various procedural codes. However, code provisions on enforcing foreign judgments refer to judgments of

[160] Norske Atlas Insurance Co. v. London General Insurance Co., [1927] 43 T.L.R. 541, 542.

[161] As reported to the authors by a leading firm of solicitors in Sydney, Australia.

foreign "tribunals," which, it may be argued, is sufficiently broad to embrace arbitral decisions. At least one United States commentator assumes that the same Latin American code provisions and requisites for enforcement of foreign judgments will apply when enforcement of arbitral awards is sought.[162] This interpretation would mean that reciprocity and other requirements would similarly be applicable to arbitral awards. Goldschmidt, citing Argentine case law enforcing a Chilean arbitral award, indicates that if the award may be likened to a court judgment enforcement will be granted. However, if the award is considered a contract, that is, only law as between the parties, enforcement will be denied.[163] Unfortunately, he does not suggest criteria to distinguish between contracts and judgments. Nevertheless, in the absence of treaty, the alien seeking to enforce a foreign arbitral award in a Latin American nation would be well advised to reduce his award to judgment in the forum State before seeking enforcement abroad.[164] Even so, a defense of public policy could be raised if the award or judgment had been given ex parte after one party had refused to arbitrate, since in Latin America agreements to arbitrate future disputes are not always specifically enforceable unless supplemented by a submission clause.[165] By contrast, United States case law demonstrates that foreign arbitral awards, even if not reduced to judgment, are enforced by New York courts and by the federal courts sitting therein without regard to the existence of

---

[162] Goldman, *Commercial Arbitration in the Americas* 41–42 (paper presented at the Second Conference on Inter-American Commercial Arbitration, Mexico City, Nov. 7–9, 1968).

[163] Goldschmidt, *supra* note 81, at 237–39.

[164] Committee on Foreign Law, *supra* note 1, at 150. *See also* P. GARLAND, *supra* note 37, at 81–82.

[165] In Venezuela, for example, Article 504 of the Code of Civil Procedure provides that if a party refuses to execute a submission the arbitration proceeding is terminated. In Costa Rica, however, refusal to abide by the arbitration clause may result in a suit for damages. Moreover, the judge will draft the submission clause and appoint arbitrators. CÓDIGO DE PROCEDIMIENTOS CIVILES, art. 398. *See also* the Argentine CÓDIGO PROCESAL CIVIL Y COMERCIAL DE LA NACIÓN, art. 769, and Peru's CÓDIGO DE PROCEDIMIENTOS CIVILES, art. 556, which also permit similar judicial intervention if a party refuses to sign a submission clause. *See* discussion in Goldman, *supra* note 162, at 10–11. Nevertheless, the necessity of judicial intervention may neutralize one of the most persuasive reasons why parties agree to arbitration, *i.e.*, the allegedly comparative speed and informality of arbitration as compared with the judicial process.

reciprocity, provided that the award can be proven to be final where rendered.[166] In addition to documentation ordinarily required to support exequatur applications, certified copies of the arbitration agreement, of the rules followed, and of the award itself should also be presented.

Where a treaty exists, it may not be necessary to confirm an arbitral award with a court decree. Both the 1889 and 1940 Montevideo Treaties state that "the judgments and arbitral decisions issued in civil and commercial matters in one of the signatory States, will have in the territories of the others the same effect as in the country where it was given"[167] provided certain prerequisites are met. The same tests must be met for execution of both judgments and arbitral awards. That is, the decrees must be issued by a competent tribunal, they must be final, the loser must have been notified and represented or declared in default pursuant to the law of the forum State, and the decree must not violate the public policy of the State within which enforcement is sought. The 1911 Bolivarian Treaty between Colombia, Bolivia, Ecuador, Peru, and Venezuela also permits enforcement of foreign arbitration awards on the same terms as foreign judgments without proof of reciprocity, and its requirements are identical to those of the 1889 Montevideo Treaty.

An impressive effort is now being made by the American Arbitration Association to promote international commercial arbitration in Latin America by reviving the almost moribund Inter-American Commercial Arbitration Commission established in 1934.[168] Due to increasing intra–Latin American trade resulting from common-market efforts, together with an upsurge in commercial disputes, it was felt that a more responsive arbitration system would be needed. Although private commercial associations in individual nations as disparate as Argentina and Surinam already had established successful domestic arbitration procedures, a more international and uniform system was required.[169] Consequently, a series of international

---

[166] *See* M. DOMKE, THE LAW AND PRACTICE OF COMMERCIAL ARBITRATION 363–66 (1968).

[167] The identical expression is used in Article 5 of the 1889 Treaty and in Article 5 of the 1940 Treaty.

[168] Norberg, *Inter-American Commercial Arbitration,* 61 AM. J. INT'L L. 1028 (1967).

[169] The Surinamese effort was sponsored by the Surinamese Chamber of

conferences began in 1967 with the assistance of the Inter-American Bar Association, as a result of which national arbitration commissions have been established in each Latin American nation. While case loads will initially be domestic, hopefully the tribunals eventually will handle international arbitrations as well. Largely as a result of these efforts, lawyers in the Americas have become increasingly aware of the need for new legislation or treaties to assure enforcement of foreign arbitral awards.[170]

The distrust of arbitration sometimes found in Latin America is not prevalent in Europe. However, the diversity of national practice once again underlines the need for uniformity. In France, for instance, arbitration clauses are valid in most commercial matters, and even more widely recognized in international contracts.[171] Foreign awards are enforced in the same manner as domestic French awards, that is, through ex parte petition to the presiding judge of the competent French tribunal *de grande instance*.[172] The award must be based on a valid submission or arbitration clause, and the parties must have been duly summoned and have received an adequate hearing. The requirement that a foreign court must apply French conflict-of-laws rules if its decision is to be effective in France is not followed with arbitral awards whenever the arbitrator is not, by the terms of the submission, bound to follow strict rules of law. There must, of course, be no violation of French public policy.[173] After some hesita-

---

Commerce, which created an Arbitration Institute. Attorneys in Paramaribo told the authors that, since the country's commercial community was so small, it was difficult to find arbitrators who did not have some relationship to one or more of the parties. The Buenos Aires Bolsa de Comercio's Arbitration Rules avoid the problem through the appointment of a permanent panel of three judges.

[170] Interviews in Argentina, Brazil, Peru, Venezuela, and Surinam in 1968 and 1969.

[171] C. COM., art. 631 (Petits Codes Dalloz 65th ed. 1969–1970). Submissions are permissible in all matters except where relating to personal status and other matters in which public policy is particularly involved. For a general discussion see Robert, *France*, in 1 INTERNATIONAL ASSOCIATION OF LAWYERS, INTERNATIONAL COMMERCIAL ARBITRATION 241 (P. Sanders ed. 1956); 3 *id.* at 190 (1965).

[172] C. PRO. CIV., arts. 1020 & 1021 (Petits Codes Dalloz 63d ed. 1966); Robert, *supra* note 171, at 265.

[173] P. HERZOG, *supra* note 97, at 600–01.

tion, French courts now hold that an award is enforceable in France even if unsupported by an opinion.[174] If the French judge decides that the foreign award is entitled to enforcement, he grants an exequatur, but this exequatur should not be confused with the exequatur granted foreign judgments after a formal hearing. The party against whom the award is to be enforced may obtain review by a variety of rather poorly coordinated procedural devices.[175] If an award has been reduced to judgment in the foreign country, it seems possible to obtain enforcement either of the original award or of the judgment. However, because of the more liberal rules concerning awards, it may not be preferable to reduce the award to judgment.[176]

In Italy, as in Latin American nations, the same rules govern enforcement of foreign judgments and arbitral awards. Moreover, a foreign award is enforceable only if it has the effect of a judgment in the country where rendered, if both parties were not Italian nationals (unless both were domiciled or resident abroad), and if the award did not involve certain matters concerning which arbitration is illegal in Italy.[177]

Arbitration is legal in the German Federal Republic as to most "financial" (money) claims, although it is not permissible in matters concerning personal status and domestic restraints of trade.[178] Foreign awards are enforced in the same manner as German awards, namely, through a court decision rendered after a hearing. Ordinarily, the hearing is conducted quite expeditiously; in fact, the party against whom the award is to be enforced submits only written comments. Denial of enforcement is permissible only if there was no valid arbitration according to the applicable law, if the award violates public policy, and if a party was not properly represented

[174] Gerstlé v. Soc. Merry Hull, note 100 *supra*. French awards must contain an opinion.

[175] C. Pro. Civ., arts. 1023–1028 (Petits Codes Dalloz 63d ed. 1966). *Cf.* P. Herzog, *supra* note 97, at 602.

[176] *Id.* at 601.

[177] C. Pro. Civ., arts. 800 & 806 (Giuffrè 1968). 1 International Association of Lawyers, *supra* note 171, at 347.

[178] ZPO §§ 1025, 1026 (C.H. Beck 1968) (arbitration available as to matters as to which parties may make a compromise, but arbitration clause must refer to specific legal relationship); Schottelius, *Germany*, in 1 International Association of Lawyers, *supra* note 171, at 36–37; 3 *id.* at 234.

during the arbitration or did not obtain an adequate opportunity to be heard. No reciprocity is required.[179]

Austrian law also is quite liberal in recognizing the validity of arbitration clauses.[180] However, absent a treaty to the contrary, it treats foreign awards substantially like foreign judgments; in other words, unlike in Germany, foreign awards are enforceable only if reciprocity is guaranteed by a treaty or an official governmental declaration published in the Austrian Official Gazette.[181] For all practical purposes, foreign awards are thus enforceable in Austria only if rendered in a country having adhered to the United Nations or European arbitration conventions, or some other pertinent international agreement.[182]

Perhaps the most constructive international effort to date to assure enforcement abroad of arbitration awards is the 1958 United Nations Convention on the Recognition and Enforcement of Foreign Arbitral Awards.[183] There is no need under the Convention to confirm the award by judicial action, and the party seeking enforcement need only present to a court in a contracting nation certified copies of the arbitration agreement and the award, with translations if necessary. Unlike the 1923 Geneva Protocol on Arbitration Clauses,[184] the burden of proof is on the defeated party to prove that the agreement to arbitrate was invalid or that the award has not become final, has been set aside, or has substantial defects.[185] A court may refuse enforcement on the foregoing grounds or if it finds that the dispute was not arbitrable or that enforcement would violate public policy. Moreover, the Convention attempts in Article II to compel private parties to abide by their agreement to arbitrate when it states that each signatory "shall recognize an [arbitration] agreement in writing" and that, in litigation involving matters covered by the

---

[179] ZPO §§ 1042a & 1044 (C.H. Beck 1968).

[180] Ender, *Austria*, in INTERNATIONAL ASSOCIATION OF LAWYERS, *supra* note 171, at 102.

[181] EXECUTIONSORDNUNG § 79 (10th ed. Manz 1961). *Cf.* note 104 *supra*.

[182] *See* text at notes 183–90.

[183] June 10, 1958, 330 U.N.T.S. 3. The Convention is discussed in detail in Springer, *The United Nations Convention on the Recognition and Enforcement of Foreign Arbitral Awards*, 3 INT'L LAWYER 320 (1969).

[184] *Reprinted in* INTERNATIONAL TRADE ARBITRATION 283–84 (M. Domke ed. 1958).

[185] Art. V(Ie).

arbitration agreement, courts should "at the request of one of the parties, refer the parties to arbitration."[186] To date, 34 countries have ratified the Convention, including, of the nations studied herein, Austria, France, Germany, Ghana, and Tanzania. Although the U.S.S.R. and much of Eastern Europe have ratified the Convention, the only Western Hemisphere nations are Ecuador and Trinidad and Tobago.[187] United States accession is expected after Congress passes implementing legislation.

Parties to contracts within the scope of the Convention are assured that, if their agreement to arbitrate is valid and covers arbitrable matters under the laws of the countries involved, "it will be honored in those countries, at least to the extent that the courts will decline to entertain competing litigation."[188] While the Convention does not provide a self-executing mechanism for the specific enforcement of agreements to arbitrate, it nevertheless marks a significant step forward toward resolving the difficult problems presented in jurisdictions where enforcement is either unobtainable or obtainable only after invocation of lengthy and cumbersome procedures.

The accession of so many States to the Convention strongly suggests an increasing awareness among European States of the number of disputes which may arise as a result of greatly augmented international trade, and of the practical benefits to be derived by providing for their settlement through procedures established by international agreement. Further evidence to support this thesis is found in the European Convention on International Commercial Arbitration, which is designed to facilitate arbitration between physical or legal persons in Europe, particularly in East-West trade situations where the Eastern party is likely to be a State trading agency or department of a Communist State.[189] The United Nations

---

[186] Art. II. One commentator remarks, with regret, however, that this Article "is not up to the standard of relative precision that characterizes the rest of the convention. . . ." Springer, *supra* note 183, at 325.

[187] *Id.* at 321.

[188] *Id.* at 326.

[189] European Convention on International Commercial Arbitration, April 21, 1961, U.N. Doc. E/ECE/423, *reprinted in* 3 INTERNATIONAL ASSOCIATION OF LAWYERS, *supra* note 171, at 307. For a comment see Pointet, *The Geneva Convention on International Commercial Arbitration, supra,* at 263. To improve the enforceability of awards in Europe further, an additional convention containing

Economic Commission for Europe, in addition, has adopted a set of rules to govern arbitration among the European nations.[190]

The almost total absence of the Latin American nations and the United States from these international agreements on procedure highlight the need to expand their coverage to the Western Hemisphere, if not to Africa and Asia. It is suggested that the successful European experience in this area, with its realistic acceptance of a world made ever smaller by new transportation and communication devices, could provide a useful example to those nations which, by geography, history, or philosophical preference, have tended to develop legal suborders which may become increasingly irrelevant in light of current trends in commercial expansion and development.

---

a Uniform Law on Arbitration has been drafted under the sponsorship of the Council of Europe. Jenard, *Draft European Convention Providing a Uniform Law on Arbitration,* in 3 INTERNATIONAL ASSOCIATION OF LAWYERS, *supra,* at 372. There are also various bilateral agreements.

[190] *See, e.g., id.* at 361 for the Arbitration Rules of the Economic Commission for Europe. For additional references on arbitration see *Bibliography on Arbitration Law,* U.N. Doc. A/CN. 9/24/Add.1 (1969).

CHAPTER IX

Techniques for Achieving Minimum Standards of Procedural Justice in National Tribunals

In the absence of a vertical international legal order, national courts will remain for the foreseeable future the only formally constituted tribunals in which aliens may seek redress for injuries. Historically, their function as participants in shaping the horizontal international legal order has been dictated by two principal factors:

(1) the unavailability of other types of tribunals in which aliens could seek relief; and

(2) the community preference that wherever possible disputes should be settled on a local level and not be permitted to escalate into confrontations between sovereign States.

Until the end of World War II, if local remedies were unavailable, or if access to them were unjustly withheld from aliens, States could intervene legitimately on behalf of their nationals abroad, utilizing a spectrum of self-help techniques ranging from diplomatic protests to armed coercion. This approach is no longer an accepted problem-solving modality except perhaps in extreme, isolated instances involving humanitarian intervention to protect human rights, since employment of self-help devices has been curtailed by the advent of the nuclear age and by ideological divisions. In addition, foreign offices and legal advisers, by the force of events, now may be constrained to limit their traditional functions as advocates and champions of citizens abroad, and to place more emphasis upon conciliating differences rather than upon imposing solutions. This diminished function of one of the traditional participants in the horizontal legal system, plus the failure of progress any further toward vertical international order, has placed greater responsibility upon national courts to preserve international stability in an era of social upheaval.

NATIONAL TRIBUNALS AS AGENTS OF THE INTERNATIONAL LEGAL ORDER

The alteration in the components of international legal stability, moreover, has called into question the ability of local courts to shoulder the added responsibility placed upon them by current realities. Increased "exposure" has made the courts' inadequacies and shortcomings apparent as never before. At the same time, ideologically motivated executive interference in the judicial process in various countries has led statesmen and private individuals alike to question the validity of the Local Remedies Rule, by which international law encourages local courts to settle disputes between aliens and nationals.[1]

The result has been legislation and treaties, such as the Hickenlooper Amendment in the United States and the lump sum settlement agreements, which permit complainants to bypass local courts and to appeal directly to their governments for protection. Private disputes which otherwise might be resolved on lower tension levels immediately precipitate State-to-State confrontations. Doubts as to the capacity of national courts to provide significant relief and thereby vindicate their roles as upholders of international legal order also have effected the manner in which business transactions are structured. Thus corporations engaged in transnational commercial activities regularly attempt to avoid litigation by including arbitration clauses in their contracts. Many businessmen faced with a

---

[1] The purpose of the Local Remedies Rule is exemplary. It is to permit a State to have full opportunity to do justice to a claimant before it is called upon internationally to answer to another State. The proper application of the rule results in the disposal at the local level of the great majority of aliens' complaints, where justice, if available, is bound to be more swift and less costly. Incidents of potential international irritation are contained within reasonable bounds, whether or not the State was an accomplice to the original act. National law is the repository of the remedy. It is, after all, in such legal systems that proper investigative and prescriptive machinery is found. Additionally, as O'Connell has stated: "Until there has been an investigation it is by no means clear that any injury has in fact been occasioned." 2 D. O'CONNELL, INTERNATIONAL LAW 1024 (1965). A minority of writers disagree. *See, e.g.,* C. AMERASINGHE, STATE RESPONSIBILITY FOR INJURIES TO ALIENS 283–84 (1967), who argues that the Rule is a concession to the respondent State, one which "tends to detract from the appropriate powers of the international legal system and is, therefore, detrimental to the community interest."

choice of litigation in a foreign court—especially in a developing country—will instruct their legal advisers to attempt settlements out of court in circumstances where, if in North America or Europe, they would sue or defend without hesitation. They do so in full knowledge of the theoretical advantages to the international community, and indirectly to themselves, of strengthening legal processes through greater use of local courts.

Nevertheless, the Local Remedies Rule still retains juridical validity,[2] as demonstrated in a recent decision by the United States

---

[2] The Local Remedies Rule, with impeccable theoretical and jurisprudential credentials, still is regarded by the International Court of Justice as "a well-established rule of customary international law. . . ." *Interhandel Case* (Switzerland v. United States), [1959] I.C.J. 6, 27. Its rationale, according to Brierly, exhibits good common sense. "A state is not required to guarantee that the person or property of an alien will not be injured, and the mere fact that such an injury has been suffered does not give his own state a right to demand reparation on his behalf. If a state in which an alien is injured puts at his disposal apparently effective and sufficient legal remedies for obtaining redress, international law requires that he should have had recourse to and exhausted these remedies before his own state becomes entitled to intervene on his behalf." J. BRIERLY, THE LAW OF NATIONS 281 (6th ed. C. Waldock 1963).

The Rule applies uniformly, regardless of variations in legal systems. Moreover, all available remedies must be pursued. "It is the whole system of legal protection, as provided by municipal law, which must have been put to the test before a State, as protector of its nationals, can prosecute the claim on the international plane." *Ambatielos Claim* (Greece v. United Kingdom), [1956] I.L.R. 306, 336. Hence all remedies, administrative as well as judicial, apparently must be exhausted. "[H]owever contingent and theoretical these remedies may be, an attempt ought to have been made to exhaust them." *Norwegian Loans Case* (France v. Norway), [1957] I.C.J. 9, 20 (separate opinion by Judge Lauterpacht). In most instances when a State is involved directly in the commission of an injury, the injurious act probably will not be remediable in the municipal sphere, but if a government can be sued in its own courts an action must be pressed to its conclusion.

In some instances, the Rule is inapplicable, as when a State injures an alien who at the time of injury is outside of that State's jurisdiction. State responsibility under such circumstances is immediately of an international quality: the State cannot compel an alien to submit his claim to its local courts for they would be without jurisdiction and hence incompetent to handle the claim. Meron, arguing that such a situation forms an exception to the general rule, notes that "it would be very strange indeed if a State which interfered illegally with an alien, who did not—except for that interference—have any connexion with it, should be allowed to derive any advantage from its illegal acts." *The Incidence of the Rule of Exhaustion of Local Remedies*, 35 BRIT. Y.B. INT'L L. 83, 96 (1959). On the Rule generally see Head, *A Fresh Look at the Local Remedies Rule*, 5 CANADIAN Y.B. INT'L L. 142 (1967).

Supreme Court[3] and by its preservation in international agreements such as the European Convention on Human Rights[4] and the United Nations Resolution on Permanent Sovereignty over Natural Resources.[5] The ratification of the multinational conventions examined concerning legal assistance and the arbitration of disputes acknowledges and underlines the importance of the Local Remedies Rule, national courts, and other tribunals. It is, after all, these bodies which in the final analysis must enforce foreign judgments or arbitral awards. The conventions merely seek to provide a uniformity of practice among States, and were designed to assist, rather than replace, national tribunals. Indeed, the World Bank's Convention, while it provides for commissions to arbitrate disputes, specifically states in Article 26 that a contracting State "may require the exhaustion of local administrative or judicial remedies as a condition of its consent to arbitration under this convention." Moreover, in Article 54, the Convention outlines procedures to be followed in presenting awards to local courts for recognition and execution under national law.

In view of the new importance of local courts in maintaining today's international order, it is vital that respect for, and confidence in, national legal institutions and in the Local Remedies Rule be preserved and augmented. It is certainly in the interests of States and individuals alike to seek improvement of local court procedures. Moreover, aliens will not be the exclusive beneficiaries of such improvement. Rather, an upgrading of local remedies will be of greatest benefit to nationals who, simply because they outnumber aliens in any particular country, will be utilizing local courts with far greater frequency.

The problems aliens encounter in obtaining relief in local judicial

---

[3] "[T]he usual method for an individual to seek relief is to exhaust local remedies and then repair to the executive authorities of his own state to persuade them to champion his claim in diplomacy or before an international tribunal." Banco Nacional de Cuba v. Sabbatino, 376 U.S. 398, 422–23 (1964). This view is echoed in the Restatement: "A state is not required to make reparation on a claim presented on behalf of an alien injured by conduct wrongful under international law and attributable to the state, if the alien has not exhausted the remedies made available by the state. . . ." RESTATEMENT, FOREIGN RELATIONS LAW OF THE UNITED STATES § 206(1) (1965).

[4] *See* text at note 78 of Chapter II.

[5] *See* text at note 79 of Chapter II.

and administrative tribunals in the countries examined are due either to the lack of adequate, formal legal machinery, to the deficient political, economic, and social environments in which that machinery must function, or to a combination of both. Consequently, the solutions which may be proposed to protect more efficiently the rights of aliens and to improve the over-all climate of justice will differ in scope and emphasis. This study, by examination of selected problem areas, has sought to highlight those aspects of national legal systems where litigants might be disadvantaged because they were aliens. The results of our investigation suggest that certain concrete steps may be taken to improve the quality of local remedies, thereby raising the stature of local courts and encouraging their utilization by nationals and aliens alike.

Inadequacies in Formal Legal Machinery

In the nations which have been surveyed there is virtually no discrimination against aliens hampering their access to judicial and administrative relief, except perhaps where expulsion from the country or denial of entrance is concerned. Indeed, in many jurisdictions national legislation channels aliens into local courts against their will, either through the Calvo Doctrine or refusal to recognize contractual submissions to the courts of other nations. Nevertheless, any inability of aliens domiciled or doing business abroad to oust the jurisdiction of foreign courts, or appeal to their own States for diplomatic relief, would not seem unduly burdensome or discriminatory provided they suffered no denial of procedural due process in local tribunals. However, blanket denial of recourse by aliens to their own governments through extreme application of the Calvo Doctrine seems unwarranted and unfair.

Once access to a court has been obtained, serious problems may be caused by long-arm jurisdictional provisions and by relatively short time periods within which litigants must answer complaints, present counterclaims, appeal, or in other ways traverse pleadings. While nationals and aliens alike are subjected to these same limitations, de facto discrimination may result where an alien defendant resides hundreds, perhaps thousands, of miles from the court. To be sure, some nations, such as Argentina and Costa Rica, allow time extensions when distance is a factor, but other States make no such disposition. Notice sometimes may be given by publication alone, as in Venezuela, thereby disadvantaging nonresident alien defendants. Fortunately, nations usually permit notice by publication only after all attempts to achieve personal service have failed. Once a default judgment has been obtained under such circumstances, it may be difficult, if not impossible, to reopen. Nevertheless, there exists little if any evidence that these rules are manipulated so as to discriminate against aliens. Also, as a practical matter, it might be difficult to enforce abroad a judgment obtained in another State by default or on inadequate notice. Such judgments apparently contravene the basic requirements for fair trials set forth in the American Law Institute's *Restatement of the Foreign Relations Law of the United States*, to wit, that an alien must have adequate information respecting the nature of the proceedings against him, and must have a reasonable opportunity to contest evidence and to prepare and present his own defense.[6]

Rules governing international legal assistance do not seem unduly burdensome, but a grave lack of uniformity and cooperation exists between civil and common law countries. Nevertheless, this problem may be nearing resolution with the ratification of the Hague Conference on Private International Law conventions on the international service of process and on judicial assistance.[7] It is regrettable that the Latin American nations have not yet adhered to these agreements, since the Bustamante Code does not provide satisfactory solutions and urgently requires revision. Requirements for security for costs to be provided by either nonresident plaintiffs or defendants are common in the countries examined, except that Commonwealth judges may have greater discretion in deciding whether or not security is justified. In various civil law nations, failure to post security can justify a preliminary objection by the other party, a device which in France has been allegedly unfairly employed as a delaying tactic. No security is required in Germany or Austria if security would not be required of German or Austrian nationals in the alien's State. In Latin America, the Bustamante Code once

---

[6] RESTATEMENT, *supra* note 2, at § 181(b)(d)(e).
[7] *See* text at notes 85 & 86 of Chapter VI.

again has proven of minimal value; it has been argued by Latin American scholars that requiring security from aliens is, if not a basic violation of the doctrine of equal treatment, a relic of outmoded xenophobia and irrational fears that local judgments against aliens could not be enforced abroad. When the same security is required of nationals living outside the jurisdiction, discrimination would be difficult to prove.

Suits in forma pauperis are also available to resident aliens in Latin America, although this relief may not always be provided to transients or nonresidents. The Bustamante Code seeks to assure that nationals of each contracting State can sue in forma pauperis on the same basis as nationals. United States and New York law similarly provide aliens with this opportunity. Reciprocity, however, is a problem in Austria, France, and Germany. This area would seem to be another one where uniformity by treaty would be helpful.

Conditions for recognizing foreign judgments and arbitral awards set forth in the legislation examined indicate no overt discrimination between aliens and nationals, except in requirements for demonstrating reciprocity. Unlike other areas examined, a significant number of Latin American States, including Peru, Guatemala, Honduras, and Mexico, require showings of reciprocity before exequatur will be granted foreign judgments and awards. Some nations, such as Venezuela, also require that the foreign judgments not be given on a cause of action over which local courts had original and exclusive jurisdiction. Rules governing recognition of foreign judgments on the European continent seem more complex, and differentiate between matrimonial and nonmatrimonial actions. For example, reciprocity is required in Austria and in Germany only for nonmatrimonial actions. Recognition and enforcement of foreign judgments and awards may be denied on public policy grounds in the United States and in all other nations examined. Those Commonwealth countries which accord recognition and enforcement of judgments of member States through simple registration procedure possess the most admirable system.

The nations reviewed also provide in their general legislation for suits against governments, by either aliens or nationals, with no apparent unreasonable discrimination. Reciprocity showings, however, seem to precondition suit in the United States and in certain

European nations. Fortunately, these requirements tend to be incorporated liberally. There are also sensitive areas, as when the sovereignty of the nation over its natural resources is concerned, where suit against the State may not be permitted. To be sure, in the normal eminent domain cases, court procedures enable individuals to challenge the State's decision to infringe upon property rights. Appeals by an alien to his government in such instances usually would be rejected absent a denial of due process. However, where a special law is enacted taking property and not providing adequate appellate machinery or compensation, an alien, despite equal treatment with nationals, may be entitled to seek the diplomatic assistance of his own State on the grounds that there are no local remedies to exhaust and that consequently he has been denied due process at law.[8] This problem arises most frequently in expropriation or nation-

---

[8] Local remedies need not be exhausted if the absence of an effective remedy would make such exhaustion futile. The arbitrator in the *Finnish Ships Case* considered this exception to include "not only cases where recourse is futile because on formal grounds there is no remedy or no further remedy, e.g., where there is no appealable point of law in the judgment, but also cases where on the merits of the claim recourse is obviously futile, e.g., where there may be appealable points of law but they are obviously insufficient to reverse the decision of the Court of first instance." 3 U.N.R.I.A.A. 1479, 1503. The Permanent Court of International Justice also made this point in the *Panevezys-Saldutiskis Railway Case:* "The rule of international law as to the exhaustion of local remedies has never, it is contended, been held to require that a claimant should be bound to institute proceedings on a point on which the highest court has already given a decision." [1939] P.C.I.J. ser. A/B, No. 76, at 19.

Both "ineffectiveness" and "futility" were at issue in the *Ambatielos Case,* [1956] I.L.R. 306, 334–35:

> The ineffectiveness of local remedies may result clearly from the municipal law itself. That is the case, for example, when a Court of Appeal is not competent to reconsider the judgment given by a Court of first instance on matters of fact, and when, failing such reconsideration, no redress can be obtained. In such a case there is no doubt that local remedies are ineffective.
>
> Furthermore, however, it is generally considered that the ineffectiveness of available remedies, without being legally certain, may also result from circumstances which do not permit any hope of redress to be placed in the use of those remedies. But in a case of that kind it is essential that such remedies, if they are resorted to, would have proved to be *obviously futile.*

In short, the alien need not seek to exhaust justice when there is no justice to exhaust.

The mechanics of invoking the Local Remedies Rule, and of countering its application by use of the above exceptions, were set forth by Judge Lauterpacht in his separate opinion in the *Norwegian Loans Case,* [1957] I.C.J. 9, 39.

alization situations, as in Cuba, where appellate machinery never was created, or, as in Mexico, where the Supreme Court has held that amparo would not lie against nationalization measures. The substantive issues involved in property takings, *e.g.*, the standard of compensation, have been discussed at length in international public and private fora, and the positions of nations fairly well defined. Little, if any, fruitful discussion has transpired concerning the procedural aspects of the problem. To date, the only practical solution that seems anywhere near implementation is that of the World Bank's Convention on the Settlement of Investment Disputes.[9]

Formal inadequacies existing in the legal systems examined, including a general lack of uniformity in some areas, probably cannot be cured by appeals to direct governmental initiative. The amendment of procedural rules is a political act, since it usually involves legislative action, and legal reform in the procedural area, unless advocated by influential segments of public opinion, tends to be shunted aside in favor of projects with greater popular appeal. As one legislator told the authors, procedural reform is just not "sexy." Moreover, reformation and unification of international procedures governing security for costs, legal aid, suits against governments, and the enforcement of foreign judicial and arbitral awards encompass complex areas of inquiry to which the average governmental official has relatively little time or talent to devote. Responsibility for initiating procedural legal reform therefore rests largely with private interests. Bar associations, legal societies, and business associations on both national and international levels not only must urge governmental actions in general terms, but also must formulate projects, such as draft treaties, for presentation to persons in government able to advocate their adoption and implementation.

The Hague Conference's conventions on the service of process, on the taking of evidence and on the recognition and enforcement of foreign matrimonial and nonmatrimonial judgments indicate what can be accomplished by private groups cooperating with intergovernmental organizations on the international level. Greater efforts must be expended on enlisting the adhesion of the United States and of Latin American nations to all these agreements. At the present

---

[9] *See* text at note 236 of Chapter VII.

time, only Ecuador and Trinidad and Tobago among the Western Hemisphere nations have subscribed to the United Nations Convention on the Recognition and Enforcement of Foreign Arbitral Awards. Similarly, no Latin American nation belongs to the Hague Conference or has ratified the World Bank's Convention on the Settlement of Investment Disputes.

This reluctance to participate in the construction of a comprehensive international legal order reflects the Latin American tendency to regard itself as a separate legal suborder, distinct even from those European States which also subscribe to the Civil Law system. The Latin American nations regard with suspicion international attempts which they believe somehow might weaken whatever protection is afforded them by the Calvo Doctrine against overreaching alien investors. Ratification of the World Bank Convention, however, would not signify abandonment of sovereignty or the doctrine, since a subsequent specific submission or consent to the Center's jurisdiction still would be required. Moreover, once such consent is given, an investor's State is prohibited from espousing its citizen's claim, absent some denial of justice. This procedure in effect affirms the Calvo Doctrine.[10] Since the Center will grow in stature as more nations consent to its procedure, and since it is in Latin America's best interests to attract foreign investment, the International Law Association, the International Bar Association, and the Inter-American Bar Association should hold joint meetings to reconcile differences involving the Bank's Convention and concerning the other international attempts to achieve procedural uniformity in which the Latin American States have expressed little interest.

In the meantime, the efforts of the Inter-American Bar Associa-

---

[10] *See* the excellent discussion of this point by Szasz in FOREIGN INVESTMENT IN LATIN AMERICA: PAST POLICIES AND FUTURE TRENDS 104 (University of Virginia School of Law 1970). The General Counsel of the World Bank, refuting a Latin American argument that the Convention showed a lack of confidence in the integrity and independence of local courts, has stated: "If there is a lack of confidence among investors it is not a lack of confidence in the integrity of national courts but a fear that the executive and legislative branches will take politically motivated actions which the courts are powerless to deal with. This is a fact that has to be faced and one, moreover, that is not surprising in a world that is in political ferment." *The Convention on the Settlement of Investment Disputes,* 9 INT'L & COMP. L. BULL. 11, 14 (July 1965).

tion to promote national and international arbitration in Latin America should be greatly commended, as should its efforts to encourage the freedom and independence of the local judiciary. The Association's labors, however, should be expanded to include a thorough review of the procedural codes of Latin America in such especially sensitive areas as times to answer and appeal, security deposits, suits in forma pauperis, and the recognition and enforcement of foreign judgments, all in order to suggest reforms to the Bustamante Code's strictly procedural provisions. Collaboration and coordination with local bar associations on such a project would be essential to obtain a consensus. With all respect, this approach might be more effective than efforts by the legal organs of the Organization of American States which, unfortunately, seem highly politicized and too preoccupied with questions of substantive, as opposed to procedural, law.

On the national level, local bar associations can play important roles in revitalizing or changing judicial procedures. The preparation of suggested amendments to, and redrafts of, existing procedural rules and their submission to standing legislative or judicial committees should be encouraged. After all, it is practitioners who compose local bar associations and who must assert in court their clients' rights. Therefore, it is they who have a vested interest in maintaining procedural standards consistent with a world characterized by a heretofore unknown and vast movement of people and wealth across State lines. For example, the Association of the Bar of the City of New York, through its Committee on International Law, regularly formulates opinions and critiques on pending legislation which it submits to the United States Congress. It is suggested that similar tactics be employed in other countries. Two practicing attorneys in Costa Rica recently worked closely with the legislature in producing an excellent, streamlined commercial code. Such action can be emulated in the procedural field as well. Reforms contained in the new Argentine Federal Code of Civil Procedure had been discussed by local and national bar associations for some time before the code finally was enacted. The possibility of improving antiquated procedural legislation by united action from the professional bar therefore is not impossible.

Interviews with leading members of national and international bar associations suggest that a major obstacle is presented by the lack of interest among practitioners in procedural, as opposed to substantive, reforms. However, as remarked elsewhere in this volume, it is the procedural side of the law which in the day-to-day functioning of the courts is most visible to the ordinary citizen. It is his reaction to calendar congestion, unnecessary dilatory tactics, and delays in decision-making which will formulate his attitude toward law in general and his political reactions to the society around him. The cumbersome processes that characterized Spanish colonial procedures generated a saying still heard in Latin America: "For my friends, anything; for my enemies, the law." Perhaps, therefore, the organizers of bar conferences should allocate increased time on their agendas for practical discussion of procedural problems, and less to such esoteric topics as the law of outer space. More hours should be expended on improving procedures whereby States can be summoned to account for their actions violating personal and property rights, and fewer on flogging such abstract dead horses as whether or not States should offer compensation for nationalized property.[11]

INADEQUACIES OF THE POLITICAL, ECONOMIC, AND SOCIAL ENVIRONMENT WITHIN WHICH LEGAL MACHINERY MUST FUNCTION

Throughout this study reference has been made to defects in the operation of legal machinery not attributable to flaws in the law itself but, rather, to the social infrastructure within which the legal process must function. These structural defects may affect an alien's ability to obtain rapid relief and, if a sufficiently serious malfunction of the formal legal machinery results, may lay the basis for an international claim. Moreover, the prevalence in some nations of

---

[11] The question is not whether compensation must be forthcoming, but, rather, the standard by which it should be measured. Surprisingly, few studies have examined the methods by which damages for nationalized property could be measured. *See* Panel, *The Taking of Property: Evaluation of Damages*, 62 AM. SOC'Y INT'L L. PROCEEDINGS 35–57 (1968). Surely this approach to the problem is the one that needs exploration today. For a forthcoming volume of essays taking this approach, see THE VALUATION OF NATIONALIZED PROPERTY IN INTERNATIONAL LAW (R. Lillich ed. & contrib. 1972).

these defects can raise serious doubts concerning the practicality of insisting upon observance of the Local Remedies Rule.

In the developing areas of the world, ancient traditions, old hatreds, past wars, and former invasions all from time to time may combine to prevent aliens from obtaining the full benefit of otherwise adequate legal machinery. On the other hand, it can be argued that the need to attract foreign aid or the anticipated support of a stronger nation still will enable the alien arrested for homicide in a Central American nation to spend the night in a comfortable bed, rather than in the general lockup. However, when ideology becomes involved, aliens may be the particular target of government action or reprisal.

Narrowing the economic gap between have and have-not nations certainly would help in this respect, since it must lessen the impact of greed and envy upon the judicial process. Similarly, it would be of great assistance if capital-exporting nations made certain concessions which, in reality, are only important to special-interest groups in the wealthier States. Such concessions might include greater willingness to extend traditional territorial sea limits, to tolerate economic and political experimentation, and to abandon such blatantly coercive devices as the Hickenlooper Amendment, which operates to the detriment of the Local Remedies Rule.[12]

---

[12] See text at notes 73–75 of Chapter II. The effect of the Amendment is to escalate expropriation cases from domestic disputes to international incidents. The main reasons why it runs against the short- and long-range interests of the United States are discussed in R. LILLICH, THE PROTECTION OF FOREIGN INVESTMENT: SIX PROCEDURAL STUDIES 117–46 (1965). For an unpublished study of the Amendment's limited ability even to deter property deprivations see T. BREWER, THE HICKENLOOPER AMENDMENT AND CONGRESSIONAL-EXECUTIVE RELATIONS IN FOREIGN AID POLICY (Amherst College 1968).

The dispute arising out of Peru's nationalization of IPC's properties perfectly illustrates the Amendment's ability to precipitate unnecessarily the internationalization of an essentially domestic dispute rooted in a long and unsatisfactory relationship between the host State and the foreign investor. The mere presence of the Amendment immediately escalated the matter into an international cause célèbre. Other Latin American nations rallied to Peru's defense against so-called "economic aggression," and threats were made, which in some instances have been carried out, against the Peruvian properties of other United States investors. The effect of the Amendment, therefore, is just the opposite of the one the Local Remedies Rule was designed to produce. See generally Hearings on United States Relations with Peru Before the Subcomm. on Western Hemisphere Affairs of the Senate Comm. on Foreign Relations, 91st Cong., 1st Sess. (1969).

Another problem explored in this study which can and does affect the legal process is the political and economic instability permeating the developing world. Thus, emergency legislation suspending constitutional guarantees may make a mockery of human rights, and the alien as well as the national may be caught up in the police dragnet. In Latin American situations, swift appeal to the local consulate is extremely advisable, especially since recent reports indicate that occasionally the treatment of prisoners leaves a great deal to be desired. It is regrettable, but today military regimes govern 70 percent of Latin America's some 200,000,000 people, in nine countries ranging from Argentina, one of the most heavily industrialized of them all, to Haiti, the poorest of the lot. Legislatures have been disbanded and the Inter-American Press Association has declared that suppression of news media has reached its highest level since World War II.[13]

While much type has been wasted on the "modernizing" role of the military in Latin America and elsewhere, evidence strongly suggests that, if they are not front men for the traditional oligarchy,

---

In the long run, however, potentially the most unfortunate consequence of this kind of policy is the damage done to the local courts of developing countries whose processes either have not been employed or have been tried and then rejected out of hand. It is in the interests of all countries, developed as well as developing, that legal institutions be given every opportunity to function effectively and to attract a reputation of responsibility and integrity. The disinclination to employ local courts encouraged by devices such as the Hickenlooper Amendment probably will prove counter-productive to its purpose, said to be the development of a sense of international responsibility. Self-judging, unilaterally invoked sanctions tend not to project an admirable model for the conduct of international relations. One attorney with extensive experience in Latin American has concluded that "[i]t is the author's own impression that, in Latin America at least, the Hickenlooper Amendments were highly useful as a deterrent, so long as there was a likelihood of their being enforced, but that they were of little value once expropriation had taken place, and might even be counter-productive." Eder, *Expropriation: Hickenlooper and Hereafter,* 4 INT'L LAWYER 611, 628 (1970).

[13] Brocone, *The Outlook for Latin America: Persistence of Strongman Rule,* N.Y. Times, June 9, 1970, at 1, col. 7. Suspension of constitutional guarantees is not limited to developing nations. When the fabric of established order is threatened other nations, such as Canada when menaced by the terrorism of the extremist separatist elements in Quebec, can invoke these procedures, subject to legislative review, to prevent subversion by unrepresentative minorities. What is significant is that the recent Canadian proclamation of the War Measures Act was the first in Canadian history in peacetime.

they merely replace one set of rulers unresponsive to the masses with another.[14] The supremacy of the executive branch has undercut judicial independence severely, even during civilian administrations, so that, despite laws enabling suits to be brought against governments in ordinary courts, judges afraid of reprisals will dismiss cases on inadequate jurisdictional grounds. Liberal removal provisions and lack of tenure make the judge's role precarious in even the best of times. The heavy hand of the armed forces also diverts scarce budgetary funds to irrelevant military adventures and nonproductive expenditures. As a result, court buildings are often dilapidated, staff and supplies are insufficient, and personnel underpaid. Not surprisingly, corruption and bribery thus are encouraged and court congestion made inevitable. Ironically, in the long run the efficient and fair administration of justice could do infinitely more than military hardware to avert the social upheavals which oligarchs fear, and to implement the social reforms which the "modernizing" military regimes claim they seek.

At first blush, these structural defects concern the alien only indirectly, although the *Restatement* provides as one of the requisites of a fair trial "reasonable dispatch by the tribunal or administrative authority in reaching a determination."[15] However, the resident alien may be arrested and held incommunicado during a state of siege if only by mistake, his house may be searched without a warrant, or he may be shot if found on the streets after curfew. Nevertheless, the alien may have the knowledge and funds to retain an attorney, or to apply for habeas corpus or petition for the right to sue in forma pauperis; the native in the bush or on the Andean plateau does not. This denial of basic rights to nationals, either through deliberate action or by depriving them of the education necessary to learn their rights, perpetuates rather than resolves internal political and economic instability. An unhealthy climate of

---

[14] *See* sources cited in Needler, *The Latin American Military: Predatory Reactionaries or Modernizing Patriots?* 11 J. INTER-AM. STUDIES 237 (1969). In Peru, at least, the new revolutionary military government is disturbed by the slow administration of justice. President Velasco, deploring that 75 percent of the prisoners in Peruvian jails have not been sentenced, recently stated that administrative changes now under way "should speed up justice." N.Y. Times, Oct. 7, 1970, at 25, col. 8.

[15] RESTATEMENT, *supra* note 2, at § 181(h).

justice therefore should be of especial concern to capital-exporting nations, whose citizens are constantly residing or traveling abroad and whose own political and economic destinies depend so much upon narrowing the gap between the richer and poorer nations.

Given preferences of both protecting and host States that aliens should settle their private grievances without seeking espousal by their own State, one still might assume that aliens wherever possible would seek remedies to alleged wrongs by pursuing their claims in local courts. Yet they do not. The alien, and especially the alien businessman, sometimes will go to great lengths to avoid involvement in foreign legal processes in many countries of the world. The reasons given for this avoidance of litigation generally have nothing to do with the substantive or procedural laws administered, especially in commercial matters, or with the independence of the judiciary (at least in the higher courts). Rather, objections stem from the alleged general inefficiency of court administration. A lawsuit simply takes too long, even in the United States, for business or industry to rely upon the courts as an effective finder of facts and resolver of issues. Time is too costly, in terms of men, manufacturing processes, land development, and inventory to permit important decisions to be delayed three, four, five, or more years while court after court slowly engorges and then disgorges itself of the facts and the law applicable to the particular dispute. Compounding the problem is fear that even the final decision, though honestly and diligently reached, will be of little assistance to the parties by the time it is rendered.

On occasion, the standards of the judiciary and of the legal profession are called into question. In the words of one veteran African observer: "Justice according to law . . . surely demands that something approximating to the true facts should emerge at the trial, and that the judge should have his attention drawn to all the relevant legal authorities. A glance through the West African law reports will soon convince you that often neither was accomplished."[16] Nevertheless, most Commonwealth countries include in their laws a procedural system almost identical to the English model, a model which is as

---

[16] L. GOWER, INDEPENDENT AFRICA: THE CHALLENGE TO THE LEGAL PROFESSION 114 (1967).

fair as any in the world. These countries employ a system of life tenure for judges, and the level of education and experience of superior court judges is extremely high. The odd breaches of such standards, as during the Nkrumah period in Ghana, attract attention because they are so unusual. The courts in these countries can be criticized for much the same reasons all courts are criticized, *i.e.*, it is their inefficiency, not their unfairness, which is of concern.

In West Africa and in the Indian subcontinent, however, some jurisdictions are burdened with far more lawyers than are needed or can reasonably expect to earn a living practicing their profession. In these circumstances, all the evils attendant upon litigation for the sake of the lawyer rather than the client appear, including nuisance suits and frivolous defenses. Bar associations are reputedly unable to control standards of practice. As Professor Gower has written, "[t]here was no control of professional conduct except a somewhat nebulous supervision exercisable by the courts. Few lawyers kept any proper books or attempted to separate their clients' money from their own. Some ran their practices on money obtained from or on behalf of their clients and hoped to be able to stave off the claims of one client until they had been put in funds by another."[17] Even in England, however, solicitors are accused of misusing clients' funds, suggesting that peculation by officers of the court is by no means confined to developing nations.

These shortcomings of the legal process will not disappear soon, nor are they the direct responsibility of the international community. Emphasis must be given by national governments to the importance of the rule of law, to the appointment to the bench only of well-qualified candidates, to the support of law schools of a high standard, and insistence—through adequate pay and working facilities—upon efficient and honestly functioning court services. This insistence is partly one of attitude, and partly one of financial assistance. An

---

[17] *Id.* at 115. Gower was referring here to solicitors rather than barristers, but the example is equally applicable to either branch of the profession in many places. He quite properly points out, and the authors agree, that in each of the countries discussed in this study there are many brilliant, well-educated, conscientious, and totally honest legal practitioners. Even should a client engage the services of one of these persons, however, he cannot be certain that the other party will be equally well advised. In the result, prolonged litigation may occur.

excellent but all-too-rare example of proper attitude is the reproof President Nyerere of Tanzania offered to persons who criticized him for failing to intervene in what some regarded as excessively lenient sentences meted out to army mutineers. He pointed out that attempts by him to interfere with the decisions of the courts would be an abrogation of the very rule of law for breach of which the soldiers had been convicted.[18]

The local organized bar has a great opportunity to improve the national political and economic environment by identifying itself with social change rather than with the status quo. The defense by the bar of civil liberties and of the independent judiciary in the face of a military government has been exemplary in Argentina. Nevertheless, legal aid centers, staffed by law students and practitioners, should become more active and should seek to inform the underprivileged of their rights. Experiments along these lines have been attempted with considerable success in the United States. However, local and regional bar associations in developing countries require the moral and financial support of their brethren from more affluent societies.

The Inter-American Bar Association long has emphasized the value of a judiciary with tenure, independent of political influence. The same energy devoted to promoting the use of arbitration in Latin America could be utilized profitably in assisting the development of legal aid programs and continuing legal education centers in various nations, and, perhaps, in focusing the attention of the United Nations, the Organization of American States, the International Red Cross, and the International Commission of Jurists upon violations of basic human rights. Younger practitioners should be encouraged to join the Association and to participate actively on its committees. In addition, more attention at meetings should be devoted to procedural, rather than substantive, problems.

Naturally, such projects cost money. However, since 1965, when the American and Inter-American Bar Associations and the United States Department of State financed two fact-finding missions to Latin America composed of educators and practitioners,[19] there has

---

[18] *See A Stand on the Rule of Law in Tanganyika*, 20 BULL. INT'L COMM. OF JURISTS 49 (September 1964).

[19] For the conclusions of the mission sent to Argentina, Peru, and Colombia

been an increasing willingness among governmental agencies and private foundations in the United States to make funds available for purposes of the sort described above. It is strongly urged that such funds be channeled through existing bar associations or legal research institutes in the developed nations, free of political preconditions of any sort. Subventions then could be directed to experiments in selected developing nations in cooperation with local bar associations and practitioners. In all cases, great care should be taken to ascertain if such programs would be acceptable and of interest in the areas involved. Latin Americans, for example, hardly can be considered legally or culturally underdeveloped. Indeed, their contributions to the development of international legal theory have been substantial; the Calvo and Drago Doctrines have had an impact not confined solely to the Western Hemisphere. Leaders of local bars therefore should be consulted carefully concerning the areas in which private organizations from more affluent countries may best be of assistance. By the same token, Commonwealth countries, as inheritors of English traditions of fair play and proper procedure, with judges and practitioners often educated in England, are especially aware of the problems impeding the development of the Rule of Law in their new nations. Indeed, their sophisticated appreciation of the difficulties inherent in bridging the age-old differences between tribal law and imported European legal mechanisms can be of invaluable assistance to those emissaries from more developed nations who are seeking to create legal structures within which economic prosperity along with human rights can be promoted and protected.

From the authors' viewpoint, the time for such experimentation would appear opportune. A recent Agency for International Development communication states that A.I.D. has begun "to view legal development as a legitimate area of concern in itself, rather than as an appropriate field of assistance only insofar as it affected the achievement of economic growth targets."[20] The same document proposes funding three feasibility studies—in Africa, the Near East and South Asia, and the Far East—to explore the possibilities and

---

see Dawson, *Professional Interchange Among Lawyers in the Americas*, 53 A.B.A.J. 903 (1967).

[20] Schott, *Assistance in the Field of Law and Development* 1 (May 1970).

value of assistance to law schools, reformation of government institutions, modernization of procedural and substantive law, and changes in the role of the lawyer. A similar viewpoint has been expressed by the Canadian International Development Agency. Until recently, Western governments have presumed that a higher standard of living in developing countries automatically would ensure open societies and respect for the Rule of Law. Experience should make us realize that this assumption is by no means justified. The legal institutions necessary for the nurturing and protection of the rule of law cannot be expected to spring into being automatically as the gross national product passes upward through some critical horizon. In each country the necessary web of practitioners, courts, legal advisers, and law schools must be provided from the beginning with the means of keeping in step with the social and economic order.

The developed world is becoming increasingly aware that economic and political problems may be linked intimately to deficiencies in national legal systems. While resolving structural legal problems will not, of itself, necessarily cure economic or political ills, it may help promote a climate of justice and dependability, of faith in court systems and legal procedures, which will prove attractive to the much-needed foreign investor. More importantly, it will benefit directly the local citizenry which has more occasion to utilize the courts, and will raise the stature of the country itself within the international community.

CONCLUSION

The day has long since disappeared when aliens could turn to extraterritorial courts to seek the local application of the law of their own States. Instead, they now have available in almost all countries local courts and tribunals to which, by and large, they share equal access with the citizens of their countries of residence.

A number of publicists have expressed the view that, under international law, a positive obligation rests upon States to open their courts to aliens. The obligation has been described as the granting to the alien of "procedural rights in his State of residence as primary protection against the violation of his substantive rights. These procedural rights amount to freedom of access to court, the right to a fair, nondiscriminatory and unbiased hearing, the right to full participation in any form in the procedure, the right to a just decision rendered in full compliance with the laws of the State within a reasonable time."[21] Whether the obligation is as articulate, as extensive or as comprehensive as this definition suggests should be the case may be arguable, but there is nevertheless considerable evidence of broad acceptance of the principle. Indeed, the Local Remedies Rule, which seeks to avoid international disputes by requiring aliens to exhaust all reasonably available avenues of recourse in their host States before invoking the protection of their own governments, would be of little relevance if States did not accept the obligation to open their courts and tribunals to alien litigants on a nondiscriminatory basis with nationals.

This study began with the premise that it is in the mutual interest of all nations, be they host States or potential protecting States, to promote the settlement of controversies at local court levels rather than allow them to grow into international disputes between sovereign States. As revealed throughout these Chapters, there are certain areas where, unless greater clarification and uniformity are obtained, formal procedural inadequacies, reinforced by the extralegal factors discussed herein, could produce denials of justice and thereby precipitate international claims. Nevertheless, the evidence indicates that, in the main, aliens' fears of foreign legal systems are groundless and founded more upon ignorance than on fact. This does not, however, mitigate the need for improvement of national court procedures, since world order must for the forseeable future depend upon a fragile, horizontal interaction between local tribunals, foreign offices, and national institutions of varying complexity.[22]

It should be recognized clearly that private practitioners must bear a major responsibility for the efficient, fair, and smooth functioning of the international legal order. In these unstable times the role of the lawyer of necessity must extend beyond mere private, pecuniary interests, to encompass active participation on realistic, procedural levels in developing and preserving techniques by which

---

[21] A. ROTH, THE MINIMUM STANDARD OF INTERNATIONAL LAW APPLIED TO ALIENS 186 (1949).

[22] See generally Lillich, The Proper Role of Domestic Courts in the International Legal Order, 11 VA. J. INT'L L. 9 (1970).

aliens and nationals alike may be assured the widest possible enjoy-ment of basic human rights. Just as attorneys are considered "officers of the court" in a domestic setting, they also must learn to regard themselves as agents or officers of the international legal order, with obligations transcending national boundaries.

Index

zania, 88; legal aid, 156, 157; in legal system, 193; national emergencies, 88; ownership of land, 257; seen as repressive, 113; *see also* Calvo Doctrine, Equal Treatment Doctrine;
—expulsion of, 66–67, 88, 99, 110, 220, 295;
—foreign exchange regulations, 249–56;
—foreign judgments, 269;
—*forma pauperis*, 150–51, 152, 153, 297;
—influence of, 105, 114;
—injury to, 2, 41n36, 292n1, 293n2; by state, 293n2, 294n3;
—international legal assistance, 184;
—jurisdiction of national courts, 19, 115, 116, 172–73, 174;
—legal aid, 154, 155, 156, 157;
—legal process, 54, 57–58, 60, 64, 79, 119, 123–29, 170, 192, 295–96, 303; time periods, 179–83;
—litigation, 122, 123, 134, 256; attitude toward, 245, 306; counsel, 132n102; in Commonwealth nations, 112; in Great Britain, 112; in France, 101; in United States, 124–25, 127;
—military personnel, 109;
—nonresident aliens, 123, 124, 125, 144, 145, 146, 148–50, 163n10, 189, 250; distinguished from resident aliens, 194, 203; foreign exchange regulations, 250, 255; *forma pauperis*, 297; jurisdiction over, 171; plaintiffs, 135; procedural discrimination against, 296; *see also* Long-Arm rules, Notice, Service, Procedural time;
—notice 176–79;
—protection of, 2n5, 8, 89; constitutions, 88–89; contract, 3, 7n21, 5n11; courts, 83, 89, 90, 94, 99, 103–04; force, *see* Forcible self-help; legal remedies, 63; own government, 292, *see also* Diplomatic protection, Forcible self-help; treaties, 3, 7n21, 5n11, 9, 243n225, 244;
—privileged position, 8, 16–17, 18, 30n10, 32, 37, 45, 59–60, 74, 105, 172, 174, 214, 243n225, 243; foreign exchange regulations, 256; judicial system, 107, 137; legal process, 303; nationalization, 241; reason for, 303, 305;

—residency permits, 220;
—residency requirements, 125;
—seamen, 125;
—security, 146, 220, 297;
—service, 172, 176–79;
—rights, to *amparo*, 211; to *beneficio*, 269; to challenge constitutionality of act, 216–17, 225, 230; compensation from nationalization, 115, 241, 243; to habeas corpus, 217; human rights, 192, 201, 211, 213, 214, 217, 223, 223n139, 226; to contest nationalization, 238; to inherit, 54–55, 54n76, 64, 263; to judicial assistance, 117; in Europe, 130; in Latin America, 115–19, 237; in United States, 214, 216, 241; to own land, 237; to own property, 236, 241; procedural, 13, 17, 27, 116, 117, 118, 128, 134n114, 310–11; to prompt justice, 115, 117, 119; to review of administrative decisions, 219, 222; substantive rights, 13, 129, 310; to sue, *see* Aliens, litigation, Aliens, suit against sovereign; *see also* Human rights, Minimum standards;
—suit against government, 192, 193, 194, 215–16, 225, 228; *see also* Sovereign immunity, Government liability;
—taxes, payment of, 118;
—transient aliens, 118, 119, 120, 147n181, 145, 170, 202, 203; *forma pauperis*, 152n208, 297; ownership of land, 237n203. *See also* Aliens, nonresident
American Arbitration Association, 285
American Bar Association, 308
American Declaration of the Rights and Duties of Man, 206n60
American Revolution, 123n64
"American System," 221n131
Amparo de Libertad, 210n81
Amparo, writ of, *see also* Habeas corpus, 6–7n18, 105, 169, 204, 214, 214–215 n102; limitation on 205–06, 207, 210, 211; procedure, 204–05, 207, 209, 211; in Argentina, 209–11; in Brazil, 213–14; in Colombia, 208–09; in Costa Rica, 207–08; in Guatemala, 208; in Honduras, 206–07; in Mexico, 204–06; in Nicaragua, 206; in Peru, 212–13, in Venezuela, 211

Stare decisis, 161, 278n142. *See also* Precedent
State action, under statutory powers, 195; under its prerogative, 195
State of seige. *See* National emergency
State responsibility, 2, 3, 8, 20–21, 40, 41, 41n36, 42, 48, 175
State responsibility, law of, 48n56. *See also* State responsibility
States, equality of, 68
State Trading Corporation (Establishment and Vesting of Interests) Act, 233 n176
Status of Aliens, Convention on, 132
Status-of-forces treaties, 109
Statute of Westminster. *See* Commonwealth of Nations
Statutes, enforcement of foreign judgments, 258–59
Subpoenas, 185; service abroad, 185
Substantive law, 131, 135, 306, 310
Substantive rights, 13. *See* Human rights, 13
Succession States, 26
Suez Canal, 44, 232
Sureties, 139

Taking of Evidence Abroad in Civil or Commercial Matters, Convention on the, 188, 190–92
Tate letter, 28n4
Tax courts, 226n153
Technological revolution, 36, 48n56
Territoriality, principle of, 263–64
Testimony. *See* Evidence
Third Party Liability in the Field of Nuclear Energy Convention, 149
Third World, 38–39, 40, 43, 44n45, 49. *See also* Developing nations
Tort, 171, 194, 195, 263; basis of jurisdiction, 274; liability of government in, 196, 197, 198, 215; non-fault liability, 220, 227; nonpecuniary losses, 220. *See also* Actions
Trade, international, 1, 48n56, 103, 148, 171n27, 260, 289, 292, 301; agreements, 1; colonial period, 1–3; Middle Ages, 1; Spanish monopolies, 1, 5; restrictive practices, 25

Trade, regional, 260, 285
Trading banks, 255
Transients, 118, 119, 120. *See also* Aliens
Transnational litigation, 154, 173, 192; problems of, 157. *See also* Jurisdiction, aliens
Treasury bills, 252. *See also* Foreign exchange regulations
Treaty, 130, 131;
—as law, 174; as internal law, 228n160;
—concerning, access to courts, 132, 134, 216, 260–61; alien access to courts, 109; aliens, protection of, 293n225, 241; aliens, reference to, 113; aliens, treatment of, 139; arbitration, 285, 288; brankruptcy, 279; civil procedure, 172 n33;
—corporations, legal personality of, 134;
—divorce judgments, recognition of, 280;
—foreign judgments, concerning, 269;
—foreign judgments, recognition of, 257, 260, 267, 278–80
—judgments, recognition and enforcement of, 279;
—international legal assistance, 184, 280 n153;
—investment disputes, 246;
—jurisdiction, 174, 279; legal aid, 155; matrimonial matters, 279; nondiscrimination clause, 149; notice, 176; reciprocity, 225, 228, 261, 271; territory, newly acquired, 132n101
Treaty Establishing a European Economic Community, 77
Treaty Establishing the European Atomic Energy Community, 279n147
Treaty Establishing the European Coal and Steel Community, 147n279
Treaty Establishing the European Economic Community, 279n147
Treaty of Friendship, Commerce and Consular Rights (Austria–United States), 134n115, 139n134, 243n225
Treaty of Friendship, Commerce and Consular Rights (United States–Honduras), 132, 260n33
Treaty of Friendship, Commerce and Navigation (Argentina–United States), 132, 260n34